# Like Two Mexicans Dancing

A memoir

Angela J Dawson

Like Two Mexicans Dancing
Copyright © Angela J Dawson 2016

All rights reserved. Printed in Australia. No part of this book may be used or reproduced in any manner whatsoever without written permission, except in the case of brief quotations for critical articles or reviews.

**Book Cover design**: Derek Murphy (derekmurphy@creativindie.com)

### National Library of Australia Cataloguing-in-Publication data:

Creator: Dawson, Angela J., author

Title: Like Two Mexicans Dancing / Angela J. Dawson

Subjects:
1. Fish John West Reject (Musical Group)
2. Musicians-Tasmania-Biography
3. Artists-Tasmania-Biography
4. Tasmania-Biography

**ISBN**: 9780646965451 (paperback)

First Edition: December 2016
**Printed by: IngramSpark**

Twenty five years ago I wrote my own story about love.

For Mark, the other half of my story.

However far away, I will always love you

However long I stay, I will always love you

Whatever words I say, I will always love you

I will always love you

The Cure, *Lovesong*

# Contents

Yours Truly 1992 ................................................................................. 1

Work and home ................................................................................. 9

Dave and the Gorge ........................................................................ 18

Crossing paths ................................................................................ 23

Rosie's Bar ...................................................................................... 33

Ripples ............................................................................................ 40

Liffey Falls ...................................................................................... 44

Gordon River and the West ............................................................ 51

Wineglass Bay ................................................................................ 69

Orion ............................................................................................... 78

Patience and Telepathy .................................................................. 94

Casualty ........................................................................................ 120

Brunswick, fish and rain ............................................................... 133

It's time ......................................................................................... 155

Crossing the Strait ........................................................................ 172

Melbourne .................................................................................... 176

July 1989: Winter ......................................................................... 189

Launceston letters ......................................................................... 200

September snow ........................................................................... 203

Studio time ................................................................................... 206

Touring with Brian ....................................................................... 213

The pace of Summer .................................................................... 234

Touring Sydney ............................................................................ 239

She'll be Apples ........................................................................... 267

Music by the beach, St Kilda ....................................................... 286

| | |
|---|---:|
| Red, red wine | 301 |
| Autumn 1990 | 307 |
| Michael and Ballarat | 314 |
| Making history on Triple J | 323 |
| Counting Down | 330 |
| Roddy and Parkville | 340 |
| Bananas and sugar cane | 347 |
| TISM, Stanley and Fin | 369 |
| Gigs, media and recording, 1991 | 374 |
| Royal Derby Hotel | 387 |
| Winter and Jesus Jones | 393 |
| Ride | 400 |
| Helvelln | 403 |
| 18 October 1991 | 410 |
| Rood and Roods | 416 |
| Always | 428 |
| Addendum | 432 |
| So the story goes | 433 |
| Author's note | 440 |
| Acknowledgements | 441 |
| List of inserts | 442 |
| Music | 443 |
| About the Author | 444 |

## Yours Truly 1992

EVERYONE in the village had thought it was a long way to go. Shopkeepers, neighbours, even my own cat, who'd flicked her tail disapprovingly when she realised I would be leaving her behind.

"On your own?" the Milkman had asked, standing on our doorstep, his hands deep in his duffle coat pockets, rattling coins. He was waiting for his weekly payment.

"They speak English there," I offered, with a lame shrug.

"Below the equator," he sighed, as if imagining that distance via milk float.

"Below the Tropic of Capricorn actually."

I smiled, not because I was clever. I'd read it in my Lonely Planet guide book.

"Well then," he said.

It had been an echo of many other conversations, although this one had stopped short of the usual segue into comments about abandonment and my Poor Mother. They'd all had opinions, and they seemed certain I'd be back in a month. I wasn't.

I hadn't ever planned to be in Melbourne, and yet there I was, renting a house in the city. It was Christmas Eve. Although it was summer, the evening was only just warm enough to be sitting outside on the front balcony of the old Victorian terrace I shared. The champagne glass was making my hand cold, but I was drinking absently, peering through the cast iron latticework of the balcony railings and focussing on the pouring rain falling in the dark.

Occasional cars scooshed-by with a hiss on the wet road below, briefly overriding the comforting hum of the hospital across the road; the low drone of a place that never rested. Someone had found my old cassettes, and through the open sash window I could hear The Go-Betweens, *Cattle and Cane* filtering out to where I was sitting in the flickering candlelight, contemplating the year ahead. Mark had compiled that mix-tape for me a couple of years earlier, from Harvey's floor to ceiling vinyl collection. Harvey had shelves of records, measured by the metre.

It must have been the sound of unremitting rain that set a mood for reflection, stirring my memories of the past, and making me remember cold British winters. I was imagining my family inhabiting a totally different time zone for their Christmas. They'd soon be waking to a crisp, frosty morning as I sat contemplating the warm evening rain in Melbourne. On the far side of the world, I had lived the day they were yet to experience. Nostalgia nibbled at the edges of my thoughts, but not only for my English home. With a sense of longing, I was also thinking of my first Christmas in Australia five years back, in December 1988.

By then I'd already been in the country for nine months, having flown the arduous twenty hour journey from Manchester to Sydney on Air India. Fresh out of college, with a bag and a work visa, I'd had no-one to please except myself, exchanging my northern hemisphere winter for the brilliant sunshine of the harbour city.

I'd headed south for the first few weeks, through Sydney and Melbourne, hugging the contours of a flat, dry continent filled with deserts, and then cut across the stirring seas of the Bass Strait to the smallest of the six states. Captivated by the sprawling wilderness and mountainous terrain of this isolated island, I had unpacked my bag and stayed.

Having found work, I'd made friends, and I spent the weekends exploring the historic towns, the local markets, and the eastern beaches along the pristine coastline.

My first Australian Christmas had been in Launceston, under the wide blue skies of Tasmania. I had settled there, in the north of the island, and was trying to adapt to summer temperatures in December; a month that brought back memories of the cold, dank and typically grey days of an English winter. Although I'd made a home for myself, I always expected it to be temporary, limited by the terms of my visa. But then Mark arrived.

In the shadows of the balcony I sipped my sparkling wine, and felt the cool fizz on my tongue. At this lofty height the overhang of the roof shadowed the red brick façade, and offered protection from the weather, the darkness affording a further intimacy, and making it almost impossible to be seen from the street underneath. As the hospital droned with distant life, and the rain drummed steadily in the darkness, my thoughts were flicking through the memories of that first year. My old diaries held all the details.

Leaving my seat, I stepped inside through the window's gape, crossing the room to the dim, lofty hallway, and heading to my bedroom at the rear of the house. I groped for my desk light on the small writing table that crouched next to the doors of the rear balcony, flicking the switch down with a click. Its bowed head cast a surprised yellow oval of light onto my postcards and scattered papers, eying them with a well-defined stare as I searched. I'd kept diaries since I'd left England, and I soon found the one I wanted. With a torch, I returned to my seat on the front balcony.

Thumbing the creased pages, I found an entry for January. It had been written at my favourite vantage point on a rocky outcrop in the Cataract Gorge. A steep backdrop of sandstone cliffs loomed all around me, carved into a flawless sapphire sky, their lofty peaks creating hard shadows in the afternoon sun.

*2nd Jan 1989 - A new year has begun, and I'm sitting on the rocks at the waterside. High in the late afternoon sky, the sun is casting dazzling light across the water. Dragon flies hover uncertainly at its surface, momentarily suspended before dashing away, the water rippled by the warm winds of a summer day.*

There was a further entry, for December.

*On the 24th, as I pushed my way through the Christmas shoppers in the mall, I heard a familiar riff filtering through the shifting crowds; and changing direction towards the sound of acoustic guitars, I found myself standing alongside two buskers.*

Both of them were playing guitars and singing a Jonathan Richman song, *My Jeans*, occasionally stepping forward to shadow the more affluent looking pedestrians and ask them to deposit some money into the open guitar case on the floor.

I stopped to watch the two fair haired boys. Although I didn't recognise either of them, their style was familiar, and I was trying to decide if they were from one of the bands I'd seen before in the city.

The song was the perfect choice for busking that day, about a pair of disintegrating jeans, ripped and torn, and slowly falling apart. Between the verses they occasionally shouted remarks about needing cash to replace their own tattered jeans, pointing to the frayed material barely covering their knees.

I smiled as people kept speeding-up and darting around them, the boys continuing their rowdy banter, undeterred by the faster moving targets who slipped past.

Laughing at their effrontery, I continued to hover for a few more minutes until they reached the chorus. That morning I was wearing tiny, round sunglasses, under a froth of curly blonde hair, and a pair of shabby jeans that my Mother had tried to throw away more than once. Despite being threadbare they'd survived several dozen washes, and I was proud of their frayed knees and bleached patches. I rummaged for a few coins in my purse, and tossed them into the guitar case as I stepped away.

"Very entertaining. But I think my jeans are in a worse state than yours," I said. At the sound of my voice, one of them wheeled around, sizing me up as he moved towards me.

That's how it had started, in that moment, from that simple decision. I sometimes wonder about it, about how I could have just wandered past like any other pedestrian, and everything would be very different.

"Hey, you're not from around here."

Looking down, I let my hair fall around my face. I hadn't expected him to address me, but I liked the soft sound of his voice, the way his lip curled slightly as he talked. I couldn't seem to move from the spot.

"No, but I'm living here at the moment."

"I like your glasses. Very John Lennon."

"Thanks," I said, fiddling with the metal frame on the bridge of my nose. My legs felt boneless and uncooperative, but I listened as he continued to speak to me. Concentrating on his words, I heard him say he was in a band that had played in Launceston a few months ago. I'd guessed as much when I'd heard the distinctive guitar riffs. We must have chatted for a few minutes then, and as I turned to leave, he asked my name, before offering theirs.

"I'm Mark.... and this is Martin, one of the Witheford brothers," he added.

"Oh, are there many of them?"

"I know there's at least two. But then most people in Tasmania are related. Who knows?" he added, plunking a string with a solemn expression.

"Yes, I'd heard that. All the inbreeding." I raised my eyebrows, and he laughed, strumming thoughtfully at the guitar hanging by its black strap from his shoulder.

"Actually, I'm wondering," he said, pausing, "...well....there's a party on George Street tonight if you can get there. I'll be there later, after rehearsals. I hope you can make it."

I noted the address, knowing that I didn't have any plans for Christmas. Although his confidence was disarming he had a sincerity that had brought a flush to my cheeks. I already felt nervous at the prospect of meeting him again.

As I walked back along Charles Street to my lodgings I thought back a few months to August, when I'd seen some unknown band play at one of the clubs in town. Afterwards, I'd bought a cassette which was being sold for five dollars at the venue that evening. It was entitled *Shy But Wild*, and contained a mix of traditional, original, and cover songs, some of which had been recorded live only months earlier. The band had sung all of those songs that night when they'd played their raucous set.

In my room I rifled through my scant possessions and found the tape, putting it into my Walkman so that I could play it as I lay on the bed. Yes of course. Without the cassette I might not have recognised the music as I strolled through the mall on that Christmas Eve afternoon, but I'd played it many times since then and I could recall the evening I'd seen them perform.

There had been posters around town advertising a band called The Fish John West Reject and their 'acoustic pop thrashabilly', so a group of us had decided to go and see them play at Night Moves. The air in the club had been a fug of smoke and heat and I'd danced all evening with Paul and Dave, the two reckless Maloney brothers, watching them stagger around in a haze of inebriation, on an endless beer quest.

It had been an adrenaline charged frenzy of deafening music and jostling crowds, and at the end of the evening, buoyed by alcohol, I'd gone to the stage and expressed my appreciation to the fair haired vocalist as he crouched, packing away equipment. It had been Mark. I remembered clearly. He'd been polite, and had thanked me.

My curiosity was aroused as I listened to the cassette playing. I'd almost forgotten that fleeting moment, but realising we'd met before made me more intrigued about the Christmas encounter.

Lying on my back as the Walkman played, I took the paper sleeve out of the cassette shell and tried to read the scrawl: *A product of 'River filf' Winter 1988*, it said. I loved the exuberant songs, with their raw passion. But it wasn't just about the music now. I could barely make-out the details of the band members; just some first names in the credits – Mark N, Mark A, Andrew and Graham.

The only thing I knew about this bold musician with the striking eyes was his first name. I felt the nudge of providence. There was something about this second encounter that was difficult to ignore, and it was making my heart race.

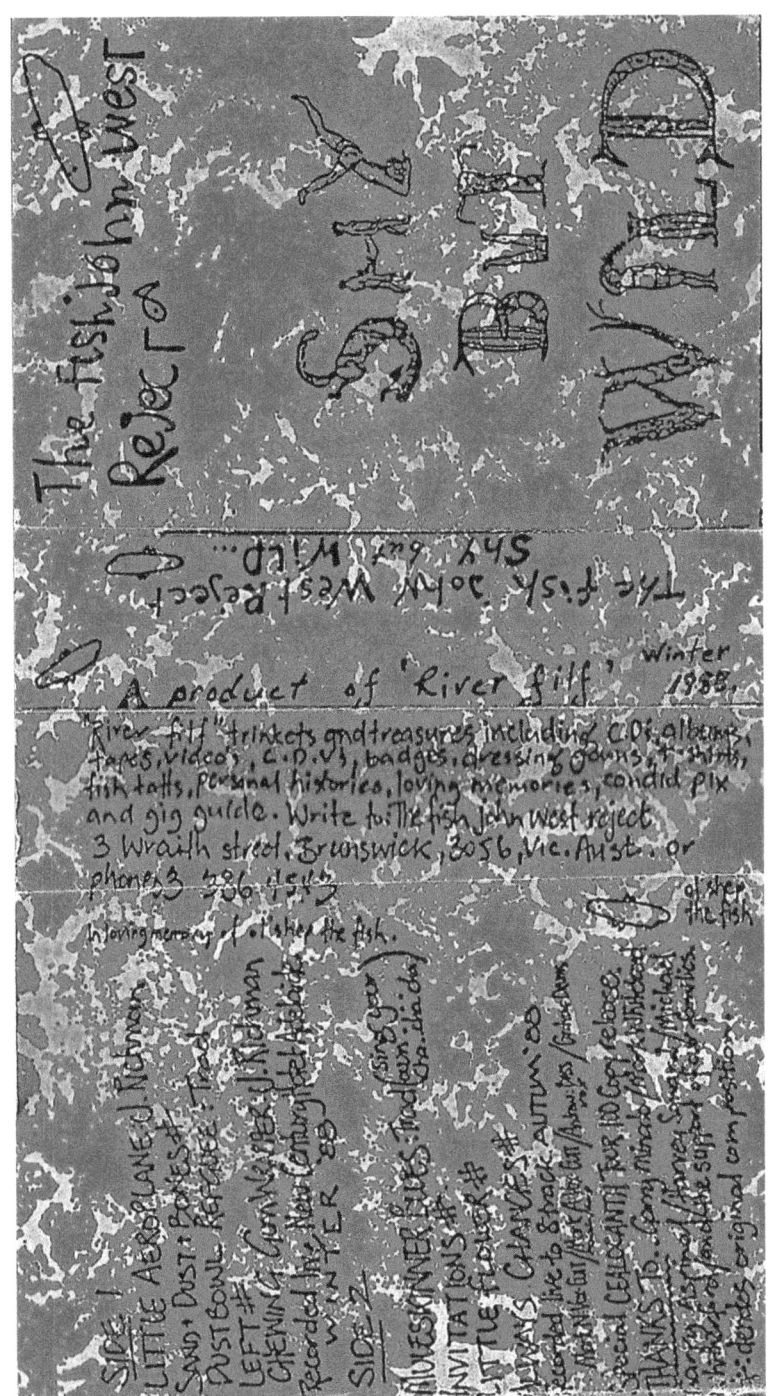

*Angela J. Dawson*

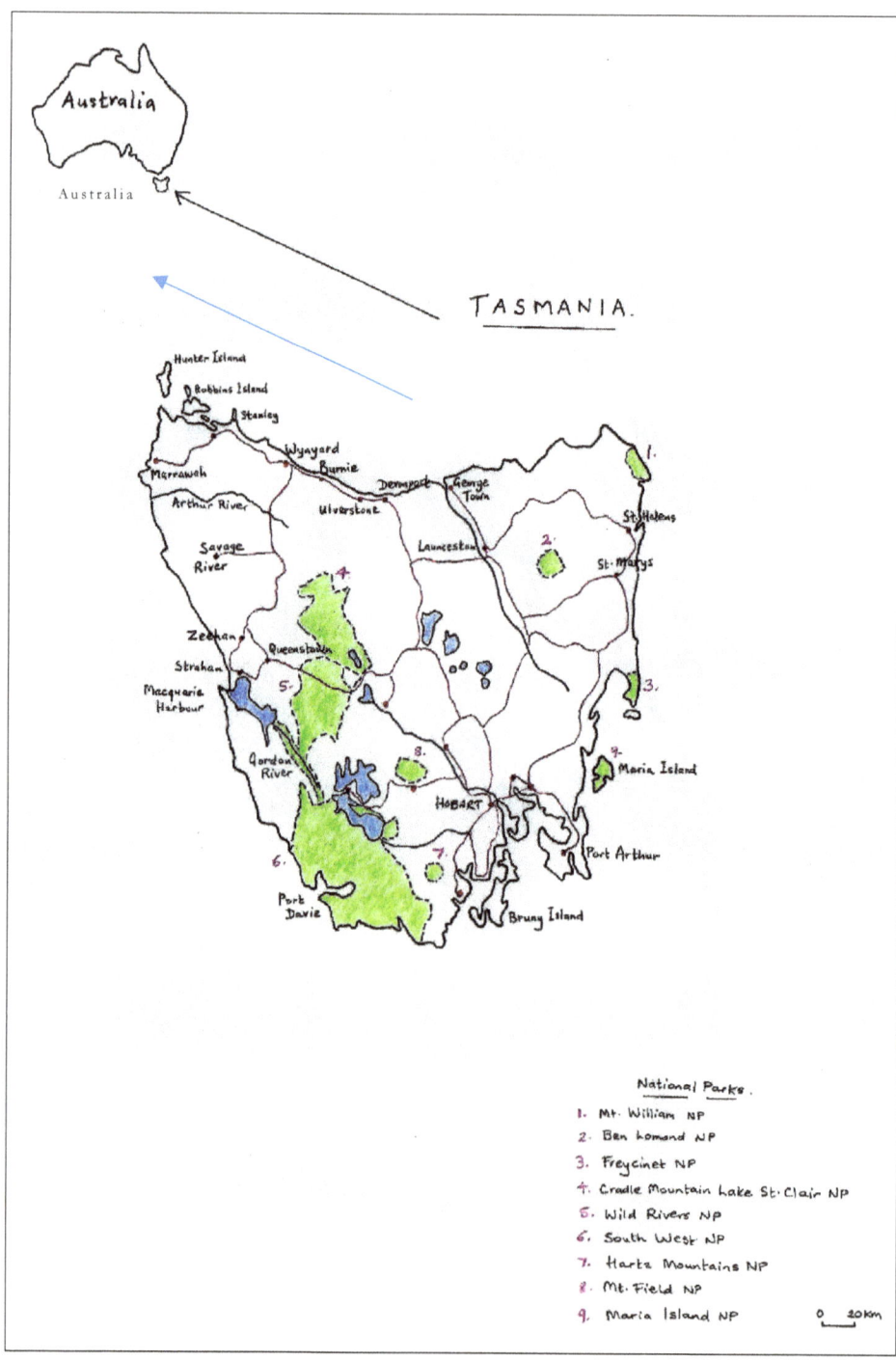

# Work and home

WITHIN WEEKS of leaving my English home my money had dwindled but I'd managed to secure my first job as a Physiotherapist at Launceston General Hospital, in the heart of the city. Since April I'd been living in the residential accommodation provided for hospital staff. They offered very cheap on-campus facilities at the Nurses' Home, hostel-style, with furnished rooms and shared facilities.

The Home was part of an old set of red brick buildings filled with long corridors and sash windows and conveniently located at the top of a steep incline overlooking the hospital, on Charles Street. From the upstairs bedroom windows there was a panoramic view of the humming hospital complex stretched out below us.

There were many disorderly days there before I met Mark that summer. I spent my time bushwalking with my new nursing friends and swimming the chilly, surging waters of the South Esk River in the thin autumn sunshine. At The Gorge, where the water collected in a natural basin, we would wallow, sunning ourselves on the rocks, gorging on ice creams from the nearby kiosk as our skin became various shades of pink.

On the weekends I'd hover in the lounge room to catch people between shifts or wait for them to return for their morning and afternoon tea breaks.

"Any one checked the mail yet?"

Some of them were in uniform, shoes kicked-off, debriefing the morning's dramas on the wards. Others were in dressing gowns, bleary from yesterday's late shift.

"Can you get me some bedsheets if you're going over there?" one of the girls asked through a mouthful of pins, in the throes of a needlework project. Everyone seemed to knit or sew, or have some complicated piece of tapestry they were embroidering.

"I'll come with you," Dave said, unfolding his lanky body as he stood, and shaking out his gangly legs.

Home Three mostly housed the teenage Student Nurses and occasional paramedical personnel like myself, whilst Home Two was for the Medical

Students. The permanent Nursing staff seemed to live exclusively in Home One. Dave was the nursing half of the Maloney brothers and he was usually behind any sort of disturbance in the Home. There were many rowdy and memorable moments when he was living there.

"Who's on the desk today?" I asked warily.

"Not Clakkers," a voice said.

"I think it's Mrs Mitchell," someone added.

The Homes were all interconnected via long hallways, or you could cut to the outside, taking the more direct route on the covered walkways in the lee of the buildings. There was a central office located in the Home One foyer, and in changing shifts until the early evening it was staffed by a succession of Supervisors, from stern to easy going. One of the most adept and fearsome was Mrs Clark, fondly referred to as Clakkers by some of the residents.

I looked at Dave.

"Come on then. You can help me carry the sheets."

Clakkers seemed to have the ability to move almost noiselessly, often materialising in the lounge for random checks, and she was an expert in sniffing out prohibited boyfriends or other contraband.

"Let's see if we can get some snacks out of her too then," Dave joked hopefully, thinking of Mrs Mitchell's kindly disposition.

The Supervisors restocked basic food supplies to our kitchens and directed housekeeping needs, like the laundry of uniforms and bed linen. They logged the signing-in-and-out of visitors, sorted mail for the residents, and they also had the grim task of stitching shrouds for the deceased. If you were nearby you could always hear the subtle morse code of their sewing machines for this never-ending task.

As Dave and I reached the end of the outside pathway and stepped into the foyer housing the Supervisor's alcove we could hear the sewing machine clattering.

"Hi Mrs M!" Dave called out.

With a welcoming smile she stopped sewing and slid her glasses from her nose, letting them dangle on their chain.

"Hello David…. Ange… How are you?" She looked like she should have been baking pies in a warm kitchen.

"We're all out of biscuits," Dave said, appealing to her maternal instincts with a sorrowful expression, "and peanut butter. Maybe even a loaf, if you have any?"

I elbowed Dave before he pushed his luck too far.

"We're just looking for any letters," I said hopefully, thinking of my lifeline to news from home. Checking for blue airmail letters was a daily mission. Sometimes it felt like I was off the radar, as if I'd slipped off the edge of the world, or been lost at sea. Ignoring the distinctive drawl and obvious differences in vegetation, it felt like I'd bobbed up again in another England, but with better weather.

She rummaged through deliveries, and handed over a couple of items, plus a jar of peanut butter.

"Nothing from overseas though." She smiled apologetically.

"Okay, well, I'll just pick up some sheets then," I added, rounding the corner to pull starched single bedsheets from the shelves and pile them into Dave's arms.

Our two storey Home had its own small kitchen, stocked with staple provisions for breakfast. In our block there were a couple of large bathrooms with shower stalls, and a spacious lounge room downstairs filled with natural light from tall bay windows. In one bright corner its cluster of beige vinyl armchairs overlooked city views and an old television. Under the bay windows we had a large wooden table and chairs striped by sunlight, and at the far side, an off-key piano in need of repair and tuning.

I strolled back along the walkway with Dave, hovering at the entrance to the lounge which, as always, was filled with plants and books, cast off cardigans, knitting projects, and a changing assortment of cups and plates.

"What are you up to tonight, Dave?"

Looking to my right I could see the cityscape cresting the skyline, with its sweeping roads and historic Victorian style homes. Corrugated metal rooftops gleamed their rich terracotta red against the dense green ridge of trees on the far hillside. At night, the city lights could be seen like pinpricks against a darkened horizon, almost mirrored by a vast hood of stars above.

"Dunno yet." He flashed a devious grin. "I'm waiting for my cousin to call."

He'd offloaded the sheets into my arms as we'd re-entered the building, shaking out his limbs like he was trying to loosen them from their sockets, and flashing Cheshire cat teeth. He glanced at the telephone booth as someone hung up the receiver, and exited. The booth was in the high traffic area between the kitchen and lounge and it was our only link to the outside world. Whoever heard the phone ringing between shifts would answer, and leave a written message on the board outside. This of course relied on someone being around to pick up the call. When the phone was in constant use, no-one could get through, and no-one got any messages

"I think Tina has a new boyfriend," Dave said, rolling his eyes with a maniacal laugh, and indicating the half empty message board. She'd just moved from her vinyl armchair and was approaching the booth to make a call.

That was the reality of sharing one phone between all of us. Not that anyone really minded. Living with so many people offered plenty of social opportunities, and provided a constant source of entertainment, particularly when Dave lived there. He loved the movie, Pee-wee's Big Adventure, and had seen it enough times for him to emulate Pee-wee Herman's voice perfectly. He could quote large chunks of the dialogue from the film.

Before Tina could get to the phone, Dave dodged in to grab the handset, delivering his favourite line with characteristic melodrama.

"Shhh…. I'm *try-ing* to USE the PHONE…!" he uttered in a sing song voice.

Tina sighed, and pushed her glasses back up along the bridge of her nose, waiting until Dave charged off into the kitchen.

We were all used to Dave's modus operandi. It mostly involved bolting, stampeding or tearing around the Home. He discharged his boundless energy with a certain crumpled charm, his dark hair usually in defiant tufts. Lately, he'd been initiating water pistol fights in the lounge room when everyone was relaxing between shifts. That was partly why he didn't live there all the time.

I couldn't read his expression to work out what he might be planning next.

"You know there's every chance that Clakkers may be on tonight?" I warned, thinking of when the Supervisors would be changing shifts.

Dave had a history of rebelling against the house rules and perpetually playing his stereo loud enough to get himself expelled.

"You're not having a big night *in* are you?" I asked, thinking of previous occasions.

He was the only one I knew that would try to have a party in his room, which like all the other rooms, was barely large enough to comfortably accommodate one person and a single bed. Worse still, he seemed to always fill it with all the most undesirable people in Launceston. After his eviction, he would stay with his cousin for a while, and then contritely reapply to move back in. Strangely he had regular success, despite continual infringements, and within a few weeks he'd be back.

"Nope," he replied, without elaborating.

Narrowing my eyes at him, I wondered what sort of mischief he intended. Pointing at the telephone board I indicated some scrawled messages at the bottom.

"You wrote those didn't you?"

Dave liked to fill the telephone message board with notes to himself. He shook his head until his hair assumed the same swivelling momentum, but his eyes said otherwise.

"And what about this one?"

It read, All Dave's friends (and he has a lot of 'em) rang to say that he's a Top Guy.

"Nah," he said, still swivelling.

"So I suppose you know nothing about that either?" I indicated an area behind him, on the lounge walls.

On a couple of the rockstar posters there was some lewd graffiti, a bit of extra bulge in the tight leather pants, and a couple of large penis sketches. It was typical Dave, the sort of thing he found entertaining.

"No idea."

He'd been seized by a compelling itch, and was scrabbling all his fingers through his hair as if he'd lost something. I was familiar with his diversionary tactics.

"I know it was you," I declared.

"Are you up for a raid later?"

"Don't change the subject."

"There're lots of new med students," he tempted.

Medical students in the adjacent Home were considered fair game. Dave was the instigator of the hilarious raids we carried out, despite the risk to my on-going tenancy if we were caught. Given the continual rotation of students on placement, it ensured new faces every few weeks, and plenty of victims. I remembered the last batch.

"Come on," Dave had hissed on the most recent of those nights, "fresh prey."

We'd appropriated some old linen from the laundry supply cupboards, and had cut eye holes in the bedsheets. Armed with water pistols, we crept ludicrously down the hallway in our ghostly disguises until we spotted a door that had been left ajar.

"There's one," Dave breathed, indicating the light falling from the open doorway.

Bursting from the shadows with a yelp, we stood like gunslingers, spraying arcs of water and drenching the unsuspecting occupant at their desk.

"Bahahaha!!" Dave jabbered as he stippled the room from his pump action pistol. In those few seconds there was barely a chance for the person to stand before we flapped away, shrieking down the looping corridors like ungainly spectres. The initial shock of our appearance was often enough to prevent chase or capture but it left us wired and unfulfilled.

"No-one's coming!" I shot back at Dave as I watched from the final corner, panting from the full pelt running. Minutes had passed.

"Let's go again!" Dave trilled as the adrenaline still coursed through us. He didn't care that initiating a re-run would reduce the element of surprise. The thrill was in the chase, but first we had to get them away from their books.

We were never caught, despite a rather ambitious third run on one weekend. Perhaps we were just too quick.

Our best effort was again in Home Two, in the early hours of one morning. We zig-zagged toilet rolls between door handles like a dense mass of celebratory streamers and blocked the entire length of the corridor. We buried room doors under layers of paper towels taped together like wallpaper, we covered the toilet bowls with a clear film of Glad Wrap, invisible until you're mid-flow, and then we stole all their shower curtains. We were suspected, but never proven guilty, and it resulted in a general warning to all the alleged culprits. If they didn't reverse their prank within twenty four hours all the occupants of our Home would suffer the consequences. It was a triumph; and it became our zenith.

"Don't think that a raid'll get you off the hook," I chided. "You'd better at least try and erase some of the penises." He just grinned. "Or buy some more posters," I added.

From the lounge room I could see Perspex roofing that sheltered a walkway from the crest of the Nurses' Home into the rear of the hospital. Given the Home's lofty position on the incline of a hill, the path actually connected with the upper hospital floors and intensive care ward. Further stairs would take you down to street level.

"Let's go and check out lunch at the café," Dave suggested, having had limited luck with Mrs Mitchell.

Sometimes you just didn't want more hospital food, but at least live-in staff had all meals provided. Fortunately the cafeteria was just beyond the walkway.

"I've got to go over to the department first. Come for a walk?" I offered.

Below us, the hospital was effectively split in half by Charles Street, the campus sprawling on either side of the busy road. In order to connect the two halves of the hospital an elevated walkway had been constructed above Charles Street. Even in bad weather there was no need to take a coat when you left for work in the morning. A five minute walk took us straight to the Physiotherapy department at the far side of the hospital complex. Dave didn't look convinced.

"I'll get you a beer later, if you come," I tried.

"Where?"

"At The Oak."

The Royal Oak Hotel was our pub of choice, on Brisbane Street, the place for ample counter meals, and a rotating schedule of live music.

"Who's going?"

"Does it matter? There'll be beer."

"Be quick then," Dave conceded, "or all the best dessert'll be gone."

IN THOSE WEEKS after Christmas Dave was often around on the wards, at The Home, and during mealtimes. He sat with me in the staff cafeteria one lunchtime, watching with a puzzled frown as I held my knife and fork to attention, fists either side of the plate, staring disinterestedly at my hospital food.

"Do you want mine too?" I asked, stabbing at something with my fork. I was already freefalling, living on endorphins, euphoria and air. When love arrives, it has a sly way of undermining all the unconscious functions that are designed to keep you alive; things like breathing or the predictable rhythm of your heart. You become aware of all their limitations as their tides and pace become disrupted and erratic.

"Are you alright?" Dave was staring at my flushed face.

At full potency the intensity of love can be your undoing entirely, sabotaging all composure, leading you to lose time, sleep, and sometimes the ability to speak; and yet for every one of its apparent shortcomings, despite its life threatening impact on our very existence, the desire for it remains unsurpassed.

I stared back at him. "I'm not hungry. I don't want anything."

Sometimes even my love struck thoughts were able to throw all these normal functions into chaos. I could feel the somersaulting in my stomach as my mind raced.

"You have to eat, Ange," Dave stated earnestly, in a rare sombre moment. He rested his head in his hands across the table and frowned at me. By then it was impossible to eat, and I couldn't sleep even when I was tired. People in the Home had started to notice.

But I've digressed. I'll need to go all the way back to the week before Christmas to explain how it happened. Then it'll make more sense. It actually began just after the evening I slept under the stars with Dave, the same night that I declared I'd never fall in love.

Dave posing in my improvised lounge room 'studio'

# Dave and the Gorge

AFTER A NIGHT of drinking port and whiskey at a friend's house a few of us were talking in the lounge, scattered on the vinyl chairs before the old television. We were sharing our collective ideas about whether love existed and contemplating the sort of activities that would prolong the warm summer evening.

"Not ever? You haven't *ever*, not even just a bit?" Dave slurred as he spoke.

"I'm pretty sure I've never been in love," I spelled out slowly to emphasize my point, and to get the words out clearly. "I mean, I'd know if I had, wouldn't I? It'd just stand-out wouldn't it?" My brain felt fuzzed by the port.

Dave nodded, as if he followed my illogical, alcohol-induced reasoning. "Yep...like dog's balls, yeah."

He continued to nod his head, as if caught in the rhythm of it.

"I'm not certain I even believe in it. Not in that can't-eat-can't-sleep sort of way," I persisted, my tongue sluggish as I tried to articulate what my brain had already decided.

Dave had started to get that crazy look in his eyes and I had the feeling he'd already tuned–out and moved on from such lofty thoughts. I rubbed my sleepy eyes.

"Well, *I'll* never fall in love anyway." There it was. I'd said it. Never.

Dave was grinning, but not at me. He was evidently lost in the excitement of his next great idea.

"What are you thinking about?" I probed.

"Let's go for a ride."

"Now?"

Earlier that evening I'd watched as Dave and his friend had balanced together on one bike and tried to establish enough intoxicated equilibrium that they could dither their way back to the Home. It had been a precarious but short trip back as they teetered along the incline of Charles St, arms and legs flailing, reflexes slowed and dulled by alcohol.

From the lounge room I looked out at the shadows, feeling the cool breeze curl under the open sash windows, waking my senses, beckoning us outside.

Given it was only December the warm months were all ahead of us. Nights were mild and during the day gaping blue skies vaulted high above us. Christmas was approaching.

"Where to?"

"The Gorge. Come on, it'll be great in the dark."

"What about work tomorrow?" I mithered, thinking of all the hills, and how long it would take to get there, and how long to get back.

Dave was rubbing his hands together, smirking and pacing from foot to foot as if the ground was hot underneath his shoes. I'd seen that before. It meant he was charged and ready to go.

"Bikes aren't allowed on the Gorge tracks, Dave," I griped, feeling my resolve weakening.

"Nope."

\*

The smooth surface of the walking track cut a precarious course midway up one of the sheer sides of the Cataract Gorge. In the moonlight our wheels seemed to cover ground more quickly as we negotiated the sharp twists and bends of the steadily ascending pathway set above the water. I was behind Dave.

"Look out!" he warned, ducking his head down.

On the right we had the heavy boulders of the rock face. Overhanging the track at unpredictable heights there were jutting sections on which to clout your head if you leaned the wrong way on a turn. On the left we had the wire fencing and metal handrail guiding our passage in the dark. It indicated the threshold of the path and the vertical drop below should we misjudge a corner somewhere.

As the path levelled out at the top of the slope we looked back to the shadowy features of the steep gorge, its huge elongated sandstone mosaic of rocks broken by the irregular shapes of scattered eucalyptus trees. Free-wheeling down through the park area, breathing heavily from the uphill exertion, we crossed a wooden platform over a faint shimmer of water and then up over the suspension bridge which gently swayed as we wheeled over the wooden slats. The river was sleeping in a blackened menace, a negative of its daytime self, spreading below the bridge like a shiny floor.

On the other side of the bridge the path took us down to a wide expanse of grass and the outdoor swimming pool, its shape defined like a rectangular black hole in the darkness. There, Dave quickly shed most of his clothes and to my surprise, tossed himself and then the bike into the unlit inky waters with a dull splosh.

"Eeeeeeaaargh!"

He'd surfaced. In the dark his howl sounded life threatening, but I was relieved to hear him splashing around.

"Dave, are you crazy?!"

"Farkin' swimmer's dick," he yelled, "it's freezing in here!" and he laughed hysterically, to show that everything was relatively normal.

"What are you doing, Dave? I can hardly see you."

Only his head was visible as if he was treading water, his breaths rasping slightly above the water's sheen.

"Trying to find my dick…it's gone so far up I don't think I'll ever see it again. Aren't you coming in?"

I stooped to feel the cool water with my fingertips and shivered. "Not likely." Most of the heat of the day had gone by then so the idea of swimming didn't seem very appealing.

In the half-light I could see his head bobbing above the surface. I realised he was holding up the bike and riding it underwater to propel himself, his legs pedalling furiously as he tried to keep himself, and the bike, afloat. Heading for the side of the pool he began a sequence of throws, hauling the bike out of the water, and then tossing it back into the deep end so he could dive-in and retrieve it again from the bottom. After a particularly enthusiastic throw there was period of panting, repeated diving, and then a dismayed silence of treading water in the gloom.

"Fuck… I've lost the bastard!" his voice resounded through the quiet dark.

I began to laugh.

"No, really, I can't find it," he spluttered as his words snagged on the surface.

But before I could offer a suggestion he was gulping and diving again, groping around the silent depths of the pool.

We'd decided earlier, when we left the Nurses' Home, that we were going to stay out all night and watch the sunrise, favouring the idea of blankets and sleeping bags so that we could sleep in the grass by the pool. Before long Dave dragged himself out of the water, sufficiently chilled by his solo aquatic bike racing. As he hopped around, shivering and dripping, he began preparing his bed for the night.

"You did bring a towel didn't you?" I asked.

"Nah," he replied, steeped with the sort of optimism that alcohol can induce.

He gave me a lopsided smile as he moved to his chosen patch of grass, unfolding a cylindrical nylon holdall with a dramatic flourish. It looked empty. It didn't surprise me that he didn't have any spare clothing either.

"Where's your sleeping bag? You did bring one didn't you?"

"Nope." I could make-out the teeth of a grin, the whiteness implied in the shadows.

He was stepping into the soft nylon bag and lowering himself into its compact interior like a magic trick, managing to cram most of his six foot height inside it. It must have been just over a metre long when zipped up to his chest, leaving his head lolling from the open end.

I marvelled at how much of him fitted inside it as I hunched in my sleeping bag on the hard ground. He seemed blissfully unaware of the discomforts, quickly slipping into an alcoholic slumber and snoozing peacefully in his bed. All I could see was his head and shoulders protruding from the holdall, all four limbs somehow folded within. It looked like some sort of chrysalis casing, as if there might be a metamorphosis during the night that would see him emerge as something else. I watched his head bobble and droop as I wished restlessly for sleep, hoping the morning would come swiftly.

It was a damp and chilly wait for the dawn, listening for the peacock chorus from the park near the pavilion. *Tay-oool... tay-oool....* they seemed to be saying, shrilling their call into the morning skies. Their singing began around 6am as we were stirring stiffly on the cold ground. We'd decided to build a fire to try and get warm, but with only twigs and debris we couldn't really get it started or get any substantial heat from it. Undeterred by the lethargic flames Dave stirred the sparks with his customary enthusiasm, believing he could use them to dry his wet underpants. He'd managed to remove them at some point without me noticing, standing crinkly and damp in his trousers and t-shirt as he leaned over our small pyre of kindling and leaves. Having speared the briefs onto a stick he held them over the blushing embers, watching them alternately steam and singe as the fabric heated up.

The first light from a low sun had begun to vaporise the dew on the surrounding grass and in the glimmering yellow of a new morning he began whistling, and then singing unselfconsciously. It was his signature tune by the Beat Farmers, *Happy Boy*. As he chanted the repetitive chorus and shuffled his feet like some strange Native American Indian dance the sound hovered somewhere between a complex throat clearing exercise and the low chug-chug stutter of an outboard motor. I smiled at him, in his own little world of Dave.

Although I felt tired and cold his good mood always prevailed. His impulsiveness and frenetic energy ensured life was never dull but it could be exhausting keeping up sometimes. I stared into the fire, willing it to come to life, but it sputtered and gasped, needing less moisture and more fuel. Eventually Dave abandoned the idea of dry underwear and used the tattered remains to put out the fire.

It was a hard ride home in the damp chill of early morning, our conversation from the night before all but forgotten. As I dodged some of the residents going out to early shifts on the wards I decided not to go to work that day, preferring to steal surreptitiously around the Home in my pyjamas, feigning illness and feeling achy from lack of sleep.

However within a week of our bike ride and my solemn declarations about love, I was anxiously appraising my wardrobe, wondering what to wear. I'd been invited to a party by a blue eyed busker to whom I'd barely spoken. I couldn't understand why I felt so flustered.

*Like Two Mexicans Dancing*

# Crossing paths

I DIDN'T KNOW anyone at the party when I arrived. Fortunately Paul turned up, the other half of the Maloney brothers, although he had no idea about my motivations for attending. For most of the evening I sat with him on the tiny balcony overlooking the street, caressed by the cool summer air. Every now and then my stomach lurched when I heard approaching voices, but whenever I peered around the balcony doors I was disappointed to see more unfamiliar faces.

Wanting to stay alert, I'd been sipping the same warm beer for the last couple of hours, but Paul had been drinking with a predictable rhythm. I was trying to make sense of an absurd, inebriated conversation with him as I glanced down to the street below, casting my eyes about hopefully, still anticipating Mark's appearance.

Running my hands apprehensively across the yellow and green flowers of my favourite fifties dress I glanced at the latest arrivals and wondered if it might be time to leave. Perhaps he hadn't even remembered the party.

As I drained the last tepid inch of beer from my bottle, and squeezed my way through the press of bodies, I could see him making his way up the narrow stairs. He finally entered with an animated entourage of fashionable disciples, all of them trailing in together and energising the room. I felt small next to their colour and sparkle and decided to slip away unnoticed, leaving them piled casually on the bed. They'd all dropped there, realising they couldn't fit onto the small balcony.

As I rounded the stairs Mark appeared at the handrail, chasing my retreating form.

"Hey! Hi! Ange, you came." He smiled at me. "Do you need a drink?"

"Oh, no thanks, I'm fine, really."

"When did you get here?"

"Oh. A while ago I think." I fiddled with a strand of hair.

Paul was close behind me, swaying on the step below. I could see how it looked.

"Rehearsal went on a bit too long. You're not leaving are you?" He glanced at Paul still hovering on the stairs, befuddled by alcohol, Paul leaned in to focus on the conversation.

"Er, this is Paul," I said quietly.

Paul had insisted on walking me safely back to the Home despite being staggeringly drunk. It was only a short walk, but I hadn't been able to deter him. I felt him rest a hand on my shoulder, more for balance in the circumstances, but Mark noticed.

We tried to chat for a few minutes, but with my chaperone swaying behind me on the landing we weren't able to say much. It felt forced and awkward, and I walked home contemplating missed opportunities.

\*

For days, the encounter with Mark continued to play on my mind. I wished I'd stayed longer at the party to talk to him. Perhaps I could have returned after Paul had walked me home. I'd been studying the local gig guides for the last week. There were a number of places around town that featured live music, and I checked to see where the band would be playing.

Most of the venues were within walking distance, and I soon perfected the ability of arriving with a degree of nonchalance that belied the level of planning beforehand; as if my being there was some strange coincidence.

For a few snatched minutes we met incidentally on several occasions around Launceston, but there were always too many people, and it was impossible to determine if I'd misconstrued his friendliness.

One late Sunday afternoon gig, when the band had finished playing, I was approached by a young girl who introduced herself as Cathy, the drummer's girlfriend. As she chatted, I realised she was inviting me to join them all for a meal after they'd cleared the equipment from the stage.

"I'd really like to have proper food," she was saying, with the intent of being overheard by the band. "With knives and forks. And real plates. I'm so sick of take-away food."

I waited as the doors at the rear of the stage were opened, and guitars and drum cases loaded into vehicles outside. My presence had finally been noticed.

Despite Cathy's request we ultimately had to settle for take-away in the wholesome setting of Princes Park. This was, after all, Launceston on a

Sunday afternoon, and the choices were limited. So we sat in the leafy square of the park with our pasta and pizza in plastic takeaway containers, opposite the bronze fountain, resting on the peeling painted wooden benches, chatting as the light faded into the cool evening, and feeling the chill in our perspiration damp clothes.

Mark was staying with his parents, somewhere just outside the city.

"We'll be here for the Christmas holidays and there are venues lined up for the next few weeks, all across the state. We'll be in Tassie for a while," he said.

I liked him, the gentle way he spoke, his smile, the way my heart raced when my eyes met his.

"It must be a big tour then?"

"It's not all work," he smiled. "I'll be staying on for the summer, but the band'll go back to Melbourne after the gigs."

As everyone eventually stirred to leave he offered me a lift home.

"Can I drop you off somewhere?"

I didn't know if he was just being polite.

"Oh thanks, but I only live up there." I pointed vaguely beyond the park, towards the top of Charles Street.

As soon as I said it I regretted my reply, but it was barely three blocks to the hospital from the park. I wished we'd been on the other side of the city so that it would have seemed reasonable to accept.

Watching them all head off together, I wondered if they thought I was just another fan. Perhaps Mark saw me as a groupie that kept turning up at gigs and shadowing the band. The only way to find out was through the music. The only way to get to know him would be to keep turning up. At least I knew where to find him.

Fading Fish poster, outside Princes Park, Launceston

## Like Two Mexicans Dancing

**F**INALLY, at the Launceston Hotel's Club 107, something changed. When I arrived the bar upstairs was already crowded. I'd seen Mark immediately but decided to wait and see if he would seek me out. I bought myself a drink at the counter, and found a spot where I could lean against the wall.

"Hello." He was standing in front of me, smiling, his face lightly tanned and his hair streaked with blonde from the sun. They'd been out of town, probably playing at a few venues in Hobart, but it was obvious that there had been time for relaxation.

"You look really well," I said, feeling my eyes dilate at the sight of him.

He looked genuinely surprised by this compliment, as if he'd expected a lot less of me, and we stood talking for a few more minutes before he was called backstage by the others. Some of the residents of the Home had begun to filter into the crowd and so I found the Maloney brothers to ensure I'd have dancing partners for the night, hoping that Mark and I would be able to talk again at the end of the evening.

They were a foursome of drums, bass, and two guitars, and that night was filled with all the usual musical mayhem, with sweat, stage diving and broken strings. Like their posters said, they were a little bit thrashabilly, a little bit pop, singing mostly their own songs, but with a few floor stomping covers thrown in. The harmonica and mandolin gave them the edge, and everyone playing strings could sing.

I'd seen Cathy wandering around the stage with a video recorder, in big Doc Marten boots, and wearing black and white striped stockings that reminded me of Pippi Longstocking. Everyone had thrashed and danced all night in the centre of the crowded room, with energetic verve and flailing arms. The boys had scrambled through the set with familiar ease, but the crowd was thinning now as people started to make their way home.

Mark and the rest of the band were clearing the stage of equipment, dragging cumbersome amps, dismantling the drum kit, and winding extension leads from the PA into meticulous coils to be neatly stored in their crates. The remaining handful of punters was largely connected to the band in some way - the meticulously groomed set of hairdressers, and a few other musicians from the local scene who tagged along to parties, or filtered in and out of the backstage area. I'd included myself in this group since Mark had asked me to wait, and all of us were sprawled in a rather jaded fashion on the stained carpet in a corner of the room. It was late, but I didn't mind waiting, watching him move across the room, stacking the equipment.

By the time Mark was free to sit down and talk, the bar was closing to the few stoic drinkers that remained. He tossed himself into the lethargic group on the floor, and took a deep gulp of his beer as he began to chat to a few people. Despite having asked me to stay I still had misgivings, and as time passed I began to wonder if my intuition had been wrong. I hung back, slowly dragging a resentful coat across my shoulders. Minutes were slipping away. The night was almost over despite my attempts to prolong it.

As I stood to leave I realised Mark was speaking to me directly, asking me something. I watched his lips as he spoke.

"I was wondering. Well. If it wouldn't be too presumptuous. If we could, erm... have a drink sometime?"

Definitely. Finally. At last.

I tried to leave a respectable pause before answering.

"Yes, that would be nice. I'd like to," I replied, with considerable understatement.

"Perhaps I can call you, at The Home? Can I get the number from you before you go?"

Despite the inherent risk, I was curious to see how much effort he'd make to track me down. I didn't intend to make it too easy for him.

"Sure. Look, it's in the phone book. Home Three. And there's only one Angela."

I didn't know where he was living, and I didn't even ask for his number. If he took the trouble to find me I'd know for certain that he was sincere. As I left I looked back at him smiling at me, hoping I'd done the right thing.

I had a feeling that I would see him again. My heart was beating recklessly with the gamble I was taking, but I was being guided by instinct, and it was telling me that he would call.

## Like Two Mexicans Dancing

SOME MONTHS BEFORE, in September 1988, I had met Tinka. She was a local clairvoyant who lived a short drive from the Nurses' Home, in a rather disorganised house surrounded by wire fencing and a locked gate. The interior was dark and cool like the dusty confines of an antique shop, and advertised the inclinations of an erratic housekeeper. For more than an hour I had sat absentmindedly reading magazines, waiting for my friend to step out of the visitor's room so that I could take my turn.

Tinka smiled as I entered the room, a middle aged woman, barefoot and wearing only a zip fronted dressing gown. She was smoking one of the many cigarettes that she lit in steady succession as we chatted, drinking the first of many coffees, and speaking easily and good humouredly about herself. I liked her eccentricity, her refusal to wear any clothes other than her dressing gown. She told me she wanted to fit into a smaller dress-size, and had to lose weight before buying anything.

Over the next couple of hours, as she enlightened me about current and future events in my life, I was struck by her strange insight, and frequently moved by her accurate assessment of my character. She either had prescience, or incredible intuition. I didn't know what to believe, and yet I hesitantly asked the customary questions about fortune, love and marriage. On the latter she was quite specific, and I was surprised by some of the responses about what lay ahead, particularly about my unconventional future.

In retrospect there are so many questions I could have asked, things I could have sought to clarify, landmarks that I could have used to confirm her predictions. But as she became more animated about successes that lay ahead I just listened with a sense of wonder. One of her more obscure remarks was about a pink room, a place that she said would bring me great happiness. However, at the time the comment made little sense to me. I couldn't think of a place to fit that description, and couldn't imagine it would have much significance.

Her appraisal had rattled me, and when I returned from our meeting I flopped onto my bed to contemplate everything she'd said. Casting my eyes around my room, I smiled. A month earlier, in August, I'd moved upstairs to the front of the building, promoted to the upper level of the Nurses' Home, where my room overlooked the city from the top end of Charles Street. I'd spent hours cleaning my ground floor room, a dim and cramped space to the rear of the lodgings, with a cropped outlook, mostly of the steep concrete walkway outside and its aluminium handrail. Its gradient plunged down from the street behind the Home, making it look more like a slide than a pathway. With my accumulated possessions, I ran up and down the two flights of stairs that zig-zagged upwards in a wide stairwell, the shapes of pot plants shadowed against the glass. At 1am, the transfer completed, I scrutinised my new location, and wrote in my journal:

*Wednesday morning. My new room stares at me in all its scattered splendour. A night of running between floors, up and down the shadowy stairs, my eyes sore from all the dust. But here, the glass sash slides up completely, not a meagre inch, and I have a view that spreads out across the city from my corner window.*

For the first time, in the evening twilight, I took in the colour of the room that I had so far barely noticed. It was a soft salmon pink. Lying on the bed, I looked around me, reflecting on all the things Tinka had just told me and thinking about the future she had so carefully described.

Maybe she did see the happiness I would find, and all the things that followed. I was certainly happy there. Life was uncomplicated, I had friends, and I had a room with a glorious view. From my window, I loved to watch the flaring colours as the sun slowly set in Launceston and the light faded on another day. At that elevation I could see the street lamps outlining the highway's exit out of the city towards the distant hills. In the twilight the trees formed dark, black shadows on the landscape, stark and bold against pale tangerine skies that merged softly into a perfect blue. Those were the months I spent writing and daydreaming, the months before I met Mark.

At times, I've wondered what form her visions took, and whether Tinka foresaw everything, like a series of pictures. It could have been a sequence of freeze frames spread before her, waiting for this unlived, latent future to be made history by my life. I would only need to breathe them into existence from where their story already slept within me.

Perhaps she saw the Mexicans dancing with us by the roadside, their arms outstretched as we laughed. Perhaps it doesn't really work like that. My potential was quite clear, as she described it, but the future would be made by my choices.

Many people don't believe in such things. I'm still not sure. But I think about it sometimes; whether my choices could have been different, whether the outcome would be the same.

*Angela J. Dawson*

The Weekender, Saturday, January 21, 1998 — Page 15

# The Fish Devonport crowds didn't reject

## Russell Jarvis Music

I caught up with The Fish John West Reject at Char's Bar and Eatery, City Limits, in Devonport, on January 11, and what a catch it was!

I did not really know what to expect. What could a group claiming to play a sort of pop-thrash-a-billy actually deliver?

Mention of the term "thrash", in music usually indicates the mindless abuse of instruments for the sake of a good head-banging, floor-stomping time.

The Fish John West Reject occasionally indulged in that but on the whole it mixed the music well, a bit of country, some blues and folk, even Gospel.

There were traces of so many influences it really has to be experienced first hand to be believed.

The pop element is a big part of the music but it mixed hillbilly with acoustic (guitars) modern pop for songs like Lights Out Over Launceston and Andrew Viney's Left.

The band started with acoustic rock 'n roll, in the form of Little Aeroplane by Boston's Modern Lovers and then later went back to it playing Hull's Housemartins with Anxious.

Mark Narkowicz (vocals, guitar), Mark Adams (vocals, guitar, mandolin and harmonica), Andrew Viney (vocals and bass), and Graham Rankin (drums and vocals) are all Tasmanians making a name for themselves in Melbourne and look to have made it in Devonport...they were worth going to see.

As expected there were some numbers I would not have given the time of day but others compensated.

Original compositions such as Andrew Viney's New Moon Cafe and Bees and Flowers and Mark Narkowicz' Lights Out Over Launceston and The Contrived were reminiscent of Go-Betweens and Triffids.

However they are a stark contrast to the music Graham Rankin played in his last band, The Oddities.

Highlights of the night included a traditional Gospel number, Mumbling Word. It was the best example of why the band says it plays thrash-a-billy.

Another highlight was Ann Burley's rendition of a Velvet Underground song called Femme Fatale. Anna was from Melbourne's The Killjoys, a band The Fish John West Reject has worked on the Melbourne circuit with numerous times.

Vocally Narkowicz can be likened to P. D. Heston and Spandau Bal-

let's Tony Hadley.

It was interesting to hear The Fish John West Reject dedicate a song to Noddy's Revenge, the band who gave Graham Rankin and Andrew Viney their start.

The song, Dreams of London, was written by Harvey Seward who lined up in Noddy's Revenge and The Oddities till the band broke up over differing musical points of view.

As a crowd-warmer for the first concert of the Warm Cordial Tour '98, which also took in Launceston, Hobart and St Helens, a five-piece band with so-name made its first public performance.

Five Burnie musicians — Doug Kerr (vocals and guitar), Peter Vincent (drums), David Hine (guitar), and Bruce Milne (guitar) and Bruce Milne (keyboards) — wound up from a slow start to a great version of Tequila, and an interesting attempt at Nancy Sinatra's Boots Are Made for Walkin'.

On the night, they decided to call themselves Worst Cook in Scandinavia – believe it or not.

It remains to be seen if the name sticks, and they make a second appearance.

*The Fish John West Reject members are (from left) Mark Narkowicz, Graham Rankin with daughter Vanessa, and Andrew Viney.*

## GIG GUIDE

**Burnie**
TOWN HALL. — February 16: The Deltones. March 9: Charley Pride and Doug Ashdown.

**Heybridge**
FOOTBALL GROUND — February 5: Heybridge Country Music Festival, featuring The Gottani Sisters.

**Devonport**
TOWN HALL — February 13: The Deltones.
CITY LIMITS — February 24: Battle of the Bands, Heat One. March 10: Battle of the Bands, Heat Two. March 24: Battle of the Bands, Final. MALL — February 26: Dr Jazz and the Jazzmen at the Devonport Food and Wine Fiesta.

**Ulverstone**
BATTERY PARK — Aistock (open air Christian concert) featuring Real Tears, Light Manoeuvres, Red Alert, Hearts on Fire and Straight Talk.

**Launceston**
PRINCESS THEATRE — February 17: The Deltones. FIRST BASIN — February 18: Basin Concert featuring The Talk, Boo Boo Gazoo, Dinnertime, Lounge Lizards, Don't Come Monday, The Attraction. NIGHTMOVES — Tonight: The Talk, The Detectives. January 27: Don't Come Monday. No Offense. January 28: Relax With Max. February 2: Citizen Kane, Yellow Rose, Funky Phantom. February 3: Dinnertime. February 4: The Colours. SILVERDOME — Tonight: Noiseworks, Johnny Diesel and the Injectors.

**Scamander**
BEACH HOTEL — January 29: Australia Day outdoor concert featuring The Talk, Boo Boo Gazoo, Dinnertime, Lounge Lizards, Citizen Kane, Relax with Max.

*Like Two Mexicans Dancing*

# Rosie's Bar

IT WAS a Monday evening in January when Mark telephoned, inviting me to Rosie's Bar on George Street, and arranging to meet on Wednesday evening.

Replacing the receiver in the tiny booth outside the lounge room I rushed at the wide staircase, leaping two steps at a time and hurling myself at the landing in a blur, knocking on closed wooden bedroom doors in the dark corridor as I passed them.

"He called. He just called!" I shouted, my feet almost airborne as I went skipping gleefully down the hallway. I would have cartwheeled had I known how to do it, but I just kept running instead.

Faces appeared as the occupants opened their doors to see my retreating form pelting down the long corridor and into the next Home. I was bursting to share my news and I would have shouted it from the balcony, but my friends were all at work. Somehow I'd have to fill the hours until their shifts ended, until they sagged into the vinyl lounge chairs for late night tea and toast. Then I could tell them.

He had found me. It was all I could think about. He had wanted to find me.

*

The air was very still as I walked down the incline towards the bar. A thunderstorm was looming and the low, dark clouds clutched onto an oppressive humidity. It felt as if there had been a lid placed over the sky, trapping the heat. I'd chosen a light silk dress and my favourite suede brogues, arriving early outside Rosie's Bar, already clammy and flushed after the short walk. Pausing to smooth my dress, I took a deep breath before I pushed open the heavy door.

I'd been inside before, attracted to the intimacy of its dimly lit interior. The central bar was rarely busy even when they had a local musician strumming in the corner of the room, and sometimes I'd been enticed from the street to listen to the music for a while. The cushioned recesses and wooden alcoves were so crammed together downstairs that it was hard to get out of the soft folds of the cushions or negotiate a path between the tables to the bar. Against the wall some stairs led up to a sort of indoor dining terrace where thin wooden banisters secured the perimeter. A dozen dinner tables were cluttered up there amongst a crowd of chairs, giving a good spectator's view to the bar below. I was glad that Mark hadn't suggested a meal. I felt far too nervous to eat.

There were only a couple of patrons talking quietly at the bar and at the other tables. Choosing one of the alcoves downstairs I sank into the deep cushions and pulled my diary from my bag, to pass the time until he arrived. My hand touched the copy of Viz, an English comic I'd brought with me. It was my fall back, just in case, something to talk about. I thought it might make him laugh. But it didn't end up being that sort of evening. When I heard the door swing open I knew without looking that it was Mark.

His eyes were blue, the colour of violets. It was the first thing I saw when he sat down. I'd forgotten how startling they looked and how familiar they seemed. They made something shift around in my mind, something I couldn't quite pin down. It was like one of those fleeting moments of déjà vu, and it fluttered there, that thing you can barely see and only half remember.

I kept dropping my gaze as we talked, trying to manage a galloping pulse and the brimming chaos inside me, but I was captivated by his presence, the timbre of his voice as he talked, and his gestures, like the way he swept his hair back with one hand.

He leaned in, pulling my half-finished drink towards him, fingering the glass where I'd touched it. I was transfixed by his hands, crossing my arms on the table and then seeing him do the same as he shifted position.

Before long I knew my eyes would betray me. I could feel my pupils dilating. It was like leaving a window wide open, straight into my thoughts, and I was sure he'd see what I was thinking. But when I looked up his eyes reflected the same dark intensity. I could barely see the blue anymore. The humid evening had made it warm in the bar, but that might not have been the only reason I was feeling flushed and breathless. I was discomposed by his charisma, and by the intensity of the attraction, the speed of it all. I hadn't expected it to be so compelling.

We must have been in the bar for a couple of hours before Mark made any reference to leaving. I couldn't believe we had talked for so long. It felt as if time had contracted, and yet I thought how endless it had seemed when I had been waiting to meet him.

"Where shall we go next?" he asked.

So he didn't want to end the night yet. Perhaps he realised I felt the same. I was relieved. We tried the shabby bar at Night Moves, where I'd originally seen the band play, but on a weeknight there was only a small group of people drinking and so we moved on after a short visit.

He had a red Gemini parked further up the street, and after a few minutes he began to steer it up the steep streets that climbed towards the Gorge. With the lights of the city shimmering behind us, the darkness had somehow settled in during the time we'd spent together, without us having noticed. The road opened out to the parking area above the First Basin where a few vehicles sat, dark and empty. Leaving the car there, we began to walk down the steep incline. I glanced at him. There was very little light, the night folding around us and obscuring all details beyond the paths; but it enhanced the intimacy, and made us instinctively close the gap between us, walking through a darkness contoured by a mystery of shapes.

Through the boom gate, and beyond the cafe and the chairlift, we could see a path on the left that wound around to the suspension bridge. It was lit at regular intervals by dull yellow lamps mounted on small pillars. They cast a glow across the loose rocks, and their positioning made it easier to follow the uneven path. Eventually this meandering route passed through the gardens where the peacocks wailed so hauntingly at dawn and dusk. It connected to the walking trail along the north face of the Gorge; the same trail on which Dave and I had taken our wild bike ride into the First Basin only weeks before.

I didn't take his hand as we moved slowly through the dark. I wanted to save that moment. I wanted to remain fully aware of the perimeters of my own body, and to feel his proximity. He was just out of reach. Occasionally we bumped shoulders in the dim light, stumbling on the gravel, but I kept my hands resolutely planted in my pockets as we walked. He didn't try to take my hand, but it didn't matter. I knew what I'd seen in his eyes.

"I went to Melbourne for the band," he was saying, "because you have to get out of Tassie if you want to get anywhere. But I always love coming back to Dilston and seeing the orchard. It's where I grew up after all. Sometimes the size of the place can get me down after a few weeks. You know how it is. It can be so insular; but I miss Mum and Dad when I'm away, and my dog, Panda."

"I don't really miss England. Well, not yet anyway. Everything's still so new to me here." I was keeping my eyes on the shadowy ground.

"Do you think you'll stay here?"

My heart skipped.

"I don't know. I've made some great friends, but I can't imagine where I'll end up living. I suppose I'll just know when it's time to leave here." I'd already sent off paperwork requesting an extension to my one year visa, but I had no idea if it would be rejected.

I'd been walking slowly without really seeing anything, but we'd already looped through all of the pathways meandering through the gardens.

Returning to the car, neither of us mentioned the trip home yet, despite its inevitability. We drove instead to the Corra Lynn reserve with all the car windows wide open, inviting the lethargic night air to come charging in to revive us and to make us believe that the quiet evening wasn't drawing to a close.

There was no-one else at the river bank when we stood plopping rocks with a dull gloop into the black water. I could feel the wetness of dew seeping into my shoes from the grass as I watched Mark skim a stone. We'd been talking about relationships, and I was trying to explain something.

"You know the sort of people I'm talking about, who have lots of relationships but never get serious with anyone. They act cool and say they don't want to get involved when really they're just scared of being hurt."

"They're kidding themselves," he agreed, to my surprise.

"There were people at college who acted like it was a sign of weakness to care about someone," I added.

"I know a lot of people like that. They cause chaos in other people's lives but never stick around to see the outcome."

"Really?" I asked, waiting for him to continue.

"Sure, this business attracts a lot of those people. In it for the thrill, you know? It's a seedy lifestyle. You wouldn't believe the mess people can make with each other sometimes."

"Mm," I responded, wondering if he was speaking about his own experience.

As a musician he was the object of so much attention, often faced with a throng of eager fans. Casual affairs would be a constant temptation. I checked myself. I was making assumptions of course. I didn't really know anything about him, and after such a perfect evening I desperately wanted my assumptions to be wrong.

"Well everyone crosses your path for a reason," Mark suggested. "That's what I think."

"I've got friends whose lives changed overnight after some random meeting," I said, "you know, when someone just turns up out of the blue?"

"You think we'll all meet someone like that?"

He was standing next to me, but he was looking out across the water.

"Maybe." But I was taken off guard. "I mean, who knows what could happen."

"Just out of the blue," he repeated.

I wished I could read his face to guess what he was thinking, but in the shadowy light all I had was his voice.

We began to saunter again slowly, keeping pace with each other.

"Do you believe in God, Ange?"

"Erm."

It wasn't the sort of question I'd expected, and I needed to give careful thought to my reply. As we walked by the quiet water I felt the significance of my words and how they might affect the outcome of the whole evening.

"I suppose so. I mean. I think so. Yes. I do." A pause. "Do you?"

"Yes I do." I could hear the smile in his voice.

"Why?" I said.

"Why do I believe?" he asked.

"No, I meant, why d'you ask?" I was relieved but I wondered where this was going.

"Because that's why things happen, but most people never realise," he continued.

I waited for him to elaborate.

"Like I said before, everything happens for a reason. It's not just chance," he said.

I thought of our paths crossing. Twice.

"I know what you mean."

"How else would we have ever met?" he added quietly.

His certainty surprised me. It was such a profound question. I would never have had the courage to ask it of someone I hardly knew.

The car was on the other side of the rickety wooden bridge, and as we walked over to it we peered down at the dark water we could hear far below us. I could barely see anything down there in the gloom.

My mind was racing. I was thinking about destiny and chance, and the idea that there was a purpose for you. Providence, luck, or faith? Maybe he was right. We would never have met if we'd left it to chance. We'd met across continents. We'd been brought together.

It was nearly two o'clock when Mark walked me up the gravel path that wound around to the Nurses' Home. From a jasmine bush near the doorway he pulled a few blossoms and handed them to me before he left. I knew I'd see him again. I took the jasmine to my room and sat it in a glass of water, its heady perfume settling into the dusty confines of my living.

Its musky aroma lasted for days, reminding me of the hand that had picked it, and of that perfect evening which neither of us had wanted to end.

Every spring time, as the blossoms start to appear and the sweet perfume carries on the breeze, it brings recollections of that long night we spent together. Its fragrance brings with it those tender memories of Tasmania, of Mark, and of falling in love.

With every passing year, when the buds appear, I am reminded of that time, and the way the blossoms heralded that sweet beginning; and I can hardly wait to fill my room with the heady scent of the distant past, and to relive that wonderful day.

Mark at The Gorge, on the lamp lit pathway

*Angela J. Dawson*

# Ripples

TWO DAYS LATER we were sitting at a table in Ripples, a restaurant adjacent to the art gallery, staring at a plump full moon gilding our view of the Tamar River. In the reflection, I could see the inverted image of the night landscape where the view met the water. It was a still and cool evening, calmed by the regular nodding of moored boats near the ramp and yacht club.

As usual in these situations I was fiddling absentmindedly with my jewellery and regretting that I felt so jittery. We'd been chatting for a while but it was confined to small talk. Eventually, after a more extended pause between us, Mark spoke.

"I'm sorry. I'm really nervous."

We both laughed at his declaration, but I was surprised again by his courage and honesty. Having seen his confident stage persona I never imagined he'd feel anxious about meeting anyone. His admission immediately made me feel more relaxed.

He'd collected me earlier at the Nurses' Home, arriving with the same self-assurance he'd shown on our first evening, wearing a black waistcoat over a white t-shirt, with jeans and a worn leather jacket. I smiled when I saw he was wearing brown Doc Martens. For years I'd had a theory about shoes and what they revealed about someone's taste in music. If I liked the music I usually liked the shoes, and definitely liked who was wearing them.

We shared stories about the time we'd spent choosing clothes to wear that night and found we'd experienced the same indecisions.

"I finally made up my mind, and then my mum told me to go and change. She didn't think any of this was right for a date."

I didn't agree. As we stepped outside to walk along the river bank I scanned his profile appreciatively, admiring the well-worn leather jacket on the tall musician striding beside me. He looked like he'd just fallen out of one of the posters in our lounge room. I considered mentioning my shoe theory.

"Did she at least approve of the Docs though, your Mum?"

He looked down at them.

"Oh, I have this thing about shoes, and what they say about you," I said.

He smiled, as if he already knew what I was going to say.

"They're very cool," I observed, "I like them. I really like them."

The moon had risen high above us as we made our way back to the car. Instead of opening the doors, Mark opened the boot and pulled out his battered black guitar case, flicking open the hinges. I stood intrigued, leaning against a tree as he rested one foot on the bumper and balanced the acoustic guitar on his thigh, ready to begin an impulsive serenade. With a soft riff he thumbed the strings to check the tuning and began to sing *Two People*, a gentle ballad by the Violent Femmes. Strumming the guitar, he began picking out the notes as his voice modulated through the refrain, resonating with perfect pitch, playing to a captive audience of one.

I felt myself relaxing, mellowed by the music, trying to imagine if there could be a more perfect setting. With the tranquil Tamar River as a backdrop, we had the moonlight as our guide. It watched with me as Mark packed away his guitar.

We'd decided to drive to Dilston, Mark soon pulling-over at the shadowy orchard by his parents' house. He parked at the roadside and we waited a moment for our eyes to adjust to the dark, then alighted the car so we could walk beneath the trees.

He was standing quite still, holding out a hand as I moved around the car towards him, my hand closing the distance until it was encircled by his; and without a word we fell in step, picking our way around the fallen apples in the damp grass. I was aware of nothing but the exquisite presence of that first touch, the darkness, and the cool air lingering beneath the trees. My thoughts were directed at that hand, the only point of contact between us, feeling its unaccustomed shape and its warmth, sensing my heart flutter with anticipation.

Under the branches, in the dappled shadows, we walked in hushed conversation. The only thing that mattered in those moments was the feel of his skin on mine, alive with implications, humming with life. We placed our feet on the musty ground, our hips occasionally bumping together as we wandered, settling into the rhythm. I could feel the subtle gravitational pull of our bodies towards each other now, like an inevitable decreasing orbit.

Our hands were still pressed together as we drove away under the blinking stars, neither of us willing to relinquish this first touch. I watched as he changed gears with his other hand, never once letting me go as we cut through the deserted streets.

Even at the Home we delayed parting, knowing we could sneak along the quiet walkways to the front door, just beyond the sleeping occupants.

"Come up for a while," I whispered, thinking of my beautiful pink room, with its old fashioned furniture and view of the city lights.

So we slipped noiselessly through the front door, and up the wide stairs two at a time, closing my door with a click.

"Am I allowed up here?" Mark asked with a slow smile as I flicked on a lamp and covered it with a scarf.

"It's alright, as long as we're really quiet."

Mark rested a hand on the bed, indicating he was going to sit down.

"Is it okay?"

I looked around. There really wasn't anywhere else.

"Unless you want to sit on the floor?"

I slid up the window panel as Mark lowered himself onto the edge of the narrow single bed. From its vantage under the window we could see the night sky as we murmured in the quiet, my thoughts returning to what Tinka had said about my pink room and about the happiness I would experience there.

Hours could have passed, or perhaps it was only minutes, while the moon stared attentively at us through the open sash and slowly rose in the sky. We'd gradually reclined until we were stretched out side by side, lying on our backs so we could watch the stars rotate above us, but I knew it was late and he'd have to leave soon. We'd been unconsciously closing the distance between us as we talked softly, and I could feel the lightness of his breath on my face when he inclined his head towards me to speak. Our heads were almost touching on the pillow we'd been sharing, tantalisingly close, but it was when I turned to him that I finally found a kiss in the only space that remained between us.

From behind my eyes I felt it, the softness of it, the unfamiliarity of his lips. I felt boundaries melt away and edges blur. I was lost in it, diving into the depths of it, surfacing to catch my breath. The slippery warmth of his mouth was mingling with my own. He was tasting me with his tongue, balancing over me, and I felt myself searching, swallowing that sweet sap from his mouth, taking that small part of him inside me.

For a while we became breath and rhythm and endless sensations, millions of nerve endings. When his lips lifted from mine and I saw him coming into focus, he smiled, running a hand through his hair to smooth it down, whispering to me for a while, our heads touching until he had to go.

He leaned on one elbow before standing, and then crouched down to me one last time. I watched him close the door quietly behind him as he left, my fingers resting lightly on my mouth.

I knew he would leave me sleepless from that kiss, from the memory of his searching blue eyes, and I watched through the window as he walked away, knowing that he could return for such a kiss again; leaving me waiting for it.

*Angela J. Dawson*

# Liffey Falls

I HAVE a black and white photograph of the two of us in a field of long grass. It was taken the day after our walk in the orchard, on the afternoon of our picnic, and it captures the sheer delight of our togetherness. The picture shows us lying side by side on our stomachs, propped on our elbows so that we could peer into the lens.

I look at our faces and I remember the freshness of it all, the sense of wonder. There was no longer the uncertainty and the waiting, just the expectation that follows the first kiss. It was the first picture of us together.

The summer lay ahead of us, and our faces smiled continually at the thought of it, our fingers twined together at every chance. We were moving gently, and making discoveries, and letting it all unfurl.

We'd been to Liffey Falls, south west of Launceston, walking down through the eucalypts and tree ferns to the shadowed coolness of a wide pool. To the rear of it a waterfall splashed and fed water unhurriedly from the pool to a shallow stream. We'd balanced on rocks to cross it, and then sat down in the cool rainforest, leaning against the gnarled, mossy bark of ancient myrtle beech so that we could delve into the picnic I'd packed into a small brown suitcase.

Afterwards, only a short distance from the Falls, as we steered the car into a bend in the road an empty field came into view.

"Look! Oh, isn't it beautiful," I said, seeing the waving grass on the deserted corner.

Mark turned sharply towards the verge and let the car idle.

"Shall we stop?" he asked me.

There was a tree casting its crooked shape across the scrubby pasture, the grass curling slightly in recognition of the lazy breeze. In the sunshine it looked like the perfect contrast to the chill of the rainforest shadows.

"It'd be the ideal place to warm-up again," I agreed, my skin still cool from our picnic lunch. "You don't mind?"

"Course not. I can play a few songs if you like."

So we parked on the quiet road, taking our strawberries and wine, and we spread the remains of our picnic on a white sheet that I'd brought from the

Home. Mark carried his guitar across the field and began strumming thoughtfully as he leaned against the warm bark of the tree.

"What are you going to sing?" I asked, holding my camera to my face, and taking a photograph of him. I had a 50mm lens on my Olympus then, an OM10 that I had to focus manually. Pictures had to be carefully planned when I only had 24 frames on a roll.

He was flicking through a catalogue in his mind.

"What about this."

Lying back on the sheet, I listened to the sound of his voice as he began, sensing the soft whisper of the wind in the branches of the tree above us.

I recognised it, *Something Stupid*. It was a Sinatra duet. It was a song for lovers, a song that talked about falling in love. I relished the inferences, feeling a shiver wash over me despite the sun filtering onto my skin through the leaf canopy. He sang *River of Love* then, a song by T-Bone Burnett, a beautiful haunting melody that suited the mellow timbre of his voice. The next was a love song, and the next. I could feel my heart being seduced, hoping it was more than chance, this chosen playlist.

My cheeks were becoming flushed by the wine as I watched him serenading me from the dappled shadows, picking out the notes on the guitar strings. It was sublime, lying there in the long grass and listening to him sing, watching the miniature world of insects running their errands in the low vegetation. There was a dreamlike quality to it all. Without the photograph, I would doubt it had even happened.

In between the songs, we were still cautious, orbiting around the intimations, smiling shyly, and kissing as we lay together in the wind blown, shushing grass. I liked the unfamiliarity of his body when he folded his arms around me, struck by how he made our contours meld together. Not even the breeze could find its way between us.

That was when I suggested it.

"We should take a photograph," I said, "of us."

We balanced the camera on my closed suitcase and pressed the timer button. As the moments ticked, we were left grinning earnestly into the lens, listening to the electronic beeps until the shutter opened and closed.

We lounged on the sheet for a while longer, until I was bitten by a jack-jumper, an inch long ant with large pincers on its front jaws, its bite leaving a painful red welt on my leg.  It happened shortly after we'd taken the photograph of ourselves, and eaten the strawberries that had spilled and stained the inside cover of my case with their red juices.

When we finally left the meadow we drove back into town with all the windows down, the air spiralling around us and tousling our hair.  I took another photograph of Mark in the car, seeing a smile creep across his face as I watched him through the viewfinder.  I was thinking of the photograph I'd taken in the meadow, hoping I would have a good picture when the film was eventually developed.

The songs he sang to me, and our smiles in the photograph say everything about the gentle pace of that leisurely afternoon.  The stain remains inside my case to remind me of that day.  It's like a piece of history captured in the material, although it's not quite so red after all these years.  It's like a moment of time fossilised in the cloth, and I can finger it, and smell that day, and hear him singing in the long grass of that quiet meadow.  I knew they were love songs, even then.

The picnic photograph, in a field near Liffey Falls

*Angela J. Dawson*

SOME TIME AGO I'd written to the local radio station in Launceston, 7LTN asking if I could host a programme. In Manchester I'd been one of the volunteer production assistants for *The Last Radio Programme,* Tony Michaelides' weekly indie show on Piccadilly Radio. I'd spent many Sunday evenings logging the playlist during the live broadcast, organising the competitions, answering the phones, and retrieving the cartridges for the adverts. I missed being in the studio, and hearing all the latest demos from upcoming bands.

For the last few weeks I'd watched Mark play acoustic sessions with Martin at the Launceston Hotel, reminding me of their original busking duo in the Mall. I'd sat cross-legged on the floor as they'd played *Something Stupid,* and the Proclaimer's song *500 Miles,* applauding until my hands ached. I wanted to offer a response to Mark, an acknowledgement of the love songs he'd been playing, and I had an idea how I'd do it.

When I finally received a response from 7LTN I arranged a meeting with one of the programme Managers, Mark Horner, so we could discuss options. "I've been an assistant mostly," I explained, "except for a couple of shows with another DJ. They were in the mid 80's, in the midnight to 5am timeslot. You know, the graveyard shift that no-one else wants."

We laughed.

"He ended up moving into television though," I said.

Chris Evans had looked like one of the Proclaimers, with the same distinctive glasses, and a shock of red hair. His ideas were innovative, his sense of humour intelligent and offbeat. We did a couple of Christmas shows together. It was no surprise that he had risen quickly from the lowly ranks of radio production to host the popular television programmes, The Big Breakfast and Don't Forget Your Toothbrush.

"What about the music?" Mark asked.

"Lots of local content, Ambitious Beggars, Microdisney, New Order. And we had guests like Pete Shelley from The Buzzcocks; and Martin Stephenson from The Daintees, one of my favourites."

He stared at me.

"We're probably not as up to date with our playlist," he admitted.

"Well, it was an indie show. We featured a lot of overseas bands too, like The Chills and The Bats."

Okay, New Zealand, but at least closer.

"The Triffids," I added. "Go-Betweens?"

He smiled.

"And The Church, Crowded House. Yes, we have that sort of thing," he said.

I'd left the north of England just prior to the Second Summer of Love, and before the *Madchester* music scene was getting into full throttle. The city venues were showcasing bands like Inspiral Carpets, The Man From Delmonte, and Easterhouse. A smaller club, The Boardwalk was featuring regulars like Johnny Dangerously and The Railway Children. But it was the three storey, cavernous red brick warehouse, The Hacienda that was hosting James, The Happy Mondays and The Stone Roses as they rose to stardom. As yet it was still early days for the Britpop bickering that had begun to rage between Oasis and Blur, but it was a war that would simmer on for years.

Mark Horner offered to co-host a show with me on a Sunday afternoon. He'd oversee all the technical aspects, and with two of us in the studio it would make the banter between songs more natural. It would coincide with one of The Fish's rehearsal sessions in town.

When I told Mark about the show he assured me he'd still be able to listen to most of it during the rehearsal breaks. Towards the end of the programme I promised I would dedicate a song to him. I'd already made a careful selection.

From within the tiny booth at the radio station Mark Horner and I stamped our way through two hours of self-indulgent musical choices. It was fun and irreverent, and we really didn't care if anyone was listening to our repartee between songs.

I liked the reversal of roles, the notion of Mark being my audience now. At the completion of our set I made my dedication to him, energised by the fast pace of the last couple of hours. The record was cued. We went live. In the small studio I could hear the piano introduction, and then Nick Cave's sultry voice as the song began.

*Something's gotten hold of my heart,* he crooned. It was my answer to Mark's picnic serenade.

# Gordon River and the West

SUMMER IN TASMANIA that year stretched from one day to the next with a succession of clear blue skies and unrelenting sunshine. To me it seemed like an island paradise where it never rained, with miles of deserted pristine beaches, and meandering forest trails. With its charm and unhurried pace it provided the ideal location in which to fall in love. Weekends were usually free to travel across the state, and at the end of January, Mark and I had planned a long drive to the coast on the far west of the island, to explore the harbour town of Strahan and the meandering Gordon River.

We were due to meet my friends from the Nurses' Home later that day, deciding in the meantime to drive down one of the unsealed roads that we hoped would emerge at a beach so we could relax and swim until they arrived. The dusty track and its uneven surface of rocks and craters took us on a winding journey towards an unknown piece of coastline, and even in the cooler morning sunshine the vinyl car seats were becoming hot and uncomfortable as we were jostled over the bumps and potholes. It was slow progress, but the road eventually opened out to a wide expanse of deserted beach with pale, ruffled sand, corrugated by the wind and yawning out to the distant water where irregular enthusiastic waves charged ashore. There was no-one even in sight.

"We've got the whole beach to ourselves. Do you think we're the first to discover this bit of the shore?"

Mark smiled. "Just lucky I suppose."

We unloaded the car, changing clothes and spreading our towels so that we could lie down in the sun, the sand's glow warming our backs, both of us settling down to sleep behind the orange glow of closed eyelids.

"Ow...something's stinging me," I said, sitting up and looking around.

Mark opened his eyes to a steadily increasing posse of flies hovering above us.

"Sandflies." He looked dismayed.

"Is it them?"

"Yes, but they don't sting. They nip. And they're *very* persistent." He swatted at the cloud above him. I was beginning to understand the lack of sunbathers now as news of our arrival spread through the insect population and we were targeted for an exclusive assault. We kept swiping at their continual harassment, but it did little to deter them. Eventually we were forced to abandon any attempt to relax or sleep, and opt for a swim. Even as we charged off down the beach we were pursued by a galloping mob of flies hoping for a final nip. All we could do was keep ducking and giggling as we tried to evade them, like a choreographed dance along the sand.

For half an hour we tousled with the waves, reluctant to leave this beautiful spot, finally breaking out of the water with flailing arms as we tried to avoid further nips, and then scooping our belongings into the car.

Re-tracing the route along the pot-holed road took us to the pub in Strahan where we lunched on fish and chips, eating with our hands and making froth moustaches from our glasses of beer, our skin crusted with salt from the sea. I draped a sandy leg across Mark's thigh as we ate, making little effort to break free when he tried to share his beery froth and smear his foamy lips against my own.

We were staying at the youth hostel, where we planned to meet the other two who were travelling from Launceston in Cecil, James' very battered silver Suzuki, named perhaps after a little too much E.M. Forster. We hoped Cecil would last the distance, and get them there on-time, and so we showered and relaxed in anticipation of their imminent arrival.

James and Carolyn were younger than me by a couple of years, but had quickly become my closest friends at the Home. At the end of their busy nursing shifts on the wards we would sit in the lounge room talking, fortifying ourselves with caffeine and a variety of other substances. In James' case the current favourite was pickled onions, eaten straight from the jar.

Perhaps it was the aftermath of too many bedpans, but he was the most bowel oriented person I'd ever met, quick to reference the state, regularity and satisfaction of any recent bowel movement. He took great delight in being able to ask, Hello, have you opened your bowels today? A phrase normally reserved for his patients, but guaranteed to produce a laugh from me as I sat down for lunch with him at the staff canteen.

Despite his irreverence he was perversely secretive about his own habits and hated to be disturbed during the process.

"I'm going upstairs," he'd announce, implying we should all stay away from the immediate vicinity.

Within a couple of minutes we'd send someone up on an errant task, to dawdle noisily and wash their hands at the sink adjacent to the toilet cubicle. It would be enough to interrupt his concentration.

Having aborted his mission, James would stalk back through the lounge door and huff noisily into a chair.

"Alright Roody?" I'd ask, oozing concern.

"Bah-stards," he'd reply, lighting a cigarette peevishly, and eyeballing the occupants of the room.

It could put him in a mood for at least half an hour.

When he turned twenty, James had tried smoking a pipe for a while, because he thought it made him look sophisticated, squinting through the smoke like a dark haired James Dean. But since his return from a holiday in Bali, he'd changed habits.

"What's that smell?" I asked, walking into the lounge one afternoon.

He'd taken to smoking Indonesian cigarettes, Gudang Garam, and it wasn't unusual at the end of the day to find him quietly smoking one of them at the round table in the lounge.

"It's just one of my Goodies. Too sophisticated for the likes of a sissy Pom," he said, inhaling the fragrant fog, knowing I didn't smoke.

"It smells like dope. Clakkers will be on to you."

He was at full inspiration. "It's….. cloves…." he mouthed, before a rush of expired air.

As we chatted he occasionally interrupted the conversation to push himself off the seat a few inches so that he could fart lustily, in several short staccato bursts. Despite his unassuming manner he delighted in displays of tasteless vulgarity.

"Excuse me… excuse me… excuse me…" he said after each one, in his soft, lispy voice, lifting himself up and down in the process.

When I feigned indignation it only caused a hiccupping laugh that made his shoulders shrug in a sympathetic motion.

"James! People are eating in here!"

"I can't help it. It's the pickled onions," he retorted, as if someone had forced him to eat them, continuing to laugh himself into a coughing fit that sounded like he was trying to clear a fur ball.

His habitual throat clearing cough made him easy to locate in the Home. Otherwise I would just follow the aromatic smell of cloves from his cigarettes.

Since my arrival in Launceston I'd repeatedly asked how James had acquired the nickname, Roody, but no-one ever seemed to know. In the end it was Carolyn who offered a likely explanation.

"It's because he's such a rude boy. He's *Rood*, aren't you darlin'?" she said pointedly, as she grasped his cheek between finger and thumb, and tweaked it like a doting mother.

James had gazed at her adoringly, making no attempt to evade the formidable grasp, and looking in fact quite happy with this lewd interpretation.

"She's Roods," he added.

"What?" I asked, baffled.

"Rood and *Roods*," he enunciated, pointing first at himself, and then Carolyn.

"That's confusing," I said, glancing between them.

"I'm the President, and she's the first Lieutenant twice removed."

They both smiled.

"President of what?"

"The Secret Sect," James said slowly, with a tone that suggested I really needed to keep up.

"I've never heard of the Secret Sect."

"That's because they're a secret."

"Who's in it?"

"We are."

Carolyn blinked, giving nothing away.

"You can be the second Lieutenant, 14$^{th}$ in line to the throne," James pronounced.

"Croods," he concluded, looking pleased with himself.

"Because that's not weird at all."

"We wouldn't want you to feel left out."

At nineteen, Carolyn was the youngest of us, with peachy cheeks and dark hair. She'd often be tackling the latest project, from needlework to tapestry, while she listened to our prattling with a benevolent smile. There was usually something delicious simmering away in the kitchen, or a cake that she'd made earlier. She was an expert at anticipating people's needs, and with her culinary skills and her generous heart she kept us well fed.

"What are you making now?" I enquired on one of those days, peering from the door into a flour spattered kitchen.

"Chocolate chip cookies, and a lemon crusty tea cake."

"I have first dibs," James announced, hovering territorially behind me, vying for whatever was on offer.

"Dibs on what?"

"Just generally."

"Callie?" I looked at her hungrily.

She'd started to whistle stridently, at a volume that made my ears hurt, making me back away. Like my ability to locate James from his cough, I was always able to determine Carolyn's whereabouts from the intensity of her whistling. No one I have ever met can whistle as loudly as Carolyn.

"It'll be fifteen minutes yet, and there won't be any tasting until I've done some fingering."

I stared at her. "What?"

James snorted.

"Roody...." she chided, as she squeezed past him from the tiny kitchen.

With two different types of hunger he watched her retreat to the piano keyboard and lift the lid.

"Fingering," he sighed, with dewy eyes.

The old piano in the lounge could be urged to produce the respectable semblance of a tune, despite a few of the keys being slightly flat for want of tuning, and some of them producing no sound at all. When Carolyn unfolded the latest sheet music she had acquired in town, we'd get a live performance. It was always a marvel to me that, like her whistling, she could deliver such incredible volume and pitch as she sang, and hit notes that even an opera soprano would struggle to reach.

I was keen for my friends to meet Mark at last, and for all of us to spend some time together in Strahan. Being a Saturday night we decided to go to the local pub, which seemed to be the only place for entertainment in town anyway. Had we known how the night would be ending, we probably would have indulged in a few more jugs of beer before we left.

On our return to the Hostel we were greeted by the pinched face of our host. He clearly disapproved of our prior alcoholic consumption and intended to act as our moral compass for the weekend, tapping the Christian fish symbol on the door to emphasize this first indiscretion. None of us had noticed, but in response we explained we'd just be talking for a while and having coffee now. We watched a frown deepen the creases in his face

"Lights out at eleven o'clock here."

It was five to eleven.

"Perhaps we might sit around and just read for a while then," Mark suggested, "since it's still early."

"There's no time for that now."

He was hovering by the light switch in the doorway of the living area, eyeing the four of us, and daring us to challenge him. Under his scrutiny we moved reluctantly towards the sleeping quarters, casting furtive, sidelong glances at each other.

There were a few bunk beds in a room sufficiently large to accommodate us, where at least we could talk for a while, with or without lights. As all four of us began to move towards the room the host's face registered open disbelief.

"Oh, NO. Boys over there, and girls in here," he said, pointing east first, and then west. That way we'd also be separated geographically by the living area.

Our inherently wanton proclivities needed to be managed, and this was the place to do it. With an invisible barrier, the separation of the sexes, and the deprivation of artificial light our urges could be conquered. It was out of the question that we might be able to do that all by ourselves. In actual fact we hadn't gone all the way down there for an orgy. We really just wanted to sleep.

The catalogue of house rules just kept getting longer. Like children, we were sent to bed, traipsing into our allocated areas with wry smiles, barely withholding the laughter that was ready to erupt at any moment. We hadn't even changed into our pyjamas yet. With a final reproachful look our host left, flicking the light switch as he closed the door behind him and thrusting us into absolute darkness.

"Has he gone?" I whispered into the gloominess of the shadowy room.

I could hear the others trying to smother their laughter, and noticed someone moving across the lounge. Torchlight cut a triangle into the blackness and outlined Mark's figure lounging on the sofa.

"I'm not going to sleep yet. I'm not even tired," he said obstinately, opening a book.

"You'd think we could have the lights on to brush our teeth. I mean, we are *paying* to stay here." James was trying to sound vexed, but I could hear the mischief in his voice.

"No. Don't Roody. He might come back."

"Oooo... and find out that we still aren't in bed."

He flashed the light on and off as I hissed my reproach.

"No Roody. Stop it."

"Who picked this place again?" James countered.

"I had no idea it would be like this. You're never going to let me forget it are you?"


In the morning, we found an extensive list of regulations tacked to the kitchen wall which had to be strictly observed by every patron. It involved completing numerous chores such as sweeping and cleaning, making us feel truly privileged for having been allowed to stay at all.

Relieved to have survived the ordeal, we finally congregated outside, waiting for James to pack Cecil. We'd planned to drive to the harbour and find the boat launch that would take us out for a leisurely cruise along the Gordon River. I noticed James was smirking.

"Okay, I know it'll go down in history as the worst place ever," I said, apologetically.

He looked beyond where I was standing and continued to grin openly.

"Actually, I wasn't thinking about that. I was looking at our four legged friend over there," he said.

In the adjoining paddock stood a grey donkey, browsing the grass and feeding quietly. I looked quizzically at James.

"Look again. Perhaps, I should say, at our five legged friend."

When I turned again, I noticed the enormous pink erection hanging down from its rounded belly, the donkey seemingly oblivious to this impressive physical manifestation as he grazed.

James raised his eyebrows in mock disgust, laughing and clearing his throat simultaneously, before dissolving into paroxysms of life threatening coughs.

"You would notice something like that," I claimed.

"He's a rude boy. I told you." Carolyn eyed James affectionately, and patted his cheek as she passed.

"Do you think he ever loses his balance from the weight of it?" James could hardly contain his glee at such a discovery. It was even better than asking someone about their bowels. We just had to hope that our host didn't notice this outrageous indiscretion on the part of our hoofed neighbour. It would certainly contravene the rules of the Hostel in some way.

We arrived at the wharf on Macquarie harbour for a full morning of cruising the waterways, first browsing the workshop in the adjacent sawmill that was slicing through logs of aromatic Huon pine. Picking up an offcut I pressed it to my face and inhaled its strange tang, trying to discern its layers of scent.

Our launch motored across the harbour at a breakneck pace as the Captain continued his running commentary across the loud speakers, entering the mouth of the river where the boat finally slowed until its movement caused hardly a ripple.

"…We'll be continuing at this speed folks, to make sure we minimise waves and therefore any erosion at the banks…"

I could see where the water was lapping gently against the edge of the rainforest as we nudged along imperceptibly.

"…Later we'll be disembarking at Sarah Island to see the ruins of the old penal settlement…"

James snickered slightly and tried to hide it with a cough.

"James," I chided, "he said *penal*."

"I didn't say anything." But he wouldn't look me in the eye.

For a couple of hours in the cool morning sunshine we slid snakelike across the river, its black surface reflecting the trees and ferns that tangled across each side of its curving journey. It offered a perfect mirror image, merging the bank and the water, with no indication of the line that separated them.

As we drifted slowly, the hush and isolation of the rainforest filled us with a sense of reverence, calming and quietening us after our high spirits that morning. Somehow the river had cut a determined path through this dense vegetation; the narrowing waterway overshadowed at intervals by steep bluffs of grey-white rock or hidden by banks of trees, swallowing us further into its quiet depths. We were diminished by the vast space around us.

"Imagine being lost out there," I murmured.

Mark, had his arm draped loosely around my waist where we were standing on deck.

"You'd never be seen again," I added.

"It'd be a long walk home wouldn't it?" Mark replied, staring off into the distance.

Home. The word sat in my thoughts. The quiet had made us pensive, yet below us the river had started to roil and there was a charge in the air. We were steering towards Hell's Gate where the boat met open sea, the waters beginning to churn, menaced by the winds blowing in through the narrow headland. Here the Southern Ocean separated us from Antarctica below. I imagined the sea merging into the Indian Ocean far out to the west, washing around the Cape of South Africa, and clashing with the Atlantic as its currents led it to the shores of England. I'd been away for almost a year now, and until I received a new visa, my future felt uncertain. I had to contain my hope. I had to suspend my dreams until I knew if an extension would be granted.

After a day of being flatlined on calm waters, we were keen to tumble on the rising swell. The movement shook me out of my brooding thoughts, as we all wrestled with the frenzied hair tangling effects imposed by the headwinds on deck. James was sporting a peculiar sort of rockabilly quiff.

"Vertical hair situation!" I hooted, raking my fingers through my own hair, and making my hands into earmuffs on either side of my skull.

"SHE loves it!" James retorted, energised by the wind and the lurching motion.

"We ALL love it!" I whooped.

Revelling in the hilarity inspired by the turbulent air, each of us fell about laughing at the wild restyling, trying to work out who looked the most ridiculous. As the boat shifted and lurched, I anchored myself to Mark, wrapping my arms around his body enveloped in a hug as he steadied me against him.

The newness of his body still startled me, its dimensions and its heat. Pressed together with my head on his shoulder, I could smell clean linen and sun warmed skin, letting my softness sink into the muscular span of his chest. I remembered the distinctive fragrance of the sawmill at the harbour, and the lingering scent of the wood on my fingers after I'd held it.

"How would you describe the smell of Huon pine?" I asked Mark.

"Hmm, it's sweet, a bit musty I suppose…Did you like it?"

"I didn't know wood could smell like that. It's like leaf litter and menthol, a bit like old suitcases…"

"…but it's kind of smoky too…" he added

"… yeah, it makes me think of campfires on the beach, the way the smoke always stays in your hair."

It seemed to contain the essence of the rainforest, as if it had distilled all the dampness and rich decay within, and locked it into the layers of the hard wood.

Carolyn was focussing on us with her camera as we swayed on deck, and captured our moment with a click. It wasn't until I saw the photograph after the film had been developed that I remembered all the aromas of the day. It reminded me of the smoky wood and the salty air, and the tilting deck, all of us balancing on it as the chasing clouds raced high above us.

Later that afternoon, when the boat had retraced its original course and deposited us on the wharf, James and Carolyn returned to Launceston. We waved them off before Mark and I continued our drive on the winding highway through the mining town of Queenstown, with its bare rocky slopes of sandy coloured hills, and naked gullies. We didn't stop to explore the town, or the lack of vegetation.

"What happened here?" I asked as we drove through.

"It's the result of mining," Mark replied, "and deforestation." It looked bleak.

"It's like a ghost town," I said sadly, looking across the valley at the denuded landscape.

The two industries were co-dependent. The timber industry had felled the trees to feed the furnaces. Pollution from the copper smelters had killed all the other vegetation that hadn't already been culled.

From the car window I looked out at the rich, golden colours of the copper laden soil, but the barren view had a haunting, melancholic air. Without trees to show the changing seasons there was no sense of time. Everything looked stripped down and eroded, like a perpetual autumn.

Heading north, we found a youth hostel at Stanley, where the warden gave me home-grown strawberries as we toured the aviaries of colourful birds behind his office. We stayed that night in separate rooms, declining the offer of a double bed or even a shared room.

Mark's gentleness drew me to him. It was never going to be a rushed seduction for either of us. We were careful with each other, moving leisurely, enjoying each moment. Although he came to my room to lie on the bed with me, we only talked in the flickering candlelight. I watched the skin tones of his face change from gold to orange in the flame, and then disappear behind my closed eyes as we kissed.

I let go of my thoughts. Everything became tactile, unseen, the pressure of lips and warm breath, the slide and silk of tongue, a marvel of skin and the weight of him against me.

The summer was ours. These lingering moments would be what I would keep. Beyond that there were endless possibilities.

The Hug – Gordon River

THE FOLLOWING morning we tackled the steep slope of the volcanic rock formation, The Nut which rose up to a plateau from where we could see a vast stretch of the northern coastline, the sea a rich blue beneath us. The sun in the early morning flecked the water with golden highlights as we struggled on the steep walk up to the grassy plateau, taking the circular track around the summit, the rough sea breeze bringing with it the sharpness of salt air, and washing through the spindly grasses at our feet in rippling waves.

The day was beginning to warm, and taking the coast road towards Wynyard we stretched out on the beautiful Sisters Beach, with its powder fine sand and calm, clear seas.

"Why don't I interview you?" I asked Mark. "I can draft something."

I was trying to think of ideas to promote the band, and was contemplating writing an article that I could transcribe later on James' typewriter. But lying on my stomach, one arm propped under my chin, my thoughts were being side tracked by Mark's hands. They were gliding slowly up the centre of my back as he carefully spread sunscreen across my shoulders, pausing to lean forward and lightly kiss the back of my neck. A shiver developed under his lips and stealthily curled its way along my spine, a warm glow that fluttered beneath the skin.

"Mark?"

"Mmmm..?" The noise came out softly like a question.

I was already delving into my bag for a scrap of crumpled paper and a pen.

"Where shall I say we are?" I was tapping the pen lightly against my teeth.

"What do you mean?"

"Well, I can't say we're on the beach. I mean, they might detect a hint of bias if I say I'm interviewing the lead singer of The Fish John West Reject while he rubs factor fifteen sunscreen onto my back, somewhere on a beach in Tasmania."

By now he'd moved down to my legs, tracing a thin line of the lotion onto my calf from the bottle, and extending up my thigh where the gentle strokes of his hands were becoming more distracting.

"Any ideas?"

"How about Rosies Bar, in Launceston?" he suggested.

"Our first date. Perfect." I turned to kiss him, and saw the undisguised look in his eyes. Desire. I was afraid of it, and yet I craved it, feeling myself flush and my breath quicken.

"Mr. Narkowicz, I think you should start telling me why you moved to Melbourne from this beautiful State."

So began our interview as the sand fixed itself to our skin, oily and damp with perspiration, laughing at our duplicity as we prepared our story for the press.

I sent a copy to England, to the NME, the New Musical Express, but I doubt it was ever printed:

**A Fishy Tail**

Tasmania, Australia. Images of the recent movie, Young Einstein, flash before me.

"It wasn't even filmed in Tasmania. Most of the scenery you see is of the Blue Mountains in New South Wales."

Two beers sit on the table in Rosie's Bar, Launceston city centre as I am joined by vocalist, Mark Narkowicz of The Fish John West Reject, their music self-defined as 'acoustic pop thrashabilly'; our initial downtown meeting occurring after I'd caught him playing the Jonathan Richman song, *Chewing Gum Wrapper* during an afternoon busking session.

Melbourne based for the past year, I asked Mark what induced the move interstate from homeland Tasmania.

"The first chance to see Cheap Trick," he grins with a wry smile, pushing back a stray hank of sun bleached hair from a face well covered by a five day growth. He tells me it's been cultivated over the recent Tasmanian tour.

"Actually, it was the first chance to see the Jesus and Mary Chain. Any band that can take a three chord song in the eighties and make something of it must be quite ingenious." (Then again, Stock Aitken Waterman probably pushed that idea too far.)

"Our move was really quite obvious. You just can't play original music in Tasmania. Audiences reach saturation point quite quickly; so if you want to pursue a career, you have to move away to get anywhere. It's obvious by the excess of cover bands in Tasmania. There's generally very little tolerance of the alternative scene, especially when it's original material. Music here can have particularly incestuous associations. With The Fish, we decided to move to a big city such as Melbourne because the music scene over there has had quite a healthy past, with the likes of The Birthday Party, Nick Cave, Blue Ruin. Melbourne has a gritty roots feel, reflected in a lot of the music over there."

Although established in 1985 with Mark Adams (acoustic guitars, mandolin, harmonica, vocals), the two were joined by Andrew Viney on bass shortly afterwards, with the recent addition of Graham Rankin as the drummer.

"The band broke up for a year in 1987 after which Graham automatically joined us, being already a friend of the band. Our change in direction was imminent before his addition, but it certainly channelled our ideas in a new direction. Andrew brought with him influences from the Violent Femmes and Orange Juice, and a more pop oriented sound. Before that, we were putting out a lot more folk material."

Closet hippies? He smiles. "We love hippies."

Listening to the band, there are obvious influences from Jonathan Richman, with *Little Aeroplane* and *Chewing Gum Wrapper*, but the Violent Femmes and Housemartins are also cited, the latter influencing direction, rather than actual song writing.

"Personally, early Elvis would have to be the obvious influence; and Alex Chilton, T-Bone Burnett."

With all the band members collaborating to produce individual songs, then perhaps this emphasises the surprising range, and the combination of styles within the music.

"We devised the term 'acoustic pop thrashabilly' to describe our music. Previously we were using the term 'neo folk river filf', but that was before the recent Coelacanth Tour…"

The what tour?

"…Coelacanth. It's a prehistoric fish that lives in mud on the seabed. It was rediscovered by accident."

Twenty more fish jibes please.

"Yes. It gets rather tedious. The band's name is so often misquoted and misunderstood. People hear it and immediately think of something comical. It's difficult to describe our sort of music. Perhaps early American Hillbilly, together with a modern tuneful pop sound. There're so many different styles within our songs; the common thread of course that we're using the same instruments throughout."

The new album, as yet untitled, will be coming out on their own label, hopefully in April this year. There will be some new songs, and some others taken from Canned and, Shy But Wild, both limited issue cassette releases in Tasmania.

Does that mean early Fish is unavailable now?

"Well, anyone can get the cassettes if they pay us a lot of money."

*Left* is a track that the band is currently completing for release as a single; a song about teenage rejection, filled with thrashing guitars and harmonica. On the album, the other tracks hardly compare in style or sound, with the violin and soulful lyrics of *Always Changes*, and the jangly pop sound of *Green* – which coincidentally is the title of the latest REM album, released November '88. Then there are the yee-highs of *Muleskinner* (Trad) sung with all the angst and scallywaggery of the Beat Farmers song, *Lonesome Hound*, and the homesick lyrics of *The Orchard*. Sing your own shoo-be-do-wops.

The beers are sinking fast as Mark ponders his return to Melbourne. Immediate plans lie with the single, but what about future ambitions?

He considers the neo-hippy folk acoustic pop associations.

"We just want to become Tasmania's answer to Lonnie Donegan."

That was a XXXX was it?

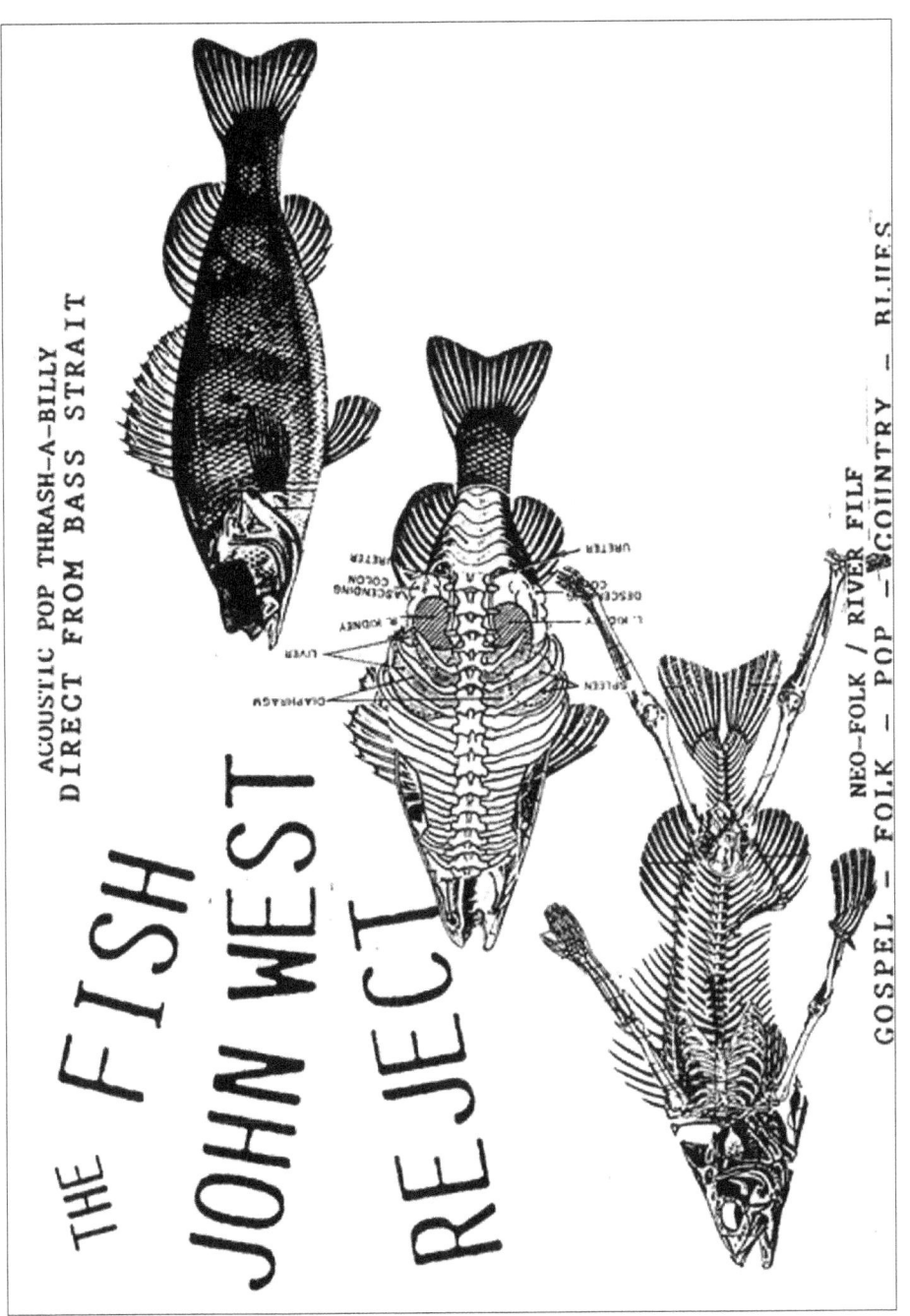

Newspaper advert for Mark and Martin, performing, as The Wetspots

# Wineglass Bay

THE SUMMER continued to unfold languorously around us, with bright sunny days and dappled blue skies that seemed to intensify our feelings of contentment. Tasmania was a place that realised every aspect of my preconceived ideas about love. Isolated from the mainland, its habits were parochial. The cities were small and charming, the roads uncongested by traffic. Launceston had one runway at the airport, and they didn't even have a luggage carousel, a fact that always delighted me.

It was the beginning of February, and we were faced with Mark's final week in Tasmania before he crossed the Bass Strait again and returned to Melbourne. In the remaining days we took a trip to the east coast, trying to avoid thoughts of a departure that we had been dreading.

His last commitment was a Thursday evening gig, with a few other local musicians at the Launceston Hotel. Mark was appearing with his fellow busker, Martin, performing as The Wetspots, and playing an assortment of cover songs. I was impressed to hear him include *Sidewalking*, a recent song by Scottish band, The Jesus and Mary Chain, as well as the usual favourites, and I whistled and cheered my appreciation from the audience.

We drove down to the coast in the late afternoon of a warm Friday, planning a weekend of bush walking in Freycinet National Park. We would be joined by two of Mark's friends that we'd be meeting at the township of Coles Bay. From there, we hoped to have enough time to take the cars to the National Park, and begin the walk before dusk. Mark had told me that the rocky track began as a steady, steep climb between the red granite mountains, The Hazards. We'd be laden with camping equipment as well as heavy backpacks, so we wanted to commence the walk in daylight, when we'd be able to safely negotiate the uneven ground.

John was a childhood friend from Mark's time in Hobart, and his girlfriend Anna-Karin, whom he always called AK, was a Swedish girl that he'd met when travelling.

We hadn't seen their car on the road, and it wasn't amongst the small group of vehicles in the car park as we drove in to look for the start of the walking track in the National Park. A dullness had begun to set into the sky, with a receding light that signified the advance of early evening, and after dawdling to change our shoes and re-arrange packs we were considering a head start in the hope that John and AK would follow us on their arrival. As we looked for the message board on which walkers could leave their details before departing, their car spluttered across the red gravel, suffering the effects of overheating from the long journey. A white Gemini. I looked at Mark's red car.

"Is it a total coincidence that you both have the same car?"

He looked amused. "I persuaded John to get a Gemini because it was such a good car," he admitted. "At least it's a different colour."

"But I thought you said it had lots of design faults, and that the heating in yours had never worked?"

"Yeah, I know. The heating's never worked in John's either."

We all shook hands, laughing at the confusion and time delays, locking our wallets and other tokens of civilisation into the car boots, and taking only the essentials for three days of camping: all things light and biodegradable.

The first half hour took us on a twilight hike up an uneven track that meandered through rocky outcrops of red-brown granite, with potholes and chips of stone littering the way. Scrub grass poked untidily between boulders, dry and spindly like the surrounding vegetation. As we turned back to assess our progress, we could only see green foliage hung over the track in a dense tangle, as if it had already reclaimed the path we'd taken.

Striding up the steady incline, we paused at a level piece of rock that plateaued off to form a wide shelf where we could drop our packs and cool-off for a few minutes. An inquisitive wallaby soon made an appearance, shuffling cautiously to within a few metres of our rest point, waiting for any scraps of food that may be offered, before leaning forward on its short front legs to stare at us beseechingly with soft brown eyes. It was clearly accustomed to seeing hikers.

Resolving to keep a steady pace, we slung on our packs again after our short break, and continued up to the saddle, an area which signified the point of gentle descent into the Park. From this summit area, even in the evening twilight, we could see the perfect crescent of Wineglass Bay, its white sandy beach curving smoothly around a turquoise sea, the tough green scrubland spreading back from the beach and smoothing the angles of the mountains surrounding the bay.

As we walked, we began to veer away from the beach path and follow another track that was obscured on either side by bushes and undergrowth. At one point, after I'd taken the lead, I had to stop suddenly.

"Wait!" I held my outstretched hand to the side like a barrier.

"What is it?" Mark asked, peering over my shoulder.

"Look!"

Ahead of us I saw a long black snake lying motionless, like a dark stocking dropped across the track. As we paused in hushed discussion, deciding whether to wait or chase it from the path, it slid noiselessly back into the bushes. I glanced back at Mark, knowing that it would be venomous, but after a minute's pause he nodded for us to continue.

Before long we retrieved torches from our packs, and casting the light low on the ground we fumbled our way on towards our chosen campsite, feeling the slender wisps of cobwebs breaking on our faces in the darkness as we walked.

The narrow path finally opened to a wider crossing that was relatively bare of vegetation, ultimately leading us to an expanse of beach that stretched long and grey, overhung by a glitter of stars in the black slash above us. There was enough light for us to relinquish our torches, and to walk in the moonlit dark without having to cast our eyes down to watch our step, the sand leading us to the camping area under some trees.

It was midnight, and in the wind there were a few raindrops from a threatened storm. I watched as Mark emptied a bag of assorted poles and nylon tent material, wrangling with the various possibilities, and inventing innumerate combinations. Meanwhile John was speedily erecting their tent, and he began to lay down mats and sleeping bags while Mark continued to display a flair for modern art and aluminium design in a contemporary setting.

All of the frame dimensions he managed to create were out of all proportion to the outer covering.

"It looked really straight forward in the shop," he muttered, dismantling the latest model with a sequence of chimes as the metal components clinked together on the ground. I couldn't help him. I'd never assembled a tent, and could only observe as he started again.

A few possums had begun to settle into the trees above us, interested in this unusual nocturnal display by a group of diurnal humans; and as seems to be the way of possums, they began to move their bowels contentedly. The sound of firm brown pellets could be heard landing dully around us, like small pebbles falling on dry leaves.

"How long is it since you've done it?" I ventured tentatively, "I mean, you must have done it before?"

I turned my eyes upwards to the stars, yearning to have some sort of shelter tonight from this mass of rods and flimsy sheeting.

"Well I've put up tents before, just not *this* tent. I hired it in town, and it didn't look that difficult when she showed me."

By now John was able to assist, and the two of them gave it their full attention as AK and myself guarded the provisions. A couple of inquisitive wallabies had begun to crowd closer to our camp in search of easy food, and under such bold scrutiny we were reluctant to leave any items unattended. They were clearly habituated to seeing campers.

Fortunately the boys soon produced a familiar tent shape out of all the components, and in this promising replica of the original there would at least be protection from the environment, and from our furry freeloaders.

We were ready to bed down for the night, but the indelicate procedures of toileting still had to be undertaken. I picked up the trowel and hesitated.

"Which way should I go? I mean, how far should I go out there to dig a toilet?" I squinted at Mark in the darkness, already stretched out in a sleeping bag.

"You don't need to go far. Just make sure it's not near a water supply or anything."

I set off in a randomly chosen direction, scratched my hole in a patch of unyielding earth that I could barely see, and crouched above it. Mid-flow, I heard a rich throaty growl within a few metres of my exposed skin, magnified certainly by my imagination, and by the dense gloom in the dark bush.

I could hardly have felt more compromised, wobbling in my ungainly squat, and willing my bladder to empty more quickly. I flicked my eyes around, but I couldn't see anything. Were you meant to whistle in situations like this, or was that just in bear country? Or was that an urban myth too? I didn't want to be eaten by anything tonight.

Without wondering about the etiquette of burning toilet paper, or covering the hole, I hastily tugged up my spooled clothing and lurched back to camp with impressive alacrity.

"Some massive thing just growled at me out there!" I hissed, flying into the tent and leaning hard against Mark, scrabbling into my sleeping bag for extra protection. As if feathers and nylon would be any defence against teeth or claws.

"Don't worry, it would've been a possum," he mumbled with complete disinterest, turning over sleepily.

I could feel my eyebrows arching up to meet my fringe.

"You mean a cute, doe-eyed thing like that…can make a noise…like a…six foot beast…vvvvomiting a pizza at high speed?" I spluttered, listening to the pellets emitted by their cousins dropping onto our tent roof.

I yanked down the zippered opening briskly, hoping the noise would scare them away. My hammering heart was reverting to a humiliated thud.

"It's alright now. Just get some sleep," he countered, rolling over to drape a warm arm around my shoulders, and drifting into a comfortable slumber.

Outside I could hear the possums scratching around our possessions, trilling and chattering amongst themselves. It really did sound like they were laughing.

Through the night I awoke intermittently to rearrange my stiffening joints on the thin rubber mat that barely concealed the lumps and stones beneath us, nudging Mark occasionally to make him turn over whenever he shifted into a higher gear of blissful snoring.

\*

When I eventually opened my eyes, our tent was lit-up the colour of fire.

Diffuse sunlight was illuminating the orange material in the early morning, casting a warm glow across Mark's face, still softened by the spell of sleep. Pulling on yesterday's clothes I crawled out of the tent, greeted by John and AK who were already boiling water for tea on their portable stove. They were surrounded at a cautious distance by several watchful native animals which seemed to be making ever decreasing circles around our camp.

After a moment, Mark emerged for muesli and tea, before we started dismantling the tents for departure to our next camp. We'd be moving deeper into the Park soon, leaving the animals to scrabble around the clearing and the remnants of our fire.

We continued to follow a path around the bay under a cloud-hung white sky, the air humid and thick on the sunless morning, all of us content with the scenery and with our private thoughts, everyone keeping a comfortable pace in the heat.

When we reached our second campsite, there was a hut made of both stone and wood, plus an outhouse that looked like a small wooden dunny. I decided to investigate the interior with cautious optimism since it was a certain Tasmanian peculiarity to find a flush toilet, even on mountainsides, even in places far removed from all signs of civilisation. Dubious about whether plumbing could extend to such a remote location, I still wanted to check it out. If it was only a bush toilet, even the long drop into a cavernous pit was a step-up from having to dig a hole.

As I peered around the half open door, and the light caught the interior, I saw movement along one wall from roof to floor. A beautiful undulating mesh glimmered in the shaft of light from the door. I stared at it as my eyes adjusted, and as the details became more distinct I could see it was a veil of spindly mosquitoes, hanging like a long curtain from the dunny roof, their legs interlinked to form a fine network, as delicate as a cobweb. In slow motion, it wafted away from the wall as the breeze from the open door lifted the free end of the fragile net, and I hastily stepped back should it detach from the roof altogether, and the insects take flight. It floated back into place as I held my breath, and I carefully retreated. Scant comforts here given the current occupants, but I'd satisfied my curiosity that it was a pit toilet. Ruefully, I accepted that I'd be digging holes again later for any toilet visits.

Once we'd picked an area for our camp, I removed my heavy backpack, my body immediately cooler, and pleasingly weightless. The breeze was now able to dry my perspiration damp shirt from where the nylon pack had clung to me, and my movements felt light as I assisted with the tents. As soon as we'd unpacked, I changed into my swim wear and set off walking to find a place to wash. I knew I'd have to bathe in the sea, but after the humid day of trekking, the sight of the empty shoreline was an idyllic scene and I waded into the cool waves, kneeling on the sandy bed as the water pushed me gently to and fro.

I could feel the salt drying in a sticky film on my skin as I walked back to camp, finding everything quiet on my return, with everyone resting for the afternoon. I decided to join Mark for a couple of hours, both of us snoozing in the glow of our orange cocoon, zipped away from any circling mosquitoes in the shadows.

We rose before dusk to prepare our food in the dank, cool interior of the hut, with its thick wooden table and empty, glassless window frames. From the rafters above we could hear scuffling, and once our food was spread across the table a pair of possum eyes became visible in the shadows overhead, watching proceedings closely and seeking any opportunity to snatch a morsel.

Around the window there were inscriptions carved into the wood by previous trekkers, and so while the others chopped and cooked, I read some of the messages in the dim light, before taking my penknife and adding my own.

"The Fish John West Reject 1989" I wrote, adding a rough picture of Ol' Shep the fish, an image that was always incorporated on their posters and flyers.

The evening brought an absolute darkness, without moon or starlight in the cloudy sky, and so we built a raging fire in a clearing near the hut, listening to a silence broken only by the sound of crackling wood and our conversation. We sang and talked until the flames died to glowing orange embers, our faces flushed from the heat and our hair thick with the smell of wood smoke.

We squeezed the life out of the dying fire before we left, slipping into an absolute darkness once all traces of it had been extinguished. Then in the featureless gloom we retreated to our tents, supplemented with makeshift mattresses of springy bracken that we'd scooped together to make a softer foundation underneath our beds for the night.

\*

Stretching in the early morning light I awoke with words on my lips, like they had somehow settled on me overnight. They were my first sensation. I could feel them on my mouth when I opened my eyes, and saw Mark's face, as if I'd made them while I slept. They spoke of a certainty that was continuing to grow. Feeling them echo within me, I didn't even need to speak, just lean across to kiss his sleeping mouth; as if I could smudge the words against his lips from mine. I love you, they said. I love you.

We had a long hike ahead of us through the Park, the day a sulking, cool Sunday with bland white skies and low cloud hanging moodily above us. We walked steadily back across the meandering tracks, calf muscles aching as our feet sank into the soft sand of Hazards Beach, leaving only our line of footprints on the deserted coastline.

Rain seemed imminent as we watched the restless skies. At times, a few fat droplets tested the descent, bursting onto the ground in rehearsal for the real thing, as if they were too heavy for the sky to keep holding on to them. They would soon erase our tracks if they gathered some momentum, or perhaps the distant sea would reclaim our footsteps, if it ever advanced so far upon the beach.

At regular intervals we stopped to cool off and drop our heavy packs, drinking the water greedily that so far we'd been rationing. Now it was just extra weight to carry as we neared the car park.

Finally, we were within sight of the steep climb back up to The Saddle. Making a steady ascent, with laboured breathing, we paused at the apex to look back at the wide crescent of Wineglass Bay behind us, its scoop of white sand corralling a flute of blue ocean. Weaving our way through the last of the vegetation, only the downhill section remained. We braced against the descent, packs cinched-in tightly, our shaky legs absorbing the natural acceleration generated by the slope until the track gradually levelled out and fed into the car park.

Although I was thinking ahead to a bath and clean clothes, I was in no hurry to return to Launceston. If anything, I wished I could stop time for a while. In a few days Mark would be gone, returning to his life and his Melbourne home. I watched him hopping around next to the car, changing shoes and searching in his pack for clothes that were a little less filthy.

I didn't want to think about how I'd spend my weekends in the weeks to follow, or how the time would drag endlessly without him. Tasmania was no longer just mine. I was surrounded by memories that we had created together. Everywhere I went would remind me of Mark. Without realising I had let him into my home.

# Orion

OUR FINAL DAYS were filled with a sense of desperation as we were faced with an indefinite separation that neither of us wanted to acknowledge.

We spent Monday evening walking hand in hand through the vast grounds of City Park, adjacent to the Royal Oak Hotel, talking quietly in the dusk and into the advancing night.

It was a place of fountains and duck ponds, and had acres of rolling gardens that stretched to the Tamar River. Its endless looping paths were often deserted at night, and it was the ideal place to walk without destination or purpose.

We passed the Victorian bandstand, and skirted around scattered statues and memorials for the Boer and Crimean Wars. The native blooms in the conservatory were little more than ashen shadows beyond the glass, and we could only see a silhouette of the monkey island. It had always seemed an odd feature of the park. A native animal enclosure would have seemed more apt. But it had been a gift from Launceston's sister city in Japan, and was normally filled with a troupe of mischievous Japanese macaques. At night, the water in the moat around its perimeter had a silvery glint, but we could see that the rocky area in which the monkeys normally tousled and chattered was empty and quiet.

Finding the swings at the far end of the park we lowered ourselves into one of the seats, our bodies moulding together as we swayed gently. The chains that held the seat to the frame above creaked in the silence as we kissed tenderly in the dark. It was midnight, and although my body was aching with desire I couldn't think of anything to say that would make a difference. He would still be leaving, whatever was said or done.

With faces only inches apart, we gazed intently, reluctant to break eye contact, memorising every feature. We were filling ourselves with each other, storing away enough detail to last through the long weeks ahead.

Mark took my hand, and kissing the back of it, held on to it like he'd recovered something he'd once lost. I looked up at the sky and the scattered stars above us, sighing deeply.

"Can you name any of the stars up there?" I asked him.

He pointed out the four of the Southern Cross.

"Why don't we choose a star," I suggested, "so that when you're away I can look up there, and see it watching over both of us, wherever we are?"

He nodded. "Okay. You choose," and he watched my eyes searching, trying to find something that would be easy to distinguish in the future.

I pointed at my selection. It looked like a brooch, almost symmetrical, with two stars equidistant from a central line of three.

"Which one?"

"All of it."

"But that's a whole constellation. Orion, the warrior. That star at the top is his head, and the three in a line are his belt," he explained pointing skyward, "then the bottom one would be at his feet."

"Well I want Orion then. It'll always be easy to pick out in the sky."

"Alright," he conceded. "When I'm in Melbourne I'll look for it. And now whenever I see it I'll always think of you."

It was symbolic really. Two stars set apart from a central strip; as if it represented our imminent separation by the Bass Strait, Mark on one side and myself on the other. We stared at it for a long time with our heads together, before we set off walking again through the park. Every now and then, I looked up to see its trajectory, to see how it moved over us as we walked.

It's the sort of thing you do when you're in love. It's the chance you take, the conviction that nothing will ever change, that love is once and for all time; that life with all its inconstancies will never divide you. I will always think of you, he'd said, his words enduring, becoming as permanent as the stars themselves.

I still like to see Orion rise, as soon as the blackness becomes absolute, as soon as I can pick out the pattern amongst the strewn glitter of stars. Far from the city lights, where the darkness is more profound, you can see the faint glimmer of a sword trailing from his belt if you stare long enough. Whenever I'm outside at night it's customary to look up and search for Orion in the evening skies, if the night is clear, the permanence and reliability of his appearance somehow reassuring, his shape so distinctive.

It has become a long practised habit, the way my eyes will stray to the heavens and linger on the dark sky to seek him out. It's like our story has been etched into the night, our love glinting there from above, amongst the stars, for everyone to see.

WEDNESDAY NIGHT was restless, with the promise of a storm. Mark was due to leave Launceston the following afternoon, and so we spent the evening at his home in Dilston. We walked through the orchard's fallen apples with his dog, Panda snuffling at the windfalls in the grass, ears always tuned for the sound of possums scratching around in the garage rafters. Even the hint of one would send her into excited paroxysms of barking.

Later, streaks and flashes of lightning began to fill the sky overhead as we returned to the Nurses' Home, the thunder growling and crashing above the noise of the car engine in the heavy air outside. The rain still held off as we parked the car, walking up the gravel track with hands clasped together, and following the path around the building towards my room.

We climbed the stairs to my pink room and stepped inside. As I turned to Mark he was pulling something out of his pocket.

"Keep this for me." It was his black and white cotton scarf. He'd folded it neatly, and was gently pressing it into my hands.

"But it's your favourite."

"I know. Have it. It's yours."

I remembered it from the first occasion I'd seen the band play in August, the previous year. He'd often worn it on stage since then.

"Thank you." I folded it into my hand, and held it to my cheek, unable to articulate what it meant to me.

Then he left, closing the door behind him with a quiet click. I turned to the window so that I could slide up the lower sash and rest my chin on the sill as I lay across the bed. It was a familiar routine. It was the way he always said goodbye.

By now he'd negotiated the stairs from the shadowy upstairs landing to the front door, and as I watched it open, he stepped out into the moonlight. Normally we'd speak in whispers, with my words and laughter floating down to where he'd stand below, his upturned face in relief, detailed by the orange glow from the night lights on the wall above the entrance. He'd promised that one day he'd bring the guitar to serenade me here, below my window.

But tonight we just looked at each other across the silence. It was his last night with me in Launceston. I felt like I'd forgotten how to breathe. As he stared up to my window, he bit his lip to contain a smile that prevailed, animating his features. Then he shook his head, and sighed, as if in disbelief. I could feel tears beginning to blur my vision as I watched his changing expressions. I wondered what he was thinking.

Lifting his chin slightly, he spoke very quietly.

"I love you."

Nothing else was needed.

He turned to stride away, his coat brushing past the Jasmine bushes as he disappeared down the walkway.

I watched the space where he'd been standing, overcome by a sense of loss, and straining to see if he'd come running back along the path. But he'd gone.

Wiping my face and casting my eyes upwards, I could see Orion staring back at me like a promise. I nodded to myself, closing the window on the hum of the sleeping hospital and on the remainder of the night, leaving the storm to wake up the dark skies. We were under the same stars now, linked together under the same sky. I would never forget that.

AFTER WORK the next day I'd decided to travel with Mark up to Devonport on the North coast, where the vehicle ferry departed at the mouth of the Mersey River. Although it only delayed the inevitable, it meant we had a few more hours together if I travelled with him. It had been an easy decision.

While Mark and the Gemini returned to Melbourne, I would be returning to Launceston on my own. I'd brought my Walkman for the homeward journey, knowing I'd feel the loss acutely in those first few hours. It would only take a couple of hours to Launceston on a Redline bus; a bus that would deliver me home, to the life that I'd had before Mark had arrived.

We talked about the band as he drove, about the imminent launch of *Left/Childless Mother*, and the release of the single on their River Filf label. But it was just distraction.

The loading of vehicles had been delayed that day, and there was a long queue at the port when we arrived, but we sat in the slow moving line until we reached the boom gates. Mark paused for me to step out of the car, and then rolled forward onto the section that led to the ramp.

"I'll see you inside," he said, squeezing my hand through the open car window.

"Okay, I'll wait for you," I said, trying to produce a convincing smile.

In the terminal, I climbed the stairs to the lounge where a covered walkway crossed over to the ferry. From this vantage point I could also see the ramp below with the cars boarding, and my eyes found a red Gemini as it made its way across, flicking back to the walkway then to watch for Mark's appearance.

A clock above me tick-tocked, clicking through our final minutes. I shifted my weight from one leg to the other, scanning the room as I twirled a strand of hair between my fingers. Over the last few days I'd been preparing something for Mark, constructing a tale in pictures and words. The narrative condensed all the highlights of our summer, using cuttings from magazines to link it all together. I could feel the rustle of the folded papers inside my bag and I ran my finger across their edges, checking the clock again and hoping there would still be time for me to give it to him. 'Gone, but not rejected' the envelope said. It was the story of how we'd met.

# THE ODD COUPLE

**IT COULDN'T HAPPEN HERE**

(or, Tasmania's answer to 'Romeo & Juliet')

This **HOT** chick from **MANCHESTER**, on her travels ALL OVER THE WORLD was at the shops one fine morning when she heard screaming fans and the familiar riffs of a song she'd heard some dirty rock'n'roller from The Fish play once...

Honestly, **The things people** do to earn a bit of cash $$ ... these days... "I wonder if it **LOOKS AS GOOD AS IT SOUNDS.**?" she thought as she wandered over; and verrily she wasn't disappointed; AT WHICH POINT she deposited her contribution to

2. the *performing* arts.

Now this was no ORDINARY girl. Nay. She fancied herself to be a bit of a **Radio** celebrity. And as she spoke to this **WEIRD BUT WONDERFUL** wild-eyed, one-legged hippy: (OK: so he had two legs really, but it sounds good) She knew that SOMETHING had gotten hold of her  ...

( We **LOVETT**. They all love it.)

**A**nd so THE SEED was sown...

She knew she would never forget     T-Bone Burnett

3. and the picnic by the falls,

**THE JESUS & MARY CHAIN** and  ...

The **TIME** came for him to leave.

" Balls. " She thought (in extremely small letters.)

Still, the **single** would be IN THE SHOPS

Soon °°°OO on independent **vinyl**.

"Well", she thought, " I'll spend at least 30 bob on that one!"

4. She knew that she would be at a LOOSE END WHEN his ASS WAS KICKED back to Melbourne, but at least she'd have BILLY BRAGG from the land of

(Evil woman)

He was DISAPPEARING, but he would RETURN..

( The UNFORGETTABLE moments of LOVE )

Until they meet again...

# The end

(Shakespeare never did it like this.)

As I stared at the walkway, willing Mark to manifest there, a figure appeared, dashing breathlessly through the dividing doors. It was him.

"I thought I'd missed you," I said, curling into the hug that enclosed me.

"The boat's not ready to go yet; and I still had to give you this anyway."

He leaned away from me slightly and handed me a white envelope.

"Oh..." I could already feel my heart racing, fingering the paper as I looked at him, wondering what he'd written.

"I have something for you actually," I said, "something I made."

"Shall I go first then?" he offered, watching me nod as I pulled out the story. "Gone, but not rejected. I like it," he said, his eyes forming tiny creases at the edges as he laughed.

I studied his face as he scanned the pages, watching the changing expressions. When I'd written it I'd imagined the tale would provide some levity in the final moments of him leaving, but despite his laughter it didn't seem enough now. Words were insignificant. Everything seemed inadequate.

"It's good. I love it," he said, but he was looking at the envelope in my hand, waiting for me to open it.

"My turn," I said, feeling more vulnerable than I was prepared to show.

Inside the envelope was a small handmade card covered with dried, pressed flowers. There was a quote in it, in Mark's handwriting, from a poem by Nan Witcomb:

> "Poets and musicians
> complement each other
> as the sea, the sky,
> as the hills, the valleys
> as the flowers,
> the earth -
> the words and the music together
> may be the soul
> of the world."

Adjacent to this, he'd written a message:

'The past few weeks have contained the most memorable moments of my life.

I cherish the moments of true love that we have felt, the moments of friendship, joy, sadness and silence.

I thank God for a full moon, for a brilliant storm, for a waterfall, and a lover's kiss.

I thank God for you and our meeting, I marvel, and I feel truly blessed.'

There was only one thing I could say.

"I love you," I whispered, pressing my face against his shoulder and trying to hide my tears, "come back to me."

I watched the slow motion walk away from me, the backward glance as he waved, and then the moment of his disappearance.

Descending the steps, I worked my way through the scattered people, the friends and family left behind, the restless children swinging on the arms that anchored them. I found a space on the dockside near the ramp, looking up to the high sides of the ferry. It was teeming with unknown faces, with bodies leaning and arms pointing, hands flapping at distant figures. Towering above the ship a heavy cloud had begun to gather, darkening the expanse of sky, and as I lifted my eyes to scan the deepening grey, I heard a shout from the crowded decks. Mark was waving far above me as I felt the first few drops of rain beginning to fall, and I waved back, scrubbing the air between us, rising onto my toes as I tried to lean to him.

The rain soon gathered momentum and began to obscure the view, hailstones beginning to accompany it and making most people run for cover in the onslaught; but I'd opened up an umbrella and intended to stay until the ship departed. I huddled on the spot, waiting as the intensity of the storm eased to a light rain, wondering what to do with this extra time when we were within sight of each other but too far away to speak.

Mark was gesturing to me, mouthing the words of a message. He was pointing first to his eye, then to his heart, where he held a clenched fist.

"I... love... " his hands indicated, and then pointed to where I stood on the dock, "....you."

I laughed through my tears and replicated the message to him, pressing my hand to my own heart. He smiled and waved again just as the boat began to move. It had to turn at the wharf so it could proceed bow first, and I walked next to it as it moved further away from the quayside, waving from under my umbrella until I could no longer see Mark's features, only the silhouette of his figure on deck.

I continued to wave even when the ship was too far away to see individual bodies, or the colours of their clothing, hoping Mark could still identify my figure standing on the dockside. I'd folded up my umbrella now, my tears indistinguishable from the rain, hardly caring anymore how hard it fell.

In the distance I could just determine a solitary figure emerging on the upper deck, a person waving their arms and running to the near side. It could have been anyone waving goodbye, but in the hope it was Mark, I stood with arms akimbo, moving them to an outstretched position, like a person crucified. The figure copied my stance, clearly visible with the evening light behind them. I moved one arm up so that my limbs formed the letter L and then reached both arms up over my head for an O, as the figure mirrored my actions. I made a V, and an E. It was Mark. I didn't have any doubt it was him reflecting my message as I spelled it out across the water. Our improvised semaphore became the final word between us as he disappeared from view.

The ship was little more than a smudge sketched into the line of the horizon when I turned to leave. The rain had stopped, but the sunlight was catching the mist in the air, breaking into a rainbow that arched across the water. It seemed unbelievable that something so beautiful could be created there, on such a sad scene.

Boarding the bus for the return journey to Launceston I pulled out my Walkman and a tape that Mark had made for me. I pressed play as we bumped along the road home, hearing the familiar introduction. Jonathan Richman. I smiled, even as I felt my eyes shimmer. The music took me back to the day I'd seen him busking in the Mall, singing this song. It was *My Jeans*. Our story had started then, even though I'd been so unsure at the beginning, waiting for him to find me.

From my open bedroom window that evening, I stared at the lights outlining the Launceston streets, and the clear night sky gleaming with stars.

I remembered something Mark had asked me.

"Have you ever wished on a star?"

"Yes," I hesitated, "have you?"

"Mm, hmm."

"What did you wish for?"

"Love," he said.

"That's what I wished for."

There was a pause between us.

"It was a long time ago," he said.

"Did you think it would come true?"

"Yes," he said, looking at me.

It was one of those romantic notions, a belief that the stars held a magic, and could make wishes come true. Long before we'd ever met, both of us had wished for love.

I looked for Orion from my window, wondering when we might be together again. Perhaps the band would bring him back here, perhaps he would just as easily forget me.

*"Perhaps one day we will be lovers,"* I wrote in my diary in the lamp lit room, smoothing my fingers over the words, and wondering if they would ever come true. As I looked out at the quiet evening skies, I couldn't imagine how that would be possible. But I held onto my belief, with an innocence that had not yet been lost.

## Orion's Belt

The moon,
An eye
In a star struck night,
A stealthily creeping
Unblinking stare;
Symbol of time
In constant vigil
To my nocturnal life.

Darkest hour
That shrouds
The city
In a shapeless black,
And folds the quiet
Of the night
Beneath a hint
Of restless sleep.
I see the winking lights
And know
That her heart
Stays wakeful,
Like my own.

The stars hang bright
That long time passed
Could be the two
On which,

We, lonely,
Wished for love;
The time before
A moon
Had faded,
And you had kissed me
Goodbye,
But left me
With your heart.

# Patience and Telepathy

THE SUMMER evenings in Launceston lay ahead of me like a waiting room of endless hours. Innumerable featureless days drifted idly one into another, the casual pace of life overshadowed by an underlying impatience that intensified with Mark's absence.

I sometimes wandered into the quiet city in the balmy night, down St. John Street, feeling intrusive as I overheard voices from the open windows of houses, murmured laughter carrying on the air with the scrape of utensils against dishes. Porches glowed seductively beyond the light from stained glass doors, throwing high shadow into the cast iron latticework overhead. The smell of barbequed meat permeated the air, and the earthy scent of a watered garden. As I walked, dandelion clocks cartwheeled delicately across the road and into the long shadows cast by the orange streetlights.

I often looked up for the moon and stars above me when the skies were black and clear. Sometimes I could see their reflection in the broken windows of the old church near Princes Square, a small park where I had sat with Mark and the band once, overlooking the illuminated bronze fountain. It looked stark and surreal in the darkness, its cascading waters and sculptured figures dappled by spotlights that had been set to define its contours.

On Valentine's Day, I received a card from Mark in which he'd quoted the passage from I Corinthians 13:1-8

"Love is patient, love is kind. It does not envy, it does not boast, it is not proud. It is not rude, it is not self-seeking, it is not easily angered, it keeps no record of wrongs. Love does not delight in evil, but rejoices with the truth. It always protects, always trusts, always hopes, always perseveres. Love never fails."

Inside the card was a ring, a brass dolphin, its body linked snout to tail. I had been sitting in the lounge room when I'd opened my mail, and James raised his eyebrows as I slipped the ring onto my hand. It encircled my finger perfectly.

"Roody, it's only brass."

"So?"

"Look, I'll call him later and ask him about it."

"Oh, whatever you like."

He pretended to read a magazine as I slid the ring up and down on my finger, reading Mark's card again, but he kept casting furtive looks in my direction. When I phoned Mark later, he remarked on a message I'd included in the handmade card I'd mailed to him.

"So, you eventually found the note I'd hidden?"

"What note?"

"On that yellow Post-it notepad."

"Where?"

"On your desk. I thought you must've copied it."

"I just wrote, 'Mark I love you, Ange'…"

"Yes, but it's the way you wrote it."

"I just doodled for a while until I came up with something I liked."

"But you doodled on the notepad of yellow paper?"

"Yes." I was intrigued.

"Well when you go back to your room, have a look at the last few pages."

When I rummaged amongst my papers later, I found the pad and flicked towards the end. His message was there, the words scattered across the page like my own. It read simply, Angie I love you Mark. But it was almost exactly the same.

I liked this strange coincidence and the weight of its significance, the way we'd shared an idea. It felt like we were humming along with the same resonance.

In his absence I hung onto every detail, and every affirmation of him having been there. I kept it all, every note and trinket, all the things that made me feel connected to him, as if I was collecting evidence. I didn't dare to hope, but every letter that arrived renewed my belief that one day he would return.

IT WAS MARCH, the first month of my second year in Australia. I'd been studying and completing Physiotherapy examinations that I would need to pass if I was to continue working in the country. Then it would be at least six weeks of anxious waiting to hear the outcome. Other hurdles had yet to be cleared, since I hadn't received word about my visa either. My fate seemed to lie in the hands of so many others, and in Mark's absence I'd had too much time to think about the obstacles.

I'd been filling my time with scuba diving lessons, to get my FAUI certificate, and had even been ballooning once, cresting the dawn skies as they began to flush with hues of orange and red. It had been a strange sensation. There was a stillness about it, despite the slow drifting; as if we were stationary in the basket below the flame-thrown heat, and the ground was being steadily rolled out below us.

One evening, there was a phone call at the Home. One of the girls came to fetch me, and pointed at the tiny phone booth.

"It's for you."

"Hello?" I listened for a voice on the line.

"Ange?" It was Mark. "The band's coming to Launceston!"

"Really? When?"

"The middle of March. I didn't want to tell you until we were sure."

They were getting ready to promote their single, and would be playing gigs in Hobart as well as Launceston.

"That's fantastic! How long will you be here?"

"At least a couple of weeks."

It had been more than a month since he'd left, and I knew my nights would be sleepless now until his arrival. He would be coming back.

*

On a Thursday evening, I was sitting on a swing in City Park, nervously expecting his arrival. He was late, and from the shadows I was aware of his voice first, calling my name, worried that I may not have waited. He encircled me in wordless hug when I stepped forward.

"Oh, I'm so glad you're here," he murmured, his arms still around me. His breath felt warm on my hair, but for an instant there was a sense of unfamiliarity about his body after so long apart. I fumbled for something to say.

"I knew you'd get here eventually," I said, feeling myself relaxing into the hug.

"I know. I was delayed, I'm sorry."

"It's okay, I've waited weeks for this." A few more minutes hardly mattered.

I stood with him for a while, letting my body speak for me when words failed me; letting my lips seek out his as he stooped over me.

We strolled back through the darkened park to the road, talking as we wandered the streets into town. We would only have a few hours before the band was due to play.

The 107 Club at the Launceston Hotel was presenting, The Melbourne Buskers prior to The Fish. This comprised the three winning acts from a Melbourne competition, the first being a comedian, Ritchie Rich. The second was a juggler who balanced on an eight foot unicycle, tossing an apple and three machetes, and progressively eating the fruit; and thirdly, there was a group of four saxophonists who played a medley of jazz numbers while they danced to them. The Fish would follow this strange collection.

After our five week separation I wanted some time alone with Mark, but at least we were in the same city again, and it was reassuring to see him across the room in the crowded hotel. I'd been relieved by the gentle strength of his hug, and the way his eyes had searched my face. He'd be leaving for Hobart in the morning so it would be another three days before we had any time together. But I could wait.

Graham was the first to appear on stage, at his throne of bass and snare drums. He drifted like a shadow into the corner, a can of beer in hand, the sneer of a cigarette held on his lip, as he sat down amongst them. Tapping together his drumsticks after the band followed him, he launched them into their mix of melodic pop songs, interspersed with frenzied guitar playing and wild harmonica. Their energy was compelling, and was soon reflected back by the eager crowd.

Mark Adams charged around the stage as the punters bumped and danced, as they cheered and sang. At times he'd exchange his guitar for a mandolin, his long hair shrouding his face in a mass of dark brown spirals. Backlit by the stage lights he was framed in perfect silhouette, hunched over the instrument in rapt concentration, and nodding in time to the music.

"Let Andrew sing!" the girls implored between songs, leaning on the stage. But Andrew just smiled at them from under his ragged fringe, holding his bass guitar low as he thumbed the rhythm.

Mark responded with mock indignation, his eyes flicking to Andrew as they worked on the girls, building the tension, making them wait. In the end, the chant became its own echoing chorus, and the demands of the girls became too great to ignore. That was when Andrew finally stepped forward to sing a few songs with eyes closed, the girls swaying to the beat, and calmed to a dreamy bliss at the sight of him.

The Maloney brothers, had arrived as the band was playing, bringing their usual chaos and energy as they careened and flailed across the dance floor towards me. I could see Paul leaping and head-butting the air, elbows out, and legs on springs. A circle of space opened up around us as we began to bump bodies and pogo jump the crowd, using each other's shoulders to gain height and launch above the mass of heads.

On stage, Mark looked relaxed, singing and raking his guitar, grinning when he'd see me dancing somewhere in the crowd. I saw him share a look with Graham, encircled by the drum kit, drumming hard and furiously, biceps muscles flexing under a black T-shirt. The set was always punctuated by a series of cigarettes between songs, and I could see the glowing tip of the one that Graham had wedged close to one of the amps while he drummed.

My eyes were fixed on-stage to the broken guitar strings and Mark Adams' larrikin antics, my mind impatiently wishing away the weekend, eager for Mark's return after the Hobart gigs. It was stifling in the room now, the air ripe with the musky smell of warm leather and sweat, of cigarettes and spilled beer.

"Oi...!"

It was Paul, and I could see his lips moving as he tried to speak over the music.

"What are you thinking about?" he mimed, following my gaze.

I smiled breathlessly at him across the noise, thinking of how my body ached to be with Mark, wondering if anyone could guess my thoughts.

"You don't want to know," I mouthed, shaking my head at him with a smile. Mark was in front of me, within arm's reach. I could scarcely believe my eyes.

\*

Sunday evening, I met Mark at Ripples restaurant by the river. He'd left the band in Hobart, driving himself back up to Launceston so we could have a couple of days together. From the restaurant I could see small boats and yachts moored between the bridge and the adjacent yacht club. They were nodding to themselves as always, listing idly in the gentle currents. The water's surface captured the blushes of the surrounding streetlights and the moon above, reflecting an inverted composition of light and colours. In the water it was varied only by the slow ripples that passed across at times, like faint shivers on its skin.

Half a moon was watching as we sat inside sipping coffee, the cool night air creeping in through the open door and mixing with the smell of pancakes cooking.

"Do you remember the first time we came here?" I asked, putting my palms flat on the table, fingers spread.

"We were both nervous."

We'd already started to document our memories, keen to remember the beginning, sentimental about the details.

"I can't believe I've been away from England more than a year now," I mused.

"Do you get homesick?"

"No, not at all. I'm having too much fun." I raised my eyebrows and felt my smile widen. "But I didn't plan to stay this long," I continued, "and it all goes too quickly, especially when I'm working."

"So you're happy here then?"

"Oh yes...but I don't think I could live in Tasmania forever."

I faltered, looking down at my hands on the surface of the table.

"I have a great lifestyle here, and some really good friends. It would be so hard to leave; but I can see that I'd probably go. Eventually."

"Go…home?" Mark probed.

"No, no. I don't think I'd want to go home for a while yet."

"What about Melbourne?"

The comment sat there for a moment.

"What d'you mean?"

"Well, would you live there, for example?"

"Are you asking me to live there? For example?" I searched the blue depths of his eyes from across the table.

His face was playful.

"Yes. I'm asking if you'd live there."

He put his hands over mine, covering them entirely; waiting, watching.

"I suppose…you could be a good incentive. For me to leave here."

My sassy answer sounded unfinished, and I blushed as his eyes lingered on me.

"But?" he asked.

"Well, there's the small issue of my visa. I still have to wait for it to come through, and that could take weeks. Months. Besides, I promised Dennis – you know, my boss - that I'd stay until the middle of the year. Which means Melbourne will have to wait until the winter."

He'd lifted one of my hands now, and was kissing the back of it, watching me intently.

"Then so will I."

My mind was reeling, beguiled by his sincerity and the realisation that he wanted me in his life. I could sense there was so much more, and I could feel the magnitude of it, and all that it might mean; but I didn't know how to say it sitting here, with his eyes looking so keenly into mine.

"Do you feel like walking?" I asked, knowing a time would come when we'd be able to say all the rest.

"Sure."

We left the restaurant then, walking across the grass towards the riverside, holding hands in the darkness and feeling our feet growing damp with the evening dew. We spoke of the band as we walked, and of what the future might look like, somewhere between Melbourne and Tasmania, my heart bursting in the shadows, as if it was a certainty, as if it was already written.

*

We drove to Hobart on Tuesday, where Mark had to record an interview with a local radio station, after which we would be seeing Billy Bragg play at the University. Originally this had been a debut support gig for the Fish, but the promoters had dropped the band from the set at the last minute and chosen a different Melbourne band. Weddings Parties Anything would be replacing them.

The Fish knew the band, having played several times with them on the local pub scene, and the Weddings boys were apologetic about this sudden substitution. It was disappointing, but there was no point dwelling on the decision. It was the promoter's choice. Mark and Andrew had decided they'd still attend as punters, and we'd arranged to meet Andrew there, just before the gig.

Mingling through the audience we found Andrew in the crush upfront with John and Anna-Karin, but all we could do was share a few shouted greetings over the noise of the music being broadcast through the PA, sipping our drinks next to the massive speakers.

When Weddings Parties Anything finally made their entrance, the Union building was smoky and crowded, with students having loud, animated conversations, everyone mellowed by the abundance of alcohol, most of it pooling steadily on the wooden floor. The band played a hard and fast set with many broken guitar strings, delivering impassioned bush ballads, floor stomping traditional songs, and favourites drawn from their folk-rock roots. Roadies were kept busy restringing and constantly retuning guitars, but as they concluded, frontman Mick Thomas dedicated the last song to the Fish by way of apology for having taken the gig. It was called *Hobart Town*.

When his set began, Billy walked out alone initially, talking under the spotlight about politics and Thatcher before he started playing any music, seamlessly changing topics from governments to condoms. Bragg, the safe sex counsellor. Then it was stories about Manchester band, The Smiths before the rest of his band joined him.

"These are the chords I learned from Johnny Marr," he said, demonstrating all three of them.

Bragg, the stand-up comedian. We laughed as he continued his story.

"...So he said to me, *Bill, every song you've written is the story of my life...* and I said, Aw, come on Morrissey..." The crowd roared in appreciation.

The set was filled with familiar songs, *Levi Stubbs Tears, Love Gets Dangerous,* some of them from the latest album, Workers Playtime, and despite the capacity crowd I was able to move freely in front of the stage, with camera held close to my face, taking photographs.

Environmental issues were brought into focus when the band played a cover version of Prince's *Purple Rain,* changing the lyrics and calling it, *Acid Rain* to the approval of any conservationists present, and all of the student population

"Let's get Weddings over to the UK before everyone starts believing that Jason and Kylie are the only worthy exports from Australia," Billy implored, to cheers and wild applause.

It was a loud and raucous gig, with all the Weddings boys joining Billy on stage at the end as they thrashed through a huge encore of *Waiting for the Great Leap Forward.* After the music ended, the crowd soon began to dwindle and filter home, and in the empty spaces we could see blood and spilled beer on the floor, and the piles of empty beer cans littering the ground.

Mark and Andrew wanted to catch Billy backstage and present him with the Fish's latest single, so we loitered until he was ready for us. The keyboard player's baby was sleeping in the dressing room, and when Billy appeared he was apologetic that he couldn't invite us inside. He didn't want to wake the baby, aware of the irony that it had just slept through the entire ear-splitting set.

I shook hands with Billy as the boys handed over their vinyl, exchanging a few words about Manchester and the North of England. It was a shrewd move to give him the single. The boys always took any opportunity to promote the band. A conversation, however random, could be the chance to make contacts in the business. A meeting could be the catalyst for other meetings. It was important to seize the moment.

In the morning Mark and I had to drive back to Launceston, both of us tired after the late night. Before leaving, we'd chosen one of the many Hobart cafés to have breakfast and sustain ourselves with caffeine, but Mark was quiet as we browsed the newspapers.

"That's *so* wrong." He had an edge in his voice that made me look up from my magazine.

"What?" I followed his eyes to the newspaper he'd been reading. It was about unplanned pregnancy.

Turning the page around to face me, I began to scan the article.

"Well they're actually looking at situations when termination's the only option."

"It's never an option."

My approach was from a medical and practical perspective, but I knew he'd be swayed by his personal beliefs. I had to tread carefully here. I could feel the tension in his voice and was beginning to feel apprehensive about having the discussion.

"It's about taking a life, Ange, killing a child."

"But what about teenage pregnancy…"

He was shaking his head as I continued.

"…or when a woman's raped?"

"It's never right. People need to take responsibility for what they do."

"But don't you think it *is* being responsible to make that decision? To avoid having a child that you can't keep because…"

"Getting rid of a baby because you don't want it?" he interrupted.

"It's not as simple as that," I said, feeling cornered. "It's a big deal getting pregnant, especially if you haven't planned on being a parent."

"But it's alive." He glanced back down at the article, looking distressed.

"Erm, look, I think it'd be a very hard decision to make, for anyone. I'd certainly take it very seriously, and I'm sure it would be a really traumatic experience. But the last thing you need is someone making you feel guilty about it as well."

Mark's anguish was palpable. He looked wounded.

"People make mistakes. It could happen to anyone," I said, trying to be gentle, to wind-down the discussion. "Whatever the decision, you have to live with it," I added, "and I think a girl should be allowed to decide what happens to her own body."

Mark was stirring the remnants of his coffee resentfully, and I hoped we'd be able to change the subject to something less inflammatory.

"Why are we arguing about this anyway?" I asked. "We just have different ideas about it, that's all."

It was obvious we'd never find any common ground in this discussion, and as I made a move to leave the café I hoped we'd be able to put aside our differences. But I'd underestimated the effects of my opinion when it challenged Mark's values. He persisted with his line of reasoning as we walked to the car, his voice raised, taking my retreat into silence as an opportunity to further emphasise his point. Even driving out of Hobart he continued with his invective until I closed my eyes and opened the window on my hot face. I was crushed by his outburst and shocked at the vehemence of his anger, allowing a silence to grow and linger between us.

After a while, I could feel him looking at me, sensing the hesitancy, both of us wanting to speak, but struggling to find the words. Nothing seemed appropriate.

I'd been broadsided and felt vulnerable after our clash of opinions. The strength of Mark's condemnation made me retreat further into uneasy contemplation. I didn't understand. It was our first big disagreement, and it wasn't even about us.

For almost an hour I gazed absently at the view, letting my thoughts scatter through the open window.

"Ange." Mark's voice cut across the noise of the engine. His eyes held a question. They were soft with concern, and held a sadness that wanted to explain; but I wasn't ready to unravel my emotions. I still felt wary and preoccupied.

"I didn't mean to…" he started, "I was just upset about…"

"…I know. It's alright."

"But…"

"We're both tired. It's okay," I said.

I kept my eyes on the road as it unfolded towards Launceston. I wanted to say that I knew he loved me, that it didn't change anything; but there was something else, more than just his words. I couldn't shake the idea that Mark had found an imperfection. He had found something which divided us; and I could feel it sitting between us, like the first stone in a wall.

IN THE DAYS remaining of Mark's visit, there was one final gig at the University College, the TSIT. When Mark collected me that evening, it was the first time we'd been together since our argument, and we were both contrite, happy to be reconciled. Although I wanted to believe we'd been jaded after a late night, I knew we'd had a major difference of opinions. I didn't want to dwell on it. I just wanted to enjoy our time together, knowing Mark would be leaving again soon.

I was wearing one of my fifties dresses, starched orange cotton with a high bodice, full circular skirt and short sleeves. Smiling in the shadows, I was standing towards the rear of the hall as Mark cast purposeful glances in my direction, playing through a familiar set of songs to a small gathering of enthusiastic students.

After the final song, he gestured for me to move up to the stage. He called over the rest of the band as I approached, and started to introduce me to the other three, hovering behind them as they spoke to me.

Even though I'd been to countless gigs and mingled casually with them at numerous city venues, I realised that I'd probably been seen as just another fan. Each of them took my hand and kissed me politely on the cheek, their faces still warm, and their clothing damp with perspiration. They were formal and courteous, receiving me as Mark's girlfriend now. This was official acknowledgement. It was a milestone.

On Mark's face I could see the same expression of contrition I'd seen on the drive back from Hobart. When I met his eyes, there was a flicker of a smile, and he shrugged. This was his supplication. It was an offering. I slid my arm around his waist and kissed him lightly on the cheek.

"Thankyou."

As they started to move away and pack up equipment, I called them back.

"Just a sec."

I rummaged in my bag. When he'd collected me earlier, Mark had presented me with a copy of their single, *Left/Childless Mother*. It had been an exciting moment, seeing it for the first time. Mark had signed the sleeve in the top corner, and it had given me an idea.

"Will you all sign it for me?"

They looked amused as I held out the cover, but someone had a pen, and they all took a turn to add their names. Perhaps no-one had ever asked them before. I didn't care. I was happy to indulge their rock star status. One day I might have the only autographed copy in the country.

"Does it get confusing, having two Marks in the band?" I asked Mark as he crouched, nestling a guitar in its case and snapping the hinges closed.

"Yeah, we have to use surnames sometimes. But we just call him Warky," Mark explained, "or Wark, we call him that too."

"So you have Mark Nark, and Mark Wark. Of course, because that's so much clearer."

"He calls me Narko mostly…" he began.

"…or you could be Mark Narkosnitch. Sneakanitch? Narkybits? Your name just has endless possibilities."

I dodged his hands as he tried to grab me. In the end he gave up trying to catch me and went back to shifting amps and winding cables.

He'd be in Launceston for a few more days yet, but the rest of the band would be departing in the morning, and as I watched them hefting instruments and dismantling the drum kit, I wondered when I might see them all again.

Mark was standing with an outstretched arm, beckoning me to follow, and as I walked towards him I shot a final glance at the others on stage, allowing myself a fleeting notion of this scenario somewhere in Melbourne.

This is how the future could look, spending evenings like this, chatting with the band, enjoying unlimited backstage access. This was their world, but I realised that it could soon be mine.

MARK stayed on in Dilston, by the orchard, spending his days busking in the Mall, and posing for photographs in settings that we contrived around the city. Under the bridge near the Arts centre we found a selection of posters advertising previous Fish gigs: the lime green print of the 1988 Coelacanth tour, the yellow of the New Year's Eve poster for acoustic pop thrashabilly at The Inn, and the white canvas whose vibrant coloured crayons launched the recent single. They seemed to be the perfect backdrop to advertise a career in progress.

One afternoon, we spent a few hours colouring-in the covers for the single. The band had decided to crayon the pictures by hand to cut costs, but it also added a personal touch to each of them.

"How many did you press this time?" I asked as I coloured carefully inside the lines.

"Five hundred," Mark replied, as he threw another completed one onto the pile.

"Wow, you're quick." I peered at his art work. "Nice colours. Some of them are even on the paper."

He glanced at his rainbow coloured smudged fingers and feigned surprise.

"Yeah, well we've all got a quota to complete," he said, referring to the other band members, "so get colouring, because you're doing some of mine," and he leaned across to thank me with a lingering kiss.

"How many have you done now?" he asked.

"Hmm, about thirty, I'd say."

I contemplated my scribbling with pride, thinking of my small, unseen contribution to the performing arts.

"I wonder if I'll ever be able to tell which ones are mine," I pondered, comparing my versions to Mark's.

Somewhere out there, in the future, my little works of art would be sitting amongst someone's record collection. They would never know.

\*

At the Nurses' Home, Mark visited me in the evenings, continuing to dodge the Supervisors, who kept their vigil at the reception desk. In theory every visitor was supposed to check-in with the Supervisor on arrival, but it was easy to arrive unnoticed and slip into our lounge room.

The house rules stipulated I wasn't permitted to have male visitors in my room, so I'd already broken the regulations. But it was a strange paradox, given James or Dave would be allowed into my room at any time. Some girls regularly smuggled their boyfriends upstairs to stay for the night, carefully evading Dot, our cleaning lady who arrived at daybreak. Several boyfriends had sneaked to the showers in the early morning, wearing a towel turban, and disguised in their girlfriend's dressing gown.

It was already late when we returned to the Home one evening, too late to be making any noise or playing music in my room.

"Dance with me?" I murmured, pulling Mark to me for a slow waltz in the space around the bed.

We moved in the silence, swaying in the dark around the furniture, before lying on the bed to watch the stars as they made their slow ascent.

"You looked surprised," I whispered, as we lay on my narrow bed.

"Hmmm..?"

"When I asked you to dance," I said.

"I was. But it was a great idea."

"We've never danced together before."

He thought for a moment. "No, that's true."

I paused and said softly, "We've never laid *in* my bed either."

He lifted his head from the pillow and moved my hair from my eyes so he could see my expression.

"Is that what you want?"

"Yes." It was barely a whisper. "We always lie down like this and I'd like to be under the blankets for once. Just lying together, that's all."

We undressed each other slowly, unbuttoning and shedding, lying down in my single bed, and fanning the sheets around us. A sensation rippled along the length of my spine. For the first time I could feel the extent of skin on skin, the touch and the caress of it. I could feel the overload of my senses, the scent of him, all the hollows and curves where we met, the silken glide and tickle of hair, the surprising heat of flesh. Under the sheets we let fingers smudge our outlines into a shared canvas of skin, slowly tracing every contour we created, and gently blurring together all the edges of our nakedness.

I lay my head on his chest, and under my ear felt the tide of breath rising and falling, the modulation of his heartbeat. I was entranced, struck by the wonder of it all, the otherness of another body and the potential that lay within it. Entwined in the dim light, overlooking the moonlit view of Launceston, we dozed and talked quietly.

It was the early hours of the morning when he left. I rolled into the warm depression his body had left in the bed and watched his silhouette dressing quietly in the darkness, feeling him stoop to kiss me before opening the door to leave. After it clicked shut, I could hear him descending the wide staircase to the outside door, and I sat up to pull open the window, sliding up the heavy sash and leaning on the sill so I could peer down to the entrance, waiting for him to emerge.

He stepped out and stood with hands in pockets, staring upwards as my whispered words floated down to him. A few times he dropped his gaze, shaking his head as if he was trying to loosen something in his mind.

"I can't believe it. I can't believe *you*..." he said, turning on the spot, before casting his eyes up for a final look.

I watched his figure retreating down the walkway towards the gravel path, leaving me high with my thoughts in the rumpled sheets. Unable to sleep now that he'd gone, I settled myself into the warmth he'd left behind and flicked on the lamp as I searched the pages of my diary. I found the comment I'd written more than a month ago, when he'd left.

*"Perhaps one day we will be lovers."*

Stirring restlessly, I stared at the page, languishing in his subtle presence, folding the bedclothes around me where the smell of his skin still lingered. Perhaps one day we would; perhaps soon. His scent was everywhere, imprinted on the pillow that I pressed to my face, waiting to see the dark sky pale into morning. Yes, soon.

Old Fish poster, in Launceston

Under the bridge, Launceston

Single cover – crayoned

Single cover – title listing

Publicity photograph, Mercury Hobart, Tasmania

## Reviews – mixed reactions

**THE FISH JOHN WEST REJECT — LEFT/CHILDLESS MOTHER (River Filf)**

*Left* floats somewhere in seas just off Housemartin Island and Proclaimers Coast. Quick, folkish beat with squeaking harmonica and jovial voice. *Mother* is a thoughtful and quiet ballad that creates quite an intense atmosphere. You can't do much better than this little pleasure.

BEAT - 13/4

**LEFT — THE FISH JOHN WEST REJECT — RIVER FILF RECORDS**

You can't help but like a single when the cover is hand drawn with crayons. TFJWR adher to the perfect left field pop formula here with driving acoustic guitar adding frantic pace to the song. Sounds just a wee bit like (sorry guys) The Proclaimers.

INPRESS - 15/4

**THE FISH JOHN WEST REJECT Left (Musicland)**

More acoustic guitars, cardboard box drums, a touch of harmonica and precious general vocals. The fish fingers pick out an alluring hook line, but no sinker. This Melbourne-based 4 piece also have an album due soon, so this is merely bait for a bigger catch ahead.

JUKE - 22/4

**THE FISH JOHN WEST REJECT Left (Independent)**

Spirited, surely well-intentioned, but unremarkable. The best thing about this is its cover, which is hand-coloured in gorgeous lime-green crayon. (Ah, the immeasurable advantages of the independent release!) The flipside, *Childless Mother*, is better — though, as the title implies, the lyrics walk rather unsteadily that finest of lines between pathos and bathos. If this is the best they can do, John West knew what he was doing.

RAM - 3/5

## LIVE

### THE FISH JOHN WEST REJECT
#### The Tote

I've been aware of a band called The Fish John West Reject for a while now. I've heard that they're from Tasmania and are quite good, and I've often wondered why on earth anyone would call themselves The Fish John West Reject — it had me stumped. I finally went along to one of the famous Tote barbies to eat free sausages and hear what rejected fish sound like.

I missed the sausages but caught The Fish and was hooked (sorry!) It's difficult to describe The Fish's music in a few words. They play an interesting blend of music with flavours of folk, blues, country and rockabilly based around the strong vocals and acoustic rhythm guitar of Mark Narkowitcz, which combines to produce a very individual style of rock 'n roll. Their harmonies were beautiful and guitarist Mark Adams used his harmonica and Mandolin to great effect.

They played a wide range of songs, from a knee-slapping country style number by Led-belly to an uplifting, arm-waving Gospel piece *See Jerusalem*. It was all very confident and happy. The music has a great feeling — I wanted to twirl, jump and leap around, instead I just jiggled along. This is one good band. Apparently they're taking off on an Australian tour soon, so catch them before they go. Don't let the name be a barrier. Old Westie must have damn high standards.

**Fiona Duncan**

*Angela J. Dawson*

# Casualty

MARK'S LAST evening in town had been spent at the Club 107, where he'd again played under the improvised name, The Wetspots. At the Launceston airport in the morning he was wearing the same suit that he'd been wearing the previous night, but I presumed he had actually slept, and changed his shirt. It was the last day of March, and we were in the lounge awaiting his departure, trying to ignore the reality that there weren't any more return trips planned in the near future. We had no idea when we could meet again, and it was a dismal prospect.

After the boarding call was made, the passengers filed down some steps that emerged into the open air and began strolling onto the tarmac towards the waiting plane. I watched them chattering in small clusters in the sunshine, making their way to the staircase that had been parked at the rear of the plane. This lack of formality in relation to passenger boarding wasn't an oversight. They didn't actually have any covered walkways for people to cross to the plane doors, or a carousel where you could collect your luggage after a flight. It was something that fascinated me about the airport, the way it felt so incomplete, as if they hadn't bothered to install everything else.

Mark jumped and waved, flailing his arms in exaggerated waves to make me laugh, but as his plane tore into the sky and receded away across the horizon I felt deflated and unsettled.

Back at the Nurses' Home I took advantage of my restless energy, deciding to tidy up the perpetual clutter that lingered in my room. Although we had Cleaners for the Home, we were supposed to maintain our own rooms, so I decided it would be a good distraction from my thoughts of Mark.

In one of my boxes under the bed I'd found an old bottle of nail varnish. I was trying to determine if it was worth saving and had been struggling for a few minutes to unscrew the cap, but it wouldn't loosen. As I put all my strength into turning it, the glass bottle suddenly snapped at the neck. The torsional force drove the jagged glass edges deep into the web of skin at the base of my right thumb, blood oozing instantly from the cut and running down my hand. It soon made a lurid red track to my wrist, where it began to form into red drips.

Without a thought to the time, I charged out into the corridor and thumped noisily on James' door with my other hand.

"James! Quick!" I said loudly to the wood in front of me, rattling the door in its frame as I knocked. I could hear him stirring, shortly appearing in his white towelling robe with sleep sculpted hair, scowling in the bright landing light. He often slept before a big night out on a Friday evening.

"Sorry, I didn't realise you were sleeping. Look," I said, thrusting my hand at him, "look what I've done."

He coughed and cleared his throat noisily, squinting at my thumb.

"How did'ya do that?"

"On a bottle of nail varnish. It just snapped."

"Well you should probably go to Casualty."

"Oh, can't *you* do anything?"

"Hmm," he said, peering, "you need to get it checked for glass. And you might need stitches. It's best if you go downstairs."

"Oh, really?" I bleated, "O-kay. Thanks anyway. I'm sorry I woke you."

But he was already going back into his darkened room, like a bear.

Taking care to keep my hand still, I covered it with a wad of paper towels from the bathroom and walked down from the Home, through the hospital, and into the quiet of a late night in Casualty. I grinned at the receptionist and waved my wrapped hand at her.

"I cut my hand," I explained. "Can I see someone please?"

"You'll have to fill in some forms first," she said, turning to the selection behind her desk and plucking out a couple.

"It might be a bit difficult. I'm right handed."

Perhaps that would get me off the hook.

"Okay. Look, I can help to fill them in for you, if you give me the details."

It looked like a lot of information. "Do you really need all that for a small cut? I'm sure I could be in and out pretty quickly if someone's free."

Worth a try.

She selected a pen, and smoothed out the first page. "Name and address?"

"Erm, here. I live here actually. I work here too, so you might not need all those details."

Surely this would score me some points.

"There's a wait of about an hour at the moment," she said with a steely expression, clearly adept at dealing with queue jumpers.

"Even for staff?"

"For anybody."

So no concessions for employees then. What else did I have?

"But there's no-one here." I scanned the empty waiting area, suddenly empathising with the patients.

"I'm sorry but all the Doctors are busy. If you'll just take a seat."

Game, set and match.

She turned back to her desk, leaving me staring at a selection of posters that I would be able to read several dozen times, and a few rows of empty chairs.

After a short time, I think I dozed off, out of boredom as much as fatigue. I must have looked pale anyway because a male nurse had manifested in front of me and was asking me if I was alright. Then another nurse appeared and led me to a side room, making me lie on a trolley for the examination. I was beginning to feel embarrassed about the diminutive size of my injury. When the doctor appeared I tried to sound casual and friendly, but he looked tired and unsmiling.

"It's only a cut," I said, proffering my hand for inspection, "but I suppose it could have some glass in it."

I looked at his identity badge as he leaned over my hand - Robert Palmer. In the hospital I'd already met Kenny Rogers working as an Orderly, and Michael J. Fox working in the Physiotherapy department, neither of them bearing even scant resemblance to their celebrity namesakes. I'd seen patients joke about Michael's name when they saw his badge, or if they heard it announced over the public address system. They weren't always convinced it was his real name.

Not surprising really. I'd heard hoax names being paged across the hospital loud speakers. It usually occurred when there was someone new on the switchboard. There was only ever a limited time in which you could dupe them. Once they'd been caught out a few times they became more perceptive about the requests. I'd tricked them myself a couple of times.

"Er, yes," I'd say to the female voice on the extension. "Can you please page Dr Jaynus. I think his first name is Hugh?"

"Paging Dr Jaynus please, Dr Hugh Jaynus."

It was always a marvel to us that they didn't catch on, even as they'd broadcast it throughout the entire hospital. Mike Rotch was a favourite; Hugh Mungus seemed just too obvious. But even Dr Tamm got through, first name, Tim.

Many of the Doctors were only a couple of years older than us, on their first placements, and we often socialised together. We were dealing with serious business most of the time, life and death, and all of the increments in between. But the valve needed to be released. I'd been pranked by the Doctors too, and I'd had some less than formal referral scripts:

'Can you assess this patient's gait please. Thanks Ducky.'

As I submitted my hand for inspection by Dr Palmer, I wondered how many times the authenticity of his name had been challenged.

"I bet people comment on your name all the time." I flashed my best smile.

"Yes." He gave me his best deadpan stare.

His face was impassive, closed for business.

"You must get sick of all the jokes?"

"Mmm."

He was looking closely at the cut under a garish overhead surgical light which he pulled closer. I doubted the merits of trying to pursue any further conversation.

After a few minutes he muttered something about an injection before selecting a large syringe, surely chosen to frighten me, and administering a dose of anaesthetic that began to numb first my thumb and fingers, and then my entire hand. It was a disconcerting sensation, but it meant I couldn't feel anything as he began scrubbing the wound and checking it for any glass fragments.

As he'd been working I'd put forward a convincing argument about stitches being unnecessary for such a small injury, and having found nothing to impress him, he taped together the rough edges of the cut with steri-strips.

The choice may have been made for speed rather than for the merits of my argument, but at that point he lost interest completely and wandered off into the domain of the apparently busy Casualty area.

He left me with a very chatty Nurse who cleaned my wound as she talked, and then began to apply a casing of bandages in ever increasing layers, from my fingers to the middle of my arm. When she was satisfied there was enough of it, she reminded me to keep the dressing dry, and told me to rest my hand for a couple of days. I thought about showering, and all the tasks I'd need to perform left-handed, chewing my lip as I considered how I'd manage.

\*

James was smoking one of his Goodies in the lounge room, still clad in his white dressing gown, when I returned. There was some embroidery underway on the table, and he'd clearly just paused from his cross-stitching so he could have a cigarette. He grinned widely at my bandaged hand as I walked in, savouring a long drag before exhaling noisily.

"Just what I need," I griped, brandishing my hand and plopping down onto a chair at the circular table in the bay window.

"Look at all this bandage! You'd assume I'd almost severed my whole bloody arm. I don't know what the Nurse was thinking. And I had a Doctor who thinks analgesia involves complete sensory deprivation of an entire limb. I won't be able to feel my hand for hours."

I tapped it against the table for effect, and to demonstrate my dulled nerve endings.

As expected, James wanted the unabridged version of events, chuckling quietly as he smoked, his shoulders shaking at my exaggerated description of the straight faced doctor.

"So much for the weekend," I added gloomily, thinking of my new limitations. "People are already giving me funny looks," I complained, indicating my bandaged wrist.

"I suppose they think you've tried to do-away with yourself," James observed.

"Don't!"

"The price of love, and all that."

"Stop it!"

"There's a lot of it about. Have you seen Dave lately?"

James' tone had changed, and a look of genuine horror flashed across his face.

"Dave? Why?"

"Well, who knows, maybe it was the full moon or something, but he had a patient defenestrate."

"What?"

"They defenestrated - threw themselves out of the window."

"I didn't even know they had a word for that. Is he alright?"

"Dave, or the patient?"

"Dave. And the patient. What happened?" I asked.

"The patient died. He hit the ground head first from the third floor. So not much chance of survival." A pause as he took a drag, "They made Dave go down and clean up the pavement." He faltered. "Can you believe they made him do that?"

"Oh James!" The idea was repugnant.

"It was a mess. It was just everywhere. Brains all over the ground," he added, in a small voice, looking distressed, and taking another deep draw on his cigarette.

"That's awful. Did he get into trouble?"

"Oh no, it wasn't his fault. He just happened to walk into the room on the ward."

"Poor Dave."

"He was pretty shaken-up. I saw him after it. He didn't look too good."

"So is he okay?"

"Oh you know, he was a bit mad for a while. More than normal. He went out on the beer, spent a bit of time in Mutacia. He's alright now I think."

Mutacia was Dave's own expression for the weekends, and occasional evenings, that he spent smoking marijuana with his cousin. He sporadically went to Mutacia when he needed to relax, which wasn't a problem unless he had an early shift the next morning.

My minor injury didn't seem particularly significant now.

"Look, why don't we take Cecil out tomorrow?" James offered, in a bid to cheer me. "We could go to the beach and stay at the caravan. Cal isn't working tomorrow, so we could all go and stay the night."

A lovely sunny autumn day by the sea, with the wind blowing through our hair. What could be finer? It would definitely be better than staying in my room all weekend.

IT WAS POURING with rain Saturday morning, drumming on the silver-grey roof of a heavily laden Cecil as James steered us northwards, towards Green's Beach. Undeterred by the weather, we pressed on, peering through the fogged car windows until we reached the Exeter bakery where it was customary on this journey to stop for supplies. Warm sausage rolls in crumbly pastry, soft crusty bread, glazed fruit tarts, and apple turnovers oozing with unnecessary cream. It was an oasis of all that was rich and delicious. James was nosing into his paper bag even before we made the dash back to Cecil, chomping down on the buttery contents, leaving a frill of crumbs on his lips.

As he drove, we all sang discordantly to a Communards tape on Cecil's rudimentary cassette player, ignoring the thin, reedy musical sound it produced, and the way it distorted on the higher notes when we played it at a volume for which it was never designed.

"Yoooou aaaare my worrrrrrld….!" We all screeched, in loud falsetto voices, each trying to outdo the other two, and producing a formidable level of noise in the tight confines of Cecil's misted interior.

The rain held back for a while in the early afternoon, long enough for us to set up a tripod on the beach and pose for self-portraits on the rocks. We wandered across the damp sand afterwards, barefoot in the weak sunshine, looking for the tiny crabs that buried themselves industriously, leaving untidy stacks of sand like coiled threads outside their holes.

The small caravan was on a block of land set off a gravel road that inclined steadily upwards from the beach. It belonged to Carolyn's family, who hoped that one day a house would be built on the block as a beach retreat. Inside, it was dusty with disuse and filled with blankets, magazines and oddments of crockery. There were also plenty of spiders that would launch themselves indignantly from their dank hiding places on spindly legs, usually next to James since he was the most averse to their presence. This was often followed by a roar and the shuddering of the caravan as James vaulted from his chair for the insect spray.

That evening, as we settled down for the night, the caravan rocked and groaned in a high wind which lashed a steady rhythm of rain on our metal roof. I lay in the dark listening to the conversational tones of the wind and wondering what Mark might be doing in Melbourne on a Saturday evening. In the morning I'd have to check with the doctor to see when I could return to work, and to have the dressings on my hand changed. The wound ached slightly and itched beneath the layers of bandage.

I turned slowly in my narrow bunk, fingering the thick binding pensively, feeling snug in my cocoon of blankets and hoping I wouldn't need the toilet in the middle of the night. The nearest bathroom was in the caravan park down by the beach, and without a torch to guide me it would be a long walk in the dark. Hunkered down in the tiny caravan, battered by seas blowing directly off the roiling waters of the Bass Strait, I didn't have much time to dwell on my convoluted and apprehensive thoughts, promptly falling into a deep and dreamless sleep.

James and Callie – Rood and Roods

1989, Greens Beach – our self-portrait

TWO DAYS later, on Monday evening, I was wallowing on the floor of Carolyn's room in the Home. I was trying to ease the discomfort of a distended stomach after an ample hospital cafeteria dinner, wondering how I'd fill the next few days of enforced vacation. Our three rooms in the Nurses' Home occupied the front wing of the building, on the first floor above the lounge, and all of the rooms shared a view of the city from the crest of Charles St.

My room was adjacent to James', and his was linked to Carolyn's room by a tiny shared balcony that could barely accommodate one person and a chair. He didn't mind his much smaller room because it meant that he could have clandestine meetings with Carolyn, thanks to the connecting balcony outside.

Carolyn was stretched out on the bed rummaging through a bag of mixed craft and sewing projects, and James had squeezed out through the hatch window to the tiny balcony so that he could smoke. Having examined my hand on Sunday, the doctor had decided I'd need more time for the wound to heal. He'd given me a certificate for the next five days which meant I wouldn't have to go to work for a whole week.

"I wish Mark was here. Then at least I could spend all this time with him. What am I going to do for five days, especially one handed?"

In the dim light cast from Carolyn's room James was glancing at the local papers that someone had left downstairs in the lounge. He gave a derisive snort that usually signified a crass comment was about to follow.

"You could go and see this band from Devonport," he said, the name of it carried off by the breeze as he said it.

"What?" I called, over my shoulder, still lying on the carpet and rubbing my full belly.

"Derek lives in a Foreskin....!" he said, much louder this time.

"They are *not* called that."

"Come and look if you don't believe me," he dared me.

I heaved myself off the floor and crawled through the window, snatching the paper from James, who gave it up after a brief struggle. Scanning the page I saw the advert for Clarence lives in a Bucket.

"Hah, made you look," he said.

"I knew you'd made that up," I said, giving back the paper and returning to my position on the floor, but this time just inside the window.

"It's a stupid name for a band anyway. My name's better," James retorted, from afar.

"I don't think that solves my problem."

"Just trying to be helpful."

He leaned in towards my reclined body on the floor and sighed melodramatically, so that I'd get the full effect.

"There's no pleasing some people. That's what Jesus said," he began, gearing-up for some full blown Monty Python quotes.

Thinking better of it, his face appeared above me like a risen moon. "You could always go to Melbourne you know." He fixed me with a stare.

"I can't do that. I'm supposed to be indisposed. Dennis wouldn't be too pleased if I took off to Melbourne from my sickbed."

My boss had an unnerving way of finding out the details of your private life.

"Who says you have to be sick in Tasmania? You could be just as sick in Melbourne. Besides, how will he ever know? If anyone asks, we'll say you're recuperating by the beach somewhere, with a rug over your knees."

The wind from the open window was blowing the aromatic smoke from his cigarette into the room. Essence of cloves filtered across to where I lay sprawled on the floor, the faint perfume reminding me of the smell of incense.

"Carolyn? What d' you think?"

She'd been concentrating on a piece of needlework that she'd found within the amassed clutter of her room, but looked down at me and smiled.

"We won't tell him."

"Hmm, no…I don't think so," I said, "He's sure to find out."

*Like Two Mexicans Dancing*

# Brunswick, fish and rain

BY TUESDAY afternoon I was in Melbourne. Delighted that we could be together again so soon, Mark collected me at the airport and drove us to Harvey and Di's place, the couple with whom he was living in Brunswick. Parallel with Sydney Road and its bustling shops and tramlines, the houses on their street were a typical assortment of fashionable inner city designs, set back from a pavement interrupted at intervals by shrubs and small trees.

Their house was made of weatherboard, with a small tangle of garden at the front, and a rear concrete yard. A path along the side of the house led to the kitchen door which was the main thoroughfare, guarded closely by their brown dog, Jessie, who gave us a delirious welcome, nosing into our clothes and bags to catch our scent.

Pushing past her into the lounge I eyed the rows of vinyl, shelf after shelf of LP's that Harve had collected over the years he'd been working for Shock Records.

"I don't think I've ever seen so many albums," I said, running my fingers along their edges, pulling out a few to check the titles.

"I'll make a tape for you when I get some time," Mark offered.

"A mix tape?" I said, gazing longingly at the selection as his arms crept around me.

"Yes, a mix tape. Perhaps it'll be Lullabies for the Lovesick, or maybe Songs for a Fireside. Something like that."

"You have titles already? I'm impressed."

"What do you like? The Chills, Lilac Time, The Waltones?"

"I can't believe Harve has The Railway Children. I used to go and see them play in Manchester," I said, fingering the album. "But maybe some Australian bands too?"

"Go-Betweens?" he asked. "*Cattle and Cane* is a great track."

Mark had a studio room overlooking the back yard, separate from the house and adjacent to the garage. It may have been intended as a workspace but it was laid out as a bedroom, its seclusion affording him some privacy, but with the disadvantage of having to walk across the open yard to use the bathroom in the house. His bed was a mattress, neatly made-up and resting on a base of wooden pallets and plastic milk crates, his room filled with musical paraphernalia, vintage clothing, and guitars. As I leaned in to view a poster on the wall, my foot kicked against something under the corner of the bed.

"What's that?" I stepped back, weighing up the ceramic edges of the hidden item.

"*That* is for the cold nights," he replied obscurely.

"What?"

Grabbing the handle on one side, he pulled out an antique basin and waited for me to catch up.

"It's… a chamber pot?"

"Exactly," he said.

"You use that?"

"Well, as you can see, it's a cold walk in the dark otherwise."

I couldn't help wrinkling my nose.

"Don't worry, I only use it in emergencies," he added, putting it back, and threatening to tip me over and tackle me onto the bed.

Leaving my bags in his room we set off on a tour of the Melbourne streets, heading first to Brunswick Street in Fitzroy. It was humming with activity in the early evening, in total contrast to the streets of Launceston on a week night. A multitude of cafés, bars and bistros were open, offering a variety of food - Thai and Italian, Greek and Chinese - filling the air with a confusing but delicious combination of aromas. I watched the fashionable clientele drifting in and out of local clothing boutiques, the steady flow of exotic patrons in the pubs and clubs, some of them elegant, others scruffy, all of them interesting. It was the cool place for musicians and artists to linger and to relax with a drink, a hub of buzzing creativity.

We browsed the jewellery shops, and wandered into Polyester. Like many of the businesses on the shopping strip, the record store stayed open until the crowds diminished late into the evening, and there were a few people browsing the stacked rows of vinyl.

Further down the street we ventured into The Black Cat Café with its high ceiling and 1950's Laminex furniture, its resident one-eyed cat just an enormous mound of fur asleep in the front window. Despite the tantalising cakes behind the glass counter, we ordered the house specialty of bagels and burritos, eating leisurely, and watching the other customers come and go in weird assortments.

Wandering back towards the car afterwards, we kept pace with the trams nudging along the busy street on their parallel tracks. We'd reached The Punters Club on its corner location, and were standing just outside the doors. I tugged at Mark's hand.

"So this is where you play?" I asked. He'd often spoken about it.

The peeling paint on its rendered exterior walls gave it an air of grunge, but its dim lighting obscured its shabby interior. From the street I could only see pool tables and a large central bar.

"Yeah, its's one of the best live music venues in the city."

I peered in at the small crowd of patrons loitering over their chosen drink.

"It doesn't seem very big," I said, trying to size up the floor space, and imagining it with an audience.

"You'd be surprised how full this place gets. It just depends who's playing. Want to go in?" Mark asked.

"Maybe next time. Let's walk a bit more."

With his hand in mine, I could feel the rough calluses of Mark's fingertips, hardened by the metal guitar strings after years of playing.

"Do they hurt?" I asked, brushing my thumb across them.

"Not any more. They get toughened up by playing, so I can't really feel the tips properly now. They only get sore if I haven't played for a while."

He slung his arm around my shoulders. "Come on, let's go home."

\*

We'd slept in tents before, we'd even been undressed before, but this was the first time we'd be sleeping together in the same bed. For the next few days, I'd be waking next to Mark, and everything about it felt unfamiliar.

We were curiously self-conscious at the prospect of our nakedness, and undressed bashfully in the lamplight. Rolling towards him in the cool dark, as he wrapped the quilt around us, I was reminded of the night in my room when we'd shed our clothes for the first time. I rested my head against his chest and felt the warmth against my cheek, focussing on all the places where my skin was in contact with his, feeling his hand gently caressing my back as he lay next to me with eyes closed.

We'd nurtured the gentle pace of a love affair that had been interrupted by so many departures and arrivals. We'd waited-out all the long intervals apart. There was a pleasure in our longing now, feeling the pull of desire, with all its nuances and demands. The time would come when we could no longer contain it.

"We've got the whole night together," I said.

"Mm, at last. No need to sneak out after midnight."

"No. No leaving, Mr Sneakowicz…"

Our murmured conversation rose above the hushed evening, hovering in the cool air seeping in from the open window. It carried only the sound of Jessie's canine sighs and stirrings from her backyard slumber, and the pulse of the wind as it wafted against the edges of the curtain. The air haunted the room as it looked for things that it could move, lifting papers idly, chasing across the floor.

I tried to listen to it before I slept, but it was more stealthy than the silence. All I could hear in the quiet suburb was the sound of Mark's breathing next to me.

### Like Two Mexicans Dancing

AS WE EXPLORED the suburbs around the city I began to look more closely at Melbourne, imagining it as the place in which I could soon be living. Browsing the antique and clothing shops in Greville Street, Prahran, with their cherished remnants of history, I imagined how it would feel to see Mark every day. I watched him disappear into a record shop to delve into dusty cardboard boxes, searching for some bargain as he stood engrossed, his face tight with concentration.

At Andrew's house in Abbotsford, I met his two year old son, Scott as we all sat around the kitchen table. Mark had accurately described Scott's distinctive lisping speech, and I watched as he pointed to Andrew's face, smiling when I heard his halting pronunciation.

"…eyesh... nozche... lipsh..."

At the receiving end of the toddler's diminutive fingertip, Andrew smiled benignly. I visualised him on stage, in drainpipe jeans and pointed black boots, his bass slung low over one hip. Here, in the kitchen, he was just a devoted young father with his son in his lap.

"Can I get anyone another coffee?" Andrew asked, with a soft toy in one hand.

*

It was on a Thursday night on Brunswick Street that I had a fleeting introduction to The Punters Club, and from that, an insight into Mark's lifestyle.

The Club had organised a gathering of all the musicians that had participated in a recent recording at the club, and it was due for release as an album, Hair of the Dog Live. A photo session was going to take place in one half of the venue later in the evening, and all the bands were being assembled for a wide angled shot at the bar.

Once inside the dark interior I could get a better sense of the layout as we wandered around, listening to the bands playing. There was a central bar split between two rooms, each accommodating green baized pool tables, and there was a low stage in the main room where The Widdershins were completing a set.

"What happened to the couch?" I asked.

Crushed by years of misuse, a squashed sofa occupied the front corner by the window overlooking the street. Next to it was a small mixing desk, and the control panel for the stage lights with its coloured dials and switches.

"It's the highest point in the room," Mark explained.

I looked around at the mingling patrons, imagining the press of a capacity crowd.

"When it's packed in here, that's the best place to stand, if you want to see the stage," he added.

The countless feet of clambering punters had moulded the sofa's sagging and rather battered shape, everyone seeking the lofty position that could be acquired by standing on the back of it. This gave an optimal view of the stage across a crowded room. In fact it was the highest vantage point attainable in the room, and if you could claim a spot, you would be elevated to a height within inches of the low ceiling.

The whole place was infused with the smell of beer, as if layers of it had spilled and dried there over the years. Posters advertised forthcoming gigs or had been left as relics of gigs from previous years, covering any available wall space, from floor to ceiling. To the rear of the room there were pinball machines next to a food hatch that served a variety of fried foods from the kitchen beyond. From the open hatch an all pervading greasy odour mingled with the cigarette haze and fused with a degree of permanence into the walls and furnishings.

This was the place that had launched the careers of countless bands. I leaned on the end of the bar sipping my drink, watching the adjacent room being prepared for the photo shoot. The length of one bar was being used as a backdrop, and the musicians were being ushered into place now for the photographs. Mark had been directed into the room with the rest of the band and their Manager, Gary, so they could be grouped together for the shot. Eventually one of these pictures would become the front cover of the album and would also be used on posters, and on postcards, advertising its release.

Huge lights had been set up and directed at the collective talents lining the counter, illuminating the faces of bands I hadn't yet heard of - The Hollowmen, Intoxica, These Future Kings. The Widdershins had also moved into place now that they'd finished playing, The Fish sitting on barstools in the centre of the shot.

Someone approached me as I sat the bar, asking me to move away from the counter as the final adjustments were made. I looked across the room to where I could see Mark swallowing from his glass of beer.

"I'm with the band," I said, pointing, "The Fish."

"Oh, okay."

There was a currency to that simple statement. Even then I could feel it, I could sense the privileges that it afforded.

I didn't get to see any of the posters. Weeks later, when Mark saw them emerging around the city, tacked to the walls of local venues, he realised there was an extra person on the left of the frame, sitting behind the manager of The Club at the far end of the bar. Mark mailed me a few copies of the postcards, but on such a small print, I can barely be seen.

*Looky here*, Mark wrote on one of them, drawing an arrow to my shadowy presence. I'm little more than a blur at the far edge, just another patron on a seat at the bar. But that was my first night at The Punters Club. I was with the band.

## Like Two Mexicans Dancing

THE DAYS passed at a gentle pace, interrupted by band meetings or rehearsals. Through my idealistic eyes the allure of this nocturnal existence was very compelling. Hip, laidback, unconventional. It was all these things.

It was a window into his life, and there were opportunities to meet people of whom Mark had spoken when he was in Tasmania. On Friday evening, we listened to Andrew and Mark Adams being interviewed on a local radio station, 3PBS by Steve, one of Harvey and Di's friends. At times two year old Scott was audible in the background, sitting on Andrew's lap, within kicking distance of the microphone, punctuating the discussion with intermittent thumps.

After the quiet lifestyle in Tasmania I realised there were so many possibilities in Melbourne, for myself, and for the band. I could understand the pull of the big city and the reasons they'd relocated. I could see their vision for the future and the opportunities here that could launch their career.

Another photo session had been planned at the spacious warehouse squat in which Mark Adams was living, to take some promotional shots that could be used for future press releases. As they set up equipment I wandered the perimeters of the building that Mark shared with the two others.

Rough wooden partitions sectioned off the areas in which each person had created a bedroom; one with an elevated bed close to the ceiling which could only be reached by a ladder, and another that had used the vast expanse of a silk parachute as decoration, attaching it to the ceiling from where it hung down in voluptuous folds. Although there was a bathroom there didn't seem to be any water, and I wasn't certain that they had any form of heating. It was a decadent way to live, offering a creative space and a freedom that was unfettered by regulations.

Andrew's wife was taking the pictures, and the fish theme seemed an obvious choice. Warky had bought a selection of fresh fish from the market that morning, and had suspended them with twine from an old window frame so that they hung down at different levels. The boys crammed themselves onto an old sofa, holding the frame in front of them, giving the impression that they were sitting inside a fish tank.

It was an interesting effect, enhanced further by the atmospheric surrounds of the warehouse. They spent the afternoon perfecting it, taking rolls of film between the customary breaks for beer and cigarettes, all of us getting chilled in the cool interior.

As I watched them, I was contemplating my return to Launceston. The spring nights were already getting colder, the daylight hours shorter, the darkness coming earlier.

The afternoon had become overshadowed by a dark sky, heavy with rain, but it didn't matter. We still drove to the beach later, watching the clouds roll in across the water and unburden themselves on the bayside suburbs from where they slouched above us. I watched the view of Brighton, washed to and fro by the flicking windscreen wipers, succumbing to the latest deluge. It seemed just the right sort of weather to herald my departure.

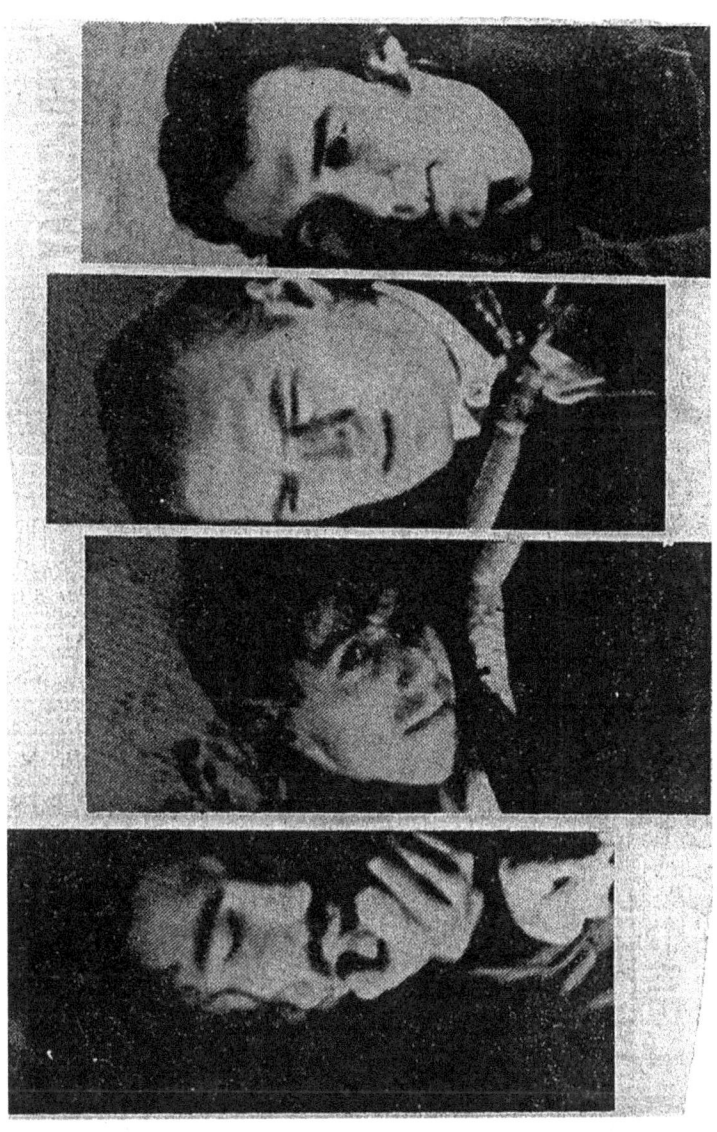

Newspaper clipping - selected fish tank shots

WE WERE huddled together in Mark's converted garage bedroom, listening to the rain falling on the roof above us. We were becoming more accustomed to sharing a bed and had staked a claim on our preferred side of the mattress.

"Don't you love the sound of rain falling when you're curled up in bed?"

I wriggled closer to Mark so that I could get warmer.

"Aah! Your feet are freezing … get away from me!"

He made an exaggerated shudder, pretending to be shocked.

"Well that's what you're here for, to warm them up again."

I was trying to rest my icy toes on Mark's shins but he kept moving away.

"Oh look, just get-it-over-with then," he said.

He gave a staged grimace, and waited for my feet to strike.

"Aaaaaaah...!" They'd touched down.

I couldn't help laughing as he winced and thrashed to the other side of the bed in a flurry of sheets and blankets. "Oh, they're not *that* cold," I said. But it had unleashed a series of impersonations.

"They're colder than Thatcher's Britain...Thatcher's *bloody* Brrrritain..." he said, in the argumentative tone used by Rik Mayall in The Young Ones. It had been a favourite show in student days. I squirmed as he trilled the words into my ear, and then felt him drop the pitch of his voice lower, until it resonated in his chest.

"Urrgh...urrrrgh... you fuckin' great poof..." he said, in his finest Peter Cook voice.

"How d' you do that?" I asked, marvelling at the rich bass of his voice.

He was smiling broadly as he rolled over to hug me. The rain was gathering momentum above us, a steady rhythm drumming noisily on the tin roof as we lay talking.

"Can't you just put some fucking socks on?"

"I could…"

"…but you're not going to?"

"Not when you do such a good job."

The insistent percussion on the corrugated metal roofing had become the sound of the city on this cold Saturday night; impatient fingers of rain that had been drumming all through the night. This would be the memory of

Melbourne that I took back with me when I returned to Launceston, the rhythm that had eventually sent me to sleep.

In the morning it had stopped. The rain had given way to a clear sky with the sort of unpredictability for which Melbourne was renowned. Over the past few days I'd tried to keep my bandaged hand completely dry. It hadn't fully healed whilst I'd been in Melbourne, but I couldn't further delay my return to work in Launceston. Taking advantage of the weak sunshine, we visited the Camberwell markets that morning, a Sunday tradition that saw the emergence of hundreds of market stalls and car boot traders. Mark drove me to the city afterwards, to take a Skybus, one of the many buses in a fleet that ran a continual service to and from the airport.

"Don't forget to write," I said, thinking of my daily visits to check for mail at the Supervisor's office. There was nothing better than seeing his handwriting on one of the envelopes. Having a letter gave me something to read and re-read in between all the absences.

"I'll phone you later to say goodnight," he promised.

"Really?" I hugged him gratefully. "The phone might be busy tonight though, so it could be hard to get through."

Everyone would be taking advantage of the cheaper rates on a Sunday, allowing them to talk for longer. The line was likely to be engaged for most of the evening.

"I won't be able to try until after ten," he said as I exited the car.

If Mark had rehearsals, or a gig in the evening, phone calls could be hit and miss. He wouldn't be free to call me, and he wouldn't be at home if I tried to phone him. A week could easily pass without us being able to connect.

"I'll wait up," I said.

Phoning from Melbourne was classed as a long distance call, charged at STD rates, and paid by the minute. Subscriber Trunk Dialling meant Mark could at least call me directly. In the past it would've involved calling the Operator, to connect from one exchange to another. I didn't mind having a late night if it meant I could speak with him later.

When I was at work, it was impossible to speak during the day. At the hospital I could only be tracked down via the public address system, and this was mostly used by the Nurses, when they wanted to locate me between wards. When I'd hear my name announced I'd call the switchboard from one of the landlines and they'd pass on the message. It was hardly ever for an outside call.

Our conflicting schedules sometimes made it a long time between conversations.

"I still have a stash of coins," I said, "so if I haven't heard from you, I'll call you before I go to bed. It'll be enough for a few minutes."

Using the payphone meant I had to keep feeding-in coins when the warning beeps sounded. It often led to a hurried goodbye when the money ran out.

"I'd love to hear your voice before I go to sleep," he said, kissing me one last time.

The airport terminal was bursting with passengers in snaking queues, so after I'd checked in I took the long walk to my departure lounge to await the boarding call. Staring at the cumbersome bandage on my hand I wondered if I'd been missed during my week's absence. I could already sense myself falling victim to the customary feelings of despair and melancholy, wondering when I'd see Mark again. However, my self-absorption was short lived.

With a kick of adrenalin I saw the familiar figure of my Boss, Dennis walking towards me. My face flushed hot, and instinctively I shrank down into my seat as he approached, briefly formulating an excuse for my trip. I could scarcely believe I'd been sprung, and on the same flight back to Launceston. I held my breath. He was almost level with me, carrying a briefcase and looking around for somewhere to sit.

Then he just walked right past me. He sat down at the far end of the lounge, took out a newspaper and started to read. After a few minutes I leaned forward and glanced to where he was seated. He seemed completely engrossed in the paper and showed no sign of having noticed me. It was an extraordinary stroke of luck.

I managed to board behind him, and didn't venture out of my seat for the brief flight, but I still had to get off the plane unseen. Although Launceston airport had a runway capable of taking international flights of 767 standard, it could only deal with one flight at a time. We would be the sole arrival.

Carolyn and James had come to meet me at the airport, but I was hovering at the back of the disembarking passengers, blending with the swarm to avoid being noticed. A Beagle had sat down opposite my feet and was gazing at my face as if I might be concealing a stick somewhere about my person. His nose twitched slightly, waiting for my move. He knew he could out sniff me.

"Any fruit or other food in your bags, Miss?"

"No." I wanted to pat the dog, but he was working.

"Quarantine," the handler said, at the other end of the lead, "I'll need to check your bag please because the dog's just indicated."

I loved the sniffer dogs in their smart Customs work jackets. They took their job seriously, and could sniff out anything edible or prohibited. My bag search revealed nothing.

"Have you had some food in that bag today?" the handler quizzed me.

"Hmm, I had a banana in there earlier."

"That'll be it."

Handler and dog moved on. That was some nose. One that could detect not only the presence of food, but where it had once been.

Luggage was being unloaded from the plane, and in the absence of a baggage carousel it was always brought around the building on a trailer, pulled by a small truck or even a tractor.

"James, can you get my bag from the trailer?"

"Is it really heavy or something?" James looked at me curiously.

It was usually a free-for-all frenzy when the tractor arrived at the side of the terminal building, as everyone grabbed their suitcases.

"It's not that I can't lift it. Dennis is here." I swivelled my eyes around warily. "He was on the same flight, but I don't think he's seen me yet."

I felt sure I'd be seen unloading my bags if I went near the trailer.

"What, from Melbourne?" Carolyn was incredulous.

"Yes! Can you believe it? But if you get my bag I can pretend I'm meeting *you* from Melbourne, and we're just collecting you from the airport."

"Good job he can't see too well," Carolyn reflected, trying to spot him.

"He doesn't miss much, despite his eyesight," I said thinking of his thick glasses.

"Okay, what does your bag look like?"

James was already elbowing into the thick of the crowd. Luck was again on my side.

After a tantalising glimpse into the life that awaited me across the ocean, I still faced many realities on my return to Launceston. It was already April, and in addition to the separation from Mark, I didn't yet know if I'd passed the exams that would permit me to keep working in the hospital. More significantly there was the threat of my visa application being denied, forcing my return home.

England seemed an impossible distance away, the flipside of the world. It was unthinkable to imagine Mark and I on separate sides of the globe. As I dug in to wait for my fate to be decided by the various factions of bureaucracy, I hung onto my memories of those cold Melbourne nights. I thought about the seductive sound of rain falling in the dark, and the warm cocoon of Mark's bed in his room behind the house. I would be going back there. I refused to believe there could be any other outcome.

## Tin Roof Rain

In the dim, naked hours
Near dawn,
A whispered kiss
Of air on skin;
Mist on the glass
Of a window
As the day
Begins to breathe.

Interchanging faces,
Hands become my own,
Our movement just a murmur
Stirring sheets,
Like pages turned.

This tin roof rain
Intimately falls,
Pulsing in crescendos
In the dark.
We tangle
Where the boundaries smudge,
And leave fingerprints behind,
Trailing them with questions
Where we touch.

Within me
I feel footsteps
Where you tread
And leave a path.
Without you
Feel the colour
Of my love
Fade black and white.

JAMES had just lit a cigarette at the round table in the lounge room of the Nurses' Home when I walked in, unwinding after an early shift at work, his hair still asymmetrical as if it hadn't been brushed since he leaped out of bed at dawn.

It was a bright May afternoon, the sun warming the vinyl of the scattered chairs around the table where it streamed in through the windows, and creating hard shadows on the floor.

"It's been a Mother of a day," he said, rolling his eyes upwards in a parody of despair, inhaling the smoke deeply and grinning at my approaching form. He'd probably been sitting in that chair since he'd finished work an hour ago, but he looked like he'd just sat down, reclining in it with the sort of wanton pleasure you'd expect for something other than furniture. James really knew how to enjoy a chair.

"How did you go being a groupie at The Tasmania Hotel?" he called out to my distant figure as I rummaged in the kitchen. My voice floated back to the lounge.

"You mean the Hoodoo Gurus gig? It was great. I got lots of good photos, and I even managed to swipe the playlist they'd gaffered to the stage. That's going into my glory box."

"You shouldn't be putting any strange things in your box. What would Mark think?"

"Roody!" I admonished, hearing the muffled snicker.

I joined him at the table with my supply of tea and biscuits, slumping into one of the chairs and offering him one of my McVities Digestives. He hesitated.

"Are they good for you or something?" He was eyeing the packet suspiciously.

"It's just a biscuit. It's the brand name."

"Oh, I thought it must be part of that bowel fodder you're always eating."

"They're English. I'm sure they're very bad for you. Why don't you try one?"

We sat for a few moments quietly munching in the cluttered room, the armchairs left as they had been vacated, set back from the television in an untidy semi-circle, the selection of wilting pot plants gathered around the windows, and the old piano covered with an increasing mound of papers and magazines. I offered James another biscuit.

"Mmm," he pushed the final piece into the corners of his mouth, holding his little finger aloft, "hmm…no, they're very one-ish."

"O-kay…"

"They have an odd afterbirth don't they?" he added, smacking his lips noisily.

"That's your cigarette. They're just wheat, you know."

He took another drag, mixing the residue of biscuit mush with smoke.

"What would I do without you, Roody?"

"Well you'll have to think about that if you're going to be leaving."

"I'm not leaving yet."

"It's only a matter of time."

"You mean if I get my visa? IF." I paused. "Fat chance. It's been ages now. Months.

And I haven't heard a thing."

"When did you apply?"

"Nearly five months ago."

"Well, either way you'll still be leaving us."

"Stop it. You're not going to make me feel guilty."

I started chewing my fingernails.

"What am I going to do, Roody if they don't give it to me?"

"Why shouldn't they?"

"But what could be taking so long?"

"Maybe they're checking your massive list of indiscretions and misdemeanours, your sordid past, you know, all the reckless and illegal things that you've done?"

But I was lost in my own thoughts.

"I'll have to go back to England."

People were drifting in and out of the room, mostly in uniform, either after, or part-way through, a day's work. They arrived as their schedule dictated, taking a break to smoke, or bringing a slice of toast from the kitchen, their knitting or some mail collected from the Supervisor in the adjacent building.

"Didn't they say it might take six months to process?"

"Yeah, but...."

"Well you've still got a bit of time to wait. No point in worrying yet."

"I know." I sighed out my frustration.

"And," James continued, "they're hardly going to kick you out of the country with Dennis sponsoring you. The hospital's already short of Physios."

"It's just hard, all this waiting. And then not knowing," I paused as James went out to the kitchen, and returned with a snack, "...not knowing when I'm going to see Mark again."

Mark's letters had recently been all about the tour to Sydney in mid-May, and other projects with the band. They'd been shooting a video for the track, *Left* which would be screened on Rage in the future, the infamous ABC television show broadcasting back to back music videos late into the night.

"He said something funny to me last time we spoke."

"Funny, how?" James asked.

"About our time apart. I didn't understand what he meant."

James waited for me to continue.

"He said *you learn to live without someone*. I don't know if it's his way of saying that you just have to get on with it, because we're apart. Or that he doesn't really need me."

"Well, have you asked him?"

"No." I wasn't sure I wanted to hear the answer.

Time enhanced my loneliness. Lately, the cloudy skies had blocked my nightly search for Orion, and I missed its presence and constancy in the quiet dark. Seeing it in the sky always reassured me; somehow it shrank the distance between us. This protracted separation was accentuating my anxiety, and although I could talk to him on the phone, I needed his physical presence to reassure me, not just his voice on the line.

"I think you're being a bit paranoid," James breathed, through his cigarette smoke, "and we all know why that is."

I hesitated.

"Oh. You heard about that. D'you think Callie will ever forgive me?"

"For going to Mutacia with Dave?"

"It was a one-off."

"Still."

I leaned on the table and rested my chin on my hand.

"I suppose it was a bit much for a Wednesday night," I admitted. "In my defence, I just thought we were all going over to his house for tea."

I hadn't smoked weed before, and Dave had been rolling cigar sized joints with his cousin. After a while I'd realised that my body had gone completely numb and I'd slipped into some strange dialect of Swahili. The only skin that I could still feel was around my lips. I'd been trying to tell Dave that, in my garbled incoherent hemp language. There's a reason they call it dope.

"I can't understand you. What are you talking about?" Dave had shrieked, laughing hysterically; which of course had kick started all the giggling. Around that time I'd seen Carolyn stand up and leave.

"She doesn't approve," James warned, stubbing out his cigarette.

"Well I know that now."

I hadn't seen her in the last couple of days. James seemed to read my mind.

"She's been on a late, late," he added, referring to her shifts, and the reason I hadn't seen her in the lounge, "but I suggest you talk to her soon."

"I was a bit wound-up about the whole visa thing." It sounded lame, even to me.

James had been snacking consistently between cigarettes, with complete disregard for all the conflicting additives and MSG. Feeling the sudden burst of hyperactivity it had induced, he disappeared out of the lounge and up the stairs where we could hear him thumping around in his room. Minutes later he reappeared wearing his sunglasses and a make-shift cape. It was going to be an evening of Darth Vader.

"*HHHHrrrooooaaaaaaarh!*"

He exhaled a loud, forced breath that resonated around the room. It had an appropriately chilling and blood curdling sound about it. I could always rely on James for entertainment when things were getting too serious. The other residents seemed oblivious, ignoring him and continuing to chat and as he breathed heavily behind them. He flapped menacingly between the chairs before stalking out to the corridor.

"Don't worry," he threw back as he left, "it'll all work out."

*Angela J. Dawson*

Byron Smith recounts the problems that expatriate Tasmanian band THE FISH JOHN WEST REJECT have faced over their name.

# A FISHY TALE

"...We tried, oh how we tried,
Until we became incestuous.
Too many combinations,
Becomes like a Chinese meal in a prison cell,
Well I'm Launcestonian,
I have a double cranium,
And you've got none,
You've got none,
I may be inbred, but I've always heard it said,
That two heads are better than one..."
- "Launceston", The Fish John West Reject, 1988.

Yes, The Fish John West Reject come from Tasmania, but before you ask them to show you their scars, remember that they've heard it all before. They've even written a song about their mythical little, ahem, idiosyncracies. (See above).

The fact that The Fish can laugh at themselves and still take themselves very seriously at the same time ("...our minor mainstream success is so *i-r-o-n-i-c*...") is an unusual irony. But then again, The Fish John West Reject aren't your usual band.

Who do you think contacted John West's Australian head office in Sydney and asked for permission to use the name — but didn't stop there — they also slipped in a *tiny* request for sponsorship?! Who coloured every one of their debut single labels in by hand, with crayons, simply 'cos you thought they'd have to be different to have a name like *that*.

Actually, a lot of people do that and a lot of people show up to their gigs expecting some wacky covers band.

Bassist Andrew Viney explains the dilemma, which is gradually disappearing -
"It has been a problem. People expecting some kinda party covers band. We've even thought about changing the name because of that, but we've stuck with it. Once people have heard the band — heard the material — it's OK."

Singer/guitarist Mark Narkowicz blows some bubbles:

"There seems to have been a nice little bit of hype created through the name. I've talked to people and said 'why'd you come to the gig?' and they've said 'oh simply on the name'.

"In places like Adelaide for instance, where we played the Fringe Festival, the name, as well as the Tasmanian element, provided a novelty that really helped in getting us press coverage".

The Fish John West Reject started out as a busking duo (Narkowicz and fellow guitarist/singer Mark Adams) in the streets of Launceston in 1985. In the following year the pair picked up a rhythm section (Viney and drummer Graham Rankin) and began playing Tassie's tiny pub-circuit and colleges. The band's roots in busking carried through into the four-piece outfit, which bore a strong acoustic/folk sound, that's still a major component of the band's projection. In the same year they accepted invitations to festivals in Sydney and Canberra, before releasing an indie tape called "Canned". After a short break, the band began playing again in the latter half of '87 and by the beginning of '88 they'd moved base to Melbourne.

The Oddities came to Melbourne from Tassie to split-up. Wild Pumpkins At Midnight and Bigger Than Texas migrated north to Melbourne and are still going, and there are countless individual Tasmanians in bands all around the mainland.

So why do so many Tassie musicians, become Apple Isle expatriates?

Viney: "You can reach a stagnation point in Tasmania very quickly. There just isn't much of a scene there".

Narkowicz: "You can really tell, every time the band goes back to Launceston that there's a saturation point in terms of audiences. Hobart is getting bigger and every time we go there, it's getting more and more like Melbourne, with more diverse subcultures and so on, but there's still a saturation point. The band scene that's away from the mainstream gets very incestuous and you find people popping up in different bands all the time — which is a bit of a shame — but it's the only thing that can be done really, if you wanna keep the music scene down there from suffocating in its own slime".

The Fish recently released their debut single "Left" b/w "Childless Mother", which was recorded during LP sessions at Melbourne's Sing Sing studios with producer/engineer Mark Woods, last November. The album is expected to emerge later this year, if the band is successful in their efforts to secure an appropriate release deal.

The recordings and the pressing of the single were self-funded by The Fish for their own "River Fill" label. The labels of every single were individually and skilfully scribbled upon by crayon-wielding Fish members.

Viney: "One guy who really likes the band bought ten copies of the single, 'cos he's convinced that they're collectors items. And the fact that the singles look a bit different has helped us to be noticed by radio programmers too".

Who's your most outrageous fan?

Viney: "Oh the Incredible Screaming Man was pretty bad".

Who?

"The Screaming Man. This guy who very early in our careers, used to come to the gigs and then he turned up in Adelaide when we played there. He just stands down the back of the room and goes 'YYGGGAAAAAAAAAGGGHHHHH!'".

Narkowicz: "He'd just stay there and scream at the top of his lungs, right from the very start of the gig when people were still sitting down, right 'til the end when they were leaving".

THE NAME JOHN WEST ACCEPTS

When The Fish John West Reject moved to Melbourne, they encountered one major problem... there was a mainland band who appeared to have "borrowed" their moniker. This, along with the fact that they hadn't received permission from the John Tuna himself, had the boys a little worried for a while, so they decided to get themselves registered as a business through the appropriate government "channels" (get it?).

Narkowicz: "In an attempt to get ourselves registered as a business — so we could have some form of protection of the name — we had to receive written permission from the Fish John West company, to use the phrase (The Fish John West Reject...). So we wrote to them and cheekily asked for some sort of sponsorship as well! But they wrote this letter back and said 'yes, we have no problem with you using the name at all, but we can't give you any sponsorship, because it doesn't fit our marketing plan at the moment. They said 'however, any time you're 'gigging' in Sydney — give us a contact and we'll be happy to have you play for a staff dinner', which is really good!"

## It's time

ON MAY 26TH my visa arrived. I had collected my mail after work as usual, discovering the official envelope amongst the assortment and running excitedly across to Home Three to tell Carolyn and James. By the time I reached the upstairs landing I was breathless, expecting the doors to their rooms to be open as an indicator that they were home.

"James! Callie!" I panted, rounding the corner and seeing James' door wide open.

I looked inside. "Roody?"

His room was empty which meant he could be anywhere within the three homes. Then I heard the toilet flush in the adjacent bathroom and turned to see him leaving the cubicle. I realised, guiltily, that I must have disturbed him in those precious moments of imminent bowel movement.

"Sorry, Roody."

He went to wash his hands at the sink.

"Sucked it right back up there. I'll probably be constipated for weeks."

But he flashed me a sly smile.

"Look what's arrived!"

I followed him as he headed straight towards his room, and watched as he began rummaging in a large pile of possessions behind the door.

"I've got it! See, I'm a Resident!" I was waving the papers at him but he was engrossed in his search, eventually pulling a rubber plunger out of the pile and returning to the bathroom.

"Oh, so you'll be leaving us to become a groupie and get your leg over in Melbourne?"

I shadowed him into the bathroom. "You know I wouldn't leave otherwise."

It was true, I was finally able to leave Tasmania, and I knew that it would bring mixed feelings despite the initial excitement. This had been my home for more than a year, and although I was keen to be with Mark my friends were all here.

James was staring into the shower recess.

"What are you doing?" I asked, looking at the plunger.

"You know I can't be too excited for you. It means you're going to be leaving us, and I'd rather you didn't."

He'd begun to pump away at the plughole with the plunger, drawing up a putrid concoction of stale water and matted hair.

"Look at it!" he shouted breathlessly above the noise of suction and regurgitation, his arm moving in a frenzy.

"Aren't the cleaners meant to do that?"

I couldn't help laughing at his crazed figure bent double in the dark shower cubicle, at the obvious pleasure he was deriving from the whole process. He stopped and looked at me, slightly out of breath.

"You may laugh, but it's blocked," he retorted. "The water doesn't drain down the plughole properly because of all the years of crap festering away down there, and I'm sick of standing in this shit every time I have a shower."

"Yeah, I noticed it was getting worse."

"Don't tell Cal about the plunger though. She'll think I'll get an infectious disease or something from all this stagnant water, and that'll be an end to doing any rude things."

He watched the water drain back out for a moment before standing up, apparently satisfied with his efforts.

"So, are you still coming away with us this weekend?" he asked.

"To Hobart?"

He nodded. "We've booked a caravan."

"Of course. I could never miss a weekend with the Secret Sect."

Since my earlier induction and naming, the three of us often referred to ourselves as the Secret Sect. I'd soon found that it had absolutely nothing to do with religion, and everything to do with Monty Python, which had become apparent after one of those hyperactive evenings in the lounge room. James had *Life of Brian* on video and after multiple viewings he'd perfected the falsetto voices, and had adopted the characteristic greeting so often repeated in the film. It hadn't taken me long to catch up, and to start implementing our favourite catchphrase.

It was obviously never a sect, and it certainly wasn't a secret given our loud conversations and all the noise we made. We couldn't really pin down when it had escalated, but most of it was incited by James, and he was responsible for all the Python vernacular. He was the one who'd initiated the wearing of identical outfits, having found second hand grey overcoats in the local thrift shops. Whenever we went out for day trips it was a strange fusion of Enid Blyton meets the Blues Brothers as we roamed our destination all dressed the same, in our coats and dark sunglasses.

His ideas hadn't ended there. I'd come home one day to see him fiddling with his latest acquisition.
"What's that?" I asked, staring at the components of the relic on the table.
"It's an old screen printer," he said through his teeth, trying to unscrew something recalcitrant and rusted.
"What do you need that for?"
"I thought we'd hand print a Sect T-shirt logo."
"We're not going to be much of a secret if you advertise us on a T-shirt."
"People will be intrigued by our inscrutability."

In the end, it all proved too much for the old printer, and its broken parts were discarded, along with the idea. On reflection, I was sure he would have been relieved, knowing we could maintain an air of ambiguity and elusiveness, which was after-all his preferred modus operandi.

James was an expert at operating by stealth; that was part of his charm. It was evidenced by his partiality for all sorts of clandestine behaviours, and by the various skills that he'd been honing lately. These included stalking down corridors in near silence, and trying to enter the building unseen. If I was reclining in the lounge room enjoying the sedative effects of the television, he'd be able to manifest behind me as if he'd been energised into the room via teleporter.

Employing his full lung capacity, he'd emit the sort of stertorous exhalation that would elicit an animalistic and unconscious loosening of the bowels. I couldn't have been more scared if Darth Vader himself had been revealed next to the piano.

In addition to the *HHHrrroooaaaaaaarh* that regularly tested my sphincters, James had other Pythonesque phrases to make my heart stop, shrieking them at ear splitting pitch in a bid to tumble me out of my chair. My terrified shrieks often heralded the end of another successful mission.

"EEEERE..!" he'd screech, with sudden proximity to my ear, in the most piercing falsetto tones, making my teeth rattle in their sockets.

I'd seen him creep up and similarly eject the resident sleeping cat from the beanbag a few times, delighting in the wet spot that it incautiously emitted due to the shock, certainly resulting in the loss of one of its nine lives. I knew how it felt.

*

When I greeted James on the morning of our Hobart trip, it was in a voice that would have shattered glass.

"ERE!" I cried, "are you ready!?"

"ERE!" he shrilled, like an echo, "Cecil is ready, and has been waiting for you. You luc-ky, luc-ky Baaaa-stard."

In keeping with the tradition of Sect weekends we set off with a generous supply of food, stopping regularly for further unnecessary supplies, but eventually arriving at the open air Salamanca markets in Hobart. The entire harbour front was a mass of colour and market stall canopies. Everything from handmade clothing, pottery, and antiques, to leather goods, and of course plenty of home produce and local cuisine for us to sample.

Crowds snarled the gaps between rows and clogged the pavements. Towering sandstone warehouses provided a backdrop, containing galleries, café's and more shops selling everything from crafts to vegetables. We browsed through the market until we reached the dock with its assorted boats bobbing in the sunshine, some with cray baskets or crates of colourful buoys piled on deck. There were so many cafes and pubs on the waterfront offering delicious variations of fish and chips that it was hard to make a lunch selection. From the sea to the plate. They all had the freshest catch of the day.

We took a brief detour south later, towards Kingston, to check out the beaches and the view across to Bruny Island.

"Are we lost?" I asked, looking out of Cecil's windows as we kerb-crawled the streets. "What are you looking for?"

"Oh, you know, snacks," James said vaguely.

He was peering at the passing shops, some of which didn't look open for business.

"Let's just get something back in Hobart," I suggested.

I felt James mash the brakes and we veered off towards a parking area.

"What's here?"

"I need a minute to use the facilities," he admitted, alighting the car swiftly.

Callie and I shared a look. All the usual difficulties would arise with using public toilets, mostly from the coming and going of other patrons. Although he dealt with his patients' bodily functions every day he remained surprisingly covert when dealing with his own.

As we stretched our legs, James made his dash to the small brick outhouse. There was no-one around, ideal for total privacy. Within minutes of retiring to the toilet block he reappeared at the car looking rattled.

"Dirty little slut..."

He was trying to light a cigarette with shaking hands.

"What's the matter, Darlin'?" Carolyn asked.

"A *cat*," he sputtered, inhaling the smoke as if it was oxygen, "...a bloody cat got into the cubicle. I was just getting started, and this black thing brushed against my legs." He shivered.

"Here?" I asked incredulously, looking at the empty beach surrounds.

"Didn't you see it go in?" I asked.

"No, it was too dark. It must've slipped under the door."

"He's a *one* isn't he?" Carolyn made a contented sound in her throat, like a hiccup.

"So have you, erm…been, or not?" I probed.

"No I bloody haven't. It could've been anything in the dark, and there I was with all my nethers exposed. I'm not exactly going to hang around and find out what it is, am I?"

"Well d' you want to find another toilet?"

"I don't think I'm in the mood now." He let out a petulant huff of smoke.

"You need to open your bowels, Darlin'…" Carolyn implored, ruffling his hair.

"I'll just save it up until I get home, thank you. I'm too crabby now."

"We can wait, if you want to try again," I began, with my best deadpan face.

"No," he said, having decided to withhold his deposit, "it's hard enough, without dealing with that sort of stress. I can wait."

At the end of the day we took the winding road that led from the city towards the hills, inclining steeply to the summit of Mt Wellington. The drive induced a more pensive mood as we passed the lifeless remnants of bush fires on the roadside. Skeletons of twisted trees passed our windows as we climbed, their silver, leafless branches creating a stark, surreal quality to the landscape, fading in and out of the low cloud that hung like a fog across the mountain. As it shifted we could see the view of the city far below us, and preserved by the cold air, there was even snow at the roadside.

"That's the first snow I've seen in Australia!" I exclaimed, as Cecil wheezed up the incline, battling the rising gradient.

"You can ski here you know," Callie said, "They get quite good falls in winter."

But James was still thinking of creature comforts and bodily functions.

"I think they have a good toilet up here," he stated hopefully.

At the windy peak we left Cecil in the vast car parking area, striding out to see the views from the plateau on the boulder strewn summit, buffeted by the updrafts of gusty air. More than 1200m below us the Derwent River was making its way into the Tasman Sea. Everything was in miniature, tiny Lego houses and hotels, the angular shape of the harbour, its moored fishing boats and yachts that earlier we'd seen bobbing on the waterfront.

At this elevation it was much cooler than the temperatures at sea level, and it wasn't surprising that snow could fall here.

"One day, all this could be yours," James quipped, ad libbing from The Holy Grail and waving his arm with a flourish, as if he was selling me the entire panorama.

In the lively wind, I squinted off into the distance.

"If you decided to stay, that is."

He'd lit a cigarette, and as his exhaled smoke drifted up it was snatched by the air gusting around us.

I shivered involuntarily. Melbourne, and Mark, lay to the north, more than 700km away. Without question, that's where my future lay.

I WAS EXHILARATED by the news. The band's schedule would be bringing Mark back to Launceston for a few days in the middle of June. The timing was perfect.

Night after night the rain had been washing against my bedroom window in noisy gusts, clashing relentlessly with the wind in the dark. It had been a week of stormy weather, but his arrival was preceded by a glimpse of sunshine.

Having spent the first few days touring Devonport and Hobart with the band, he'd travelled back to Launceston and arranged to meet me outside Ripples restaurant. I found him there in the late afternoon, lounging in the crook of a tree overlooking the river. After coffee and cake at the gallery café we walked by the river, watching the light fade; but the city was quiet on a Monday night, and we decided to return to the Home for the evening.

"Happy birthday," he said, kissing me softly.

Gifts had been arriving for me. The sunshine, and Mark's appearance, had added to the celebratory mood of the month.

"This is the best present," I said, folding my arms around his waist.

A plump moon was gaping at us from a cloudless sky, its face turned to reflect a distant sun. It looked like a gilded mirror catching the light from a far corner of space. We were standing in my room in the darkness, looking out at the lights of the city, my presents still unopened in a corner of the room.

His visit was particularly meaningful this time. In a couple of weeks I'd be leaving Tasmania to join him in Melbourne. After so many months of waiting it was hard to believe we'd finally be together in the same city. It was an exciting prospect, but it was tempered by my sense of loss. This would be the last night we'd ever spend in my Launceston home, the last visit Mark would make to my room.

Turning to kiss him I felt overwhelmed by a mixture of sadness and anticipation. So many significant things had happened here, on this small island. It was the place in which we had unexpectedly fallen in love, and I wanted to savour the last few hours before he left.

I began to undress Mark slowly, feeling his eyes on my face as I looked down to fumble with the buttons of his shirt. His face was full of questions, but still he didn't speak. In the dim lamplight I watched his expression change from curiosity to tenderness, confused by my boldness, but returning my kisses and slowly dropping my clothes to the floor.

When we lay down on my bed I felt my apprehension tangling with my desire, but as I grazed my lips against his, I could feel the arousal becoming more urgent, kissing him ardently until I felt him draw away from me. He rested on one elbow so he could look at me.

"I'm not going to make love to you, Ange."

I searched his face for an answer. "Why not?"

"Because it's not the right time," he said softly, "Not here."

"You don't want to?"

"Oh yes. I do; but not like this. It's too important to me."

"I just thought it would be more special here." I felt oddly relieved.

"So you were going to seduce me?" There was a tenderness in his eyes.

"Well. Yes. That was the plan."

"The plan?" he teased, "You planned it?"

"Sort of. Not really. I got a condom just in case. But I knew I'd be too scared to go through with it."

He sighed out a long breath, and held me closer.

"You know I'm scared too don't you?"

"Are you?" I was surprised.

"Of course I'm scared. I want this more than anything. I want it with you…" He pulled away so he could see me again. "And I want *you*, you know that …when the moment's right." He paused. "We'll know when it is."

I hugged him gratefully, feeling his warm body against my own, his hand gently stroking my back.

"Where did you get the condom anyway?"

"From James," I replied into his chest, resting my head in the soft, downy hair. "It's under my pillow."

I could feel myself relaxing, lying with his arms around me.

"I'm so glad you said no. I'd been worrying about it all night," I said. "I think I'd just decided that you expected it, and that it was me who was holding back."

"No." He turned my face towards him. "No, of course not. I'd never think that."

He lay behind me, so we could see the night lights of the city through the window.

"I love the outlook from here," I murmured, "I'll miss it."

"We'll be back again."

"Will we?" I asked, turning to look over my shoulder

"Of course. To see my family, don't worry."

"But we won't be here, in my room with a view."

We listened to the sleeping night for a few minutes, watching as the wind stirred through the tall conifer alongside the path and shivered its limbs.

"Hey…your birthday presents," Mark said, pointing at the floor. "You still haven't opened them. Shall we…?"

Piling up my presents, we opened them together, lying in bed and reading the cards in the diffuse light, ripping open the brightly coloured paper and scattering it across the floor.

I watched him set off along the dark walkway, memorising every nuance of that final moment until he disappeared. My body ached to follow him, yet with some trepidation I considered the uncertain future into which he was leading me.

My mind was filled with images as I lay thinking about Tasmania and all the months I'd spent there. Even though I'd grown to love the island's wild beauty and isolation, the rainforests and the clear waters, I'd sometimes wondered what might draw me away from its shores. There had been a time when it would have been inconceivable to leave, when I could never have imagined relinquishing the place that I'd let into my heart.

I had arrived there, and chosen it as my own, this outpost on a vast continent. I had flown in and made it entirely mine, constructed it twig by twig, and created a home. Mark had become the reason for me to let it go, and although in some ways I wanted to stay, he'd finally made it possible for me to leave.

NOW that I'd resigned from my position and finished working at the hospital, my remaining days were free to finalise my travel arrangements. I had time to revisit favourite places, and to lie awake for hours watching from my window as the city blinked and settled down to sleep at night, the line of orange lights that traced the highway receding into the distance. It was a time of reflection. Listening to Mark's lyrics, I could understand his love for the place.

"*Watching the lights going out over Launceston...*"

His voice was unmistakeable, even in song. I imagined him writing those words in a past that had not foreseen me, watching the sleeping city as I had done before we met.

The Gorge was always in flood at that time of year, and walking the pathways in the Reserve helped me to loosen some of the memories of those mellow afternoons. Up river, turbulent and swollen white water was cascading through the deserted ruins of the old Duck Reach power station, charging down to the wide expanse of water below and into the First Basin. As a result of this excess flow, the water in the Basin had been stirred into a brown opacity, skimmed with a grey-white foam that drifted to the edges and lay like clusters of snow around the bushes at the waterside.

Standing on the suspension bridge I looked up river, thinking of the summer days when Mark and I had laid on the giant slabs of rock at Duck Reach, with eyes closed, letting the sun warm our skin. Its remote location often ensured we were the only hikers in the afternoons. I could recall the way my skin flushed and tingled as his lips and hands wandered my body in the sunshine, the erotic sensation of being caught there, out in the open, as Mark found gaps between my clothing through which to caress and kiss. It had been a drowsy, deep arousal, a gentle ache and a slow meandering desire. Under the sky it had felt like we were uncontained, made daring by the sultry day. But we were just two innocents. As we circled one another with our love, we were still only in rehearsal.

Turning around to look at the vast Gorge and its wide pool I watched the water churning violently underneath the suspension bridge, far below my feet. It normally only trickled over a concrete ledge in the summer, forming a gentle waterfall into the Basin. Now the floodwaters were roaring through. Beyond the bridge, even the boulders at the perimeter of the river were submerged under the rising waters.

On the hottest summer days, when I'd gone to swim with friends, we would lie on the grass close to the kiosk and the outdoor swimming pool. Sometimes we sunbathed further away on the high vantage point of the boulders, adjacent to the bridge.

If we wanted to swim in the Basin, we had to clamber barefoot across scorching, uneven chunks of rocks at the shore, moving unsteadily with arms outstretched until we found an entry point. The soft mud squeezed between our toes as we waded, floating with arms sprawled like starfish, eyes closed, letting the water fill our ears and muffle the sounds of the day. It whispered secrets from below, as the sun warmed our faces and left an orange glow behind our eyelids.

Sunbathing on the boulders had its drawbacks. Sprawled on towels on the flattest of the blocks, we basked there until we were driven almost mad with thirst. But too lazy to walk all the dusty trails that led to the kiosk, we dropped down into the moving river and took the most direct path across the Basin.

It was a cold swim, and even as the sun speared the surface it couldn't infiltrate the murky depths that faded into a cold blackness far below our kicking legs. We had our coins tucked into one cheek, lips closed on their metal tang as we skimmed the freezing pool, feeling them rattling against our teeth until we could make the final dash across the grass.

There were stories of giant eels living there, ready to twine themselves around our feet and pull us under; but we weren't deterred, wedging soda cans into our bathers, and sliding in for the return with briefs bulging like gun holsters, feeling them drag as we backstroked away from the shore.

I'd moved from the bridge to the far side of the Basin, where a dead tree that I'd once photographed had been felled. Only a stump remained. When I'd taken the picture of it so many months ago I'd been captivated by its twisted beauty, resting inert by the waterside like an exclamation mark against the skyline. As I wandered the winding trail that cut into the cliff above the water I wondered how things would change in my absence, and what I might find when I returned.

In the Cliff Grounds, the lamps alongside the pathways had begun to glow, lighting the way through a rising gloom. It was time to leave. The musty smell of dusk was in the air, and the peacocks had begun to shrill in the gardens in the early evening, their mewling refrain piercing the drowsy twilight.

"Tay....oool, Tay....oool," they wailed, their voices resonating across the spaces between the lofty sandstone cliffs.

My bed was perfectly level with the window frame, and from its position against the wall I could easily slide up the panel. I was still awake with the curtains parted, reluctant to shut out the last view of the city, resting my pillow on the sash of my open window so I could stare up at the star glitter from my corner bedroom.

Everything was packed, even though I knew there were some things that I just couldn't take with me. I couldn't bring myself to go to sleep.

## Softly

Love walks
A moonlit path
By river bank
And orchard shadow,
Coveting time
In the moments
Of an offered hand,
Or the touch
Before a kiss.
Each step weaves
Its intricate way
To the place
Where footsteps merge
And tread together.
Launceston,
Where I found
Myself
In you:
The place
Where my heart
Was,
Is,
And always
Yours.

Launceston, Cataract Gorge: the cliffs, & path, above the South Esk River

Launceston, Suspension Bridge, across the First Basin

Walking trail to Cliff Grounds Reserve, and First Basin

*Angela J. Dawson*

# Crossing the Strait

THE following day, on a bright Friday afternoon, James and Carolyn drove me north to Devonport from where I was due to catch the ferry, The Abel Tasman across to Port Melbourne.

I'd decided to take the overnight sea crossing rather than the short flight, not entirely due to my fear of flying. I wanted some time alone, to reflect and gradually absorb all the changes occurring, and the long journey across the Bass Strait was perfect for the slow transition.

We bumped along in the cramped confines of the tiny silver Suzuki, Cecil chasing the fading light, all of us subdued by our individual thoughts. The noise of the engine filled the space, but our collective brooding seemed to preclude any meaningful conversation. In the rear of the little car I sat with my legs stretched out on the backseat, my back to the window, gazing absently at the passing scenery. After a while I noticed James was reaching up to his face with increasing regularity. He was quietly wiping away tears. I didn't know what to say. Carolyn glanced at him, hunched at the steering wheel, staring intently at the road as it slipped away beneath us. She reached across and rested an arm on his shoulders, leaving it there as he drove.

"Roody, I really wish…" I began.

"…don't…I'm sorry…I can't help it," he said

Carolyn moved her hand up, and rested it behind his neck.

"Darlin'…" she soothed.

"I just wish you weren't leaving us," he added.

Carolyn was looking for something in her bag, and when she turned around she handed me a small box from a jeweller's shop.

"We bought you something, so you won't forget us," she explained.

I opened the box. Inside was a round silver locket, and there was an inscription on the back. *In sectdom, Love R & R's*

I could feel my eyes filling with tears and my throat tighten.

"You can still change your mind," James said quietly.

He sniffed, and cleared his throat noisily.

I opened the clasp and put the chain around my neck, fingering the locket where it hung from the necklace.

"Thankyou. It's beautiful."

"The man doing the engraving thought it was for a wedding or something," Carolyn said, over her shoulder. "We had to write it down so he could understand it."

"I really love the inscription," I replied, trying to control the feelings of sadness that were beginning to overwhelm me. The evening alone on the ferry would help me to organise my thoughts and calm my jangling nerves.

At least there would be work for me in Melbourne. Mark's friend, Di was a Nurse, and thanks to her enquiries I'd been able to secure a locum position at The Royal Women's Hospital in Carlton. I would also have somewhere to live, given I was entitled to lodgings in the adjacent Nurses' accommodation. But having relinquished my network of friends I was aware that Mark was my only contact now as I moved into this huge city.

When we arrived at the ferry terminal for the dusk sailing, I boarded immediately so that I could find my berth and stow my baggage. My room was on B deck, so low in the depths of the boat that I was below the waterline, and I could hear the creaks and groans of the hull as it shifted in the water. The lack of windows added to the timeless, claustrophobic atmosphere of the tiny berth, but I'd only have to spend a few hours there when I finally needed to sleep.

Returning to the lounge, I located James and Carolyn in the crowded room, the three of us standing together looking sombre and uneasy.

"Oh, why couldn't you get the plane?" James complained. "It's so much less painful than all this hanging around."

"You know I hate planes. It makes me feel sick to even wait at an airport for someone else's plane."

He sighed. "I can't even have a cigarette in here. You did it on purpose didn't you? Oooh, you're a callous, wicked thing."

He succumbed to a hug from Carolyn without objection, his arms hanging limply at his sides.

The final announcement for boarding was being repeated, and the last few remaining passengers were heading along the walkway to the ferry.

"Thanks so much for driving me up here. And thanks again for the locket."

I reached out to hug each of them in turn, struggling with those last awkward moments before departure.

"Make sure you write to let us know you're okay," Carolyn said.

"Yes, we expect a letter every day or I'll get really crabby and renounce your membership," James threatened, watching Carolyn kiss my cheek again.

"Of the Sect? You wouldn't do that."

He gave a sly smile.

"I would... and I *can* actually, because I'm the President."

"I'll call you tomorrow night, with the phone number of the Home."

"She'll forget us when she gets there and becomes a full time groupie," James said, releasing me from our hug.

"No I won't, and I'll write all the time, I promise. I'll really miss you two. So much. You have no idea…"

I could feel my voice cracking. There really weren't any words that could describe what they meant to me. Turning away, I moved tearfully towards the walkway and gave them a final misty glance before boarding.

Somehow I managed to find my way along the passageway to the outside deck, flicking away tears as I looked for a position from where I could wave as the ferry pulled away.

As I stood looking down at the crowd of faces on the quay, I remembered how I'd felt a few months ago when I'd watched the ferry draw away with Mark on board. First was the sense of loss, and then the acute loneliness at being left behind. I began to wave and shout when I singled out their faces, waiting for them to see me before I began to gesture. I pointed to my right eye, then held my clenched fist over my heart before pointing to where they were standing. I could see them smile, understanding my message, and then wave back in recognition.

The ferry had moved away from the quayside, but I could still see James occasionally touching his face where, at this distance, I assumed there were tears. The two of them remained huddled together, becoming smaller, until they were ultimately swallowed into the shadows of the dusk. I was left alone on-deck, being blown by the wind, straining my eyes across the blackness of the dark ocean. I stood for a while, watching the last of the lights on shore flicker out, and until I was too cold to linger any more. There were striped deck chairs in the draughty shelter of the observation deck so I went back to my cabin to retrieve a coat and my Walkman.

For a while I sat out on deck, letting my thoughts drift as the ship nudged onwards, keeping my coat wrapped tightly around me in the dark. An old man tried to speak to me, unaware of the headphones, but I wanted to be alone with my tears. He eventually wandered off to find more interesting company and I was left with just the nausea that had begun to churn in my stomach. The rising swell on the open ocean had begun to rock the ship, and as my music played I waited for the bile to settle in my empty stomach.

The joyless assortment of food in the café didn't lift my spirits. After a snack I still felt queasy, but I knew the ship kept medication for passengers. Seasickness was nothing new to the First Aid Nurse on board as she dished out tablets. The crossing was often rough, and as people staggered across corridors on scissoring legs, I could see I wouldn't be the only one in need of assistance.

By the time I returned to my shared cabin the other occupants were already lying quietly in their bunks, and I had to undress in the dark before climbing up to my top bunk. Despite our low berth I was aware of the vessel lurching and crashing through the rough seas above, feeling the motion of the ship rocking me in my bed.

I rested my hand on the locket, with a thought to the pictures inside, embodying everything that I had found in Tasmania. On one side was a black and white photograph of James and Carolyn, and on the other a print of Mark's face, illuminated by one of the lamps that lit the pathways through the Gorge.

They condensed a year into a glance. I could see everything in the locket that I had ever wanted, then and now. Friendship and love.

*Angela J. Dawson*

# Melbourne

THE ENTRIES in my diary during those transitional weeks from Launceston to Melbourne were infrequent. We were in the heart of winter, and the rain was falling generously on the city in July. My new home was a high rise structure on Grattan Street in Carlton. The Nurse's quarters occupied a few floors, but the building itself wasn't exclusive to hospital staff. The upper floors, from level 8 to 12 accommodated a range of students, undertaking subjects from journalism to science. Its u-shaped configuration obscured any view of the city from my room, so to obtain the best outlook I had to take the lift up to the twelfth floor to access the rooftop.

At night, exposed to the cold air and chill winds, I would huddle in my thick coat, leaning against the rails as I pondered the vastness of the spreading city lights; watching the trams below executing perfect ninety degree turns on parallel tracks that ran meticulously around the building, into Swanston Street.

As we'd done in Launceston, we worked out a way for Mark to access the building so that he could occasionally stay until the early hours of the morning. He referred to it as breaking in and breaking out again, and it did seem like a covert operation when he wanted to visit me. The security was stringent, and more formal than our previous matronly Supervisors, but we carefully mapped a way through the back doors and hospital corridors so that he could discreetly avoid the curfew.

The slow pace and simplicity of life in Tasmania had given way to the insomniac ways of a diverse and fickle city. Although I'd lost the serenity and safety of the carefree days in Launceston, I tried to focus on all the opportunities now that we were able to live in the same city. Mark hadn't spoken of us living together, and I was grateful that the initial hospital accommodation afforded me some independence. Despite my quixotic expectations I didn't know what lay ahead of us, and even as I nurtured my ideals I knew there were no guarantees. I needed to find my own way.

Earlier that month I'd been to the art gallery where I'd been captivated by Imants Tillers' huge canvass entitled, Quest: I the speaker 1988. On it he'd copied a quote from Ecclesiastes, the emptiness of all endeavour. The words seemed to describe my current situation, and the cycle of life as the days unfolded.

"*.. The sun rises and the sun goes down; back it returns to its place and rises there again. The wind blows south, the wind blows north. Around and around it goes and returns full circle. All streams run into the sea yet the sea never overflows; back to the place from which the streams ran they return to run again.*"

There was a satisfying repetition about it, the way things continued unremittingly. But there was also a sense of futility and inevitability in those words. Everything would eventuate at its appointed time, as if nothing could be changed, as if we are locked into our future. The final quotation stirred other thoughts:

"*....So I applied my mind to understand wisdom and knowledge, madness and folly, and I came to see that this too is chasing the wind. For in much wisdom is much vexation and the more a man knows, the more he has to suffer.*"

Ignorance is bliss, I thought. Sometimes it can be better to live in blind hope.

My locum work had not yet started, but as I settled into my new life, James ensured I received regular news of Tasmania with a string of unpunctuated, misspelled and often graphic letters. They were sent in bulging envelopes, written on scraps of paper, and filled with a pertinent reference to bodily functions. The first one was written on the back of a notepad that he had somehow procured from TasGraphics Professional Photographic Laboratory, and it began with the usual greeting.

"ERE, Show us your growler, said with a nasal drawl and a sinal constipation. How do I feel? Let me count the ways -

1. like shit
2. like death
3. like shit

Yes, you guessed it. I have a head cold, Roods and I have just had a rip-roarer (fight)... many a loud word was exchanged ... and I come home to find my friend and confidante is still in Melbourne, so I guess I will have to wallow in self-pity. The others are having a bitch session about a nurse in the Home but as yet no-one is bad mouthing you. Thank God for that or they would suffer the wrath of Darth HHHHHrrr - said with mystery and a spine chilling tone.

Thank you for your jotting full of intrigue and lust. "We love it". We have booked for Bali and will doss in Melbourne overnight so expect us EREing with childhood abandon at the sight of you. By the way, do you still look the same? It's been so long... don't you know... me and your mother are worried sick about you. Are you eating properly, brushing your teeth and cleaning behind your ERE's..? Oh, and don't forget clean underwear. You never know when you may be run over by a maverick tram, and there you'd be lying on a trolley in casualty with some strange person looking at your particulars only to find soiled undergarments. Tsk, tsk.

Oh, pardon me, I just farted and you can smell it if you lightly scratch here. → ≅. Go on try it. It can only bite you.

By the way, how's your growler? Pretty happy I guess (and with good reason) I mean, you know growlers... give 'em an inch and they'll take a mile!!

By the way again, thank you for the phone call. It's really great to hear your voice. It helps to remind me that my memories are just that, and not only imagination. We really did have some good times didn't we, the Not-so-Secret-Sect? But the memories of those times and our corrospondence will suffice until we are together once more as a Sect. I'm beginning to "fill up" ... but life is about growing and these things equip me "spiritually, mentally and emotionally" to cope and learn (Christian Ad on TV).

Anyway enough morbid wallowing in a mire of self-pity. We will be re-united and scream sectal profanities once more."

The note continued a few days later:

"I am at present couching-it after an ordeal not unlike crucifixion - having had my hair cut - it now looks like Jason Donovan. I have just returned from yet another study session. My brain won't cope. All it wants to do is dream and sloth about in its cranial confines. Not too much to ask I feel, all things considered. Dave is asleep on the couch, surprise, surprise. Still the same old David, but I suspect there is even more indulging and visiting Mutacia."

I smiled. Dave's continuing desire to spend evenings in Mutacia caused endless trouble, especially when he smoked in his room, and the unmistakeable smell of weed filtered down the corridors.

James continued:

"Say no more. I really think that he indulges too much, but I wouldn't like to say anything. How's Mark and The Fish? And are you getting any? How are your girlie problems, and how's work? The hospital here is now 'No-smoking' except for some of the cafe and the foyer of the lecture theatre in which they've turned the air-conditioner onto supermelt in an effort to evict us. But you know us smokers are a hardy and determined lot, and it would take more than heat to drive us out.

It's that time of the night and my trusted friend and confidant is missing, so I guess I'll make a mental note of the things we would discuss and bash the hell out of your ears when you return. You will be pleased to know that I have not experienced any self-pitying bouts of jealousy for ages. Perhaps I'm cured. It must come with maturity. Snicker, chortle, grunt.

What the hell...GUFFAW, GUFFAW. Maturity! I wouldn't know it if it came up to me, introduced itself and pissed in my eyes."

The last section was again undated, written on different paper and I could only assume a time lapse of several days:

"Anyway, on to sop and tears. I have been looking at the stars and miss you terribly. It's really not the same. I have just mentioned this jotting to the lounge room occupants and they say your letters will dwindle and you will stop writing. BLASPHEMORS... Stone them quickly.

A slight pause as I sip demurely on a hospital coffee, light up a cigarette, and draw on it with an air of confidence and assurity. Ah, that's better. He loves it, but Callie doesn't. Smoking that is. Well the commoners are watching some tacky little video in the lounge now.... Oh, I live with a bunch of socially bereft waifs.

The sink in our bathroom has finally given in. It has succumbed beneath head hair, pubic hair, toothpaste and other assorted grime... and not even my trusty plunger will fix it. So we are doomed to face spit and hair constantly and ominously swirling before our eyes – not to mention festering!!

I wonder if you noticed - I had another pause to do some cross-stitch? Honestly. Life. It's all go, go, go.

Oh, what a reck I am... stubble on the face... believe it or not... unshowered... but none the less all pooed out.

Sorry, I do go on, but honestly. My word. Strike it down in history. Consider yourself privileged that this must be the longest letter ever to roll out of your pen (yes, I stole it) through the deft action of my fingers and wrist. My hand is quickly fatiguing hence the quality of my writ and I'm fast running out of things to say so, ERE, you're not the Messiah you're a very naughty girl!! Write soon or else you'll be sorry.

Yours in Sectdom,

Roods. (President, Secret Sect.)"

I could always count on James to make me laugh; but his descriptions of life in the Home emphasized my sense of being lost in the big city, and I missed my friends. Melbourne was vast and exciting, but my lifestyle was now transformed, having moved from the provinces to the multi-cultural shores of the mainland. I felt like a very small wave on a long stretch of coastland.

Melbourne trams on St Kilda Rd

DESPITE THE SEASON, Melbourne could deliver a haphazard array of changeable weather. It was a bright, sunny day in the second week of July, and the band had headed to WA for a few gigs, taking the arduous journey west across the almost treeless, featureless desert climate of the Nullarbor Plain. Instead of the train, they sometimes elected to drive across the bottom edge of the southern state, taking the Eyre Highway which hugged the coastline, arching over the Great Australian Bight, taking it in turns behind the wheel as the others slept. It was a gruelling two day slog of rostered sleep and non-stop driving; definitely one that I was happy to miss.

During Mark's absence, as the band toured around Perth, I explored the city on the extensive network of trams, spending an afternoon in St. Kilda where I could smell salt on the sharp coastal breeze cutting across the water in Port Phillip Bay. Hazy sunshine was spreading a path of golden sunlight over gentle waves, and from its low position it was making silhouettes of the distant shapes against the skyline: the gantry cranes at the Port, the jetty's wooden platform, a boy with his dog on the littered beach. Two trawlers skimmed across the sea where it met the sky, as if balanced precariously, high on this sharp edge of water on the horizon.

Although I relished my solitude on days such as these, I was looking forward to Mark's return. I'd arranged with Di to stay at their house overnight so that the next morning I would be sleeping in Mark's bed, to surprise him when he arrived home.

He was due back at six o'clock but I awoke in the night to hear him approaching from across the backyard, listening to his voice as he paused to speak to Jessie, and then her throaty growl at being disturbed. Switching on the lamp, I propped myself on one elbow as he let himself into the room.

"Hey," he said softly, "what a nice surprise."

"You're early." I smiled at him sleepily, and lay back down to keep warm, watching him undressing quickly in the cold room.

"I decided to get an earlier flight so I'd get to see you a bit sooner. Okay, move up."

The wooden pallets under Mark's double mattress made quite a firm base on which to sleep. It had been a comfortable night, but my own body warmth had only heated up one side of the bed.

"No, that side's cold, you can have it," I said, as he tried to nudge me across the chilly sheets.

"It's my bed!" But he was getting in anyway, and hustling me to one side.

"I'll get out then," I dared, tossing aside the doona.

"No you don't! Come here."

He pulled me back so that both of us were lying in the warm depression I'd left, kissing me slowly with silken tongue and cool lips, his chin stubble grazing my face.

"I really missed you," he said tenderly.

As his fingers traced across my skin, I lifted his left hand to my lips to kiss the callused tips, the ones he pressed to the strings.

"Mmm, I thought I'd keep the bed warm for you while you were away," I said, locking eyes, searching his face.

"Good idea. Thanks." Another kiss. "You smell so good." He was inhaling the scent of my skin at my neck.

My body was starting to warm to his touch, even though I was barely awake, lying across his naked skin, focussing on the sensations humming between us as we twined together. I could feel a glow of desire starting to take hold. There was a charge between us, something I hadn't felt before.

"Ange?" I could see Mark looming over me, his face serious. "Are you sure?"

It was a moment that I'd imagined for so long, and I feared it almost as much as I yearned for it.

"Yes, I'm sure," I whispered, as I felt his arms scoop around me.

He made love to me tenderly that morning for the first time, in the quiet dark of the early dawn. It felt as if we had met again in a different way, like we'd moved beyond the limitations of skin, blended into each other, and become something more. It was a connection that would bind us together forever, like a promise that can never be broken.

We were idealistic, but we were never reckless. It was a communion into which we spilled our essence, the deepest unknowable part of ourselves. But we did it freely, and with certainty, knowing it was something we are divested of just once in a lifetime, stripped bare by love, after which nothing is ever the same again.

We were too young to think ahead, to think about a time when we may look back at those days with such yearning. In the first light of that morning we had irrevocably merged the two halves of ourselves together.

## Like Two Mexicans Dancing

THERE WERE occasions when I felt so lonely in the icy heart of the city, moments when I longed for Tasmania; when the intermittent rain in Melbourne left a damp sulphurous smell in the air and made me crave the crisp Launceston days, heavy with an earthy redolence. After the rain in Launceston the air would be filled with the smell of apple wood, burning in the open fireplaces.

Sometimes I took the elevator down to the deserted lobby of the nurses' accommodation and sat at the piano in the semi-darkness, letting my fingers drift across the keyboard, improvising meandering melodies, pouring my sadness into the music. My locum position hadn't yet commenced, but I hoped it might fill the void left by my absent friends.

Mark and the band were my only contacts. Although I knew this would change when I started working, I was aware of the gamble, the tenuous basis for my upheaval and relocation. Conscious of my sense of loss, Mark tried to help me adjust and acclimatise to big city living. After all, he'd had to do the same when he had moved to Melbourne with the band; but I think both of us missed the small island, and its easy lifestyle.

Before my days became fixed into the hospital routine I had time for sightseeing with Mark by day, and for the twilight activities of the music scene by night. The Botanical Gardens in the city contained a meandering expanse of pathways and lakes, and it had a huge array of birds, and banks of native plants overhung by a canopy of trees. In filtered sunlight we spent our days sauntering through the huge parkland, along the edges of the curving river. At night we spent our evenings at The Punters Club, permeated by a haze of cigarette smoke that mingled with the lingering aroma of things being fried in the kitchen.

The Fish played to crowds of eager fans packed tightly around the stage, dancing wildly to the music, however dubious the mix. Tim would turn-up occasionally at certain gigs, the original drummer for the Fish, and I began to see the network from which all these musicians emerged, as if their lives were forever intertwined.

Mark said it was incestuous, the way people kept coming and going, forming new bands from the remnants of the old; all the divided loyalties, and no-one ever really leaving the scene entirely. It was the allure of commercial success that kept them there.

Some of them had already achieved a degree of notoriety and public acclaim, and played regularly to full houses of ardent fans. Careers could be made on crowd sizes. This alone might have been seen as proof of a band's achievement, but the crowds could be as fickle as the music business itself, and sometimes punters would begin to gravitate elsewhere. A change in the line-up, a different sound, a new band on the scene; they could transfer their devotion without warning. It was a strange roulette sometimes.

Yet gigs for The Fish remained crowded and full of energy. Enthusiasm was high, they were popular, and after the recent years of playing and touring, a recording contract could be within their grasp.

One Saturday evening we were invited to Mark Adams' warehouse. It had evolved since my initial visit, with a fluctuating number of people living there now, and a more structured interior. The toilet flushed but paradoxically, there still wasn't any running water. There were a few more partitions dividing up the main living area, ensuring everyone their own private space, and the eclectic rooms created by the dividing walls had all been decorated with found objects, and colourful fabrics.

Warky had brought in a PA system and some enormous amps for a couple of bands that would be playing there later, and a long table had been set up for plates of food. He had plenty of friends, and the place soon began to fill with an elite crowd of musicians and artists, leather jacketed boys, girls in beads and tie-dyed clothing, shadowy Goths with bloodless faces. My eyes lingered on the homologous troop of raven haired night creatures. They'd accumulated in one corner like an uneasy group of androgynous vampires, all draped in black.

We didn't stay for the band at midnight after we heard the first song distort the speakers to a conversation impairing volume, feeling the pain in our eardrums however far we retreated towards the back of the room.

Outside it was drizzling as we walked through the back alleyways to find the red Gemini. As we walked, Mark's arm crept around my waist.

"Will you be *mine*?" he said in a Texan drawl, stretching out the syllables.

"Yes," I laughed, "I will. I am…"

"…and I'll be your cigarette smoking, beer drinking toad."

I shot him a look.

"Well it's just how I feel sometimes. All this shit with the band. It's not always very glamorous, and you never complain."

"I enjoy it." There was a pause as he cast me a dubious look. "I do."

"Well I really appreciate you putting up with all this anyway, all the sound checks, the hanging around, all the seedy venues we have to play at…"

"…the meeting of amazing musicians, the photo opportunities…" I added, smiling.

"Yeah, that too," he conceded.

"Look, I love all this stuff, the music, the touring. This is probably the closest I'll ever get to a rock star."

Our hips bumped together as we walked. "Thanks anyway," he said.

"It's kind of ironic that I end up going out with a musician. I was such a groupie at college, going out to see bands all the time. Besides, think of all the pictures I've taken. Maybe they'll make *me* famous one day too."

"So you think I'm going to be famous?" he teased.

"You never know in this business I suppose."

He nodded, frowning slightly.

"But you've got a better chance than I have at the moment," I admitted.

As we fell into step in the rain I was wondering what sort of life we'd have in Melbourne. We'd reached the red Gemini, and at the passenger door Mark fumbled the key into the lock so he could let me in. Images of summer trips around Launceston flooded my thoughts, of Mark driving us to the orchard and the Gorge.

"I love this car," I said, my hand resting on the door frame as he walked around to the driver's side. He looked at me dubiously as he keyed his door open.

"It reminds me of how we began. You have to keep it forever you know."

He smiled before entering the car.

"Sure ma'friend. As long as its wheels keep turning."

The first album, *Swim*

*Like Two Mexicans Dancing*

# July 1989: Winter

THE ALBUM LAUNCH for Swim was due to begin in the third week of July at The Club on Smith Street. It followed the unofficial preview during the tour of Perth earlier that month, and preceded an imminent launch in Sydney, where they had gigs planned at the University. The band would be leaving at the end of July and staying there until early August.

At The Club, more than five hundred people clustered around the stage. As the band played I weaved in and out of the crowd with my camera, looking at the set and how the lights changed so that I could get the best pictures. The audience seemed to be a mass of arms and eager faces in the shadows, like one enormous body dancing to the music, blowing cigarette smoke up to the red and orange lights, pushing and thrashing to the beat.

Moving to the front of the stage I waited for the moments in each particular song that would capture the frenzy and the passion, watching Mark looking for me in the crowd, his eyes searching all the upturned faces until they met my own. As he winked or smiled at me, I'd see his lips move. I love you, he'd mime, and a few people would turn around to try and locate the recipient of this endearment. But I was elusive amongst the crowd, only recognisable to punters who regularly attended gigs and had seen me taking photographs.

The band was my life almost as much as it was his, and I enjoyed telling people that Mark was a musician, watching their faces light with recognition on hearing the band's name, or begin to ask the usual questions. I'd often see their posters around the city: old ones that were torn and partially covered by the latest flyer for some other band, new ones in bright colours under the bridges on traffic heavy Punt Road, on lamp posts and along the chilled out strip of Brunswick Street in grungy café windows. Occasionally they'd been pasted hurriedly and illegally onto street lamps on Kingsway, when someone had been able to dodge the seamless traffic, or find a place to pull over before the road swept around towards St Kilda.

There were still a few days remaining before the band had to leave for Sydney, and on Saturday morning, the phone rang. It was Mark.

"Can you be ready in an hour?"

"For what?"

"For a trip. I thought you might like to get out of the city for a while?"

"Where to?"

"It's a surprise; but pack a bag because we'll be staying overnight."

After Mark had collected me we headed west towards the tail end of the Great Dividing Range, leaving city life behind and driving into the relative tranquillity of the open road. As we headed further along the Western Highway the traffic diminished, and within a few hours we were entering the bushland and forest of the Grampians National Park. Mark had booked a room for us at a small guest house in Halls Gap, and after checking the handful of businesses and cafés in the tiny community, we only had time for a short walk into the damp forest before nightfall.

Returning along the track, under the canopy of trees and ferns, the air had already become heavier and darker. Far from the city lights the night was descending into a total blackness under a spattering of stars. As we emerged from beneath the foliage, I cast my eyes skyward and drew in a deep breath.

"I feel like I can breathe here," I said, the taste of the forest in my mouth. "Isn't it wonderful?"

For a few minutes we let the silence complete us, Mark no more than a hand in the dark, a soft exhalation in the gloom.

An open fire lured us into the lounge room after our meal. It was empty at that hour of the evening, but Mark ushered me in, promising to return in a few minutes. When he walked back into the room I felt a quickening below my navel, then a blur of adrenalin that spread to my face and limbs.

"I didn't know you'd brought your guitar."

Every part of my face was beaming, my skin already flushed from the fire and the wine. With hands clasped to my chest, I watched him settle the case on the floor, its battered black exterior covered with an array of coloured stickers and gaffer tape.

"As if I'd forget."

He kept his eyes on mine as he flicked open the hinges.

"So you're going to sing for me?" I asked softly.

"What would you like to hear?"

"Ohhh..." My breath fluttered out in a sigh, "It's been so long. You haven't sung to me since our picnic; and you always promised you'd serenade me outside my window in Launceston. Don't think I've forgotten that."

He'd taken out the guitar and was strumming it lightly to check the tuning.

"Can you play *River of Love* for me?" It'd become my favourite T-Bone Burnett track.

I knew he would indulge me. I loved to hear his voice, particularly the songs that had meant so much to us, watching his fingers pick out the chords, looking at his mouth as he sang.

At times the other guests wandered into the lounge to listen, knowing that I was being seduced by a lover's serenade in the firelight, smiling and then slipping away quietly, leaving us with our songs in the sleeping forest.

*

The morning brought a light mist. It hovered in the cold air without a breeze to whisk it away, the grass still glossy with dew when we made our way down to the waterfall after breakfast. Deep steps had been cut into the earth like shelves, their front edges boxed in by wooden planks to prevent erosion. Some of them were wide enough for two strides, and others narrowed to a foot's length as the path turned a corner, making it difficult to keep a regular pace. But we trekked steadily downwards under the fluctuating cover of the forest, our features dappled by shadows as fingers of light tried to reach through the canopy.

The sound of the McKenzie Falls had been getting gradually louder, becoming a clamorous rumbling as we drew closer. They reached their full pitch at a rocky ledge adjacent to the waterfall, where the water was surging through with a deafening roar.

We paused, overwhelmed by the torrents washing over the ridge, a primordial mass of white opacity churning and crashing into the pool below. There was a timelessness there. A sense of something ancient but ageless; unstoppable. Where the water pummelled into the pool, the rebound splash rose up like a fine mist and fluttered on the air. I could feel the droplets settling on my eyelashes, on my hair and clothes.

Rainbow prisms were forming in the spray, and although the noise of the water made it impossible to talk, I turned to Mark to see if he had noticed.

He was already watching me, but with a cool detachment, as if he'd been looking at me for a while. I stepped towards him so I could take his hand, but his eyes moved to the falls, and he put his hands in his pockets. Something about the gesture made me hesitate.

I tugged his sleeve, and pointed at the prisms, seeing him smile and nod, then turn back to the view to watch for a while. The sights and scents of the forest reminded me of the Tasmanian bush, and as Mark stared wistfully I wondered if he was thinking the same.

Gesturing at the steps, I indicated that I was going to start the ascent, and he nodded, letting me go, his face impassive now, unreadable. As I plodded slowly up the steps, I felt a sense of relief as he slid his hand into mine, turning to glance at him for evidence of what I'd seen on his face. But it had gone. I could feel the shape of a question in the back of my mind, and I was trying to unpick it as we climbed.

"You looked," I paused, searching for the right word, "pensive. What were you thinking about?"

"Just…thinking, you know."

But it had been implicit in his expression. There was something more.

"Is it about the Sydney tour?"

"No, nothing like that. Just…stuff, you know."

As the minutes passed and our breathing increased with the steady incline, the sound of the falls diminished behind us. The noise had distracted me so much that I'd almost missed it, but I was certain that I'd glimpsed something in his eyes in that brief moment and it made me uneasy. It was guilt.

THE FIRST OF SEPTEMBER meant spring had finally arrived. We continued to share a nocturnal existence, dictated by the band's activities, but our days had become discordant. Mark's morning often began at midday, when mine was already underway, ruled by the constraints of the hospital timetable. When I had free time on the weekends, Mark was often tired after late night gigs. There was a frisson of tension thrumming between us, like the dissonance on a plucked string.

The fleeting emotional disconnection that I'd first seen at McKenzie Falls had become more entrenched, and Mark had continued to be guarded and distant. I was bewildered by his muted disposition, certain that there must be a reason for his altered behaviour, something I'd overlooked.

But there were things I didn't know. There had been an omission, and I'd sensed it long before he admitted it.

"There was this girl in Perth," he began, carefully.

An icy chill spread through me as the words settled. He'd just returned from the Sydney tour.

"What?"

"It was just a kiss. Nothing happened."

Infidelity wasn't something I'd ever considered, despite all the nights away on tour, and the girls who hovered around the band at gigs.

"You kissed a girl?"

"No, she kissed me."

"What's the difference?"

I could feel something shattering inside me, breaking into shards that would be hard to piece together again. I had always trusted Mark implicitly. There were so many questions that I wanted to ask, but I couldn't get beyond my outrage. This explained everything.

Stunned by his admission, I hadn't been able to pursue the details; but a few days later, I was ready to hear what had happened.

"How could you do that, Mark?"

"She was hanging around the band all night. Just another groupie really."

I could hardly bring myself to ask.

"And?"

"It was only a kiss, Ange."

"Where? Where were you?" I challenged, trying not to imagine the scene.

"It was in a café, at the table, and she…she sort of caught me off guard."

"So…it wasn't just at the gig? You went with this girl afterwards? To a café?"

"I guess I was flattered," he admitted. "We were just talking. And she leaned forward and kissed me, but that's when I told her about you. And I said I already had a girlfriend in Melbourne, so I couldn't, you know…"

"And that's it?"

"Nothing else happened."

"And you're telling me that now?" My words were like barbs, striking out, wanting to wound. "Is it because you feel guilty?"

"Yes, I feel bad about it. That's why I'm telling you."

"You would've been loving all the attention. How could you have put yourself in that position, and been so reckless?"

I was struggling for breath, consumed by my emotions, devastated by his admission. It didn't matter that it was only a kiss. Still protected by the conviction and security of romantic love, I'd been blindsided, shocked that this could occur within a few weeks of me moving to Melbourne. Suddenly I missed the safety of the Nurses' Home, and my friends.

"It won't happen again, Ange," he assured. "Please. It was a mistake. I'm really sorry."

Perhaps I should have been thankful that it had been nothing more. But I hung onto this betrayal keenly, feeding the insecurity that it provoked. I used my anger to steel myself against the shock and duplicity, the deep sense of disbelief that rumbled through me. We could no longer bask in the simple trust that I had taken for granted. I felt forsaken.

*

At The Punters Club on a Friday evening there were a couple of bands playing an acoustic session, and as usual we'd dropped in to check out the music. But underneath the veneer of normality, my thoughts picked at the edges of my misgivings. They kept my new wound fresh, and renewed the ache that I felt just below the surface.

I looked through the dim, smoky haze of the main room with its shabby interior and faded posters. The air felt old and rebreathed, overwhelmed with too many odours. In the corner, a shadowy game of pool was underway, suggested by the crouched figures and the snap of resin when the balls were smacked apart. A large hood hung low over the table, illuminating a spot-lit rectangle of green light in the gloom, and in the fringe of reflected light other patrons hovered, waiting for their chance to play. There was always someone waiting for a game as soon as the one being played was over.

In the other room the battered red sofa slumped inertly by the window, repaired in cross-hatched patches with the ubiquitous black gaffer tape. We were waiting for the next band, leaning against the bar and watching the set being changed. Equipment was being lumped on and off the cramped stage, little more than a platform elevated a few inches off the floor, littered with speakers and sound equipment. A girl with a white fur collar and a black eye patch was drifting around the bar, and as she passed, I nudged Mark.

"Look at that."

The collar was twitching a curious whiskered nose. It was actually a large albino rat.

"I can't believe it doesn't jump off and try to escape," I added.

The rat was sitting at eye level, curled around her neck, clinging tenaciously to one lapel, but no-one seemed to have noticed it. Maybe they were just more interested in the pool.

After the gig, I leaned into the car after Mark had dropped me off at the Nurses' Home.

"What time should I be ready?"

"Ready?"

"Tomorrow. We were going to go away somewhere?"

"Oh, I'll call you in the morning, when I'm leaving."

I was looking at my packed bag as I held the receiver to my ear. I'd been waiting since breakfast, and had finally decided to phone Mark.

"Are you on your way?"

"Er, yep, just getting ready." His voice sounded low and thick with sleep.

"Have you just got up?" It was midday.

"Yeah I….."

"We should've left by now."

"I won't be long. I'll just grab a few things and jump in the shower…"

A tut slipped out with my words, "It'll be too late to go anywhere by the time you get here." It was met with a hard sigh, but I pressed on. "You said we'd go somewhere today and I've been waiting ages for you to call me."

"Well. Okay. Where do you want to go then?"

"I'd like us to have some time together. I don't care where we go. But I only have the weekend to get away from the city, and it's half over now."

"I'll be there as soon as I can, Ange. Alright?"

We'd succumbed to a resentful silence as we sat in the car. Mark had arrived after two o'clock, pointed the car towards the Nepean Highway and started to drive towards Sandringham.

I wanted to ask him where we were going, but I just stared out of the window as he continued further around the bay, driving for hours, passing Mornington and Dromana. Finally he had to stop where the highway ended at the tip of the peninsula, and the bay met the open sea. We were in Portsea.

I followed the coastal pathways with my hands deep in my pockets, straggling behind Mark as he tramped ahead of me. The beach looked beautiful, with white surf roaring along the length of the coastline. But we stood apart, watching it wordlessly, blinking in the bright spring sunshine while careless, tatty waves tore in and raced across the sun bleached sand.

The drive homeward was worse. My face was hot, and the car felt too small.

"What's the matter, Ange? What's this about?"

My pulse quickened, my teeth scraping against a dry tongue. I couldn't articulate it. I hadn't realised the extent of my underlying rage. For the last few days I'd been trying to ignore it. I thought I'd buried it.

"Talk to me. Say something."

I tried to swallow. My head ached and I needed a drink.

"Anything. Just don't sit there in silence."

The need to speak was overwhelming, the urge to form the first word and then fall into a sentence, to offer some explanation. I stared through the windscreen, I fiddled with my seatbelt.

"Please, Ange. What's wrong?"

I'd been clinging to my resentment, feeding it with any grievance, however small, until it threatened to erupt. Perth, I thought. That's what's wrong. That's when it all went wrong. In Perth.

His hand was resting on the gear stick only inches from my arm, but I wound down the window to let the frigid air slap against my face, propping my head on my hand and succumbing to the numbing pain.

So it wasn't the act itself. The illicit kiss wasn't the thing that muttered endlessly, and tugged at my thoughts. It was the intent. The fact he'd been tempted. That's what was wrong.

It was a relief when we reached the outskirts of the city.

"Can you just let me out here?"

He stamped so hard on the brakes that I heard the tyres yelp, waiting for me to slam out of the car into the street, and then drawing away before I'd even closed the door properly. I heard a few words tossed from the open car window.

"....so let's just forget it then....."

Everything in my chest clenched. I tried to breathe deeply, my heart drubbing beneath my ribs, tears welling up in my eyes. Groping towards a low wall, I sat down for a moment feeling stunned, wondering if he'd meant it. This is the end, I was thinking. This is how it ends, like this.

The car travelled away for a few metres, but then it pulled over. The driver's door opened. He was coming back. He was going to walk over and pull me into his arms. For a breathless moment Mark loped towards me, for the time it took a tear to make its gilded track towards my chin. It dripped as he raised an arm.

"Your purse...." he said, throwing it for me to catch, "...you left it by the seat."

"Oh, I...." But he'd already turned away to stride back to the car.

\*

"I wish you were here," I said, sighing. "Better still, I wish I was there." Four days had passed. I was fiddling with a pile of coins by the payphone, stacking and restacking them. There was a deep inhalation along the static of the line, the sound of air being breathed into the receiver.

"Mm," James was smoking, "what are you going to do?" he asked.

"I don't know. I just wish…"

What? That I didn't know? That he'd never told me?

"Do you want to be with him or not?" James said.

"I'm not sure he wants to be with me."

"You have to talk to him."

I pulled at my lip with finger and thumb.

"You need to decide," he continued.

"If I want to be with him?"

"If you want to forgive him."

"You mean, if I can."

"No. If you want to."

I looked at my feet. "Mmm."

"Look, I understand how you feel about it, but it sounds like he made a mistake, and he's admitted that," James stated.

My indignation rippled. "I can't imagine what he was thinking. Letting her…just…"

"Does she live in Melbourne? Is he likely to ever see her again?"

"It's not just that, Roody. What about the next time, at some other gig?"

"Didn't he say it'd never happen again?"

I'd pushed a finger into the coiled spirals of the wiring leading up to the headset.

"So," James asked, "do you believe him?"

There weren't many people in Fitzroy Gardens after dark. We'd been talking for more than an hour. As we'd been walking I'd felt Mark closing the distance between us, brushing his hand against mine. I had an urge to feel the squared tips of his fingers. This was atonement.

"I want us to get past this," I said.

There were still choices.

"When you said it was nothing…" I began.

"…I said nothing happened…"

"Well, it wasn't nothing."

He nodded.

"It was something," I said.

His hand was swinging loosely at his side, curled upwards like a hook, like an upturned question mark. I let my fingers latch onto his.

"My dad calls this a fisherman's grip."

I felt his hand closing around mine, then slowly reeling me towards him, and for a while, we stayed together in a wordless hug.

"I promise you…" he started.

"I believe you," I murmured, feeling the bulk of him, the solid reality of him standing next to me, "I do."

I would never forget what had happened, but I'd made my choice. It was what I wanted.

*Angela J. Dawson*

# Launceston letters

I CONTINUED to receive colourful missives from James, inventively structured and spelled, and scrawled in his disorderly handwriting. They kept me abreast of all the events in Launceston, the mini-dramas at the Home, and James' days spent on the wards:

"...Hello, how are you today? Just follow me and we'll pop you on the scales and see how much you weigh... could you sit down now and I'll take your blood pressure. Good. Did you bring a sample with you? Lovely. I'll just test it. You can go back now and we'll call you when the Doctor is ready.

Sorry. I'm just so used to saying it as I've been working in Specialist Clinics... Boil urine and add two - not one, or three - but TWO drops of acetic acid and reboil. Now, let the gunge settle, measure it, taste it and throw it out!"

The letter rapidly deteriorated into James' distinctive and tasteless vernacular:

"...How the hell are you, you spotty faced twat-on-legs sissy-virgin-groupie runaway smeg breath? I'm tired as usual and passing my customary amounts of noxious fumes, commonly known as FARTS. Helen's mum sent another delicious fruit cake and suck-me-off with a turkey, you're not here to pig-out on it. We considered sending you some, but knowing the GPO, it would either arrive with bits missing or mouldy, so we've eaten it all. HA ha.

Due to my being tired I'm going to indulge in a couple of pharmaceutical lollies commonly known as 'mazzies' ... but to the Lay-Pom 'Temazapam'...."

He was making reference to a sleeping pill I'd taken once after a particularly arduous weekend shift at work. He'd given me a couple of tablets from his supply, to help me relax and unwind. But they'd induced such a degree of stupor and lethargy that I'd become almost incoherent, and he'd had to help me upstairs to my room.

"...You remember staggering up the stairs into your brothel after some of those? Say no more. A nudge is as good as a wink to a blind leper. Half a bloody denarius for my life story... there's no pleasing some people! That's just what Jesus said. Oh dear, I've just had tenesmus. Look that one up!

How are your hormones? Up I trust, as I hope is your libido."

I was certain tenesmus would be something vulgar or crass as I searched for it in the medical dictionary. A sensation of the desire to defecate, it said in the description. Sufficiently obscure for it to go undetected in everyday conversation, but perfect for bowel updates.

A few days elapsed before the letter continued:

"...The sun is shining, the wind is away and I'm on 'days off' so put that in your pipe and smoke it. Twenty eight days to go until I've got six weeks holidays, and I've been shopping, taking photos, giving up smoking and generally guffing around. AND loving it, I might add.

Melissa, Rood-one and I have just come back from Jimmys supermarket with plastic bags bursting at the seams from our combined wealth of twenty dollars. Melissa didn't budget properly and had to return things to the shelves so she could afford some cigarettes, and I emerged unscathed with sausages, bacon and a large packet of crisps. Although I had already purchased a rather seductive kimono.

Dave came up to visit God-knows-who and brought the dregs of Launceston into our home. We were not impressed... David was pissed, with cans in hand, as was the Dreg.

How's Mark and the Fish? Give him my regards and salutations. We can't wait to get over there and see you. You know, check that the hair is still vertical, clothes still obscure and growler totally discheveled and wild... you loose woman.

Well, I hope this gets there... and I might add, AND the price is going up. Forty one cents. Forty one bloody cents to correspond with a pal across the water. It's enough to turn me off letter writing for ever.

P.S. I also bought some fart inducing guff fodder...bowel cleansing stuff...raddishes.

Yes, ten of them for 99 cents. Hah. Lovely. Luxury, bloody luxury.

Love and 'eres, salutations, copulations and kisses, Rood. (President etc.)

P.S. again. Please find enclosed two photos that I thought you might like. Look at them when you feel home-sick and remember that you have friends who used to lie on the bed with heads out the window and contemplate life and everything... and miss it! I'm filling-up now so I'd best go.

Rood etc...."

It was barely a one hour flight across The Strait, but however much I missed Tasmania and my friends, this was now my home. My current room in the high-rise Nurses' accommodation couldn't be compared to the homely modesty of my Launceston corner view and its sash window overlooking the city; but I couldn't yearn for a past to which there was no return.

# September snow

THE REVERSAL of the seasons here will always confuse me. Christmas occurs in the middle of summer, replete with roast dinners, carol singing and tinsel decorated houses on sweltering forty degree days. The dark days of winter begin in June, the cold air transforming the rainfall into fluttering snow that falls on mountain ranges and ski resorts in Victoria and New South Wales. By September the snow season was almost over, but with my new network of friends at the hospital, I decided to take a coach to Mount Hotham for the five hour trip to the resort. It felt like an early Christmas.

I liked the Chief Physiotherapist, especially her irreverent and often mischievous comments as she tried to deal with the bureaucracy that came with her position.

"I'm getting mild to moderately shat off with this bloody filing," she would say, in exasperation as she shuffled the mess of papers, and pushed her sliding glasses back up the bridge of her nose.

There were other priceless moments as we prepared for the ante-natal classes.

"Look," she said, tidying up the plastic models in our exhibit of female anatomy, "we've got a twat stand." It was the sort of thing James would say.

The alpine resort of Hotham lies in the Victorian Alps of the Great Dividing Range, nestled within a sprawling valley. I'd never skied, although I'd spent many childhood winters wading through layers of snow. After our bus had climbed the snaking passage up to the village it delivered us into the sort of expansive yule-tide scene that promised log cabins and crackling fires. The view was inhabited by a winter panorama quilted in white. With more than 300 hectares of skiable terrain, the resort had more snow than I'd seen in years.

We had lessons on the first day, with hired equipment and padded jackets, learning how to snow plough in the reflected sunshine before tackling the Summit Run and the Basin. But it was on the second day that I really learned how to ski.

I set-off on an aerial chairlift to the Summit in the early morning, the wind already picking up, swinging the seat in the freezing air and clattering my skis against each other.

Rising above the brief protection at the base of the slope, the gusts of squally air became more tidal, prodding me and rocking the chairs ahead as they made the slow motion journey upwards. I huddled in my layers of clothing, turning once to look behind where I could see a series of empty chairs pitching and swaying on the labouring cable. I seemed to be the only skier heading up.

There was an increasing opacity as I ascended, and I needlessly rubbed the lenses of my goggles with clumsy gloved fingers, as if this could make the visibility better, shifting my focus to the vanishing cable and squinting to watch my progress.

At the peak of the slope I felt the full force of the wind, flattened against the backrest by the strength of it. Even hitching forward to alight the seat at the upper terminal was difficult, but I tipped myself out of it, using gravity to slide away from the tower, feeling myself pitched sideways by a buffeting slap of wind. The beginners run had become like a hurricane extreme encounter, with almost nil visibility as the foggy air had descended, the slope carved savagely by cross winds. I wobbled as I braced against the shoving air, sizing up the moguls, selecting a starting point. My stomach lurched in sympathy, showing allegiance with all my other body parts as I assessed the dismal view.

I was alone, apart from a couple of skiers on the slope further below, already being erased by the low cloud. Peering down at the precipitous terrain I inched forward and began to slide, hoping my rudimentary skills would enable me to control my descent against the tailwind. Barely able to see beyond a few metres, I had to use all my leg strength to maintain the position of my skis as the icy air whipped around me.

Accelerating gusts hastened the plunge, but I leaned hard into the gradient, digging-in the edges of my skis to slow my speed, cutting backwards and forwards across the slope to reduce my velocity as the wind tore at me. I wondered if anyone would even be able to see me from below, hardly daring to look beyond my ski tips. If I lost my balance I had no idea if I'd be able to stop, or if I'd be able to get to my feet again in the blasting squall.

The sheer descent had started to give way to a more gradual drop, and I realised that the haze of mist was thinning even though the wind was still clutching at me, trying to shrug me off the mountain. I had made it down.

At the base of the run, the other skiers had been watching my final descent as I came to a trembling halt.

"You got down alright then?" one of them said.

"Only just," I breathed.

Despite the noisy vigour of the wind, there was something missing from the soundscape. I glanced up. It was the drone and vibration of the aerial lift that had been edited out, its mechanism lying inert overhead.

"What happened to the chairlift?"

"Shut down. They've got an 80 knot cross wind up there this morning. They're not letting anyone else up there now."

It must have stopped running shortly after I'd alighted at the Summit. I could see a rising line of receding seats pivoting and reeling on the static line, gradually swallowed into a gullet of low cloud.

"It wasn't like this yesterday," I said, flexing my numb fingers.

"Alpine weather. More changeable than Melbourne," he added. "Been up before?"

"It's my first time."

"Here?"

"Skiing."

"I'm amazed you didn't walk it down with all that fog." He adjusted his goggles, ready to move off. "It can get dangerous out there you know."

I nodded as he skied away. I suppose you'd often take a different course if you knew what lay ahead, something a bit less risky. I looked up at the glowering skies. Sometimes it's better if you don't know what's coming though. It ensures you live in the moment. It allows you to enjoy the rush. It gives you something to remember.

*Angela J. Dawson*

# Studio time

AT THE END OF OCTOBER the band was due to record the B-side for *The Orchard* at Phantom Tollbooth Studios on Rathdowne Street, in Carlton. In the poky rooms, everything except the digital equipment looked shabby and dusty, and was littered with cigarette stubs and old coffee cups. Posters and photographs covered most of the wall spaces.

By the time I arrived in the late afternoon they had been doing the multiple track taping all day, and all the boys except Andrew were now sitting in a room housing the technical equipment and the mixing desk. Apart from this room and a small kitchen area, there was only a small space for the recording studio in which Andrew was putting down his bass track. Until the others were needed again they were confined to this cramped room, together with the dreadlocked technicians, Bo and Perri.

As I squeezed myself next to the others, Bo stood to look for empty cups that could be re-used for the next round of coffee, his imposing height made more remarkable by a mass of ropey braids he'd pulled back into a fat ponytail. Perri had the same shaggy head of dreadlocks, but her diminutive size was in total contrast to his lofty stature, and made her better suited to the constraints of the tiny studio.

Perri was busy at the desk, spooling large reels of tape backwards and forwards, the loose end poking out from the centre and flapping noisily as she kept winding and rewinding to find her place in the music. Every now and then she made slight alterations in levels, sliding the controls on the panel, using the array of coloured buttons to make changes.

Hours of repetition and delay had contributed to the haze of cigarette smoke that lingered in the stale air, and everyone looked tired. In fact, Graham was already dozing open mouthed in the corner, but he stirred as Andrew broke off from playing and slid his headphones forward to scrabble his fingers through his hair, his bass hanging from his shoulder by its black strap.

Perri was still fiddling with the latest mix. "You can ditch the cans for now," she said to Andrew via the speakers to the studio.

Through the thick glass we could see Andrew unhitching his bass, but before shedding his headphones he spoke into the microphone, his voice echoing loudly across the speakers in our room.

"Does it sound too staccato?"

"Too flamingo," Graham replied dryly, getting out of the chair in which he'd been slumbering, and moving around stiffly.

"Okay, look…maybe we should take a break," she suggested, "and everyone can get some food?"

This idea was met with a collective enthusiasm, Warky and Graham simultaneously rushing through the connecting door into the studio, clashing shoulders and then tearing across to the far wall. They jostled and elbowed each other against it until an outside door appeared out of the thick corrugated soundproofing of the studio wall. It opened outwards to the street, casting a long rectangle of daylight across the floor, the frame filled with jockeying limbs as both Graham and Warky struggled to get out first. I could hear them shrieking as they disappeared down the road in search of dinner, chanting the latest catch phrase like a chorus.

"Who ordered the pie … who ordered the *pa-eeeee*?"

I'd heard the story, about how the slogan had been adopted by the band after a late night search for food. Most take-away outlets had been closed after their gig had finished, but a shop had finally been located that was still open, a mixed business with a Chinese proprietor. The boys had ordered their pies and had been waiting in line at the busy shop for them to be heated.

After a few minutes, across the hum of customers, the shrill voice of the proprietor skewered through the air, spitting each syllable with fierce enunciation.

"Who ordered da *pa-eee*?" he accused in an apoplectic tone, eyes swivelling at the waiting queue. "Who ordered da *pa-eee*? *Who ordered it!?*"

It had impressed the boys so much that it was reiterated often, and with gusto, usually as a preamble to the search for food.

There would be two songs on the B-side of the single, *Minute* and *Ezekiel Saw That Wheel*, and after the boys returned with their food, Mark was next in line to lay down some vocals. Most of the instrument tracks had been recorded before I'd arrived that day, and the task of combining them and editing any mistakes was yet to be completed. I saw Perri pause the reel, asking Mark to repeat segments of his vocals, and then start it up again to drop in the new version.

The tape was primed for *Minute*, and Perri gave Mark his cue.

"Okay, when you're ready." Her words buzzed across the studio, a strange electronic voice in the speakers. They retained her comment in the final recording; you can hear it just before the bass starts, reliving that moment each time the song is played, letting the past endlessly repeat itself.

It would take a couple of weeks and a further session in the studio before the final mix was completed for the second single. Like the first, it would be released on their own label, River Filf Records, featuring the unmistakable image of 'Ol Shep the fish. It would give them something new to send to radio stations, something to put in the record stores.

As I watched Mark through the glass I was thinking about where I'd find the single on my next trip into the city. Gaslight Music was one of the oldest independent music retailers in the city, and an outlet for ticket sales, and it was usually open late for browsing. They supported local bands and were known for importing some of the more obscure labels that other stores didn't stock. The store was at the top end of Bourke Street, its dark interior filled with racks of vinyl and T-shirts, and the band had friends amongst the staff, many of them part-time workers moonlighting as musicians after dark.

The days when bands did live performances in-store were legendary, the audience spilling out into the street from the cramped interior. Somehow amps and a PA would be installed in the narrow aisles while customers sidled between rows of dusty vinyl. As the crowd swelled, eventually the press of people would become so enmeshed that there was no room to enter or leave, but it never stopped the fans from cramming in to hear the set.

Mark winked at me between takes, listening to Perri's instructions and nodding. With a second single pressed, the Fish would be ready for marketing and promotion by mid-November. They needed to garner interest from radio stations and get some airplay. A good interview would elevate their profile, sell singles, increase attendances at gigs. But they also needed to get back out on the road, start touring and ensure the music magazines were writing about them.

The lyrics of *The Orchard* reflected on the childhood years Mark had spent with his family in Dilston. They held a significance for me too, reminding me of the clean air and easy days of our Tasmanian summer. I hoped the single would be the catalyst they needed, offering *Minute* as an example of their driving power pop sound. Surely it was the perfect hook, the ideal length for radio play.

I remember that long afternoon of recording whenever I listen to the songs, everyone sitting in the studio while a small piece of musical history was created and stored. The music takes me back to those days, arousing the enduring passions and memories that seem to linger underneath the skin, stirring emotions that I have held onto unconsciously. It opens a door for an instant, letting me glimpse my former self, giving me a brief retrospective of the things that once touched my heart. For a few minutes I'm in Dilston, beneath the apple trees, under a perfect cerulean sky.

7 inch single cover - The Orchard

*Like Two Mexicans Dancing*

Flip side of single - The Orchard

RF003

**the orchard** *re-recorded at sing sing studios october 1989 engineered by mark woods produced by mark woods and the fish thanks to paul stolhard for the piano, harvey saward, andrew leihborg and michael witheford for the borrowed guitars*
**minute** and **ezekiel saw that wheel** *recorded at phantom tollbooth studios november 1989 engineered by ho, perri and the fish*

**thanks to** *john sinclair, weddings parties anything, public radio all over australia, darren christensen, mark woods, peter pilley, punters club, michael newton at premier artists, dianne ransley and raymond j. bartholomeuz*

*front cover photograph by Martin Witheford, photograph of the fish by Simon Frost, art and design by russel bradley*
**Management:** *Gary Mason, P.O Box 143 Fairfield Victoria 3078 Australia*
*original version of* **the orchard** *appears on the album:* **SWIM**

Gaslight 10% discount cards

Postcard, 1995

## Touring with Brian

THE BAND was due to tour Tasmania at the end of October and I was looking forward to a leisurely cruise across Bass Strait on the car ferry, particularly since Brian Nankervis and his alter ego, Raymond J. Bartholomeuz would be travelling with us. His debut television appearance reading poetry on the renowned weekly offering of *Hey, Hey It's Saturday* had ensured a degree of notoriety; but he wasn't always immediately recognised off-stage. It was easy to see why. When he was reading his comic verses he usually appeared in tights and a nightshirt, with a chicken tea-cosy on his head.

I had expected the overnight crossing to pass quickly, knowing we would have an evening of Brian's sharp wit and double entendres, and I was enjoying sitting in the café on board the ferry listening to the exchanges between Graham and Brian.

It wasn't particularly busy on board, a Wednesday evening, and the café almost deserted except for ourselves and a small group of shaggy haired teenaged boys at another table. They were mostly dressed in black, their callow, unfledged faces emerging from an assortment of grisly T-shirts depicting sinister heavy-metal slogans, reclining in their chairs as if they'd been dropped in them from a great height, as if they were melting over the edges. Limbs lolled under the table, fingers drummed on its surface, rearranging the sugar sachets as they talked over each other, enjoying their brief emancipation from parents in the lounge.

Having established themselves in the corner, they slithered off the plastic chairs at intervals, doing glowering laps of the café with jutting chins and swivelling eyes, seeking attention, but resenting it with equal ferocity whenever any hapless coffee drinker stared at them.

There was alot of hair and quite a bit of loud back slapping, and sudden bellows of laughter, like the screeching feedback from an amp.

Brian was discreetly following the interactions within the group, observing the swaggering behaviour and the dress code that unified them. As one of the boys did a circuit around our table Brian made his move.

"Great shirt, Mate," he said to the boy in his genuinely effusive way, his face lit-up, showing all his teeth as he smiled right up to the eyebrows. The teenager sized him up warily, unsure how to respond, surprised at the apparent compliment.

"Yeah…" he said sullenly, and frowned.

"Was that the Open-Up-And-Say-Aaah tour of '87?" Brian improvised, maintaining unblinking eye contact.

"Erm..."

The boy looked back at the others for some sort of support.

"Yeah..." he shot back, offering what he assumed was the right response.

"Good gig that…" Brian was nodding, knowingly.

"Yeah, *yeah*!"

The boy brightened for a moment, before reverting to his baseline of truculence, eyeing Brian's sincere expression with distrust. The interest seemed genuine enough, but the boy hovered hesitantly, unsure whether to offer more.

Brian sipped his drink, held his glass aloft to the other boys across the room, and nodded in their direction with a radiant smile.

"Cheers!"

We tried to keep our poker faces as the boy fell back in line, assumed his place again in the pecking order, and cast back a look of deep suspicion from the safety of the pack.

They had their heads together as Brian sat with his long legs crossed at our round table, the image of cool composure. Something had just happened and the details needed unravelling. Brian was clearly the ringleader and was far too friendly to be trusted. We left them in the cafe, still trying to work out exactly how they had been upstaged, and by whom.

When we entered the lounge, a mass of people had begun to settle down for the evening. We had a cheap passage over to Tasmania since we'd decided not to pay the extra cost for a berth, and to sleep instead in the lounge chairs with all the other budget travellers. Our group had congregated in a corner near the bar area, organising makeshift beds on the floor using either the vinyl covered chair cushions, or stretching out on the seats with sleeping bags and floral covered pillows from home.

Someone had brought a football, and so Mark Adams, Brian and Graham decided to start a game on the dance floor, this being the only area of available space that remained uncluttered. Reaching up and redirecting the overhead lights to spotlight this chosen pitch, the boys ensured we could see them as they pushed and shoved enthusiastically for a while, the rest of us winding down for the evening, absorbed by our individual routines.

Andrew was reading young Scott a bedtime story, his son levelling a solemn toddler stare at the page from his mound of pillows. Only half listening, I was settling into my own bed. I had discovered that the beer mats fitted perfectly into the square-shaped recess of the light fittings overhead, and had just secured a cardboard lid on the ones directly above my face when the Steward saw me, raced over to admonish me about the fire hazards and took them all out again.

Having tired of their game, the boys had sprawled across a selection of chairs and cushions. Warky was now a head of spiral curls under blankets, Graham must have been hypnotised when I wasn't looking given the state of deep sleep he'd reverted to in his chair, and I would be settling for the darkness within my sleeping bag, pulling it over my head to block out all sound and light.

Across the vast lounge, despite the throb and hum of the engine, a hush and peacefulness hovered over the sleeping occupants, and I could feel the gentle swell of the shifting waves rocking us slowly to sleep. For the next few hours, in the darkness, the water would shrug our ship towards Tasmania, rolling us on our passage across the breaching surface of The Strait, and taking us back to my island home. By the morning we'd be disembarking in Devonport.

Pit stop for refreshments, East Launceston
(Brian on L, Michael Hayes on car, Mark on R)

Brian in full flow as Raymond J
(Melbourne photos)

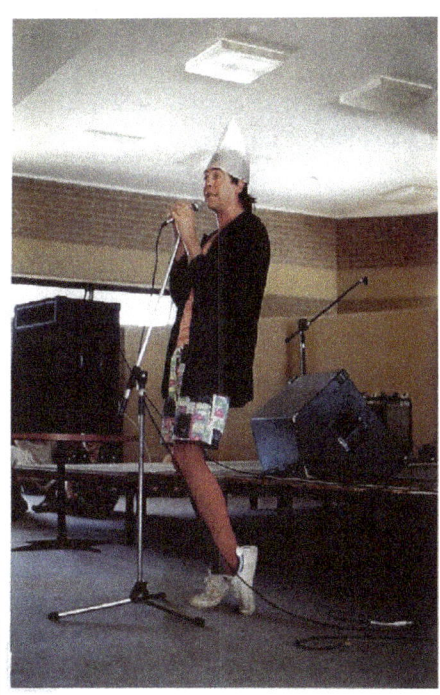

The Fish – looking very hairy
From L, Graham, Andrew, Warky, Mark

## Like Two Mexicans Dancing

IT WAS EARLY EVENING and we were in a pasta house in Hobart, a brightly lit take-away and café, with Formica tables and plastic chairs. I was standing with Brian and Warky, waiting for our food to be prepared so we could take it back to the hotel and eat it before the gig that evening.

A few lads were standing in the doorway, smoking cigarettes and glancing periodically at the three of us sitting at one of the tables. One of them finally moved forward to speak, and pointed at Brian.

"You're from *Hey, Hey It's Saturday* aren't you?" he said rapidly, and without waiting for an answer, he pointed at me and added, "…and you're famous too. I know you are…"

I smiled at the comment.

"I'm actually the only one here who isn't famous."

Glancing at the others, I realised this was the downside to public recognition, this loss of privacy, suddenly thankful to be at a take-away and not cornered in a restaurant where Brian would be obliged to chat. This is what the future looked like if the band became more successful.

We managed to retreat with good wishes and smiles, everyone laughing as we returned to the hotel, but I knew something was wrong when I saw Mark's face.

"What's the matter?" I asked discreetly, as the others were unwrapping their food.

"The gig hasn't been advertised," he replied, tensely.

"Aaah…" I said knowingly, "and if no-one knows about the gig…"

"…there won't be much of a crowd," he finished, nodding worriedly.

I had been enjoying the trip so far. Warky's impulsive antics often triggered all sorts of high jinks, and Brian was clearly enjoying having someone with whom he could share his comic genius. Their combined wit added a certain levity to even the most mundane tasks. But I didn't want to appear frivolous when Mark was feeling anxious about this setback. It could impact on the door takings for the evening. His irritation was palpable, and it wouldn't have helped that we'd all just come tumbling back into the room, laughing at some shared joke.

So far everyone had been in such good spirits, but the real work had yet to start, most of the time having been spent on the road, or perhaps more accurately, on the water. If their first night was marred by a promotional oversight, it didn't set a positive mood for the tour.

I made an effort to brighten Mark's mood by telling him what had happened in the cafe.

"We were just recognised when we went out for food. Me too. Did you know I'm famous?"

His mouth moved into a smile briefly, but his face was overcast by his thoughts.

"It was Brian's face they noticed though. Lucky we got take-away."

I wafted it enticingly in front of him, but he still looked grim. Hopefully, things would pick up later in the evening when they were due to play, and perhaps the crowd would be larger than we expected by some inexplicable turn of fate. I hoped, for everybody's sake, that this would be so.

The equipment had been set out on stage and the band was ready for a sound check, but I could see that Mark's mood hadn't improved as I watched him pace around the stage, shifting cables and tuning his guitars. Since it was likely to be a small audience it was hardly worth paying an extra technician to manage the stage lights, so I'd been asked if I could operate the panel. The controls were fairly limited, with only a few buttons to push and a selection of switches. The filters were already in place above the stage, and all I had to do was remember the colour selection and their corresponding position overhead. It was easy. I'd done it before.

As I was playing with the panel to familiarise myself with all the options, I felt a kiss on the back of my neck and turned around expecting to see Mark behind me. I was greeted instead by the wide smile of an unfamiliar face. The boy swayed a little as he leered at me, and I could tell he was quite drunk.

"Uhhhh...sorry....I thought you were my sister," he slurred, from under the fluff of alcohol, but his smile undermined his credibility.

It had been the tipping point for Mark, seeing me hassled by a punter, insulted right in front of him. It couldn't have happened at a worse time, and I was aware that something like this could create a potentially explosive situation. Mark was quick to appear at my side, looking furious, but I'd already stepped back from the boy, holding up an open palm to indicate he should back-off.

"It's alright," I said to Mark, "He mistook me for someone else. I'm sure he didn't mean anything."

But Mark wasn't convinced and viewed the boy's mumbled apology with mistrust. Perceptive to Mark's mood the boy remained defiant at a safe distance, continuing to taunt and gesture at him from the front stage area. I was worried that it would eventually erupt into a brawl, particularly when I saw Mark launch himself off the stage and charge across the room. He'd had enough.

Striding towards the bar, he stomped a straight line towards the proprietor, insisting on the eviction of the boy so the band could play without further disruption. But the publican didn't care about Mark's frustration and declined to evict one of his best patrons on such a quiet night, however unruly, or undesirable, his behaviour.

Fortunately we had Raymond J on stage first to diffuse the ill feeling, and to incite some good humour into the small crowd. Mark was somewhere back stage as Brian began the recitation of his obscure love poetry, his agonising thoughts about his first love, Gail Timmons and his profound observations on life.

"I never wait for trains..." he began, his statement punctuated by a moment of silence and a wistful look, "...they never wait for me..."

He'd perfected the dramatic pause and the melodramatic voice, a slow wavering tone and an exaggerated enunciation.

"I'm confused about noodles... one minute stiff... the next... floppy..."

Then the rich sound of Indian music filled the speakers, with sitars and the hollow jab of hand drums.

"In-dee-arrr... Guru Swami Daddy... I will listen to your chutney breath..."

It had been a very strange evening.

WE HAD ONE more night in Hobart before we had to return to Melbourne on the Sunday ferry, and the boys had a final gig at The Doghouse on the Saturday evening. It was a popular venue and usually drew a reasonably large crowd, so there was still chance to make up for the poor attendance at the previous gig.

The Hotel had offered free accommodation for all of us, but Mark and I had elected to drive back up to Dilston after the gig and stay overnight at his parent's house. We'd still need to shower though and change clothes before the band played, so we'd transferred all our luggage and toiletries and locked them into the rooms. They'd given us two rooms, allocating more beds than we actually needed, each room containing five bunk beds, and had put Warky in sole possession of the keys.

In the afternoon there was no sign of the others when we rattled the doors, and Warky's whereabouts were also unknown.

"Perhaps there's a spare key?" I suggested.

We wanted to rest for a while, knowing it'd be a late gig.

"I'll go and ask," Mark replied, disappearing down the narrow staircase. He reappeared shaking his head.

"No?" I huffed, "Why not?"

"They think it's a security risk to have extra keys."

"Great. How long shall we wait? They could be anywhere, and I really want to have a shower."

"Perhaps we can break the door down?" he joked.

"They might be back soon," I said, willing them to materialise in the corridor.

We looked at each other wearily, wishing ourselves on the other side of the door. I had an inspired thought. Perhaps breaking and entering wasn't such an outrageous idea.

"Do you think you could get me up on to that roof at the back?"

Mark's eyebrows rose exponentially towards his hairline as I continued.

"Well, not the roof exactly. Come and look," I added.

We ran down the stairs to the outside of the hotel, and around the building to the rear courtyard from where we could see the upstairs windows to our rooms. Above our heads was a green plastic corrugated carport that connected to the hotel wall just below our rooms. If we could get on top of that, we'd be standing right outside the window.

"See," I pointed upwards, "I left the window open this morning. I could just about fit through there if you can give me a leg up."

There was a small ventilation window that I'd opened after we'd left our luggage that morning, and although it was high up at the top of the window frame I was sure that I could wriggle through it and drop down onto one of the beds on the other side.

First, Mark gave me a boost onto the carport roof, scrambling up after me to walk carefully across the supporting beams where the roof was strongest. We made our way methodically towards the far wall, looking up to the open window, which from this new vantage point looked suddenly much smaller and further out of reach. It was an unlikely entrance for even the most determined burglar.

"I'll have a go if you can hoist me up to the window ledge," I instructed Mark.

"Are you sure?"

Despite his doubt, I felt compelled to meet the challenge now that we were so close, and I just wanted to get in before we were caught.

"Yeah, if I can stand on your shoulders."

Mark hitched me up from his back to his shoulders, and then to the sill, from where I was able to reach inside and unhook the latch. The ventilation window was like an elongated letter box, about a metre wide, and with the latch released I could open it outwards, towards me.

"If you go back down I'll let you in," I hissed. "Just give me a minute."

I pulled myself up into the narrow frame, surveying the options below, and balancing on my stomach midway through it, as if preparing to dive. The most difficult manoeuvre was getting first one leg, and then the other through the gap. There was a brief struggle, and some impressive callisthenics. I needed to maintain both my balance and my footing whilst wavering at a height almost level with the ceiling. The manipulation of arms and legs culminated in a sudden and ungainly freefall, and I was precipitated into the room onto something soft. My initial calculations had been accurate. I'd landed on one of the bunk beds below the window. As I climbed down I could hear Mark thumping up the stairs in the passageway outside, and I opened the door to his smiling face.

"I'm impressed," he declared.

"So am I," I said, looking up at the high window, red welts already forming on my arms and thighs. "Who would ever believe us though, that I mailed myself into our room?"

The others didn't even ask, and by the time they got back we were each enjoying our first beer, courtesy of the five dollar note I'd found on the bathroom floor. I prodded the change on the table; two dollars exactly. There I was, on the road with The Fish John West Reject and the next big name in television. Who needed room service and limousines? I elbowed Mark.

"Want to share a burger?"

The venue was crowded that evening, in total contrast to the previous gig; proof that advertising did make a huge difference to the attendance. Brian was on first, to warm-up the crowd, lurching onto the stage with the sort of hyperactive dancing you do when you're being chased by a wasp. Loud music blared through the speakers. Coloured lights flashed on and off, making a strobe effect of his movements. His arms flailed as he stumbled around to the music, grinning his toothy smile at the crowd, faking self-consciousness. There was a pause.

"Hello, I'm Raymond…" Music exploded again through the sound system, even louder than before, drowning his voice, and he frantically continued the dance, jerking to the beat, face contorting. Another break.

"I'm…" and then a surge of pounding bass and drums.

Brian resumed his breakneck dancing, more frenzied than before, cavorting around the stage awkwardly in his night shirt, a chicken tea-cosy on his head, feigning embarrassment, this apparent technical oversight all part of the act.

As if looking for assistance, he peered over his shoulder at the backstage area, still dancing convulsively. Exaggerated heavy breathing. Just as he reached his limit, the music abruptly stopped.

"I'm….I'm…." he panted into the microphone, "…I'm *fucked*."

The crowd whistled and applauded, the numbers steadily increasing as punters were seduced into the muggy interior. Everyone laughed at Brian's strange humour, and then later they all danced when the band began to play.

It was a jubilant reception, each song elevating the mood, cranking up the energy until there was a rapturous crowd pressed to the stage, nodding and bouncing to the beat. The temperature was oppressive, the steaming bodies of dancers and their hot breath transformed to condensation on all the windows. It felt as if the air had a weight to it, an elasticity that made it harder to draw in with every breath.

Towards the end of their set, Warky produced some new instruments he'd found backstage, brandishing a kitchen whisk first, whizzing the crank noisily as he held it aloft. Then it was a bowl and a ladle that he bashed together into the microphone, the crowd picking up the rhythm and dancing in a frenzy. As the song reached its climax he drew the final device from his pocket, levelling it at the crowd with both hands and pulling the trigger. Flinty sparks crackled at its tip. It was a stove lighter.

To everyone's delight, he ultimately stage dived into the crowd, an enthusiastic mass of hair and crinkly shirt, the rest of the band continuing to play as he washed around. It was wonderful to finish the tour on such a high note, and everyone was elated.

By the time the equipment was cleared from the stage and loaded into the vehicles in the early hours of the morning, it was almost 2 am. Despite the late hour, I was still glad that Mark and I had planned to drive back to Dilston on the quiet highway after the gig.

We talked softly to stay wakeful during the journey, watched by Orion from where it hung diagonally in a black sky of stars above us. We travelled unhurriedly, few vehicles passing us on the road in either direction, knowing we'd be in Launceston within a couple of hours. The deserted road enhanced the feeling that we had the island to ourselves for that short time, the absolute darkness closing around our headlights as we pushed through its heavy presence. The night refused to be startled as we fled through it, and although it acknowledged the red glow of our tail lights, it effortlessly sank behind us again, soaking up all evidence of us ever having been there.

## Hobart

THE FERRY was due to leave Devonport in the early evening, and while we had enjoyed a mellow afternoon and leisurely barbeque with Mark's family, the others were in a rowdy mood, looking dishevelled, as if they hadn't slept at all the previous night. We met in the terminal and boarded together, watching the shoreline recede as we were propelled out to sea, feeling the swell increase as we moved further into the Bass Strait.

When the wind grew colder we decided to head to the cafeteria and sample the fare on offer for dinner that evening. Everybody was hungry and in high spirits as we converged on an empty table, talking noisily, our plates piled high with food, spilling tomato sauce, chips and empty packaging onto the table. Warky was eating with his hands, tearing into his fish and chips and picking up the jug of water with greasy fingers, his face obscured as he held it up to his mouth to take long gulps. Disapproving diners watched as he sculled thirstily. We weren't making a very good impression. Things deteriorated even more when Brian decided to demonstrate his technique of neck manipulation.

"Watch this," he said, as he furtively passed a disposable plastic cup under his jumper, and settled it into his armpit, out of sight. Then at a sufficient volume to be overheard by the surrounding tables, he asked loudly, "Are you any good with necks?"

Without waiting for an answer, he placed his hands either side of his head, jerking it quickly to one side, and driving his elbow down against his ribs. There was a very effective splintering sound as the movement squashed the cup hidden in his armpit. It sounded quite realistic and was met with expressions of horror from surrounding diners. Glaring at our bad manners they shook their heads in collective disgust, turning away slightly as they resumed their conversations.

Of course, having seen this marvellous trick, we all had to try it under Brian's careful tutelage, each repetition becoming more amusing than the last. Finally, having alienated ourselves from most of the people within earshot, we moved away from our table, leaving the surface covered with an impressive array of squashed food, sauce and broken plastic cups. Other passengers peered scornfully at the debris as we departed, as if this mess was the final insult. The sight of our gastronomic abandon was not well received by the crew either, surveying the clutter with displeasure when they came to clear the tables, and casting glances at our retreating figures. I could see them frowning and shaking their heads, muttering as they began to remove our rubbish, the comments drifting back to me as I followed the band through the doorway.

"They could do with an education, couldn't they…?"

Last night, Brian and the boys had been the recipients of unfettered adulation. It was interesting to see how they were received when their identities were unknown. In an industry that fostered, and in many ways tolerated, this sort of extrovert behaviour from musicians and performers, they were just a group of badly behaved boys with terrible table manners in the café that night. A stage, and a microphone made all the difference.

In the lounge bar we were expecting to settle down for the evening, optimistically making our beds again with a spread of pillows and sleeping bags. We hoped to be able to snooze for a few hours until the ferry arrived at Port Melbourne in the early morning. However, this time there was a pianist, Tracey-Lee playing in the lounge, and it was obvious from the high attendance at the bar, and the noise from the crowd, that we wouldn't be getting any sleep for some time. During a break from playing she struck up a conversation with some of the surrounding crowd who were standing around smoking, amongst them, Andrew, who let it slip that there was a band on board the ferry. Shortly afterwards Mark appeared breathlessly, and announced that they were planning to go down into the hold to try and find the car.

"What for?" I asked, puzzled by this sudden decision.

"We might be able to get some cabins tonight, for *all* of us."

I raised my eyebrows sceptically, and he continued.

"We're going to sing for our beds."

He grinned at my expression.

"Look, Tracey says there are lots of spare bunks on board, and if we play a few songs, she'll have a word with one of the Stewards and make sure we get some beds."

I watched as Mark and Andrew left the lounge, amused at the way they could pull strings and receive preferential treatment, when only hours ago they were treated with revulsion in the cafeteria, almost like social outcasts.

The boys appeared after a ten minute absence, carrying only Mark's guitar case.

"It's all we could get," he explained. "All the cars are parked bumper to bumper down there, and we could hardly open the doors to even get this. But hopefully my set will be enough to earn us a bed."

I watched as Mark carefully checked the strings, tuning them quickly before making his way across the room to the microphone. The raucous crowd continued to cackle and drink, oblivious to the change in entertainment as Mark started an acoustic session of old and new songs. I could feel a rush of pleasure as he began T-Bone Burnett's *River of Love*, his fingers gently plucking the strings, his beautiful voice softly reciting the ballad. It was always such a pleasure listening to Mark sing, sharing this strange intimacy across the room in spite of the crowd; the music evoking such poignant and vivid memories.

Brian interrupted my reverie. He was sitting with legs crossed, looking around at the collection of people talking uninhibitedly, their conversations animated and exaggerated by the effects of alcohol.

"Half these people wouldn't know if they were awake or dead," he observed.

I glanced around at the vacuous faces, hoping we'd be able to get away soon from the crowd and sleep for a few hours. I didn't care that they weren't listening. In my eyes Mark was playing just for me.

Our promised beds were scattered throughout several cabins, the only remaining vacancies, and so we didn't know with whom we'd be sharing a bunk that night. Still, it would be a relief to just lie down in the darkness in a real bed and feel the ship riding the swell, heaving us steadily back towards Melbourne. After Mark's set we all said goodnight, and gratefully went our separate ways to bed.

In the morning, at 7am, there was no sign of Warky. Despite the succession of breakfast announcements over the ship's intercom, accompanied by loud bells and warning chimes, he had managed to sleep his way right into the harbour. We'd all woken and breakfasted a long time before the final approach into the Port, and we were beginning to worry that The Wark had gone missing.

"Hasn't anyone seen him surface yet?" I asked.

"He'll still be asleep somewhere," Andrew suggested, as the others shrugged their collective ignorance.

"Everyone just grabbed a key last night, so I don't even know where he ended up," Mark said.

"Well, we're going to have to find him; we'll be docking soon. Maybe we can get the Steward to call him over the intercom?" Brian suggested, imagining the scene if we had to search through all the cabins for our sleeping friend.

We listened as the announcement for *Mark Adams* came across the loud speakers, hoping that this would be sufficient to rouse him, watching people beginning to disembark in a steady stream as we looked down at the pier below. After a few minutes we caught sight of him pushing his way through crowds of people down one of the corridors, making his crinkly way towards the reception, red eyed and creased, moving in a blur of tousled hair and untucked shirt, and looking as if he'd slept in his clothes.

"Are we all ready?" he said.

We shared a look with each other, and turned all eyes back to Warky.

"What?" he said, taking-in our surprised faces.

"Didn't you hear any of the breakfast calls this morning?" I asked, thinking of the loud, regular chimes.

"I was asleep," he offered, good humouredly.

As the hordes disembarked behind him he was looking over our shoulders into the middle distance.

"Do you think I've still got time to grab some breakfast?"

Out on the wharf the twelve seater bus was waiting, hired, collected, and driven by Darren, who had been appointed as the band's official Roadie. He looked wired and sleep deprived, as ravaged and creased as Warky's clothes.

"Too early for you?" Andrew teased.

"Nah, too late," Darren said. "Not been to bed yet." It had been an evening of nightclubbing in the city.

"…stamina…your age…" Graham could be heard wisecracking, as he moseyed over to the bus.

Darren was a welcome sight, greeted warmly by all of the boys, and was quickly jump-tackled by a well slept Warky.

"On time too, Darren. What's going on?" Warky stirred.

Since his appearance a few gigs ago Darren had been assimilated into the social and working interactions of the band, offering his services one late evening, after a show. He was a keen fan of their music, regularly attending gigs, and was more than pleased to become personally involved with their playing schedule. His tireless ministrations to their needs had actually made him invaluable to the boys.

"…Said I'd be here. You can count on it."

Darren was in his early twenties, gregarious and reliable, with the sort of charisma that attracted a succession of pretty girls. The position of Roadie made him first point of contact when anyone wanted to approach the band, and the filter through which information passed to the backstage area. This new status was a great conversation starter with women. Many evenings were spent dealing with queries from a series of attractive girls as they approached the stage, and there were many evenings when he believed he had at last found the love of his life. Until the next gig.

"How'd the tour go?" Darren asked, already manhandling equipment, and deftly lumping it into the back of the vehicle without being asked. He radiated cheerfulness, chattering brightly as he laboured, running on adrenaline.

"Ooh, I met this beautiful woman last night. She was gorgeous…" he began, "I think she's the one."

Everyone was pitching-in to get the equipment loaded, and two year old Scott was already staring blearily out of a window in the bus.

"Hey, you know last night, I had this great idea, and I think it'd really work… I just have to figure out how I'm gonna get it started…but it'll be amazing. I reckon it could really kick-off…You're gonna love it…"

Darren was a dreamer, an idealist. I liked listening to his latest enthusiastic idea for success and wealth, knowing that he would soon move on to the next dream.

"Thanks for organising all this," Mark declared, slapping Darren on the back as they worked.

Like his appearance on the wharf that morning, Darren's services often involved driving at all hours of the day, the hiring of mini-buses, and the endless shifting of amps, instruments and stage gear. On stage, he would set up the drum kit piece by piece, organise microphones at the sound check, and during a gig he would be watching the boys move around the stage, ready to untangle the long leads to the guitars, or pick up a fallen mic-stand.

I considered him the fifth unseen member of the band, a back stage shadow, stooping to change the broken string on a guitar, or with head bowed, listening to some girl asking about the band. I became accustomed to seeing his slim profile at the side of the stage, standing with one foot resting on the step above, his hand on his thigh, ready to leap forward when someone managed to squirm up out of the crowd to stage dive.

"So, you're in love Darren?" I asked.

He coughed, and swept back his mop of sand coloured hair with both hands. "You should see her..."

This wasn't work for him. He just loved being with the band.

I looked at Darren driving the bus as we moved away, still handsome despite the hard edge of fatigue. The touring had passed too quickly, despite the slow pace of the last few days in Tasmania. We were back to the reality of Melbourne again. As the road stretched out before us, I knew Darren and I shared the same sense of contentment. Spending time with Mark, and with the band, was all I needed.

"Go on then Darren...what's she like...?" I ventured.

Darren, being an efficient Roadie, tuning a guitar

*Angela J. Dawson*

# The pace of Summer

BY NOVEMBER I was living on Nicholson Street in Fitzroy, in a spacious rented Victorian Terrace. My locum position at the hospital had finished, necessitating my move out of the Nurses' accommodation in the adjacent suburb of Carlton. News from home came via intermittent airmail letters, and was bizarrely delivered to me by Graham, who doubled as a Postman for Australia Post outside of his drumming duties for The Fish. For the first time I was living within his current delivery zone.

I planned to return to England for Christmas, and had decided not to take any further work in the few remaining weeks before I departed. I could afford to take an extended holiday after careful budgeting, and since the band would be touring Sydney soon it would leave me free to travel with them.

One beautiful Sunday afternoon I went to Brighton beach, swimming in the clear, chill waters of a sea that still held the cold heart of winter under its sun-warmed surface. The daytime heat continued to build during the afternoon under a heavy ceiling of cloud that began to expand and darken, threatening an approaching storm.

By five o'clock I was home, just as the first heavy drops of rain began to fall in the warm air, bursting on the dusty ground and lifting the earthy smell of dampened soil into the air. Released of some of their load, the clouds gathered new resolve. After a momentary lapse in the initial deluge they began to discharge waves of torrential rain and hailstone onto the parched ground. I watched in the open doorway of the house as the water formed a small rivulet, too substantial for the overwhelmed drains, washing instead across the yard and under the big double iron gates.

Still wearing my bikini, I waded out from the doorstep, catching the hailstones and paddling through the water to rescue snails caught in the current, trying to unclog the drains, and tasting the sea salt on my skin as the rain washed it down my face.

Later, when Mark arrived, we lay on my bed together listening to the rain falling on the metal roof, making love under the open window; Mark peeling off my damp swimwear, and kissing the salty skin on my neck as the curtains billowed in the breeze.

Life was uncomplicated then, without any real responsibility. With few material assets, everything could be packed into one bag with a day's notice. It was such a simple freedom, but we had no comparison, nothing by which to measure it. We could never have realised that those extraordinary days would come only once, that they would be so transient.

In the drowsy, languid days at the end of the year, as we counted down the weeks to my departure, we delighted in reminiscing about our past and guessing what might lie ahead.

It was almost a year since we'd sat nervously in Ripples restaurant beneath the expectant eye of a full moon, and fallen in love. Whenever we could, we stirred up memories of the Gorge and its peacocks, Corra Lyn, and Rosie's Bar. Launceston had been our ideal, a place that was meant for love, and for lovers; and it would be the place to which our hearts would always want to return.

With few commitments and no routine to our days, we spent our time having picnics in the afternoons. Sometimes we'd go to the vast green belt of Yarra Bend Park in Kew where we could hire a wooden boat at the historical Studley Park Boathouse, row it upstream, and drift along the river, dining on white wine and cherries.

In the city we visited the dark planetarium, sinking low in our seats so we could stare up at the domed ceiling with its mass of stars; looking for Orion, the warrior with a lion's pelt and a brilliant star, Betelgeuse at his shoulder. He was our jewelled brooch, claimed from the multitude of stars.

Having endured a long separation during the months I had been living in Launceston we savoured our time together, letting the weeks unfurl with desire and spontaneity. One evening, Mark dragged a chair outside to the darkened leafy balcony of the Brunswick apartment into which he'd moved, and we made love hidden from view by the overhanging trees, seduced by the cool night air. The sight of that swivel chair in his apartment could always make my heart flutter in memory of those passions.

But it was music that connected everything, like a recurring refrain humming along in the background, linking all the incidental moments. Studio time, and hours of rehearsal, performing and touring, radio interviews. Even the time spent watching other bands. It was all part of the process, a piece of the bigger picture.

*The Orchard* gave them another calling card, a second single that they could market, a chance to continue chasing that elusive dream. Mark and the band sought every opportunity to advance and promote themselves. It was the driving force behind everything, in a business where persistence and resilience mattered as much as talent.

In October I'd managed to secure front row tickets at the National Tennis Centre, for the Lovetown Tour, a massive U2 concert supported by BB King and local boys, Weddings Parties Anything. The extensive tour followed the release of U2's sixth album, Rattle and Hum, and the playlist that evening included many of the new tracks.

As I scanned the stadium I tried to picture a time when The Fish would be performing at these large venues. Sometimes it seemed plausible. Finding out that their peers were one of the support acts made the dream feel within their reach.

It was a rare treat having Mark next to me in the crowd to see a band, and as he scanned the vast open-air stage that night I wondered if he was imagining himself up there too. They'd started to play *All I Want Is You,* and the music floated over us under the clear skies, the notes from Edge's guitar picked out with such clarity, mellifluous crescendos seeping through the air, spiking and cresting into the refrain. Without realising it our bodies were swaying and rocking, caught in the passion of the anthem.

I'd hoped to get a few illicit photographs during the show, despite the ban on cameras. That would be more difficult on the front row, where I was so visible, but I was carefully reassembling the parts of my Olympus that I'd secreted into various pockets, using the shadow of my open jacket. As I mounted the lens on the body and loaded a reel of film, I could see two young girls next to Mark glancing at us periodically, whispering and giggling. Clearly we were the subject of conversation as they nudged and murmured breathily, taking in his leather jacketed grunge, and my recycled fifties glamour.

"Are you his wife?" one of them finally asked, smiling shyly.

I looked up at Mark, at his face, and we shared a covert smile. He took my hand, and kissed it theatrically, to their delight.

"Yes, she is," he replied; and I loved him for pretending that I was.

As the music played during the encores, Bono picked up one of the flowers that had been thrown onto the stage by the fans, drawing in its scent before he scanned the crowd to pick a recipient. Amongst so many eager faces and hands I leaned forward with an outstretched arm, watching his eyes track across the mass of bodies as he paced the massive stage; and then he made his choice, pausing directly in front of me to look at my smiling face, reaching across the empty divide of the security pit, and handing me the red rose.

My palm was resting on the soft petals in my pocket as we exited the venue, fingering the bud where I had laid it so carefully across the lining.

"I can't believe he gave it to you," Mark said, keeping me close as the crowd surged. The momentum threatened to sweep me off my feet, but I could feel myself holding my ground. I had known the flower was mine an instant before I had received it. I couldn't explain the certainty I'd felt in that moment; but as I held out my hand, I knew he would pick me. I had the same sense of conviction about the year ahead, trusting my intuition that everything would fall into place, that our life in Melbourne would continue. Without the security of a job or a permanent place to live, my prospects were uncertain. It was the same for Mark and the band, the parameters of our lives undefined, and unscripted.

All I could do was cling to my certitude and let it guide me; in the same way that I clung to Mark's hand while he steered us through the current of the fleeing crowd. Neither of us knew the way, but we were going there together.

Cassette comment: Please recycle this plastic if you think The Fish are crap and you decide to chuck this tape out

*Like Two Mexicans Dancing*

# Touring Sydney

IT WAS 6.30 AM when the mini-bus arrived to collect me. Its occupants were already regressing to varying levels of somnolence, having been wrenched from sleep at this abnormal hour, and some of them were experiencing a part of the morning that they wouldn't have seen for some time. Darren was driving so at least he was functioning at a level that included more than one faculty. He was already sounding hoarse from coughing and clearing his throat, a regular and subconscious habit. He coughed as he got out of the bus, sliding open the side panel for me to alight and join the others.

It was a Wednesday in November, and we were leaving for the Sydney tour with a busy schedule. The band had five gigs lined up over a five day period. The drive from Melbourne could take about twelve hours, and as I looked inside the bus I could see it would be a long and cramped journey.

I was the last one to be collected, and the twelve seater bus was already tightly packed with guitars, amps and a full drum kit at the rear. Graham's solid six foot frame had been wedged into the remaining space at the back of the bus, slumped on a pile of quilts and pillows, and he was already dozing, chin on chest. He didn't stir as I slammed the sliding door and settled into one of the few vacant seats.

His capacity for sleep was unrivalled, whether it was napping in the studio, on the ferry, or in any sort of chair. He always looked so relaxed, however improbable the location, or its apparent shortcomings; but he had a disconcerting habit of interrupting the conversation when everyone thought he was profoundly asleep. I liked his dry humour, and his shrewd observations were frequently droll and insightful, but always concise and well-timed. He would rouse when food was required, like a bear from hibernation. *Have we passed a McDonalds?* he'd ask, signifying the full transition to wakefulness.

For now, he sprawled contentedly, oblivious to our movements, wearing his full-length Doc Marten boots and the customary heavy black leather jacket he inhabited. Even in hot weather I didn't often see him without the jacket, unless he was drumming. Asleep in the cool, early morning he seemed to be folded into the pile of equipment, almost a part of it, nodding to the motion of the bus as we lurched away and headed for the Hume Highway.

In the confines of the bus it was easier to observe the interactions of all the different personalities. Mark never liked those early mornings, becoming exasperated when Darren broke into another full concerto of coughs, or when he started singing with Warky in a loud tuneless voice to something on the radio.

Warky amused himself with car-high-jumping. This involved diving backwards from the front seat of the bus, over the tall headrest, and onto the person behind him in a mass of arms, legs and curly hair.

Given his proclivity for extreme relaxation, Graham habitually slept through most things, even missing some of Darren's more impassioned comments. He was sound asleep as one these early morning observations floated back to us over the hum of the engine.

"Aren't trees amazing…I mean…they just grow from the ground," Darren marvelled, his eyes sweeping the arboreal view on either side of the bus.

By the time we were bumping along on the straight line of the highway, everyone had made themselves comfortable and settled in for the journey. Andrew was smiling benignly as he leaned over his young son, Scott. A hank of black hair fell over his face as he talked softly, his fringe swinging gently with the motion of the bus. Even at such a tender age, Scott had become accustomed to travelling with his father and mostly managed the confinement of the bus. It was nothing like the ferry to Tasmania where there was room to walk around, but there were other distractions. Andrew was pulling books out of one of his bags.

"Shall we have a story?"

Scott had fixed his gaze on the selection. Thomas the Tank Engine held a certain appeal. But if words weren't enough there was always jelly or chocolate on the longer road trips, when things became too challenging. With regular treats, a few games, and some stories, he coped well with the journeys, soon falling asleep on his back, his bare stomach like a full, round peach, rising and falling with the rapid breaths of deep slumber.

There had been a few toilet breaks, and we usually split up during the food stops so everyone could go in search of their own preference.

"Where's the Wark?" Graham enquired as we all hovered around the bus, waiting to board again.

"Hey dudes..." a voice filtered down from above.

We peered into the tree canopy overhead, shadowing the bus. Warky had a taste for high places, on occasions sitting on the roof of the bus when it was parked, but this time he had climbed a tree while he waited, and within the branches we could make out his black T-shirt as he made the slow ascent. Whenever he was missing the best way to find him was usually to look up.

The air became more hot and humid as we travelled further north, and the temperature in the bus rose higher, with little relief from the open windows. We were all dishevelled and damp with perspiration, but we were within a couple of hours of the Sydney CBD and I welcomed the idea of a cool shower as we neared Goulburn.

Warky was driving, everyone else lost in reveries, the blast of the warm air through the open bus windows amplifying the sound of the engine, and making it even more difficult to talk. Unexpectedly, the bus began to slow down, the noise diminishing as our speed lessened. Warky was steering to the side of the highway so he could pull-over.

"Police," he said simply, in a flat voice.

We could see his eyes in the rear vision mirror as he slowed the bus at the dusty border of the road, the gravelly edges forming a cloud behind us as he braked.

"Has anyone got anything?" he hissed, as the police car parked behind the bus.

We all stepped outside into the sunshine, unfolding our cramped legs and squinting in the brightness as the two officers checked Warky's licence. They moved around the bus, asking for the contents of the glove compartment to be emptied, then pockets turned out, and wallets inspected. Having seen the musical equipment piled high against the windows, this was going to be a drug search.

They peered through the windows at the interlocking tangle of amps and guitars, and all the components of the drum kit, pausing for a breathless moment before dismissing a search of the bus and returning to their vehicle.

I was relieved that we hadn't needed to empty and repack the bus in the aching heat of the late afternoon, and thankful that we'd avoided a considerable delay.

We kicked the gravel at the roadside as we stretched our legs and watched the patrol car pull away onto the shimmering highway, reluctant to get back into the hot bus. Graham mauled his pockets for a cigarette, lighting the tip and drawing the smoke inwards, each inhalation like a lungful of air before a dive.

"So did anyone have anything?" Warky asked again, never having had a reply.

"...Could have done," Graham muttered, swinging back into his seat, "but I ran out. Thought I'd get something when we got to Sydney." He patted the place where his wallet was situated, inferring that this would have been the storage place for it.

Mark had an expression I couldn't interpret and looked as if he was going to speak, but Darren had decided to rush Warky in a low tackle and they were scuffling noisily in the dust. No one seemed too concerned. Graham looked like he'd gone back to sleep already. Scott, impressed by the sudden activity between Warky and Darren, was pacing outside the bus swinging his tiny backpack with all of his toddler might, vigorously slashing it at the scrubby roadside grass.

"Debaser...!" he was yelling, with every hurl of the bag, "DEBASER.... DEE-BASE-ER..!" Even at two years old he had a working knowledge of American music; currently The Pixies were being played alot at home.

"He's good with lyrics," Andrew declared, receiving a hefty blow as Scott swung the bag with all his strength at his father's shins. "He knows that album really well."

Our fleeting encounter with the law had put us all in a good humour, despite the implications. We'd been lucky this time, but I wondered idly what the charge was for possession. It might have set a very different tone for the start of the Sydney tour, and been so much worse than arriving late for the sound check.

From L: Darren, Andrew. Below: Graham, Andrew & Scott

## Warky sitting on top of the tour bus (twilight)

THE PUB HOTEL venue for the gig that evening was in Wollongong, only 80km south of Sydney, but despite the provision of beds for the night the boys elected to continue on to Sydney, driving the remaining few kilometres after the gig while it was so much cooler in the early hours of the morning.

It was 1am when the bus set off, with Graham driving this time, most of us gazing sleepily from the windows as he steered us along the quiet untrafficked highway. I was still awake when we reached the outskirts of the city, absentmindedly observing the curve of the streetlights on the empty pavements and the silent and shadowy landscape of a sleeping metropolis. It was peaceful in the bus, and the boys had all fallen asleep by then, the engine providing a reliable hum that only encouraged a sense of inertia. My brain was doodling in the library quiet, but just when I started to nod I was jabbed by a throaty shriek from behind. My body convulsed, a knee jerk response. I could feel every nerve ending jangling.

"Stop…stop… STOP!!" it said, with increasing volume.

It was like a starter pistol in the muted darkness.

Catapulted into a flight or fight response, I felt my startled heart beating furiously. It was Darren. Swivelling around, I could see him staring ahead wildly, his face creased with sleep. Everyone else had been roused with a jolt, woken by the sudden noise, twitching and stretching as they moved around.

"Darren?" I was looking straight at him, "What the hell….?"

He let out a relieved sigh and leaned back in his seat, his eyes focussing now on the passing scenery outside the bus.

"Chuh…!" he exhaled, with relief, "I must've been dreaming…it's alright."

"What's going on, Darren?" Graham sounded unfazed by the eruption. He could see Darren in the rear view mirror as he turned into a main street.

"Er, yeah, sorry. I was dreaming that we were just about to crash. It felt so real."

No-one seemed too dismayed by the outburst. Within a few minutes it had prompted a litany of other remarks and wisecracks, followed by an inventory of their favourite expressions. This included a few rounds of *Who-ordered-the-pie?* after which Graham, as the driver and the one therefore most wakeful, began to think of his stomach despite the late hour.

"D'you think there's a McDonald's still open round here?"

Rosebay was our first stop, where a few of us would be staying for the night. One of Andrew's friends shared this apartment in the more prestigious and expensive part of town. The rear of the property overlooked the waters of Sydney Harbour, the bay lapping leisurely at the wall bordering the patio, the winking lights of the illuminated city perfectly duplicated on its surface, until the movement of a distant boat muddled its inverted colours.

Although we were expected, it was very late and we didn't want to wake the other occupants of the apartment. We knocked cautiously and crept quietly inside when the door was opened to us.

Mark and I were to share a room at the back of the house overlooking the bay. The window offered a full panorama of the harbour, being wide enough and sufficiently deep to fill almost the entire wall. In the moonlight it was a tranquil and romantic view, but as we discovered a few hours later, without any shutters or curtains it admitted the full brightness of early dawn light. As soon as the sun rose and illuminated every corner of the room, we had little chance of further sleep.

There was nothing unusual about seeing a tall ship skittering across the bay, leaning into the wind with capacious sails, its heavy grace distinguishing it from all the other modern cruise boats. Canoes and windsurfers sliced across the surface against a backdrop of the Harbour Bridge and the distant Opera House, watched by the opportunistic gulls and wading birds that dipped and hovered overhead. It was an affluent and much coveted location, bordered by parks and playing fields, and only a few kilometres from the city centre. The bay waters lapping at our patio were tidal, retreating during the day, and when they did we discovered that it was possible to walk across the waterlogged sand, as soft as mud, and paddle the pockets of shallow pools.

It was a Thursday and the morning was free to enjoy the sights of Sydney, to push through the commuters and the lunch-goers with all the other tourists in the city. We had decided to regroup at Circular Quay, the landing point for the harbour ferries, since Graham, Darren and Warky would be crossing over from Manly at the ocean edge of the harbour where they were staying with other friends.

Graham's dark, arresting figure was easy to spot, dressed in black amongst the brightly coloured tourists, and wearing his leather jacket in the morning sunshine. He drifted towards us across the covered wooden jetty, preceded by a montage of hair and patterned shirts, which gradually separated into Darren and Warky as they came into focus.

"Come on, let's check out the buskers," Warky urged, taking the lead.

Around the quay there was always plenty of busking talent, most of them taking up positions close to the cafés or the exit points of the ferries, in the hope of beguiling tourists to part with their money as they wandered around the Cove.

Having scrutinized their equipment and the quality of their instruments, we moved on towards the historical area of The Rocks for some sightseeing, swarming along the dockside in a conspicuous gaggle. Shadowed enthusiastically by Darren, Warky was already setting an energetic pace with a repertoire of goofy walks, charging up behind the others, and then moving full circle around them, his arms slung low in an exaggerated ape walk, clowning and tripping to amuse us, leap frogging and rushing at one of the boys in a full tackle until they were both rolling on the floor.

"It's so hot," I murmured, feeling my shirt sticking to my skin. "What d'you think the temperature is now?"

"I dunno, maybe 38, 40?" Mark replied.

The humidity had been building under accumulating afternoon clouds, their fluffed opacity trapping the heat within the sweltering city, and it made us feel breathless in the muggy breeze.

"Look!" I cried, pointing upwards.

Forked lightning sparked above us, heightening the promise of an approaching storm, the air swollen and thickening as it got darker. It gathered momentum quickly and soon began to slew the first batch of heavy droplets, casting them fatly on to the ground, the displaced air puffed upwards and carrying with it the smell of dust.

"Run!" Mark yelled.

"Where to?" My eyes flicked around.

None of us were prepared for the torrential, slaking downpour, but anticipating a solid drenching we dashed to the lee of nearby buildings, searching for better shelter. The rain was falling so heavily that I could hardly keep my eyes open as we ran across the deserted roads, dashing en masse down two flights of stone steps that went under the bridge, our hasty feet measuring an uneven stride as we clattered down the crooked stairway.

We paused briefly under the bridge, shaking our wet hair before running on towards Pier 1 with its arcade of shops and restaurants. Outside, a large Chinese pontoon was moored. It served as a permanent floating restaurant, but its gaudy colours and ornate paper lanterns seemed unappealing after the distinguished warehouses and colonial buildings along the cobbled streets of The Rocks. We charged past it into the entrance of the shopping complex, the storm clouds by then having lifted and only a light drizzle falling in the resurgent sunshine.

Slowing down now, we chose a café laid out with plastic tables and chairs where we could sit, shed some of our wet clothes, and push back lank strands of damp hair. Warky and Darren were laughing at each other, comparing their bedraggled appearances.

"You'll have to take it off," Warky was saying, watching Darren drip, and hauling his own T-shirt over his head to reveal a bare chest.

Compressing the material into a sodden bundle he wrung out the excess water, forming a small pool on the tiled floor by his chair, and then draping the T-shirt across the backrest. Everybody had started to emit a light steam that floated around us, our warm bodies vaporising the rain from our wet clothes after the exertion of running. It held the scent of sea salt and surf, wet wool and damp dogs.

"What can I get you, boys?" The proprietor looked amused as he stood at our table, notepad in hand. "Maybe some paper towels?"

We were the only customers in the late afternoon, the streets empty after the change in weather.

"Fish and chips," someone said, and there was a collective nodding of heads.

Fish with The Fish – a paradox that certainly suited the mood of the day. The food arrived quickly and was swiftly devoured, most of us trying to warm ourselves afterwards with cups of tea and coffee as we decided what to do for the rest of the afternoon.

"There's an amusement arcade down there," Warky said, licking his greasy fingers, and indicating the deserted shopping complex beyond the café. Graham's interest was piqued, and the two of them wandered off for a look, knowing they'd have exclusive use of all the games with so few customers.

We found them there, poring over the screen of the motorbike ride with intense concentration, their hair still wet from the rain. Engrossed in the track, they steered the imaginary course, barely noticing my photographs as they played, the yellow light of the game flickering on their faces.

My memories of our time in Sydney are like an album of photographs, a series of images and fragments, vignettes from those epicurean days when we pleased ourselves; eating when we were hungry, sleeping when we couldn't stay awake. Snatches of conversation, late nights and dancing, windowless, cramped backstage dressing rooms buzzing with adrenaline. I can flick through the highlights and remember the finer details, the way the sunlight fell on the water of the Harbour, the spontaneity, the laughter and disbelief that this life was ours.

Those are the snapshots that have stayed with me, not the seconds within the hours of hanging around, or on the long unfurling road, or in the cycles of setting up and dismantling, or the moving of equipment from one place to the next. All those connecting moments have faded, as if we had no grip on them, habituated as we were to the tide of their routine, all of them as unmemorable as breathing.

Graham, drying off

Bedraggled in the arcade, Mark and Graham

*Angela J. Dawson*

The colours of Sydney

Pete (Lawler) from Weddings, on harmonica – top left

Mark

Graham upfront, probably for *Tamar River*, Andrew on (bass), & Darren (R)

WE WOKE LATE the following morning, tired after the previous gig at the dark hotel in the city. Pete, the bass player from Weddings Parties Anything had been spotted in the crowd, and had therefore been invited on stage to make an impromptu guest appearance with The Fish, playing the harmonica for a few songs. But it had been difficult to see much in the meagre lighting and the cigarette haze. I rarely used flash with my camera so I'd used longer exposures for my film, opening the aperture on the lens, knowing my photographs would be grainy.

The next gig was at the legendary Kardomah Café in the centre of Kings Cross, reputed to be the sinful heart of the city, but we had a day of sightseeing before the sound check in the afternoon. For a couple of dollars we took a trip on the newly established monorail on a track above the streets, gliding away from the city centre shops to Darling Harbour, propelled away from the downtown area towards The Docks. The 3.6km round trip took about ten minutes, travelling full circle through eight stations, and linking us directly to the western area of the city.

The vast Virgin Record Store was the main attraction of the day, the boys quickly dispersing to browse the huge selection of T-shirts on display. There were rows of them on coat hangers, densely packed across more than a dozen aisles.

"Check this out." Graham had found a black Pixies shirt on the rack, and was holding it up. He was wearing his *Big G* T-shirt that day, one of his favourites, and held the new one to his chest to check the size.

"Time to replace Big G then, Gray-bones?" Mark was eyeing the Pixies logo approvingly.

Darren had been hovering nearby and as Graham melted away to the cash register he set off to trawl through the racks. We could see him moving up and down the aisles, his head bobbing up now and then as if he was taking a gulp of air. After a few minutes of rummaging he emerged with a satisfied expression and an identical T-shirt, trotting off in Graham's direction to make his purchase. You didn't get much more rock and roll than a black Pixies T-shirt then. Black Francis would have loved it.

They had an early slot for the sound check but Ed Kueper was running late.

Being the support act the boys would have to hang around until his crew had finished their sound check, and even then they wouldn't be allowed to move any of the overhead lights, the microphones, or the drums. They sometimes used the headliner's drum kit, particularly if the stage was too small to accommodate both sets. Ultimately they could have whatever space was left, but sometimes that was just the front few metres of the stage in which to cram their equipment, with a curtain separating the two areas.

We settled down for the long wait. I'd spent many afternoons like this, watching the ritual of guitars and amps being unloaded, the unspooling of coils of electrical cable for the microphones, the adjustment of stage lights on the ceiling boom, and the construction of a drum kit from the many separate components. In a frequently spacious and empty room I would sometimes wander to the sound desk to watch the Technician operate the array of coloured buttons and sliding controls, trying to determine how they calculated the required levels.

The lighting desk was more interesting to me, and if the crew had finished mounting and resetting the lights above the stage I liked to play with the panel. There were buttons for the backdrop effects, colours that could be flashed from lamps covered with thin plastic filters, or I could bring up the spotlight, fashioning a circle of stark, white light on the stage floor.

These were the hours of work that went unseen by the audience, when strings were changed and guitars tuned, when Roadies walked between microphones saying, "…one, TWO, one, TWO," as technicians perfected the sound quality. This was when I'd learned the language of the road crew, hearing them talk about fold back, guitars that had been DI'd, whether there was enough drum fill, and who had the gaffer tape.

The boys had resolved themselves to the delay. A girl was improvising a Biro tattoo on Warky's upper arm, colouring in the ballpoint outline while he sat with an air of resignation, squinting closely at her intricate handiwork in the dull glow of the basement lighting.

Without warning Warky jumped up out of his seat. He vaulted across a couple of tables, dodged around the scattered chairs and produced a water pistol from somewhere which he began firing indiscriminately around the bar.

"Don't fuck with me. I'm a Puerto Rican…I've got drugs and I know how to use them," he whooped. He wasn't, and he didn't, but it hardly seemed to matter.

A scuffle ensued as the others were stirred into action, but the attack soon dwindled in the absence of suitable ammunition for the opposition. Before an adequate counterattack could be initiated they were called in for their sound check.

In contrast to the long wait for Ed Kueper's set up, the boys completed their rituals in less than ten minutes, with everybody except Warky looking slightly damp from the earlier drenching. As usual everyone was then free to spend their next few hours seeking food, socialising and changing into stage gear. Sometimes they did this together, but if they went their separate ways they'd usually meet backstage later to accept the rider, the customary pre-gig drinks provided to the band.

Given it was a Friday night there was an impressive crowd in the basement of the Kardomah Café that evening. The Fish played a tight and almost flawless set, with plenty of on-stage antics from Warky and sharp wit between songs from Mark and Andrew. They didn't wait to see Ed Kueper when he came on stage. They'd be able to see him after their second gig with him the following evening. The consecutive gigs meant they could leave all the instruments on stage without having to lump equipment into vans after the show. So for once, everyone was free to enjoy the evening. They were all in high spirits, heady with success, and tonight they had their own triumphs to celebrate. None of us hesitated, emerging exuberantly onto the busy Kings Cross streets with clammy shirts and salty skin.

We regrouped again in the city on Saturday morning so we could head to Paddington markets. They'd made up a batch of about three hundred handbills advertising the next gig at the Kardomah, in the hope of boosting the attendance, and Paddington seemed an appropriate location to distribute them. We browsed the market stalls selling kaftans and pop art, second hand clothes and handmade jewellery, and wandered into the food hall where delicious vegetarian food was being sold by androgynous vendors with mounds of matted, dreadlocked hair and decorative nose rings.

For a while I joined a crowd encircling a busker who was juggling machetes and riding a unicycle, shielding my eyes from the sun with one hand and glancing back periodically to see if I could locate Mark amongst the scattered stalls.

There was a girl in tie-dyed clothing wandering from one stall to the next, barefoot in the heat, and I'd been watching her until I caught sight of Mark. He was standing at a music stall rifling through the boxes of records, occasionally pulling one of them out to examine the sleeve. I smiled to myself as I began to walk towards him, looking at his face as he stood engrossed in the notes on the cover of the album. He was frowning slightly in the brightness, his upper lip curled as he read the information. It was an obvious place to find him in the crowded market.

I'd been next to him for a few moments before he realised, his face transforming into a relaxed smile as he met my eyes.

"Hello ma' friend…" he said softly, putting a hand on my shoulder.

"I was watching you from over there. Find anything?"

"Not yet. Where've you been?"

"Oh, just wandering, taking pictures. Have you given away all the leaflets yet?"

"Yeah, Warky had most of them," Mark added.

The main objective had been achieved, but his eyes had wandered back to the sleeve that he was still holding and I guessed he hadn't finished browsing.

"I'm just going to look over there," I said, pointing indiscriminately into the market.

"Okay." He glanced up at me briefly as he said it, and flashed a smile.

I drifted back into the market with my camera, allowing myself to be absorbed again into the crowd. After a few steps I turned to look at him, but the mask of concentration had settled again, and he was reading with rapt attention, lost in all the music.

Saturday night gigs started late and were always busier. Enhanced perhaps by our leaflet drop, a good crowd had gathered, further encouragement that things were going well for the band.

After The Fish had played another set filled with mayhem and thrashing guitars, they infiltrated the crowd with the remains of the rider and joined the fans for the rowdy second half. The two gigs there had been such a buzz, and it felt like everyone was on a high, keen to have a big night. Probably a good thing. They had to wait until Ed Kueper had finished his set in the early hours of the morning before they could retrieve and dismantle their remaining gear on stage and load it into the van. It was almost 3 o'clock by the time we crept home to our Rosebay bed.

Only a few hours later we were woken by croissants. It was Andrew's son, Scott offering food, his tiny hands tilting the plate of pastries over our snoozing heads. His schedule hadn't changed, and he was ready to have breakfast with his dad at the usual time, even though all of us had only just gone to sleep. Andrew had been rummaging in the kitchen and appeared behind Scott, looking rumpled, with sleep wrecked hair.

Coffee anyone?" he enquired wearily.

On mornings like these, life on the road just didn't have the same appeal.

THERE WAS ONE last gig on Sunday evening before our return to Melbourne, and after the succession of late nights it was a low key performance at a pub in the suburbs.

Scott had been allowed to stay up and see the band play and he'd been placed on a tall stool next to the poker machine, staring at the flashing lights and coloured sequences offered in the game. In the near darkness of the bar the colours danced across his features as he sat transfixed, slightly hunched as he endured the protruding foam earplugs that someone had thoughtfully applied, to protect his hearing.

A few people danced as the band played, even an old man who must have been one of the regulars, lurching unsteadily to the music as he held his unspilled glass in one hand. After the final song, he staggered over to us and muttered a few words of appreciation, and on his breath I could smell sweet, yeasty aroma of the beer he'd been drinking. Darren had started to dismantle the equipment on stage, and it was a relief to see it being packed up and loaded onto the bus for the last time.

Outside it was still balmy from the day's heat as we stood on the pavement, the smell of warm bricks and alcohol filtering towards us from the hotel. We spent a few minutes debating the trip back to Melbourne in the morning, some of the boys electing to stay another day, and then make their own way home. On such a warm Sydney evening, it was difficult to believe that I'd be returning to cold weather and a frosty English winter in a couple of weeks' time.

There would be one more gig in Melbourne before I left the country. My eyes drifted across to where Mark was standing. I could still remember the acute feeling of estrangement which had accompanied each parting in Launceston. It would be February before we would be reunited, the beginning of my third year in Australia. Already my heart quickened at the thought of my return, eager to envisage the end of that separation. But it was the thought of where we'd be meeting that really made it race.

As we departed and the bus drew away through the streets of a warm Sydney evening, it evoked a litany of farewells that I'd chosen to forget, and yet stirred too the recollection of so many sweet reunions. Andrew had sung about it in their song, *Invitations* and now I understood the words that I'd heard him sing so often.

"... *The return makes one love the farewell.... So many farewells...*"

*Like Two Mexicans Dancing*

Scott, by the poker machine

MARK WAS DRIVING east of Melbourne towards Burnley College. It was situated in a green belt comprised of the City of Richmond golf course and the Burnley Gardens. The College itself was almost completely surrounded by the Yarra River since it was positioned within a deep curve of the channel, the water scooping around the campus, and then continuing to flow west towards the Port.

It had been a week since the Sydney tour, and back in Melbourne it was a beautiful languid evening at the end of a warm spring day. We were only a few days away from December, but the mellow temperatures had breathed sufficient heat into the afternoon and the warmth still lingered as the light faded.

When Warky arrived he was wearing a fantastic old straw hat. His trousers were rolled up to mid-calf level and held up by braces on his naked chest, his bare feet already dusty, no doubt from a day spent without shoes. The rustic appearance made him look as if he was ready to do some barn dancing rather than get up on stage to play with the band.

The lighting and sound equipment had already been set up in the gardens for an outdoor gig, and with such a small gathering of people on a Tuesday night there was an air of intimacy as local boys, Helvelln opened the set with one of their original songs. Jeremy Gronow had met his bass player, Andrew Papadopoulos at school, and they'd been playing in bands since then, recently joined by Nick Green on drums after they'd lost both their singer and their drummer. Although they'd intended to find a new vocalist, Jeremy had ended up with this role, and the band had become a trio. They'd become friends with The Fish having crossed paths with Mark when he'd been on the panel of a Battle of the Bands contest they'd entered, and it wasn't the first time I'd seen them play in the city.

The night was perfect for lingering outdoors, with clear star-filled skies above us and soft grass underfoot. Tiny flies spiralled around the hot stage lights, a crowd of black flecks that withered in the excessive heat as they hovered too close. They dropped delicately like punctuation falling off a page, forming an increasing layer of singed bodies on the equipment below.

The Fish had been playing for a while now, microphones had fallen over, a bass string had been broken, and I'd been listening dreamily, leaning against the warm bark of a gum tree and watching a few people in the crowd dance enthusiastically.

As they began to play *Birthday* the mood became even more mellow, the dancers subdued to a gentle waltz by the lilting tune.

Mark was watching me as he performed and I smiled shyly as people occasionally looked at me, the recipient of this attention.

"*...I'm sitting here with my fear, my quandary, my shadow and my eff-i-gy...*" he sang.

As the music continued I saw him move away from the others, who were still playing the melody softly. He stretched his arm towards me, his palm open, beckoning me to go to him. Shaking my head I continued to stand by my tree, but Mark waited unmoved, his guitar still strapped to his shoulder, his arm extended towards me.

Under his gaze I advanced slowly, passing between the other dancing couples who were swaying gently to the music, reaching for his hand and feeling his arm scoop my body against his as I leaned into him. I smiled contentedly, burying my face into his shoulder, waltzing with him. Between us we embraced the guitar that he'd slung across one hip so that we could dance, still plugged in to a long black cord that tethered him to the makeshift stage area.

For minutes I was floating with him, lost in thought. I was thinking of the many ways Mark showed he loved me, suddenly overwhelmed by my own feelings for him. I was thinking of his upturned face in the shadows below my window, his puzzled look as I undressed him, the way he pushed back his hair with one hand as he crouched over my nakedness in the lamplight. He seemed to have so many different faces, and I understood why I'd fallen in love with all of them.

Warky suddenly broke the spell, smiling engagingly as his voice echoed through one of the microphones.

"Are there any religious people in the audience tonight?"

He paused in the stillness as everyone waited. They all gazed for a breath held moment. I looked at Mark questioningly.

"...Anyone who religiously gets out of bed in the morning...anyone who drinks beer religiously?" he added, with a hand on one hip.

Laughter rippled through the crowd, everyone brightening as the band prepared to change the mood again, the introduction to the next song offering a boisterous contrast to the previous slow number.

Our moment had passed. Mark moved away from me, walking back towards the others and leaving me amongst the dancers again. I smiled at him as he began to play, throwing himself into the thrashing tempo. He was my poor, gifted, gentle musician, my friend, and my lover; the one I chose to take me home.

Before I left for England, we drank wine and made love again in Mark's apartment; Mark leaning in to me as he pressed me to the wall and kissed me everywhere. In the lounge we let ourselves become slowly entwined on the swivel chair, clinging together in the darkness, and dreading the separation that would follow.

As we parted, he gave me a card in which he'd written the words of T-Bone Burnett:

> "*I love you more than dreams*
> *and poetry*
> *more than laughter*
> *more than tears*
> *more than mystery*
> *I love you more than rhythm,*
> *more than song*
> *I love you more with every*
> *breath I draw.*"

I knew I would come back.

PART TWO

*Angela J. Dawson*

## She'll be Apples

IT'S A STRANGE expression. I'd been confounded by it when I first arrived in Tasmania. Sometimes people would smile and say, *she'll be apples*, meaning everything's alright. But I'd also heard it used as a polite refusal.

"No thanks, Mate, she'll be apples."

The versatility of the phrase continued to intrigue me, but I was left wondering about the derivation.

Tasmania was often referred to as The Apple Isle, exporting fruit from its abundance of orchards, so it was easy to see the analogies; but I'd reached no conclusion about how the phrase had fallen into the local vernacular. Having never heard it in Melbourne I'd assumed it was an island phrase, and one of the many local idiosyncrasies that I had grown to love.

It was January 1990 and I was eager to shed my winter layers and wear summer clothes again, to feel the sun gently warming my bare skin. I'd had weeks of dark days and bitter December winds in the north of England, visiting old haunts and favourite places, keen to see how Manchester had changed while I had been on the other side of the globe. In the music magazines, The Stone Roses had made it to the front cover of the NME. Band of the Year, the paper declared in its 23/30 December issue, full of praise for *Fools Gold*, the Manchester band's latest single.

People were shopping for tie-dyed T-shirts at Affleck's Palace and wearing Reni sun hats, and they were buying their dance music at the Eastern Bloc record shop. But on city streets there was a Liverpool scally subculture, and a football casual look, that was influencing local fashions. There were shaggy basin haircuts with heavy fringes, widening flares and floral shirts, beads and hooded tops.

Even though the Second Summer of Love had been happening while I'd been in Australia, the *Madchester* music scene had continued to embrace alternative and psychedelic rock, and electronic dance music was still pumping through the clubs.

Driving into the city centre with a school friend, I'd made the nostalgic trip to The Hacienda, FAC51, famed for its association with Factory Records, New Order, and Tony Wilson, but with the techno rave dance scene in particular. Lately it had become notorious for its gangs, drug dealers and shootings, but the club was still where the crowds gathered because the music was loud and you could dance all night.

On a chilly Wednesday evening, close to midnight, that's why we were there, folding ourselves into the warehouse interior of The Hac, squeezing through the crush of punters in hooded tops, the air hot and muggy, congested with the sweat of damp bodies under the strobe lights. Once we'd found a point of entry to the dance floor we flung ourselves into the throng, moving to the rhythm of the hypnotic music. Sweat poured down our faces and necks, dancers undulated around us on the factory floor, pulling us into the wash, more dancers on the stage writhing in a convulsing mass.

People were blowing whistles that hung from rope necklaces, nodding and shrugging to the beat, freeze-framed in the strobes; the space compressed by a wall of noise as songs were blended seamlessly in an addictive mix, blurring all sense of time. We had no idea how long we'd been in the pack on the dancefloor. But we were dancing. Arms aloft, eyes closed, we were caught in the throb and the bouncing masses, lost in the fug of dry ice and humidity enveloping the undulating press of bodies.

Hours later, and finally too thirsty to keep dancing, we oozed our way towards the edges of the crowd and fell out into the freezing dark, tumbling into cold streets that were empty but for the long and ever present queues outside the nightclub. That's why The Hac never made any money. Most people were already high, the music was too good, and no one ever stopped to buy a drink.

During the closure of the University and Manchester Poly, the majority of students dispersed across the country to their respective home towns in the winter holidays. Most bands were out of circulation during the cold weeks of the Christmas break, however, the smaller venues were still featuring local bands.

At college, I'd favoured Johnny Dangerously's mini LP, You Me and the Alarm Clock, playing his ballad *Black and Blue* on repeat on my turntable. He'd produced it after Ignition, had split, and the rest of the band had gone on to become Ambitious Beggars. When I saw them listed in the local gig guide, it was a night I couldn't miss. They were playing at The Boardwalk, with The Man From Delmonte, and New Fast Automatic Daffodils.

Music here was just as incestuous as Mark had indicated about the Melbourne scene. Everything overlapped and interconnected. The New FADs had been signed to Playtime Records by then, a label that had been set-up in 1988 by Paula Greenwood, one of the other production assistants for Tony's show on Piccadilly Radio. His programme was still running on a Sunday evening, profiling the latest bands. I listened to the familiar patois one night, as local musicians dropped into the studio for interviews, played a few songs live-to-air, and offered tickets for various gigs.

During the time I'd worked on the show with Paula, unsigned bands often sent reels of demo tape to the studio to be played on air, and Tony always gave them a chance. Many came and went, with only fleeting success before they slipped away again into obscurity.

After the programme one evening in the mid 80's, I'd been told to clear out old reels of tape from Tony's overflowing cupboard. As I sorted, I hesitated over the psychedelic patterns decorating the entire surface of one of the boxes, casting my eye appreciatively over the colourful artwork. For a moment I considered saving that one tape for myself. The Oldham band had been around for a couple of years, and had become popular. I turned the box over in my hand thoughtfully, aware I didn't have the right equipment on which to play it.

Looking down through the aircraft window as we prepared for landing, I smiled at the recollection, knowing now that it would have been the one to keep, the hand coloured demo tape from Inspiral Carpets. It had gone into the pile, to be discarded.

The plane was circling over Launceston some fifty minutes after leaving Melbourne, and I recognised the landmarks as we passed over them. I had taken an arduous international flight back to Melbourne in the new year, stayed in the city for a couple of days to recover, and then taken the short flight to

Launceston, to reunite with Mark. He'd been staying with his parents in Dilston for the summer holidays and I was eager to join him after our time apart.

It was a clear sunny day and I could easily see the features of the Gorge, and then the long highway tracing a thin line between the city and the airport as we banked around to land. Mark had arranged to meet me at the small terminal and I knew I would have no difficulty finding him amongst so few people.

I joined the other passengers walking down the mobile staircase that had been attached to the side of the plane, and across the tarmac in the sunshine to the terminal building. Once inside, we waited a few minutes before the tractor appeared, its trailer laden with our suitcases. The airport looked quaint and unsophisticated, particularly after the vastness of the terminals I'd passed through on my return from England. Without a thought, I stepped outside to where the tractor had parked so I could rummage on the trailer for my case.

As I walked around to the front of the building, my eyes searched anxiously for Mark. I couldn't see him anywhere in the crowd. I scanned the faces, feeling steadily more nervous about the long separation and about what could have happened in my absence.

Then, from the road I saw a car draw in and Mark step out, hurriedly moving towards me, his overcoat flapping with the speed of his stride. For those few seconds I stood riveted in the sunshine, sensing the chill in the cool wind, feeling oddly distant, as if I didn't know how to behave. He was too far away for me to see his expression but I watched him approach, taking in his presence, trying to read his body language.

Wordlessly he took hold of me and gathered me to his body in a hug.

"Ange…" It sounded more like a sigh as he said it. I held on to him, gripping the fabric of his clothes, burying my nose in the scent within them. He looked the same, but I felt as if my body had forgotten the shape of him in my absence.

"I'm sorry, I was running late," he murmured.

He leaned back so that our eyes could meet, reconnecting us as we gazed at each other. I looked into those familiar eyes. They were such a piercing blue in the sunlight, taking me back to that first meeting, to the way they'd made my heart stumble.

"I really missed you," he said, and up close like this, I could see the small gap in his teeth at the front, and the slight bend in the bridge of his nose.

"It was a long time wasn't it?" I said, feeling the heat in the parts of my body that were pressed against him. "Too long."

In the gentle warmth of the sunshine we stood for a while in that timeless hug, my body moulding into the soft contours of Mark's embrace. It was long enough to realise that I was in the right place. I was home. We could have been standing anywhere together and it would have felt the same.

I knew Tasmania would always induce recollections of my first summer in Australia with Mark. Perhaps that's why it felt like a sanctuary, a place where all my memories could be kept safe. Just as it was after every other separation, I felt that moment of recognition as I stood in his arms, that moment when I knew him again, as I sometimes felt I'd always known him, with an odd familiarity.

I felt our chests rise and fall with each breath. I had crossed the world to be here, under this clear blue sky, and had no idea what I was going to do next.

ALTHOUGH MARK had planned a few trips we spent the first few days revisiting some of our favourite places around Launceston, listening to the peacocks crying out at dusk from the Gorge, and walking through the orchard in the evenings.

Mark had contacted his friends in Hobart, John and Anna-Karin, and he'd organised for all of us to go bushwalking again for a few days, hiring a tent from a local camping shop and researching a couple of destinations within the surrounding National Parks.

We'd chosen Maria Island off the east coast of Tasmania, and for that we'd managed to borrow a car from Mark's busking friend, Martin who lived in Launceston and worked at the hospital. He'd been in a few bands over the years with his brother Michael, but at the moment he was playing a few acoustic Billy Bragg sessions around town. These were the infamous Witheford brothers that Mark had mentioned the first time we'd spoken, forming bands like Another Script, and Blackboard Jungle; bands that had played long before my arrival in Australia.

When we visited Martin's flat to collect the car keys I was surprised to see the collection of guitars and equipment he'd accumulated over the years, including a white Rickenbacker. I hadn't met many musicians who worked full-time, but Martin's day job as a Microbiologist had no doubt helped to procure his impressive guitar collection.

His car was an old and battered BMW, and we welcomed its unaccustomed comforts as we drove out of Launceston. Winding down all the windows in the stifling heat of a late afternoon we let the hot wind whip through our hair as we travelled. It gave us little relief as we headed down towards Triabunna on the east coast where we'd arranged to meet John and Anna-Karin. From there we intended to take the ferry across to the Island, staying within the camping grounds near Darlington, once the site of a penal village. Although I was curious to see the remains of the settlement on the Island I was beginning to feel reticent about sleeping in a tent on such an oppressive and muggy evening.

By the time we arrived at the small resort of Louisville our shirts were wet with perspiration, and I welcomed a chance to get out of the car to stretch and let the hot air dry my clothes. Since the others hadn't arrived yet we began to slowly unload some of our supplies and then sit lethargically in the car with all the doors open, feeling drained by the heat. We cringed as we eyed our nylon backpacks, knowing our shirts would soon stick to our backs again when we began our walk to the campsite, burdened with the hefty packs in the sultry air.

I was sitting with my head against the backrest of the car feeling weary, my eyes closed, when I felt the wind suddenly drop and an eerie stillness fall over us. I turned to look at Mark but he was resting too, with eyes shut.

After the momentary calm I felt a draught of air blast overhead and the wind resumed with new vigour, but even as the first gust passed over me I could feel the drop in temperature. It was so cool and refreshing after the hot day that I could feel my energy returning. Standing by the car I turned my face from side to side letting the chill air brush across my skin. It felt like a door had opened somewhere and the cold wind had come charging in. The change was so abrupt that the cold front must have passed over our heads as we sat in the car, and as I looked up at the sky I imagined the striped isobars on a weather chart sketched into the air above us.

While we were marvelling about the dramatic transformation to the day, John and Anna-Karin arrived, driving into the car parking area. It was good to see them again, but after shaking hands and chatting briefly we were eager to reach the boarding point of the ferry, realising that the squally wind had begun to raise an impressive swell on the water as we came within sight of the sea. Our ferry was actually a small boat, probably large enough to carry twenty passengers, with a central covered area so that we could retreat below deck for the journey.

John looked pale and grim as we begun a lurching, determined passage across to the island.

"I think I might get a bit sea sick," he confided, the scarce covering of a patchy beard barely hiding his draining colour.

With her fair Scandinavian complexion and slight build Anna-Karin looked demure and composed. In stark contrast to John's anxious vigil, she watched our progress quietly from her window seat, her gentle mannerisms and the way she tipped her head reminding me of Meryl Streep. She offered John a piece of Dutch salt liquorice with a beguiling smile, hoping it could quell the nausea, but he shook his head and smiled weakly.

We'd been told that the trip across to the island would take about half an hour, but that was in calm seas and without a strong headwind. The water by now was roiling and heaving vigorously, stirred by a wind that was creating a huge swell, and as the boat motored uselessly towards the island we clung to our seats and peered out of the windows. At times I could see the horizon levelled off in the frame of the window, watching it disappear as we were tossed up on the crest of a wave, leaving only sky in its place. Then it would reappear briefly at a diagonal slant when the sea began to shrug the small boat off the crest. For an instant we'd have an oblique view of the island before it was snatched away, the vessel plunging down into the trough of the next wave until the outlook was replaced by a full frame of the dark waters.

It took almost an hour to reach the shores of the island, by which time John was staring at a point on the floor and swallowing regularly. He oozed relief as the boat finally won the battle and we began to approach the wooden jetty at the landing point to the National Park.

The cooler temperatures had prevailed as we stepped onshore, unloading our packs and provisions, and hauling them up the short walk to the campsite. In addition to their camping equipment John and Anna-Karin had brought a large plastic Esky full of food which they hefted between them, taking a handle on either side.

"Are you going to be able to carry that around with you?" I asked. "It looks pretty heavy."

"This? No," John said. "We'll be leaving it in the tent. We've got our day packs for when we go bushwalking."

I raised my eyebrows defiantly at Mark, thinking of how he'd advised that we take only minimal supplies.

"Trust me," he'd said the night before as we carefully measured cereal and sugar by the spoonful, "I've worked as a bushwalking guide and you really don't want to take more than you need. It can make all the difference when you have to carry everything."

Mark looked sheepish and I could tell that he felt duped. We'd obviously been too frugal with our supplies but we'd thought we would be walking all weekend. We hadn't expected we'd be able to leave provisions at a base camp.

In less than an hour we had reached a relatively open area of scrubland that was only interrupted by the contours of a couple of water tanks. There were already a few tents pitched in this camping area, but there was still enough flat ground available near a tap. It seemed odd to see the metal tap protruding from the ground amongst all the scrubby grass and open paddocks but it meant we'd have abundant supplies, which was a welcome thought if the hot weather returned.

It was rumoured to be a very quiet and picturesque island, certainly an ideal location for its original inhabitants. It had been a penal settlement given its isolation and the difficulty of reaching its shores, something we'd experienced first-hand on our earlier crossing. We'd been told that the only car on the island was used by the park rangers, so we knew we were unlikely to be disturbed by any noise other than the waves onshore.

On the way from the jetty we'd passed the ranger's lodgings, little more than a wooden shack, with a hint of smoke weaving up from the chimney to confirm its occupancy. The lodge and the water tanks appeared to be the only concessions to civilisation.

After setting up our tents we did a quick sweep of the area to check the layout of the camp before dark. To our surprise we found a large dining hut. It was a wooden structure, just a roof on stilts above a group of long benches and tables, but it housed a couple of gas barbecues on brick stacks. It would be much more efficient than trying to cook on our portable camp stoves, so we retrieved our food from the tents and returned there while there was still enough ambient light to move freely.

Slicing our ration of vegetables we eyed John's slabs of steak frazzling juicily on the barbecue. The wooden canopy was starting to cast long shadows as the light faded, and our supper was giving off plumes of steam from its plastic bowls, like tiny chimneys.

It was almost dusk by the time we had finished eating and stacked our dishes, but there would be enough light to move around without torches for a while.

From the hut we could see a glowering orb of sun sliding behind the hillside, sending a flare of orange into the skies, and we wanted to chase it to the very edge of the day, before it was lost.

We set off running on the grassy slope, skittering the wallabies that had been grazing there in small clusters, forcing them to skip away a few metres before stopping to watch our progress. Resting on muscular haunches with ears forward they nudged at the air with soft noses, curious about our breathless flight. At any moment the beautiful colours would change. We didn't want to miss the final smouldering descent of the sun as it dropped away and pulled at the threads of the night sky.

As our noisy scramble hastened us to the peak of the small rise, we emerged to a full panorama of sky arching above us, panting in the twilight as we twirled to see the view. The shapes of trees on the far horizon were fading into silhouettes, and in the expansive darkness we saw meteors flashing curved parabolas across the night skies in tiny bursts of light.

By the time we returned to our campsite there were more stars than I'd ever seen. Before I zipped the outer flap of our tent I lay on my back in the gloom staring at the gleam of planets like sequins on the blackness, the shooting stars, and the circling satellites, their distant lights drawing a steady line as they swept across the sky. From the cocoon of my sleeping bag I could hear the nocturnal wanderings of the native possums.

"Did you put away all our food?" I asked Mark.

"Mmm."

"Only, I can hear them rummaging." There was a clink, like the sound of metal. Like a spoon or a knife. "I think they're eating our breakfast."

"I don't think they need utensils for that," Mark said, from within his own cocoon. "It's fine, really. Come on, let's go to sleep."

WE AWOKE to find John and Anna-Karin moving their tent to a spot about thirty feet away, underneath a leafy tree.

"Morning!" John called out, "How about eggs and bacon?"

"You have eggs and bacon *as well*?" Mark threw back, watching them move to and fro with their possessions.

"Sure. We always camp in style," John answered, heaving the closed Esky across to the new location and sitting down on top of it.

"Why've you moved?" Mark asked, standing by the tree now with his hands in his pockets.

"Well it's probably the best spot if it rains later. More sheltered. Some other campers just left here so I thought we'd get in before anyone else had the same idea."

Mark was looking up at the tree, scrutinising the foliage.

"It's a walnut tree," John said before anyone could ask.

"Aah, of course," Mark intoned, continuing to study it.

Anna-Karin was nudging John to get off the cooler so that she could start cooking. She'd appeared with a frying pan and had already set up the trangia camp stove so we could dine by the tents.

"Do you want to move your tent over here too? There's plenty of room," John suggested, addressing Mark.

"Yeah, okay. I guess it'll be better here if it does rain," Mark said, studying the sky overhead for any clues.

We relocated as the bacon fried enticingly on the camp stove, finally breakfasting under the picturesque and leafy canopy of the walnut tree.

"What's in that?" I asked, indicating a plump canvas bag hanging above us. John had tied it to a tree branch by a length of rope, from which it swung like a pendulum.

"Bread."

"Ri-ight. Why's it there?"

Anna-Karin was smiling as she loosened the bag and reached inside it.

"I'm sure you heard the possums last night?" she said.

We nodded, thinking of the clattering sounds after we'd retired.

She held up a frayed crust, neatly punctuated with crescent shaped bites.

"Well they got into our bread, even though it was inside the tent. They must've got under the outer shell."

"We'll figure out something else for tonight," John said resolutely.

"But you'd better keep everything well wrapped," Anna-Karin added, "or maybe we can squeeze your things into the Esky too. They won't get in there."

"Toast anyone?" John asked, shaking out the frilled bread and spearing it with a fork.

We spent the rest of the day following paths that led to the beaches on the shoreline, carrying a few provisions in our small daypacks so that we could picnic on the sand. John had also brought two snorkels, so we took turns to float belly-down in the cool water. The facemask was like a mini television screen revealing a scene in slow motion, green seaweed washing in jewelled shafts of light, its soft filaments inhabited by shoals of tiny fish hovering in the sway. With the sunlight warming our backs we drifted along the shore, swaying to and fro in the underwater currents, getting chilled by the cold sea as the others slept lazily on the beach.

On our third morning it was drizzling steadily when we awoke. Despite the shelter of the walnut tree the tents were thoroughly soaked, and there was a damp chill to our clothes as we dressed. We didn't linger over breakfast, knowing the rain would persist, packing our sodden possessions before visiting the remains of the penal village.

Bennetts wallabies were grazing leisurely on the grassy hillside under a vast expanse of grey clouds, apparently oblivious to the rain, their fur bedraggled and clumped together in sharp spikes and tufts. Despite their nocturnal inclinations the group was browsing serenely in the morning light, occasionally sitting up to scan the area for sounds, and shaking their heads lazily with a flip flop of ears.

The resident native hens were more excitable when we passed, running away from us with exaggerated importance, their long legs and oversized feet bearing them off on some urgent mission across the scrub grass, leaning into the turns, veering off on an invisible zigzag course. The way they changed tack and speed with such comical precision made me think of the cartoon character, Road Runner. I could almost hear the meep-meep as they lurched away.

The ferry trip was much less dramatic on our return, for which John was the most grateful. The sea was flat and apathetic under the whispering drizzle, its surface ruffled only by the steady rainfall, and overhung by bland white skies.

Within half an hour, we had chugged back to the mainland, sustained by the idea of a shower and a real bed, and a choice of restaurants in Hobart's city streets.

*

WITH ONLY a few more days left until we returned to Melbourne we had a final trip with John and Anna-Karin. There was an area in central Tasmania in the Lake Country, about an hour and half from Launceston, where we planned to walk in the Walls of Jerusalem National Park.

It had been another scorching day and we arrived in the late afternoon fully equipped to tackle the steep ascent to the summit from the car park. It was oppressively humid as we began the walk, too sheltered by the trees and vegetation to receive even a slight breeze and suffocatingly hot in the sultry air. Eyes to the ground we plodded up the almost vertical pathway to the first peak, encumbered by our heavy nylon backpacks.

Fortunately it began to rain as we were struggling up the final part of the steep track, and this served to dampen some of the heat; but it forced us to tramp with heads down, unable to take in most of the distant scenery, our field of vision narrowed as we peered out from under our rain hoods.

We arrived at our chosen campsite just before it was fully dusk, hurriedly pitching our tents and starting to cook while there was sufficient light. There was little point in lingering after dinner in the persistent downpour, so we left all the dishes for the rain and the possums to clean and went to our respective beds.

When I woke in the morning it was to the metronome of rain falling steadily outside. Mark was still asleep as I rubbed my eyes and focussed blearily on the domed roof of tent above us. There was enough daylight passing through the fabric to cast a dull orange light on Mark's sleeping face, but something didn't look right.

"Mark."

I nudged him, and he stirred and yawned.

"Wake up. Look."

I pointed to the roof of the tent as he squinted in the direction indicated by my finger, trying to keep his eyes open against the light. It had obviously been pouring down for most of the night.

There was a large collection of water sitting on the inner lining of our tent, which had begun to sag down heavily with the weight of the accumulating pool. It looked like a full hammock straining above our heads. Evidently the outer layer of the tent was damaged, letting the rain seep through, so I reached up towards the middle of the pool intending to release it.

"No! Don't touch it," he said, quickly grabbing my arm.

Instead, he poked one finger against the fabric just adjacent to the pool, raising the material slightly so that the water ran off to one side.

"Lucky that nothing in the tent was touching the inner layer," he said thankfully.

"What would've happened?" I asked, glancing around.

"It would've started dripping on us during the night," he explained. "It'll probably fill up again but there's not much we can do about it now."

We lay back in our sleeping bags, staring at our leaky roof and listening to the percussion of rain tapping its morse code rhythm on the canvas and surrounding leaves.

"We're going to have to turn back aren't we?" I lamented, measuring my disappointment but thinking of the alternative if we stayed. We'd be walking in the rain, and then pitching a damp tent on wet ground in the evening.

"It might clear up," Mark said hopefully. "We should see what the others want to do."

By the time we unzipped our tent, John and Ann-Karin were standing under a tree wearing their rain proof jackets and spooning-up cereal from plastic bowls. Once outside we could see the extent of the weather. Overhead, the cloud was so low on our hillside location that it hovered in a white mist all around us and blotted out any views of the horizon. There was an eerie isolation to our campsite, and a loss of all perspective as the steamy haze hung in the air and obscured the terrain.

Mark had pulled up the hood of his jacket and he made a dash across to the others under the tree. I could hear snippets of John's reply to Mark's questions and guessed that as a seasoned camper, John wouldn't be deterred by a bit of rain.

"... might improve... wait to see if it clears up... walk on a bit further..."

I joined them as soon as I could crawl out of the wet tent, pulling my hood forward to shield my eyes as I walked.

"You're not thinking of staying are you?" I asked.

"We think," Mark paused, looking at the impenetrable white above us, "it could clear up a bit later."

"Or it could keep raining all day," I added, squinting at the sagging skies.

"We could walk a bit further and just see...?" Mark ventured.

"It's so beautiful up here normally," John observed, looking around at the determined rainfall. "You should be able to see for miles in every direction."

"I'm sure it is…but we're not going to see much on a day like this. And after yesterday's rain as well, I haven't got any more dry clothes," I admitted, looking at the dripping trees, "or dry boots…"

"Might be a bit hard to build a fire later," John said, kicking at the sodden ground, "and there won't be any dry kindling anywhere."

"I suppose the tents will be a bit tricky to manage when they're wet. And a bit heavier. And once we pack them up they won't just be wet on the outside," Mark speculated.

"They're not likely to dry out before we sleep in them are they?" I asked, "And did Mark tell you that ours has sprung a leak?"

There was much discussion of the options then, and general speculations about the sort of bucketing rain you could expect in a place like this. It was called Lake Country for good reason.

"I think perhaps we could come back another day," Anna-Karin suggested, much to my relief.

"Yes…please?" I implored, hoping to convince the boys.

"I thought you Poms were used to a bit of rain?" Mark teased.

"I am, at a cellular level. I'm just not used to camping in it."

"I suppose if the rain's settled in… it'd be a hard day of walking," John conceded, chomping on the last few mouthfuls of his cereal. "If the girls want to head back, then let's do it."

After we'd all eaten something we rolled up the sodden tents and retreated along the path back to the car park. It was an easy walk, but underneath my jacket I could feel my clothes starting to absorb the rain as it seeped through.

Underfoot we stepped over strange luminous green mosses and colourful lichens on the scattered rocks, some of them white like flat watermarks on the surface, and others yellow and more intricate. From the confines of my hood I could only see the ground and the falling rain. However, within a couple of hours we were beginning the descent along the steep path that only yesterday we had climbed in the staggering heat without any idea that we would be returning so soon.

Launceston was just over 100km away but we should've been on the plateau somewhere, walking through the bush. This was supposed to be our last hurrah before we left the island. It felt like we'd been fast forwarded, and I just didn't feel ready to leave.

I WAS SITTING on the back porch of Mark's family home in Dilston, overlooking the garden. The next morning we'd be leaving the island. The weeks spent in Tasmania had been intimate and relaxing and I was aware how the seclusion had made me forget the reality of Melbourne. It was February, the last few days of the summer months, and I'd have to start considering the practicalities of life in the city again.

Just under the porch roof, high up in a corner, there were two fledgling swallows perched on the lip of their mud nest, waiting to be fed. With their wings tucked in, their fluffy brown bodies looked like two fat monks staring down at me. We'd been watching them for the past few days, knowing that their first flight must be imminent, and noticing how they'd become more inquisitive. Today they seemed quite content to wait for their parents to continue the supply of food, and had been staring down at me accusingly whilst I'd been sitting outside.

It was so peaceful at the house with the shadowy orchard extending all the way to the road, and cows grazing in the paddocks beyond the back fence. A huge tree overhung the garage, and as the wind raked spirited fingers through the branches it played crescendos of leaf stirred melodies, carrying their whispering on the breeze. There was enough sunshine from the white skies to cast faint shadows on the driveway, and as I watched their outlines darken and pale I allowed my mind to wander.

Mark and I were continuing to explore what it meant to be in love. Sometimes we struggled with the powerful emotions that it evoked, sometimes we succumbed to flights of passion. But they led to such tender reconciliation. There'd been such an evening, when we'd argued and I'd left the house, taking flight to the dark orchard hoping Mark would follow me. But he hadn't.

When I returned alone to the house, I'd seen light still emanating from the lamp in the lounge, and could make out Mark's figure in the shadows. Remorsefully I'd sat down next to him on the couch. There was a moment when we may have spoken, or perhaps we only touched, but somehow it became a tearing need, and we were suddenly on the floor making love, and I couldn't remember how it started, just that there was a raggedness to our passion and I wasn't able to stop it.

An echo of that desire still hummed within me, and I could feel a shift as something moved to accommodate it, to welcome and preserve it. We had both changed, but we were also changing each other, letting our love arouse and inspire us, and hold us together.

As I sat on the porch in quiet reflection, I realised the fledglings had gone. Despite my vigilance I had missed them leaving the safety of their nest for their first flight, and they had slipped away unseen. Some people believe it's a sign of good luck if a swallow builds a nest under the eaves of their house. I smiled as I scanned the garden for them, thinking of all our hopes for the year ahead. But I'd heard other views that were far more circumspect. Just because a swallow has appeared, it doesn't mean that the dark days are over, and summer has come to stay. The good times may have arrived, but they shouldn't be taken for granted. The thought made me uneasy as I searched the cloudy skies, still hoping for a final glimpse of the birds.

I tried to shake off the feelings of foreboding, about the unforeseen difficulties of leaving home, about the many obstacles that might yet lie ahead. These young birds had left their home with nothing more than their wits and the will to survive. Is that why I felt their loss so acutely, wondering if, like me, they would find their way?

The disappearance of the fledglings was a stark reminder that there was no room for complacency. In the pursuit of love I had endured so many separations and absences, but there were never any guarantees, and I realised as I scanned the empty skies that loss can come suddenly.

Mark was moving through the garden towards the porch, and I watched as he approached my chair. I couldn't command love any more than I could hold back the fledgling swallows. Whether love would cleave me, or make me whole, I could only hold onto my half.

*Like Two Mexicans Dancing*

Mark at home, in Dilston

*Angela J. Dawson*

# Music by the beach, St Kilda

ON FEBRUARY 11th the international news delivered an incredible story. In South Africa, Nelson Mandela had been released after 27 years of imprisonment. He was 71. The mood was ecstatic, with people dancing in the streets in Cape Town and across the country, and there was an enormous sense of disbelief and joy across the globe. It was referred to as a day of triumph, the making of history, the biggest human interest story the world had ever seen. His walk to freedom filled television screens, and stories of this landmark moment ran on-loop for days.

It was a heady start to the year. The jubilant mood was filtering across the world, and with it, the knowledge that something impossible had just been made possible. A hopeless situation had now become one of hope. It was easy for everyone to feel more optimistic about the future.

The annual St Kilda Festival started in the middle of February, and this little piece of history was being made with an open-air concert on the beachfront. It included music from Nick Barker, Paul Kelly and The Fish, and although it wasn't an eminent event in global terms, it was still cause for celebration.

It had been a day of high humidity and blistering sunshine. By the early afternoon the walls and pavement had absorbed the heat and were reflecting it from every building, increasing the already oppressive temperatures. Mark and I had set off early Sunday morning, the vinyl seats of the Gemini seeming to melt against our skin.

Once we reached the backstage area we hoped to join the others and take advantage of the free refreshments, and having brought my camera I hoped to take some shots of the band later. The crowd was already amassing on the grass adjacent to the stage and as we crossed from the car with the guitars we could see a couple of the others waiting near the marquee.

The entrance to the backstage area was defined by the sort of free-standing poles that are used as a temporary barrier, linked by nylon sashes. We could only gain access to the enclosure by showing a backstage pass to the security officials at this informal gateway. However, we discovered that we hadn't been allocated enough passes to allow Darren or myself backstage with the band.

As we watched the guests filtering through and lingering at the entrance there was an obvious solution. We realised it would be easy for the band to enter and then discretely hand back their passes to us when the officials were too distracted by the flow of people to see the exchange.

The plan worked, and once we were all inside the marquee we found an empty table close to the supply of drinks at the private bar. From there, Warky was able to indulge his predilection for Malibu, and we were in a favourable position to watch the influx of local celebrities. Most of them looked startlingly unimposing in the daylight, especially under the harsh glare of the sun – Paul Kelly, Jimi the Human, various actors from Neighbours.

When Nick Barker arrived, he looked pale and diminutive, his pasty features hidden behind heavy concealing make-up. A colossal man strode across to greet him, lifting him clear of the ground and encasing him in a smothering hug.

"Nickie...baby...!" he roared, swinging him around in a flamboyant circle, Nick's boots inches above the grass. They flashed dangerously close to the shins of the surrounding crowd before the man planted him carefully back down, some distance from the original lift-off. The others in his entourage then began a raucous ceremony of back slapping before being absorbed into the crowded backstage area.

The effects of alcohol and heat soon induced a feeling of lethargy amongst us, but there were a few hours remaining before The Fish would be on stage. Inserting a roll of film into my camera I wandered off in search of photographic opportunities.

In front of the stage the crowd had gathered into lively groups scattered on the grass, their diverse fashions forming odd patterns as they intermingled, gradually covering all the exposed ground until it was just a clutter of shapes and colour.

I panned across the sprawling bodies with my zoom lens, stopping as I caught a group of Bikers in the viewfinder. The heavy black leather jackets made a startling contrast to the sheer summer fabrics worn by other people adjacent to their group, and I paused to focus and compose my picture, seeing one of the bearded men toss back his head to drain the last of his beer in one deep swallow.

When he dropped his chin he was still holding the can, but he'd fixed his gaze on something and he narrowed his eyes as he watched it intently. I wondered what had caught his attention until I zoomed in, until his face filled the frame perfectly and I was looking right into his eyes. No lip reader could miss it.

"F-u-c-k o-f-f," he mimed, with measured enunciation, his teeth gripping his lower lip for full effect.

I twitched the lens away from my face and flashed a glance across the crowd. I was standing about a hundred feet away but through the zoom lens it had seemed as if he was staring right at me. From his position on the ground, he was lying propped on one elbow, glaring in my direction from his kingdom of black leather. I didn't risk a second look.

It was three o'clock in the afternoon by the time The Fish were on stage, and the heat had peaked in the high thirties, with heavy humidity and a hot wind that offered little relief. On a day like this, the sweat would soon soften Graham's calloused hands, and he was drumming wearing black leather gloves to prevent them from blistering.

At the front, the crowd was pressed hard against the barrier and I knew if I went out into the audience I'd have little chance of squirming through it to take photographs. The stage was about five feet off the ground, no more than a makeshift platform with wooden struts supporting it underneath, and a curtain of black material as a backdrop.

Standing at the rear, in the narrow gap between the backdrop and the stage, everything was at eye level and all I could see was feet and amps. For once the privileges of being backstage offered neither any comforts, nor a better outlook.

Shouldering my camera I hoisted myself up behind Graham's drum kit. Since he was elevated further on a small rostrum I would be out of sight if I stayed low, lying flat on a narrow ledge of stage and peering around the drums to take pictures.

I spent almost the entire set crawling commando style along the rear of the stage, teetering on an area little wider than a bookshelf. On one side I had the swaying drum kit as Graham thrashed out a steady rhythm to the music, and on the other the sudden descent over the edge if I misjudged my position. There were times between songs when I saw Graham peer behind him to check that I hadn't actually fallen off.

Towards the end of the gig I could see the clouds starting to thicken overhead, preventing the heat from escaping, until the wind picked up at last and began to create peaks and crests on the surface of the sea.

The band poured offstage after an energetic set, wet with perspiration, and headed thirstily to the backstage marquee for drinks. There, Nick Barker's drummer was limbering up extravagantly, stretching like a cat, twisting his arms behind his back and then resting one leg on a stool so he could press his forehead onto his thigh for full effect. His flexibility was impressive, but it looked like he was preparing to dance rather than drum.

It was a balmy evening as Mark and I drove home with all the car windows rolled down, the St Kilda streets still busy, cafés full and people spilling out onto the pavements or seated at scattered tables. I was filthy and hot, embracing conflicting feelings of tiredness and elation, my bare legs sticking to the vinyl seat. I knew there was nowhere else I would rather be at that moment.

I looked at Mark driving and saw a slow smile creep across his face when he became aware of being watched. He reached across and squeezed my leg affectionately.

What would it be like if you were famous, I thought? What would *you* be like if you were famous? I left it unsaid, wondering what the future might bring.

"What are you thinking about?" Mark asked, his eyes on the road.

"Hmm…. I don't really like Nick Barker," I said, wrinkling my nose.

"Really?" he laughed.

"No. And all that back slapping," I huffed scornfully. "You won't be like that will you?"

"What do you mean?"

"In the future, you won't be, you know… all showy and brash?"

"Showy?"

He reached across for my hand, and kissed the back of it with a dramatic flourish. "You mean… like this?" he said, making me laugh at the gesture, his eyes flashing mischievously.

"You wouldn't do that if you knew where these hands have been today," I said.

"Tell me," he said, slowly enveloping a finger with his lips.

I could feel the silken heat and intensity of his mouth, and it made me forget the rest of my body for a moment.

"I should get danger money you know, for taking all these photographs."

But his lips were too busy to reply.

My heart felt full. Just don't let it change you, I thought, feeling myself tethered by Mark's hand. Just don't let it change us.

St Kilda Festival: lying behind Graham's drum kit

The drop at the rear of the stage

*Angela J. Dawson*

I LOOKED AT EVA in the car, gripping the steering wheel with slender fingers. Neatly brushed red hair fell about her shoulders, a short fringe curling above the delicate arc of her eyebrows. Even without make-up she was captivating. It was a couple of weeks after the St Kilda Festival and we were driving in her car to Sydney to meet the boys, who had left a few days earlier. As the road fell away behind us she was telling me how she'd met Warky and fallen in love with his playful humour.

It was easy to imagine the attraction to his inimitable charm. I'd often been grateful for his impulsive games during the long sound checks, for his exuberance and sense of fun on tour, and the way he took pleasure in the smallest things.

It would take about eleven hours to reach the city from Melbourne and we were prepared to take frequent rests, stopping along the highway at service stations so we could stretch and buy cold drinks in the hot afternoon. We shared stories about recent gigs with Raymond J, and the open-air gig in Warrnambool with the Wild Pumpkins At Midnight. The Fish had played again with Nick Barker at Melbourne University, and they'd been recording new songs at Whirled Records in Richmond. So many things had happened since my return from England a few weeks earlier. I still hadn't found permanent employment, but that meant I could go to Sydney and stay with the band at whatever accommodation they'd arranged.

The boys had rented a large unit in Darling Harbour for the weekend which had sufficient space to sleep about ten people. However, the gig that evening was in Blacktown, 40km from our city accommodation. After our arduous journey from Melbourne, Eva was having some difficulty finding the hotel venue in which the band would be playing. We'd been circling the streets slowly, looking for the pub and trying to fix our location on the map, when we saw a familiar lanky figure striding out on the pavement a few metres away.

Warky was setting an impressive pace as he walked, a black dinner jacket blowing open in the wind, the familiar shoulder length, dark curls tossed back with the force of his stride. Apart from the formal jacket he was dressed in a T-shirt, his casual pants rolled-up at the bottom. Eva sounded the car horn and accelerated across the short distance between us, pulling up alongside the kerb and calling out through her open window.

"Mark!" she shouted, but he was already crossing the road towards us.

He leaned forward, resting one elbow on the car door, thrusting his head inside and smiling warmly at Eva.

"Hey Dudes," he said, his eyes checking over the inside of the car, "just got here?"

"Well, not really. We've been looking for the hotel you're playing at tonight, but I think we've been driving round in circles for a while," she replied,

"You're nearly there," Warky assured us, "and you're just in time to give me a lift."

He opened one of the rear doors and settled himself amongst our bags and cases, indicating the next turn to Eva as she moved off. Rounding the corner, we travelled a few metres before Mark called out.

"There it is!"

Eva braked sharply, pulling the car over to the pavement to park and grinning at our ten second journey.

"Lucky I found you," he said, heaving himself out of the cluttered car, "or you might've missed the gig."

We indulged him by smiling broadly, and began pulling out some of the luggage.

"You might as well bring everything, and then you can use the shower in the band room if you want?"

The entrance to the night club looked like something you'd see on the streets of Hollywood. There were fairy lights along each step of a staircase that led up to the venue, high above street level. As we reached the top, the light inside the club was dim and the smell of stale beer crept towards us, as if all the spills had seeped through the carpets and been preserved in the floorboards underneath.

Despite the scarcity of people at the bar, the wide dance floor was filled with a dense cloud of dry ice fog through which we had to pass to reach the backstage rooms. We rapidly lost our sense of direction, blundering through it and aiming ourselves roughly towards the opposite side of the room. As I followed the others I saw them vanish momentarily in a fresh blast of dry ice discharged gratuitously into the already foggy room. I held my breath involuntarily expecting it to sting like smoke, but it just left a strange taste in my mouth. As I came through the other side, I saw Warky opening a doorway to admit Eva into the space beyond.

The backstage band room was tiny, made smaller by the number of people already crammed inside. It was more like a corridor than a room. There was a workbench, like a counter along one side, above which a wide mirror filled the entire wall. The mirror helped reduce the sense of claustrophobia, but the room was evidently not intended for more than one or two people. Mark and Andrew were sitting on the counter with their backs to the mirror, Darren was standing, and Graham was lolling on an old plastic chair, handing out cans of beer from a stash piled on the floor. Our arrival meant that everyone was required to move limbs and shuffle around to some degree to make way for three more bodies, but everyone welcomed us and adjusted their position without complaint.

A corner door led to a small bathroom where Eva and I took turns to wash and change before re-joining the boys in their anteroom. But by then the air was filled with a haze of cigarette smoke, and I knew my sense of being clean and refreshed would soon become undone. The heat of the day was lingering in the bricks of the club walls, and it was likely to be smotheringly hot once the crowd started to compact on the dancefloor.

It had been an uneventful night, and I was eager to escape the smell of dry ice, cigarette smoke and stale beer. I wanted to breathe some cool, clean air, but when we stepped out onto the street the humidity was still high and the night air offered little relief.

Warky and Eva decided to depart immediately after the gig, taking Mark and I with them, and leaving the others at the bar. It would only take about 40 minutes to reach our Darling Harbour accommodation if we took Eva's car, leaving the van behind for the equipment, which the boys could load after they'd finished their drinks.

There was a swimming pool at the unit. We saw it when we quietly checked in after midnight. Knowing it would be difficult to sleep on such a hot night we all changed into bathers, creeping gratefully into the water and splaying across its cool surface. We must have stayed there for at least an hour, until our skin felt chilled, but when we returned to the unit, the rest of the band still hadn't arrived. So we chose our beds for the night, and fanned the thin sheets over our chlorine scented skin, and eased into an exhausted sleep.

At some point in the night the others had materialised, and in the morning they were sleeping heavily in their beds at the other end of the unit. Warky seemed keen to go to Paddington when he saw me breakfasting with Mark.

"Hey, d'you guys want to come and check out the markets with me and Eva?"

I was waiting for the kettle to boil so I could make some more tea.

"What about the others?" Mark asked.

"Yeah. We might leave them to sleep-in a bit," Warky replied quietly, glancing back over his shoulder.

"Have you eaten anything yet?" I asked. He was hovering near the door.

"You'll have to hurry if you're coming," he added.

Mark stood up to stretch and shrugged at me by way of acceptance.

I nodded. "When did they get back anyway? Did anyone hear them?"

"Pretty late," Warky admitted carefully, inching Eva through the open door.

It was only when we departed that we discovered why he was so eager to make himself scarce. The others had finally made an exasperated and raucous arrival at 7am, having spent the night hunting for the keys to the van. The keys had unfortunately been in Warky's trouser pocket, a fact that he'd forgotten when we'd all shed our clothes and left the unit for a swim. This wasn't something he wanted to recap to a group of people who hadn't slept all night, and he clearly didn't want to be around when they woke. I didn't dare ask how they'd finally got there, but wondered if it had involved someone having to make a round trip to pick up the keys.

After some sleep, a swim, and an unwholesome array of fast food, everyone was in good humour when we returned from the market in the late afternoon. However, after the chaos of the previous evening, it was no surprise that The Fish's support set was laden with technical problems that night. Microphones cut out periodically for seconds at a time and guitar strings snapped in succession, mostly when Darren wasn't paying attention. I could see Mark getting frustrated when Darren failed to notice the damage, or when he wasn't ready with a second guitar tuned and ready to exchange, leaving Mark playing with the broken string dangling uselessly. Their tired performance was in stark contrast to the band that followed.

Hunters and Collectors were magnificent that night. They moved on to the stage with a sudden eruption of music, Mark Seymour leaping and swaying, menacing the audience. *Throw your arms around me* he sang, and we did. We were all entranced.

Mark had found me in the crowd, his initial despondency fading as he too was transported by the atmosphere within the room, swaying involuntarily to the throb of the music. We were mouthing the lyrics, we were dancing, we were becoming like one body with a multitude of arms, the lights changing the mood, shifting us between sinister reds and cool blues.

Deafened by the crashing noise all I could do was turn and grin at Mark, bracing himself in the crush of bodies. The room had become like a field of cane in the wind, bodies swaying, arms punching the air. I could feel the bass resonating in my chest, shivering through my hair, and I could feel Mark's hand on my waist, stabilising us in the muddle and chaos, my hips rocking in time with his. The strobe lights flashed over us, deleting moments of movement, the room blinking with missed seconds. They'd begun *When the river runs dry* and it felt like we couldn't go any higher. But while the music played we didn't need anything else.

We only existed as the audience now. We were the ones applauding and holding our arms aloft, and clapping fervently, and pushing our fingers into our mouths to whistle noisily. We were the ones bellowing our approval beyond the smoky ceiling, and high up into the summer skies.

A FLOURISH of sultry summer temperatures in Melbourne had made me reluctant to venture outside in the stifling heat unless it was to swim at a beach somewhere, but in March I finally secured some casual hospitality work at a bar on Queen St frequented by wig wearing Barristers from the local courthouses. It meant I had to travel to the city by train and then toil across scorching concrete for several blocks before I reached the cool basement of the tavern.

One afternoon, in the calm after the lunchtime rush, a large bouquet of flowers was delivered to the bar. Checking the card I was surprised to find that it was addressed to me. The handwriting was familiar, and opening the note inside I saw it was from Mark. As I read it I could see the admiring glances from the other staff, curious to know about the sender and asking whether it was my birthday. Listening to their murmured approval with flushed cheeks, I folded the note into my pocket, excited by his promise of a picnic the following morning. Despite all the gigs over the next few evenings he'd made time for us to have the day together.

In the morning when he collected me he already had a picnic prepared, although the sky was ominously grey and overcast, and he'd chosen a destination as he set off around the Peninsula towards Mornington.

"I hope the weather holds out," I warned, looking at the leaden clouds.

"Oh, I don't think it'll rain," he smiled confidently, intent on following through with his promise and daring the weather to contradict him.

The slate skies became steadily darker but we arrived in Mornington ready to brave a chilly beach. Walking out onto the cold sand we spread a blanket, unpacking our basket of paté and cheese and looking out at the restless seas, fingered by pouting winds. A few glassy droplets began to spatter from the waterlogged clouds but we continued to sit resolutely, willing the rain to hold off for a bit longer.

"I don't think it'll rain much," Mark reassured me, crunching a cracker and trying to ignore the increasing volley of droplets. The shower soon began to gather some momentum and after a few minutes we saw the futility of trying to withstand the intensifying deluge, tossing the food into the basket and making a dash for the car.

"Grab your coat!" Mark said, undeterred, shaking out his wet hair as he retrieved his jacket from the back seat.

"Where are we going?"

He pointed towards the Esplanade, still clutching the basket of food and holding his jacket over his head.

We made a shrieking dash for the beachfront where Mark had spotted a deserted wooden shelter under which we could take cover. It was large enough to shield us from the rain, and although there was no seating we could at least finish our picnic undercover, sweeping the beaded water from our sleeves as we huddled together.

Across the sea the flat line of the horizon had become serrated by the driving rain, and we listened to the drumming rhythm of it on the shelter as we watched fat droplets dripping off the edges of the roof.

"I don't think it'll come down for long," Mark said hopefully, but with less conviction now, as we watched puddles forming on the saturated grass of the nearby park.

Retrieving umbrellas from the car we wandered along the pier for a while, glancing into the buckets of the various fishermen to see if the catch was good that day; but the downpour seemed to be keeping the fish from biting and the majority of buckets were empty.

"Thank you," I said, taking Mark's arm as we walked slowly, "for today."

He was striding alongside me thoughtfully, his hands plunged deep into his pockets, ruminating over the contents. I could hear coins jangling.

His eyes scanned the grey horizon. "It hasn't really worked out the way I'd expected."

"It doesn't matter. You can't do much about the weather," I said, leaning into him.

He gently spun me round so he could take my hands. For a moment he looked down at our interlocked fingers then lifted one hand so he could kiss the back of it.

"So much for all my plans."

I waited until his eyes shifted to my face.

"I don't mind the rain. Really. I'm English."

He smiled, sadly I thought, his disappointment more palpable than he would admit.

"It'll probably change in a minute anyway. You know what Melbourne's like," I added.

"All seasons in a day," he quoted, peering up at the dense clouds. "If you don't like it, just wait for a minute."

He was still holding my hands, turning them over and studying their shape as he folded them into his own. He used them to pull me towards him for an embrace, opening his jacket so he could wrap it around either side of me.

"We can do it again," I said. "You know I always love a picnic."

I lifted my head to look at him, feeling the warmth where our chests were touching. His eyes were on the rain soaked horizon, but he was miles away.

"Mark?"

"Yes, some other time then," he said, starting to walk.

I could feel him steering us towards the parked car.

"Come on," he said tenderly, "we might as well head back."

Despite the distance we'd travelled to get there we didn't linger, driving back to the city in the late afternoon to watch it come alive with the three day Moomba Festival. Every year the event offered a weekend assortment of carnival rides and sideshows, all of it assembled alongside the Yarra River and adjacent city gardens. Plus there was the Birdman Rally where people flew home-made gliders from a high platform over the river, hurling themselves in winged costumes into the water for the sake of charity. At the end of it, there was live music and a big firework display at dusk.

The band would be playing an outdoor gig at the festival that evening, in Alexandra Gardens, and when the others arrived to set up the equipment we were thankful that the city remained free of the heavy rainfall that had been falling further down the Bay.

It was an infrequent pleasure, watching the band perform in the open-air, free from the usual cigarette haze and the stifling heat that would build in the confines of a hotel gig. It was a balmy evening, the grass was soft underfoot, and it didn't matter if I was backstage or in the audience as long as I had a clear view of them on stage. Mark still seemed disappointed that our picnic had been rained off after all his careful planning. I waited quietly through the sound check, giving him space for his thoughts, knowing he was preoccupied with their busy schedule. The Sunday gig at The Punters Club tomorrow night would be a big one, and a special night for Mark Adams. In fact, by all accounts, it would end up being a weekend to remember.

# Red, red wine

IT WAS a capacity crowd. I recognised a few faces in the congested room. Martin Witheford had flown over from Launceston for the Moomba weekend and I could see him standing in the crush inside The Punters Club on Sunday evening, joining the enthusiastic audience that was filling the Club. So many people had arrived to see The Fish that people were pressed together all the way from the stage right back to the rear windows.

The band had been in high spirits as they played, buoyed by their excited reception and careening about on the low stage, only inches above the eager throng.

Shortly after that energetic and inspired performance, Warky was taken aside and told that he was out of the band. The Punters Club gig had been his last. It was a tense moment, compounded by the knowledge that they'd also confiscated his guitar and mandolin as payment for money he owed.

Discovering the boys had organised his removal so secretly must have been a hurtful mutiny, and the deceit made me feel uncomfortable. I hadn't known about it before the gig, but the timing couldn't have been worse. The band had just secured the support for a big international act, and in a couple of days they'd be touring with them across several states. It was a tremendous achievement and should have been a time of great excitement, but everything was marred by all the upheaval.

Evidently the band had made their choice, and even though I wasn't aware of the reasons, I knew I wouldn't be the only one saddened by the news. Warky was very popular with the crowd and I couldn't imagine The Fish without his mandolin and harmonica, or his mad antics on and off stage. It would be a turning point for the Fish, the end of an era, and I was certain he would be greatly missed.

Martin's arrival that weekend had been no coincidence. He was there as Warky's replacement. A few weeks earlier Mark had sent Martin a cassette, and he'd been practising the songs the Fish had been playing that night. He'd discreetly brought his guitars with him from Tasmania, careful to keep them out of sight. If anyone had seen them they may have asked questions about the timing of his arrival. He was ready to slip seamlessly into place now, for a week of touring. The Fish were going to be the support band for UB40. They were set to play at venues all around Adelaide and Perth, starting with a night in the spacious Festival Hall in Melbourne. There, Martin would make his debut as the new rhythm guitarist for The Fish. It would have been a bitter pill to swallow.

*

When Mark phoned the next day his voice still retained an edge of tension. He was excited about the UB40 tour and the opportunities it could offer, but the last few days had been particularly stressful. Everyone was still trying to assimilate the changes and come to terms with what had happened. There was one more evening before they left for the tour, so he asked me to meet him for a walk through the Carlton Gardens in the city.

A round moon hung in the festival sky and the city was still buzzing with activity. The Moomba fireworks were fizzing in the distance, bursting brilliant colours into the blackness of the sky.

As we walked hand in hand in the shadows Mark was very quiet, and after a while I made a comment about it, trying to draw out his thoughts. He let out a deep sigh.

"I'm really nervous actually," he said, nibbling at his bottom lip.

It wasn't what I'd expected.

"Why? What are you nervous about?" I asked, thinking of Martin, and what could be happening with the band.

"Erm, I've been thinking for a while now, you know…even before the picnic…but that day I'd decided… and then of course it rained so much…and, well…"

I focussed on his voice in the moonlight.

"…Ange…will you marry me?"

I felt the small tide of my indrawn breath and a flush of heat shrugged over me. The question had arrived so unexpectedly. Surprise coursed through me, bolting along my veins in jagged waves. There was nothing but the sensation of my own heartbeat and the cool night air on my face. I could feel the rush, and the freefall in my chest, and the slow breath out.

A full moon was spooning the darkness out of a corner of the sky as I turned to look at him. I wanted to plummet deep into the blue irises of his eyes, to wade in and search within. My answer lay there. It always had. Even in the gloom I could see it.

"Yes." The words came freely, and with such conviction. "Yes, I will."

There was a gentle exhalation as he released his breath, and I felt the warmth of it from his mouth as my words still blurred through the air.

He was leaning in now, letting his body meld into mine as we kissed, filling each contour until there was no space left between us. The night had paused for us, waiting to tip us into a new beginning, letting us hold onto our moment in the stillness.

When my senses began to tune-in to the night creatures again, I noticed the bats and possums and the unseen rustlings around us. The soundtrack of the park had been turned back on as they stirred again in their hidden places. I could hear the increasing volume of their collective hum, as if they'd been listening, as if they'd been waiting for the answer.

Casting my eyes around, I could see the Moomba rockets exploding in the distance, erupting in an avalanche of sparks and embers. It looked like the day and night had collided, and pieces of sunlight were fluttering down from the sky.

Resting my head on his shoulder, I thought about our drive to Mornington and the flowers he'd sent to the bar.

"So you were going to ask me at the picnic?"

"Mm. If only it hadn't rained so much."

"I wondered why you were so quiet."

His hands had been resting in the curve of my spine, but as he pulled away and we began to walk, he draped an arm over my shoulder.

I thought of our first touch, where it had all begun, when he'd taken my hand in the dark orchard at Dilston. Those footsteps had taken us here. They had led us to this question, and to the answer.

EARLY MORNING. It was March 13th, two days after the Punters Club gig, and the band was assembled on the train platform at Spencer Street station where the nine o'clock Overland train was due to leave for Adelaide. Their equipment had been loaded and they had a few minutes before the train departed, so they were having a last minute cigarette before boarding. Mark and I had stepped aside for a murmured farewell while everyone else was standing around chatting to the band's Manager, Gary.

From the far ramp that led up to the platform we suddenly became aware of a group of people striding resolutely towards us. They were being led by Warky, his hair flying back as he walked, his face transformed by anger and becoming more animated as he neared the boys and started to shout. The crowd of station personnel that Warky had gathered together were trying to determine their role in the drama that was unfolding, evidently advised that there had been a theft of some description, but realising when faced with the perpetrators, that the situation was actually more complicated.

I moved away, embarrassed by the confrontation, anticipating that it may deteriorate into a fight as a result of Warky's impassioned demands to unload the equipment from the train and his escalating anger at the continued refusal.

I could see the staff nodding as they spoke with Gary, although I was too far away to hear anything. Obviously they were satisfied with the explanation and although Gary turned to speak to Warky, it was too late; he had spun around and was stamping away, back down the ramp and out of sight. The station personnel moved off and I moved back towards Mark.

"That was awful," I said simply.

"Yeah. He'd told them we'd stolen his guitar, but when Gary explained they refused to unload anything from the train."

"I can understand him being upset."

Mark didn't say anything, but his eyes agreed with me.

"The way he was told, the way things have worked out, you know," I added.

We all knew. It was sad that their departure for the tour should be overshadowed by such reproach instead of being remembered as a turning point in their career. I hugged Mark sadly.

"Have a great time," I said, but my words sounded flat and tired.

"I'll send you a postcard," he replied and squeezed me reassuringly.

"Will you?"

"Sure ma' friend."

I revelled in the strength of his hug for a few moments before pulling away. "See you in a week then."

*

Mark dropped in to see me the weekend after he returned from Perth, evidently galvanised by his week on the road, and talking about taking a morning drive to Hanging Rock so we could have a picnic.

By then he was renting a flat in Brunswick, and I had moved into Di and Harve's place. I'd been grateful for their offer of a room until I found permanent work, and was glad I'd been absorbed into the circle group of friends and musicians that lived in Melbourne. His apartment was only a short distance from their house and I could easily walk there.

As we sat in the lounge discussing our picnic plans he reached into his waist coat pocket and pulled out a small green box. Wordlessly, he held it out to me. It was the sort of box that contained jewellery, hinged on one side with a sticker underneath that read, Lucy Parrot Antiques. He smiled as I glanced at it, and then raised my eyes back up to his.

"What is it?" I asked, despite its traditional shape.

I lifted the lid tentatively. Inside was a delicate sapphire and diamond engagement ring, the stones set into a small gold band. It had been a week since he'd proposed. I hadn't anticipated that he'd act so quickly. I was lost for words. Easing the ring out of the box, I fingered the dainty band, turning it over in my palm.

"I found it in a shop in WA," he said, watching me.

"It's…. it's beautiful," I said, with trembling hands, "Mark…"

"You didn't suspect?" he asked, watching me shake my head.

My mind was racing as I looked at it. I wavered for a moment, feeling his eyes on me, and then slipped the ring onto my left hand. It fitted my finger perfectly.

"You got the size exactly right. How did you know?"

He looked pleased that his measurements had been accurate.

"I'd tried one of yours, on my little finger."

"One of my rings? When did you do that?"

"A while ago. I can't remember…" he laughed, running a hand through his hair.

So he'd been planning this for far longer than I'd imagined.

"O-kay," he paused, "so does this mean we're engaged now?"

He was smiling broadly as he sat on the edge of the chair.

"I…well…yes." I looked down at the ring on my finger. "It's lovely, Mark. I don't know what to say. I had no idea…"

"…Only, I want to call my parents and let them know," he interrupted, moving towards me on the couch and wrapping me in an embrace.

My head was reeling but I could feel myself nodding. I hadn't even thought about a ring until this moment. There was a feeling building in my chest, and I tried to slow my breathing and calm my thoughts. I just needed a bit of time to catch-up. It was the shock.

My heart was thudding as he hugged me, and I held him close as I looked over his shoulder. It was a relief to press my body against his, so that I didn't need to look at him, so that I didn't have to look into his eyes. It wasn't because of what I'd see, but because of what he'd see in mine.

## Autumn 1990

WHEN I THINK of that autumn in Melbourne, I remember the feeling of breathless anticipation. Something was always happening around us that whispered of promise and opportunity. There were writers and musicians circling our lives, helping us to reimagine our grand ambitions and to keep our goals in sight. No-one could take the stars from our eyes.

In April, after a two year absence from the scene, Sydneysiders, The Church appeared at the cavernous Metro nightclub on Bourke Street in the city, across the road from Gaslight Records. Mark and I had been intrigued enough to get tickets for the legendary band, and from our position at the back, we could see Marty's guitar catching the light as he played, sending laser beams across the heads of the crowd. A bearded Steve Kilbey looked strangely moody that night, illuminated by purple light, his left leg constantly beating time to the music, the stand-in drummer lost somewhere in a fog of dry ice.

Many of the old favourites were rolled out, like *Under The Milky Way*, *Reptile*, and *Myrrh*, the familiar opening riffs inciting the passion of the fans as each song began. But there was no joy in it, even when they returned for an encore, giving us *Tantalised* as the strobe lights flashed. It had been a night of very little stage banter, and more than a hum of tension, so it wasn't a surprise when Steve finally snapped. The house lights were being turned up and the DJ had started to play a record even as Steve was still hovering moodily at the microphone.

"Dance is dead," he uttered in a barbed monotone, scowling at the DJ as he leaned into his microphone.

The encore wasn't over, and the blunder had incited Steve's wrath. The record was cut short, the band resumed their places, and *Blurred Crusade* came charging through the speakers.

There was something unsatisfying about the gig, despite the large crowd and city location. Whether or not it was just his stage persona, I couldn't help feeling that Steve sounded jaded. Perhaps it was the price they paid for commercial success, when so many other pressures and obligations impacted on their performance. Glancing at Mark, I hoped he never reached that point, when playing live ceased to be enjoyable. Despite having seen the grind of touring and some of the pressures they endured, it was hard for me to imagine how such a coveted lifestyle could become so burdensome. I held the thought in my mind as I clung to Mark's hand, jostling in the stream of people exiting the building, grateful to reach the cool air on the street outside.

The Fish had maintained their eagerness. They strived to be noticed, and they had the drive to succeed. As they waited for their break, they continued to hold their nerve, despite the fickleness of the music business. Although the budget was tight, they lived in hope, even as they lived with financial hardship. Any employment they acquired always had to be flexible, to allow for the band's schedule, and touring. Mark had secured a few hours of work in the afternoons, providing on-site after school care. It allowed him to sleep-in after late night gigs, but it only provided minimal income.

After the UB40 gigs, it had seemed reasonable to think that further opportunities could start to materialise. An international support was good exposure for a local band, increasing their profile and perhaps generating some interest from a record label willing to offer that elusive recording contract. Representatives could have been mingling in the audiences at any time during the tour. But the on-going silence was like white noise.

The ring had become a thorny topic that we tended to avoid. Mark had found it difficult when I'd started wearing it on my right hand, and then on a chain around my neck, to avoid the inevitable questions from all our friends. The questions were usually about marriage. I tried to articulate my thoughts to Mark, about the premature arrival of the ring, but this inevitably raised issues about commitment; and before long I'd placed the ring back in its box and ceased wearing it altogether.

There were plenty of other diversions. Life had started to change pace in those early autumn months, influenced by my home life with Harvey and Di. There were always musicians visiting the house in Brunswick, and this was mostly due to Harve's work at Shock Records and his musical origins in the four piece Tasmanian band, The Odolites. However, when the Melbourne comedy festival started in April we had some unexpected visitors from Sydney.

I was surprised to find them all inside the house when I came home one day, languishing fully clothed on all the beds, tired after a long interstate drive. I had no idea how they'd gained entry without a key, but they assured me they were old friends who had known Harve and Di since school days.

Scott was a writer, Guy was a violinist, and Doug was the versatile musical talent of the trio, singing, drumming, and playing bass and clarinet. Draping himself across Harve and Di's double bed, Scott was so tall that his feet and ankles overhung the end of the mattress. He lay grinning from under a basin haircut, his hands clasped behind his head while I made some tea, refusing to disclose their method of break-in. Their arrival was timed for the festival, and for a show they'd been developing with the comedian, Glynn Nicholas. It was a collaboration that was very successful, and which would ultimately continue for many years.

All these people came and went, a collective talent flirting with their aspirations and reminding me how closely I guarded my own. Mixing within this circle seemed to light the touchpaper of our dreams, showing us they could become real. So many of them had forged connections and already received recognition. The transition from obscurity to success seemed possible.

Yet there was something shabby in the background to which my mind kept returning, and it undermined the shine. Melbourne was never infused with the essence of romance in the way that Launceston had breathed it into every day. The gritty reality of Melbourne, with all of its demands and distractions, was never going to be anything like the gentle pace of life in Tasmania.

The years spent away from England had assured my eligibility and acceptance for Australian residency, so I was free to stay in the country. However I'd eventually have to make a choice about how long I would stay, and determine which would be my future home. My reluctance to relinquish connections with either left me brooding over the decision and agonizing about the right choice. My loyalties were equally divided. England was home, but then so too was Tasmania, and now Melbourne. Home had therefore become a word I used to describe the place in which I was currently living.

We had our first big argument about the ring outside Di and Harve's house. I tried to describe the pressure I was feeling, and the extent of my dilemma.

"Everything's different now. Everything's changed since you asked me. *You've* changed," I insisted.

"Well why don't you give the ring back to me," Mark retorted, "and I'll return it to the shop next time I'm in Perth."

"No! That's not what this is about. I've told you that."

"But you never wear it," he snapped.

"It was just…so…fast. I didn't think we'd be telling everybody straight away."

We were sitting in his car, separated by the console and the lever of the handbrake.

"They kept asking if we were engaged, even when I wore it on my other hand."

"I thought we were," he said, bitterly.

I sighed, thinking of how quickly things had moved since the ring had appeared. There seemed to be a tension between us all the time now.

"We talked about that, and you know how I feel."

"I thought I did," he said pointedly.

"People expect you to get married once you're engaged, and I can't stand everyone asking me about it all the time. They keep pushing things along a bit faster. Dates and dresses and all those things."

"You said *yes*," he was exasperated.

"I know. And I meant it. But not right now. Not yet. I thought it would be in the future, you know, when I have a job, and when we both have some money. I didn't know you'd go out and buy a ring like that."

"But we can still make plans can't we?"

"Why couldn't we have made plans without everybody knowing? Without all the pressure? It's easier for you anyway."

"What d'you mean, easier?"

I didn't intend to sound glib, but he didn't have so many choices pulling him in different directions.

"Mark, all my family are in England. You're asking me to make a commitment to live here, on the other side of the world. It's a huge decision, and I can't promise to do that right now, especially without permanent work. I just don't know what I want to do yet."

"I'd go and live in England with you," he declared.

"You wouldn't," I sighed.

"I would."

"What about the band? I asked, quietly. "You couldn't just leave all this. And I would never ask you to."

I wouldn't have allowed him to let go of his aspirations for the band, but I wondered if the offer was really a token gesture. In reality I doubted he'd abandon his goals, having fought so hard to reach them.

"Everything's so unsettled at the moment," I continued, "I just need to get a job and let things settle down a bit. Get into a routine."

He couldn't hide his frustration.

"Why can't you at least *wear* it, even as a sign of friendship?"

"The ring again," I said, my words coming out like a sigh, "it's not just about that. I haven't changed my mind. I just need a bit more time. I had no idea there'd be such a rush when I said yes. I suppose…I thought…I don't know what I thought."

My voice trailed away. It was a divisive subject. Even though I could see he was upset, I felt compelled to continue.

"I'm just not ready. It's too soon for all of this."

He didn't reply. I tried to think of something more, so he'd understand.

"Look, it's," I thought for a moment, "…it's like asking me to decide if I want my right arm or my left arm." My voice dropped to a whisper. "And I can't. I want both. I don't know what else to tell you."

We seemed to have reached an impasse, unable to solve the question of where our future lay. Before long we stopped searching for a solution, and just left everything unresolved. However, I began to feel an increasing resentment now that this issue had come between us and forced a confrontation. I blamed Mark for not foreseeing the practical obstacles of me living permanently in Australia, a country on the farthest side of the globe; I even blamed him for my own inner struggles, as I tried to balance my needs with his.

As the weeks unfurled, I felt the pressure to constantly prove my commitment, to show it was equal to his, but I just didn't know how to measure it. Having bought the ring, it seemed as if the scales were forever tipped towards Mark, and nothing I could do would ever restore the balance.

One day I received a beautiful photograph of Mark, arriving unexpectedly in the mail. It wasn't one of mine, but I recognised the tenderness in his eyes as he stared at the lens. His face was highlighted by the butter rich hues of autumn sunshine, threading his hair with gold. I wondered where it had been taken.

On the back of the picture he'd written a short comment, his words reminding me of my own when we had argued. It felt like a plea:

'I haven't changed – I still love you.'

Melbourne, May 1990

*Angela J. Dawson*

# Michael and Ballarat

AS WELL as regular gigs there were so many other things happening with the band, and Mark and I allowed ourselves to be distracted, taking the focus away from our personal lives. At The Old Greek Theatre they played the support to Harry Dean Stanton & The Repo Men, after which Martin persuaded Harry to autograph one of the cherished guitars in his collection, his white Rickenbacker, using a thick black marker pen. In July the band spent time in the studio again, working with Producer, Mark Woods at Whirled Records. This time it was for 3RRR. The radio station was producing an album of cover songs, Used And Recovered By, and The Fish had been asked to record their version of the track, *Sooner or Later*. It was good to see them so focussed, and engaged in creating their music, rather than just the grind of continual gigs.

My search for employment had initially resulted in locum physiotherapy work in the city, but this had been cut short when I gained permanent work at a community hospital, north of the city in June, a day before my birthday. It was commonly referred to as PANCH, and the acronym made it much easier than writing the name in full – Preston and Northcote Community Hospital. My days would soon become a ritual of the Sydney Road tram cutting straight up through Brunswick, and then the Bell Street bus, heading east, and stopping outside the hospital doors.

In addition to my new job, I also started black and white photography classes in the city. I was fortunate that I had the band as willing subjects and so many opportunities to practice all the latest techniques. I loved being able to manipulate film, push the processing time, experiment with double exposures. It was like painting with light. Watching the pictures materialise within the trays of chemicals in the darkroom felt nothing short of miraculous. Taking pictures of fast moving figures on a stage, often in near darkness, was an exciting challenge; but it was only in the darkroom that I'd discover any mistakes.

The boys made a surprising announcement in the middle of the year. Andrew had decided to leave the band, and they would need a new bass player.

I thought of all the girls who would be disappointed, the ones who always pressed to the stage and implored him to sing. The boys each had their fans, and losing someone else could affect their future audiences. It meant that Mark would be the only original member of the band now, since even Graham had taken over from Tim, their first drummer. A solution wasn't too far away though, and they'd already initiated plans for the new line-up. The new bass player was a skilled musician and a music journalist, and he would help to consolidate their sound.

Mark had been sharing his flat with Michael, the other half of the Witheford brothers, so it had seemed the natural choice to ask him to join the band, putting the brothers together again for the first time in years. Before Tim had joined The Fish he'd drummed in a Launceston band, Another Script with the two brothers, Michael and Martin. These musical connections stretched far and ran deep.

Andrew's loss could be a chance for the band to embrace a different style and a fresh perspective. Mark had already featured a couple of Michael's compositions at previous gigs. One of them was a beautiful song called *Isobel* that I'd heard them play a couple of times. The change in the band's style was becoming more obvious. They were moving away from the original folk sound, and embracing Michael's interest in English bands with their driving power-pop sound. His addition to the band completed their transformation, and they even began to discuss the possibility of a new name.

THE BOYS HAD decided to welcome Michael by inviting him on-stage at the next gig, allowing Andrew to officially hand over the bass guitar to mark the occasion of his own departure. However, the next gig was in Ballarat rather than at a city venue where they would have had a larger crowd of fans to witness the event.

Mark had invited me to travel with the band to Ballarat so that I could take some photographs of the exchange. I'd been feeling lightheaded for a while and when they arrived to collect me, the floor seemed to tilt when I stood up from the couch. I ignored the sensation as I walked down the long hallway, assuming it was from skipping lunch. We'd be eating after the sound check, and I could wait until then.

Once seated in the minibus the feeling subsided, but every time I moved my head things seemed to wobble slightly. As we headed west of the city, I smoothed out the starched cotton of my frock, listening to the banter as we hit the highway. I'd dressed up for the occasion, having rifled through my wardrobe to select a brightly coloured fifties frock, and a fur trimmed vintage Blin & Blin wool coat.

When we eventually arrived in Ballarat the dizziness returned as soon as I left the bus. I waited for a while, until the boys were busy unloading the equipment and preparing for the sound check, and then slipped away to stretch my legs and have a walk. It was a special night, a chance to showcase the Witheford brothers together for the first time, and I wanted to make sure I'd feel well enough to get through it. Perhaps I'd be able to find a medical clinic nearby if I walked down the street.

Outside, the road stretched out in either direction without even a shop to break the monotony of the line of houses. I looked to the left, and then peered to the right, making a random choice and starting to walk unsteadily along the pavement. It was a pleasant evening, still quite light, and I kept glancing behind me to check the distance that I'd walked, ensuring that the hotel remained in view.

There was a junction at the far end of the road and after a fifteen minute walk I reached it, relieved to see the luminous sign of the Ballarat Hospital a few hundred metres to the left. Being familiar with hospital routine, I knew I could see a doctor in Casualty. However, I hoped it was a quiet night in the emergency room, and the wait would be short.

There were a few people in the waiting area but I had no idea how many others were behind the distant curtained cubicles, further ahead of me in the queue. I addressed the woman behind the counter hopefully.

"Would I be able to see a doctor please?"

She glanced down at her appointment book.

"There's quite a wait, Dear."

"Oh..."

"What's actually the problem?"

I spoke quietly in the hushed waiting room, aware of my voice breaking through the silence.

"I've been feeling dizzy, and I don't really know why; but I've been like this for a few hours now, and it doesn't seem to be going away."

She frowned slightly.

"Just a minute." She glanced over her shoulder, "Hang on."

She walked away from the desk into the department behind her, which was calm and empty, and where nothing seemed to be happening. It always looked deceptive from this side of the desk. Probably behind the curtains people were having a variety of mortal emergencies. Even if tonight, they were having them very, very quietly.

She reappeared at the door adjacent to the counter, clicking it open as she released a button on her side, and surprisingly she then beckoned me through. I was guided by a nurse to the other side, watched by the resentful eyes of people who had been waiting for hours already. I must have looked worse than I thought to have skipped the queue so effectively. Maybe something really was wrong. Maybe something was about to rupture or break, or otherwise fail me.

The nurse chatted to me pleasantly as she steered me into a cubicle and drew the curtain with an efficient swish, asking me to lie down, taking my blood pressure and connecting me to a heart monitor. Then she left me lying on the trolley with a blanket over my legs, promising the Doctor would appear soon. I wasn't sure that all this mechanical scrutiny was really necessary for just a bit of dizziness but perhaps I'd missed something.

Half an hour passed before a young Doctor appeared. I'd been anxiously watching the clock, and hoping Mark wouldn't be too worried about my prolonged absence. I always managed to keep myself occupied during the sound checks but this time I hadn't mentioned where I was going.

The Doctor glanced at my fur trimmed coat with a look which said I was overdressed for an evening in Ballarat, and started to ask a few questions in a bland voice. I explained the sudden dizziness, and the evening drive from Melbourne to Ballarat with the band. He'd been scanning the diagnostic pages of his mental checklist. The mention of musicians had made him hesitate, and

I could see him changing tack.

"Have you been drinking?" His voice was flat, but non-accusing. He was just trying to eliminate one cause.

"No, nothing. I never drink much anyway," I smiled.

"And have you taken anything?"

"No," I responded hastily, retaining a bemused expression.

"Any drugs?"

"No!" I said, more sharply. He'd said drugs; *drugs*, not medication.

"Nothing at all? And you haven't smoked anything either?"

"*No*. I don't smoke."

I frowned. One trip to Mutacia hardly counted.

I shifted uncomfortably, annoyed at his assumption that it must be a self-induced state. Mention of the band had certainly provided the basis for that suspicion.

"No, I haven't smoked, taken, or drunk anything. I just feel a bit dizzy."

He glanced at the heart monitor and moved forward to listen to my breathing and then my heart with his stethoscope. There was nothing to impress him in there, and he continued with a few more possibilities.

"You're not diabetic?"

I shook my head.

"Hmm..." he said, "or on any medication?"

No again. I folded my arms. I wondered if it was appropriate to share my paramedical knowledge at this stage, although I doubted it would improve his opinion of me.

Cleared of relevant organic or narcotic causes, but nevertheless reeling from the implications of social deviancy, I waited for his final diagnosis. He took a small instrument and peered into my ears.

"Hmmmm."

A much longer hmm this time, I thought.

I felt like a miserable fraud. Perhaps there was nothing wrong with me. I was certainly wasting his time when he could be doing things that were more worthy of his qualifications. Returning the instrument to his top pocket, he looked at me like I was a disappointing jigsaw that he had finally finished.

"Otitis media. Ear infection"

I knew he wouldn't appreciate it if I asked him if he was sure.

"Are you sure?"

"Mmm, hmm." The inflection was upwards, signalling that he'd finished dealing with me.

He turned to write on a prescription pad, wilting over the pages and releasing a steady outbreath through his nostrils as if he was slowly deflating. I'd let him down with my dreary ear infection. If only I'd arrived with something more diagnostically challenging, something urgent or life threatening or rampantly contagious. Evidently there were too many quiet nights in Ballarat casualty. My otitis media seemed so inadequate. I wondered whether I should apologise.

Before he wandered off, I accepted the prescribed pills graciously, wanting to appear at least grateful for his ministrations; besides which I wanted to hurry back to the hotel. I'd been away for almost two hours.

After a brisk walk back to the pub, I emerged breathlessly at the top of the stairs just in time to hear the boys playing a song. It usually signified the end of the sound check. Once all the lighting and equipment had been set-up, the boys would be playing-in their guitars to stretch any new strings, and to have the sound levels set at the mixing desk.

The music was resounding thunderously around the empty room, and during the usual preoccupation with drum fill or fold-back on stage it was difficult to attract Mark's attention. After a minute or so he noticed my arrival, and smiled. At the end of the song Mark swung the guitar strap over his head, propping the guitar in its stand. He walked over to me and kissed me lightly on the cheek.

"It won't be busy tonight."

I'd expected some curiosity about my absence. Maybe even some concern.

"That's a shame," I offered.

"What d'you fancy for dinner?" Mark asked, moving towards the door.

I stared at him for a long moment, and then followed.

"I'm starving," Mark continued, glancing back at me.

"Yeah. Me too."

Mark narrowed his eyes, "Are you okay? Sorry it took so long. Did you get bored?"

"No, I had a very interesting walk up the road actually, while you were all busy."

"Oh, great. Did you see anywhere good for dinner?"

"Not really." I was measuring my words carefully, and fiddling with my camera. "Good sound check though? Everything was okay?"

"Yeah, no problems. Come on, let's go and eat."

He held out a hand, and as I reached out I could feel the pinch of one of the adhesive electrodes still stuck on my chest from the heart monitor. I must have missed it in my haste to leave.

"Which way?" he asked, as he steered me out of the hotel.

"Not that way," I said smiling. "There's nothing much down there. Except the hospital."

Witheford Brothers – Martin and Michael, Ballarat

Mark and Martin

*Like Two Mexicans Dancing*

## Making history on Triple J

IT HAD BEEN raining all day. The wheels of the car were making a wet sound on the road, like waves washing on-shore. Mark was driving us to the ABC television studios on Gordon Street in Elsternwick where we planned to meet the rest of the band. It was a dark afternoon in June, and the rain showed no sign of stopping as we entered the studios. In a few hours the band would be making radio history. They'd been invited to take part in Triple J's first ever live broadcast to Tasmania.

The station's broadcast range at that time encompassed Sydney and Melbourne, but this début programme would mark the first time they'd be on the air in the southern state. A local station in Hobart had been equipped to receive the initial transmission, and thereafter Tasmanians would be able to tune in to Triple J on their radios.

Fellow Tasmanians, The Wild Pumpkins At Midnight had been asked to play, as well as Rob Clarkson who appeared with a cleanly shaven head that accentuated his elfin features. There was a crowd of people ready to participate in the broadcast, most of whom I didn't recognise, but the studio was capacious and uncluttered so everyone congregated in the central area, setting up an island of equipment for the rehearsals. I noticed Darren had arrived to help with shifting instruments and assembling the drums, and as everyone made their preparations I melted into the background, moving around with my camera and taking pictures.

Although it was going to be a live broadcast the musicians had to tape their tracks so they could be used for playback during the show. When the Producer indicated he was ready and The Fish were called to start taping, I went in search of the recording booth where I'd be able to watch them on the studio floor. They had six songs to record for their session and I knew it might take a while.

I sat with the Technician at the control panel, watching as the boys donned their headphones, the floor a muddle of electrical cables in snaking highways around their instruments, the excess pooled in neat coils by the drum kit. Mark hadn't told me which songs they'd chosen, but I recognised the introduction when I heard them start to play *Caution Rings*. It was one of Michael's songs, although Mark had changed a couple of lines in the chorus. The narrative of the song was strangely evocative of our first meeting in Launceston, and for this reason it would often bring a pang of nostalgia when I heard the words.

"*...She looked up and moved towards me, slender as a naked flame,
I watched her pass, I couldn't say a word,
I know my fears are quite absurd....*"

If it was on the playlist at one of their gigs I would always watch Mark's face as he scanned the audience to find me. Even in the most crowded venues I would see him searching until we could make eye contact, and he could sing the words to me across the room. It was like a moment of our history being endlessly relived.

From the studio, I saw him looking across to the booth as he sang the refrain, watching me smile at him through the glass. It felt like an affirmation every time he sang it.

"*...With the twelve string overlay, the sixties go straight to my brain,
Makes me think of a brand new colour, makes me think of Angela-la-la...
When caution rings, a bell in my head says 'hold everything',
My paper nerves would tear right up if I talk to her...*"

After the Technician had fiddled around for a few minutes and then indicated they could move on to the next track, I was surprised to hear them begin a gentle love song, *Poetry*. It was a recent composition written by Mark, and the band would have only played it a few times. It was written after a quarrel, and like all good love songs it was filled with remorse and heartache. After we'd reconciled he'd played it to me as we sat on his bed, drawing the melody out of his guitar as he sang softly. It had brought tears to my eyes the way it captured those moments of longing and regret. I was pleased he'd included it for the special broadcast, and I hoped we'd be able to get a copy of the soundtrack so that we'd have an official recording of the song.

Before the end of the session everybody was instructed to congregate around the microphones in the centre of the vast studio. I was told to put down my camera, and technicians and roadies were all instructed to join the group. We were given some lyrics, an unofficial Tasmanian National Anthem that had been written earlier, the words crudely scrawled on sheets of paper, and told to sing for the finale.

After our rousing chorus it was all over. We were free to leave. Yet, in the absence of any cheering or applause, there was nothing by which to gauge the performance. It seemed an abrupt ending. In the huge, empty studio everything felt strangely quiet and disconnected. During a gig it was the crowd that always conveyed the mood of the show. Without them all you had was the silence. Somewhere out there lay our unseen audience. The broadcast may have been a landmark occasion, but it could just as easily have been transmitted unnoticed into the world.


Walking away into the night along the quiet streets, packing guitars and drums into cars, I could feel a light rain still falling delicately in the darkness. I narrowed my eyes and cast a look back towards the studio, but it looked closed and dark. I tried to imagine the sound engineer inside, filing-away the taped recording of the session, perhaps boxing a spool or a cassette and cataloguing it with hundreds of others.

The Fish had completed so many different musical recordings over the years. They'd made local and interstate radio appearances and done newspaper interviews, they'd been photographed and videotaped. Hours of Mark's life had been preserved like this.

"It must be weird," I began, "being able to re-live moments of your life, you know, from all the recordings and pictures."

"Yeah, so you can remember all the bad hair days and daggy clothes you used to wear," Mark laughed. "How about this - I actually saw *Left* on Rage the other night."

I was still living in Tasmania when they'd been making their black and white video in Melbourne. It was submitted to Rage, the legendary late night music programme, around the time they released their single, *Left/Childless Mother*. It had been a model of budget movie making, showing the boys assembling a go-kart, riding it through the city and then crashing it at the end of the song.

"It's all good exposure if it gets you a deal in the end," I suggested.

"You know, Jeremy thinks Mushroom might be showing some interest in taking-on Helvelln," Mark said, referring to the record label.

"That's great! Have they made an offer?"

"Not yet, but it sounds hopeful. And not only that…John said they might have something going on soon as well."

John was Mark's upstairs neighbour, and keyboard player in the band, FOM.

"I'm sorry," I said quietly. It would be so difficult being on the side-lines and watching everyone else get ahead.

"No, it's good. It's okay," he said, smiling, "I'm really happy for them."

"Do you think the new line-up might make a difference for you?" I was thinking of the Withefords.

"Yeah, I think it'll give us chance to try something new, you know, with Michael's songs."

It was time to change and adapt. Their music was already evolving and taking them in a new direction. They had different players now, even though their goals were the same. Martin and Michael were bound to each other as brothers, but they also shared a musical history. They came from that complex web of musicians, a collective that kept expanding and overlapping, and remodelling itself. It felt like a solid foundation on which to build the band's future.

I peered through the fogged up car windows as we drove away from the studio, trying to visualise the transformation that lay ahead, and how it might alter the course of Mark's life. He was my link to all of this, the one that kept me connected to this network of people. By choosing to align my life with his I'd already accepted that I would need to embrace the challenges they all faced. As they reinvented themselves I knew I would also need to adapt and evolve if I was to continue on the journey, but I was compelled to see it through. I had made my commitment and I had unswerving faith in their ability.

## Poetry

*You don't need a knife to cut me up;*
*Just say nothing, I'll turn it to something,*
*Before I mess it up.*
*I don't need a knife to cut you up, just one misplaced word,*
*And that's enough.*
*I couldn't tell a lie, I didn't want to hurt you;*
*It's so unkind when honesty, it turns against you.*

*You don't need an axe to break my heart;*
*Just say nothing, I'll turn it to something,*
*Before the teardrops start.*
*I don't need an axe to break your heart, just one misplaced word,*
*And that's a start.*
*I couldn't tell a lie, a twisted kind of virtue,*
*Bitter, on my tongue, and it flies through the air;*
*Now I don't deserve you.*

*I feel that I've found some truth, and now I live a lie;*
*I betrayed you, hope betrayed me,*
*I kiss it all goodbye.*
*All I need*
*To make me bleed*
*Is a story,*
*A picture,*
*A memory,*
*A photograph,*
*Poetry.*

Song, *Poetry* copyright © Mark Narkowicz

ABC studios – Darren, below R

The Wild Pumpkins At Midnight, ABC studios

*Angela J. Dawson*

# Counting Down

JUNE brought another opportunity their way, something that would be remembered as a highpoint for the band. I was at work when I heard the news, but I could hardly believe it, sharing my excitement with anyone who would listen.

The Fish had secured a guest appearance on ABC television's *Countdown Revolution*. This was the thing that could finally open so many doors.

I didn't grow up watching Molly Meldrum hosting *Countdown*, the original incarnation, but there would be few people who hadn't heard of him. His 30 minute show had aired at 6:30pm on weeknights, and had been the most popular music program on television, maintaining a huge audience. It was filmed at Melbourne's Metro nightclub and featured a high number of Australian acts, which consequently got the attention of local radio programmers who followed Molly's instinct for the next best thing.

It had all ended in July 1987, after 14 seasons, and more than 500 episodes, but in its heyday it was considered the best platform to get noticed, and it had been the perfect showcase for many bands to launch their careers. Local and international acts had often hosted an episode, but it was Molly's shambling monologues that were remembered, and which had ultimately endeared him to just about everybody.

When the idea was resurrected and it returned as *Countdown Revolution* the concept was short lived. It began in July 1989, with programmes hosted by Tania Lacy and Mark Little. By then Molly had moved on to prime time television for *Hey Hey It's Saturday,* although he still had some contact with the programming schedule as a consultant. By the end of 1990 it would all be over.

It was in these final months of the show, just before its demise, that The Fish had appeared playing their latest single *The Orchard*. At the time the hosts were involved in an on-air protest, taking issue with ABC's policies that barred live performance and forced bands to mime to their own backup tracks. For a breathless moment the boys were asked to support the industrial action, effectively cancelling their own appearance. But they weren't about to be remembered for contesting policy.

The hosts were ultimately fired by the ABC for their unauthorised campaign, but the show continued on for several months until it was finally cancelled in December. The Fish at least had had their chance to be part of it all.

When the programme screened, the camera panned over a crowded studio as the song began. Walking slowly through the dense audience playing their guitars, the Witheford brothers joined Mark and Graham on stage, with Andrew featuring as an extra on tambourine and harmonica. There was a lot of hair and heavy fringes, and a surreal rolling footage of leaves and trees playing out in the background, and they'd also included some Lees Orchards signs on stage. In the end Mark did a very effective job of lip synching and making it look like he was singing live, even in the close-ups.

I couldn't help wondering which industry moguls might be watching the show, which record labels might be contemplating signing-up the band and preparing their contracts. The boys just had to be tenacious now, and wait for the right offer.

For Mark, I knew it was a dream realised, appearing on a show that he'd watched as a child, but it was only one ambition from a list of many yet to be fulfilled.

There they were on national television, The Fish John West Reject, at last. Could this really be their moment that I was watching? My fair haired busker had become a television star.

*Angela J. Dawson*

ROCK

# FISH MOLLY MELDRUM ACCEPTED

**Funny name, deadly serious attitude.**

**The Fish John West Reject have had a slow haul in gaining the respect they deserve, but mainstream success is looming.**

**The Tasmanian quartet has always been embraced by the west, and next week The Fish visit Perth for their fourth tour in 12 months. MICHAEL DWYER reports.**

Picture this.

You're sitting at home watching *Countdown Revolution*, hoping the neighbours can't hear you, when suddenly you're attacked by fish. No, just any fish, but four fish John West had the common decency to reject.

Lead singer of said fish, Mark Narkowicz, is sheepish about his band's tentative foray into mass culture, but ultimately unapologetic.

"Yeah, it's one of those things you dream about when you're a kid but when you finally get there you do wonder, 'hey, am I perhaps a bit of a dickhead being on this show?'

"No, really, the whole Countdown team was really good," he says defiantly. "They work very hard to make you look as good as possible, very friendly and very concerned about everything. I admire the way they've taken the time out for a lot of young bands to get national exposure — and Countdown's still the best national exposure a band can get.

"Sea Stories, Killjoys and us are three bands who are on the verge of mainstream success, and Countdown has given us that break. It's a great way of getting to that under 18 audience too, because otherwise they just don't see you.

"I used to be easy to work out where a band fit in the grand scheme of things and Countdown was a major reference point. Today, it's not so easy. The Fish John West Reject are hardly mainstream, but surely they deserve a break as much, if not more than Mossy."

The opportunity arose and The Fish leapt, fins aquiver. It was a remarkably pragmatic, business-like act for a definitively 'Left' band (indeed, that was the name of their first single), and a band which many still ignorantly throw into the 'novelty basket'.

"Our name has caused us some problems," Mark explains. "Sydney has been the hardest one to crack for us, Perth and Melbourne were relatively easy. In Sydney the press was really scornful at first — I think because of our name — until they sent somebody down to see us live. It's taken us about eight trips to get a bit of respect and a decent following there."

Respect is in no short supply from the converted Perth has embraced The Fish in three tours since June last year, and the fourth gets underway next week. The band's debut album, *Swim*, was widely praised for its striking originality and intelligence. Consequently major label interest is brewing and The Fish aren't being too precious about their Indie roots.

"If any band was offered a major record deal compared to an indie deal they'd be mad not to take it, depending on how good the deal was," Mark says. "If it's $100,000 compared to $20,000 you'd be silly not to consider it.

"And it doesn't mean you're selling out," he says, pre-empting criticism from the 'serious music' subculture which often equates success with a lack of quality. "Plenty of bands' make the switch and still maintain their integrity. It's a question of whether you make good music or bad music, and we make good music.

Today the good music is in the hands of a new line-up, brothers Martin and Michael Whiteford taking over from the recently departed Mark Adams and Andrew Viney.

"Andrew left in May," remaining Mark (Narkowicz) explains. "He made the honourable decision to be a full time father rather than a full time musician. And Mark Adams was replaced. That's all I'm going to say about that."

Replacing half the band has obviously had some effect on The Sound Of Fish.

"It has definitely become more electric based," Mark agrees. "The mandolin and harmonica have gone. I still play the acoustic guitar but Martin has a stupendous electric guitar collection ranging from a Gretsch Country Gentleman to a Gretsch White Falcon to a Rickenbacker 330 with three pick ups and a whammy bar... Martin's a collector. It's definitely more important that he looks good.

"Also there's more influence from newer music, Michael being an ex-rock journalist is very up on a lot of current stuff, especially English bands. I guess now we're all real music lovers, whereas before only half the band was interested in a lot of new music.

"I've it's still really dynamic, really energetic, as it always has been," Mark is quick to point out, "but the band's a bit tougher now. We still keep that thrashabilly kick thing, but it's far more a guitar pop band now. Quite Technicolor guitar pop.

So when choosing new band members, what does a Rejected Fish look for in another Rejected Fish?

"It's all a matter of whether they're Tasmanian first, Mark explains, getting all parochial, whether they have a scar on their shoulder where the extra head was removed... then I guess it's to do with the state of the fish's gills, the bowels, how much sewer sludge is in there from the Tamar River, they're all mitigating factors in choosing a Rejected Fish.

"What about musical prowess?

"Nah, bollocks."

*The Fish John West Reject. In Perth from August 3.*

## Like Two Mexicans Dancing

**B**ETWEEN tours Mark and I took short trips, driving out of the city to visit the National Parks or heading for the sea, seeking air and open spaces. It allowed us to get away from the schedule of gigs and allowed some normality out of the spotlight, away from people and performance and noisy smoke-filled hotels. When we went west around the Bay, we'd head for the surfing town of Torquay then follow the endless, narrow ribbon of the Great Ocean Road and its beautiful coastal scenery.

Hugging the cliff edges it was a road that cornered precariously, cutting narrow turns and tight hairpin bends as it scribbled along the coastline, overlooking open sea that rolled in from the Bass Strait. Surf beaches, bushwalking tracks and campsites dotted the seaside towns, and the backdrop of State Parks promised hidden waterfalls and lookouts. Sometimes from the curve of the hills hang-gliders would be hovering, catching the updrafts coming in from the sea, their coloured sails drifting down like sky confetti.

In Lorne, the stately Erskine House became our favourite place to stay in the off-peak season. It was a huge, old fashioned guest house set in its own grounds, its six hectares of immaculate gardens encompassing tennis courts and trim lawns on which you could play croquet. Inside, the three storey brick residence was equally spacious, with long echoing corridors and more than 30 rooms within its sprawling configuration. The vast ground floor dining area was as big as a ballroom and overlooked the rear lawns and the open ocean, its long trestle tables laid in an open plan configuration with rows of bench style seating so that everyone breakfasted together. It reminded me of school days, walking across the wide room to fill my plate.

In late autumn or winter the town would be relatively deserted and we could chase across the beach within metres of the rear lawns, zigzagging across the whipping sand often with only hardy dog-walkers for company, feeling the nip of the sea breeze as it dashed under fast-moving clouds.

If it rained, there was a free standing shed in the garden that contained a damp and musty games room, and in there we could flail through endless rounds of table tennis as our breath misted in the chilly air. Or we would rummage around for the heavy black lawn bowls, the golf putters, or the croquet mallets so we could play on the lawns before the thin wintery sun set on the horizon. But on a cold evening it was the deep vintage baths in the communal bathrooms that offered the most relaxing and hedonistic diversion. We loved the antiquated washrooms at intervals along the corridors, with their frosted glass and inscribed door panels, still separating the Ladies from the Gentlemen. We could have a bathroom each.

The guest house had retained the old style lavatories and porcelain fixtures, the wide pedestal hand basins, and the enameled cast iron baths that were so deep you could fill the water up to your chin. At that time of year there were few visitors and we knew we wouldn't be disturbed, so we could each have a long soak, slapping the adjoining wall between us as we had boisterous conversations.

There were cafes along the beachfront, and dinner was usually a late dash across the road for freshly grilled fish and chips folded into paper, their radiant heat warming our hands as we ate them on the darkened beach. But we didn't embrace any of the Lorne nightlife at the bars and hotels. With so few occasions to share a bed, we chose to spend the evenings in our simple room with just a bed and wooden furniture in which to store our clothes. We'd curl in our beachside bed and listen to the gossiping waves bringing us endless rumours of the sea, talking to us until we fell asleep. We were just the city flotsam, washing up for the weekend, and leaving on the next tide.

IN JULY, with the snow season underway, Darren had finally taken a step back from the band and started to pursue his other dreams. I never had the chance to ask him, but maybe he had finally become a ski instructor. We certainly saw less of him. I wondered whether all the changes to the line-up, especially the loss of Mark Adams, had been the catalyst for his decision. It was a different band now, and perhaps being their Roadie held less appeal if it meant foregoing those friendships. It was another absence that I felt keenly, and I knew that everyone would miss him at future gigs.

The machine of touring continued, the band travelling the full span of the country to the far western shores, and then across to Sydney in the east. While they were in Perth they spent time in Planet Studios recording *Exile/Sick Inside*, planning to release a single and also an EP, using additional tracks that they'd recorded in February at Whirled Records in Melbourne.

It was exciting to see them pressing more vinyl and embracing their recent transformation. The tracks *Sick Inside* and *Mother Hold My Calls* were instantly recognisable as Michael's compositions, melodic and haunting, and leaning towards the British sound. I could imagine them being played on the radio in Manchester. Even the covers reminded me of the sort of artwork being featured on album covers by bands like The Smiths, who favoured legendary stars of the screen like James Dean and Alain Delon. The Fish single featured Pier Angeli.

One afternoon, as the daylight hours began to lengthen at last and our thoughts turned to spring, I found an envelope in the mail from Mark. Inside was a short poem that he'd written for me. It sounded like a pledge, and it was a tribute to how far we'd come.

> without question
> you took my hand
> and led me into a dream
> a reality
> a mystery
> my destiny…
> as freely as you give your love
> equally I give my thanks
> without question
> you became the answer
>
> (August 1990)

EP cover for Sick Inside / Exile

## Sleeve details

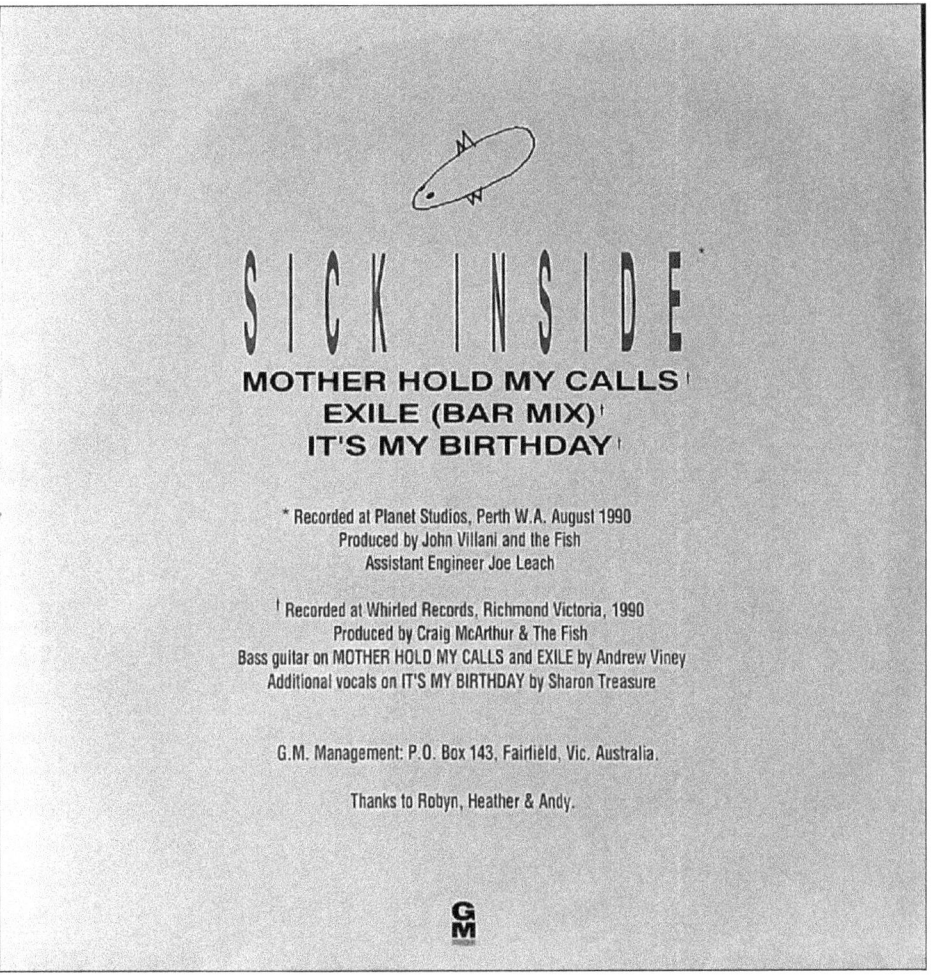

7 inch single cover – Exile / Twenty Ways

Dear Ange,
From your #1 fan... with love,
Monkey
xxx

*Angela J. Dawson*

# Roddy and Parkville

ON THE VERY last day of winter on the 31ˢᵗ of August, Mark and I were standing inside The Palace in St Kilda on a cool Friday evening. We were waiting for a twenty six year old from Glasgow to begin his performance, and we were both beyond excited to be there. Mesmerised, we watched as he stepped up to the microphone with his guitar.

"Hello, I'm Roddy Frame," he announced, from under a choppy fringe.

That night was a high point, getting to see the only Aztec Camera gig in Melbourne. It was their Stray tour, promoting their fourth album of the same name with just one gig at The Palace. It began with Roddy's acoustic set, a Bob Dylan song, "…for my friend at the front, Barry," and a slightly different rendition of *Birth of the True*.

"This is the 90's version…so you can all take drugs and smile at each other."

As he strummed his guitar the band gradually joined him onstage, keyboard first, bass, guitar, and finally drums, filling the place with sound, right up to the high ceiling.

Gary Sanford played like a legend, dipping his guitar and tossing a mass of golden hair, breezing through *Oblivious* and *Walk out to Winter*. We recognised *Crying Scene*, and watched Roddy put down his guitar and move up to the microphone for the lyrical, *How Men Are*.

There was no sign of Mick Jones when they started *Good Morning Britain*. Roddy had asked the guitarist from The Clash to perform the song with him as a duet in the European leg of the Stray tour, but it was a long flight for one song. We hadn't expected him.

Two hours later they were swooping through a charged encore of *How It Is* to fortify us for our journey home. We spilled out into the cool sea air, filled with lofty thoughts and the usual aspirations. Mark would have loved to play the coveted support act for such an illustrious band, but it was as close as we'd get.

*

DURING the initial weeks of spring that followed, there were changes to my home life. The routine of full time work and a permanent contract had brought a sense of stability, at least in one area of my life. I had enough income now to consider something beyond my current room and board.

I found lodgings in an adjacent suburb, moving to the Parkville residence in which a few years later I would begin to write this story; the big, old terraced house with cast iron railings on the balcony upstairs, overlooking the grounds of the Royal Melbourne Hospital. The street intersected the tree lined avenue of Royal Parade, where trams rattled past the University campus and on to the nearby city. Back then it was the ideal location. It was close enough for forays to Brunswick Street, for insomniac excursions to cafes and music venues, and to view the succession of gigs at The Punters Club, only minutes away. It was also only a short tram ride up towards Sydney Road and Brunswick, where I could alight and walk to Mark's flat; or during the week I could continue north to Bell Street for work.

Since my move to Melbourne fourteen months ago I'd relocated my belongings to four different addresses, and spent time in England and Tasmania. Although an itinerant lifestyle held some appeal for me, the sheer size of the sprawling metropolis and its unlimited choices had made it difficult to settle. With so much practice, I'd become skilled at living out of a bag.

I saw my move to Parkville as a chance to unpack, an opportunity to further my own social network, and a chance to finally step outside our network of friends. Having lived in Nurses' accommodation for so long, I had little to offer in terms of kitchenware or other household items; but moving into shared accommodation meant that I needed few possessions. Mark's situation was similar. He had a mattress and a few personal effects, but his flat was light and airy, and fitted with built in wardrobes, blinds and storage cupboards. Nothing else was needed, and by maintaining a Spartan lifestyle it made it easier for both of us to move out at any time. Perhaps the austerity of our lifestyles said more about the impermanence of our existence and the uncertainty about the band; a truth that I strived to ignore. We all expected them to succeed.

But for the first time I had chosen a place of my own. It wasn't in residential accommodation, or someone else's spare room, and although this was a step towards establishing myself in the city, I was aware of an underlying ambivalence about it. It would be inaccurate to call it homesickness, which implies a yearning for a place. My longing was more about the concept of home, and the feeling of belonging.

News from England filtered across to me via blue Airmail letters, and in the evenings I hungrily scanned the television news reports for global content. I didn't have any plans to go back, but I hadn't reconciled the dilemma about staying either.

International phone calls were expensive even with a landline into the house, which meant I still had to watch the clock as I chatted. I no longer had to save coins but I still had to wait for the cheaper rates. Contact felt metered-out and rationed, and staying in touch was constrained by geography, time zones and costs. Even the tremulous vibrato of the dial tone sounded faraway, purring on the open line like a distant fuzz of static, like the trill of a contented cat when I held the receiver to my ear as I dialled. In the evenings, it would be office hours in England and no-one would be home, which left the weekends to try and reach friends and family. Our disparate lives were divided by so many continents, and as I tried to work within the constraints of the time differences I often felt the distance acutely.

Living in a house that was owned by the University and which also stood opposite the campus made it relatively easy to get flatmates. When someone moved in with an Apple Macintosh we were fascinated by its capability and its bulky boxed monitor. We were still hand writing notes in patients' files at the hospitals, and I didn't know anyone who had a personal computer at home, or who could actually touch type. Everything about operating this oversized device seemed complicated and laborious, and the rest of us would peer at its screen warily, wondering exactly how to use its complex and sluggish search engine. We weren't amongst the people who knew anything about the internet, a concept that was on the cusp of its inception and wasn't publicly available anyway. In fact it would be another year until the World Wide Web went live across the globe, in August 1991.

At the end of September I had an invitation from some friends in my photography class. They'd secured tickets for The Big Gig on ABC television, and suggested Mark and I join them in the cramped studio for the filming of an episode in the fourth series. The sketch show had been running since 1989 with stand-up comedians like Glynn Nicholas and Wendy Harmer, and there were regular feature acts.

We had Flacco wearing his kilt and shrieking his strange observations, his face a cadaverous white, a single black curl of hair fashioned like a huge question mark on his bald head.

"My, nothing flies when you're not having any…" he observed.

But it was the Allstars who stole the show. When I saw the trio across the studio in their military style uniforms I nudged Mark.

"The Doug Anthony Allstars. I saw them last year. A few days after I met you actually."

"In Launceston?"

"In Hobart. They were busking. We didn't know who they were then. It was New Year's Eve," I said. "We'd gone down in Cecil, for the fireworks." Mark looked blank. "You know, James' car - Cecil," I added.

"Oh, right."

We'd spent the morning in Salamanca browsing the market, and had been drawn to a huge crowd and the sound of live music. It was Paul, Tim and Richard singing and bantering, performing choreographed routines as they played, lampooning onlookers who dared to stop.

"They were really funny," I whispered, keeping an eye on the boom sweeping over our heads in the studio. "At the end, they told us to throw $2 coins at Paul's head…"

Mark shot me a look.

"…wrapped in five dollar notes though. That's what they told us to do. They got a lot of money."

They were so good that we ended up buying tickets for their show that evening at The Peacock Theatre.

Technicians in headphones were hovering around the monitors, and I could see them speaking with Glynn Nicholas.

"Six degrees," I hissed, thinking of all the connections.

"What?"

"Of separation. Less actually. From you to Harve and Di, then Scott, and then Glynn Nicholas." It felt like I'd been standing in that outer circle right from the beginning, moving towards Mark and his friends, drawn to this destination.

The taping had taken a few hours, and despite the laughter and high spirits Mark hadn't said much.

"What's the matter?" I whispered.

"Nothing," he said but he was slumped down in his seat, hands in his pockets.

"You've hardly said a word to my friends all night," I ventured.

In a couple of days he would be leaving again, to spend a week in Sydney with the band.

"Is it the tour?" I prompted. "I thought you'd be looking forward to the trip?"

If I hadn't been working, I would have loved to go on tour with him again.

"Can we get going now? I'm really tired," he said. He had an edge to his voice. People around us were starting to file out from the studio, and as we left our row, Mark hung back, standing behind me as I thanked my friends for organising the evening. Outside, my irritation flared.

"They wanted to know about the band. Couldn't you have made a bit of effort?"

"It was the same old questions."

"They were just interested," I said, but he shrugged dismissively, "and it would have been nice to have more than one word answers."

His strange mood had eclipsed the evening, and we parted on bad terms. I regretted my temper later, knowing that I wouldn't see Mark for a week. Life on the road was not as glamorous as many people expected. I'd experienced their schedule first hand and I knew it could be gruelling, with limited funds for any real comforts. Making enough money to sustain the band and keep them financially afloat was a constant stress for all of them. Poorly attended gigs, inadequate equipment, bad mixes, delays, late nights. There could be so many unforeseen events that could affect the quality of their performance and influence how the band was received by an audience. Mark rarely burdened me with that sort of information. There was a lot at stake, and many things that were outside their control. I had no idea of the pressures they were facing at the moment. I hadn't even asked.

*

THE REMAINING months of the year started to gather a more positive momentum. Harve had returned to playing live, deciding it was time to come out of musical abstinence. His new band, Tender Engines made their debut at The Tote in Collingwood in September, with Andrew as his bass player, the gig including appearances by The Sugargliders, Captain Cocoa and The Fish.

In November The Fish went back into the studio for a full fifteen days to record tracks for their second album, *Fin* at Whirled Records. Jeremy from Helvelln joined them on guitar for one of the tracks, and John from FOM was featured playing keyboards. It felt like progress.

It would have been a great debut release if they'd been picked up by a label, but there was no-one knocking at the door yet, no contracts looming. In the end, it was released and distributed by Shock Records, giving them all the assurances of a local independent label, and someone who was a friend to the band. They'd still have to promote the album and fund the next round of touring, but perhaps having Harve looking out for them was better than being with a major label; better than ending up as just small fish in a big pond.

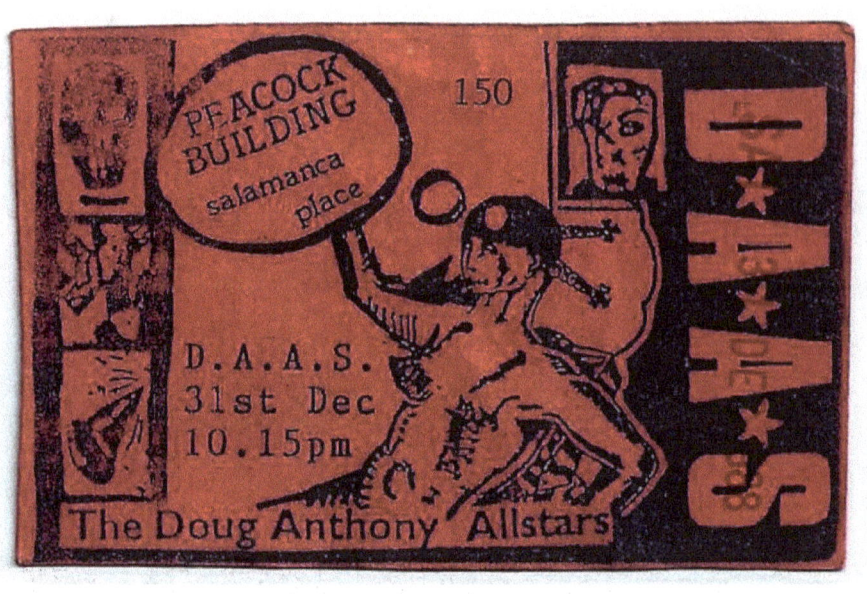

New Year's Eve 1988: Ticket for Doug Anthony Allstars, Hobart

## Bananas and sugar cane

THE HEAT was escalating rapidly as Mark and I left Melbourne and headed north in the red Gemini towards Dubbo. We were on our way to the 35km strip of beaches that comprised The Gold Coast in Queensland. It was only the first week of December but we hadn't expected the temperatures to be so high when we'd planned our road trip, and we were already too warm in T-shirts and shorts, even with all the car windows wound down.

"Go on, shoot!" Mark yelled over the noise of the racing engine as we gunned along the highway.

"Where do you want it first?" I shouted back.

"Here," he said, pointing at his face.

"Take off your sunglasses then," I hollered back at him, in a moment of clarity. I wanted to be careful that I didn't obscure his vision while he was driving.

I pressed the trigger, and pumped it a few times in his direction.

"Fantastic!" he roared, turning his face from side to side.

To cope with the heat we were dousing ourselves with a fine mist of water from a plastic spray-bottle. It made our bare arms and legs glisten, cooled our faces and necks, and quickly evaporated in the muggy air blasting from the car vents and the open windows. We'd also laid towels over the car seats to avoid any skin contact when the vinyl became blisteringly hot.

It would take two full days of driving to reach our destination, crossing a couple of thousand kilometres of open, dry Australian countryside. From the car I watched the plane of the flat horizon, scattered with a ground mosaic of open grassy vegetation from sun blanched shades of green to the colour of straw. Sometimes there were scraggly gum trees giving dappled shade to whatever sought it, the twisted limbs of Eucalyptus crouching at lean-to angles, wind-blown shapes on the hardened dirt. But mostly there was an absence of tree canopy, with various types of tussock grasses sprouting in thick clumps and tufts, some of them high enough to graze your knees with their spindly blades. Spring wildflowers still dotted their yellow and pink petals amongst the stiff spears, and there were fluffy fuzzed pompoms of Wallaby grass that made me think of dandelion clocks. I wondered whether you could scatter their downy heads too, with a single breath.

As we left the outskirts of Melbourne I glanced at Mark, his hair lashing around his head in the air streaming in from the windows. The noise of the engine together with the clashing air currents around us made talking difficult unless I raised my voice, and so I'd just been watching the familiar Victorian landscape unfold as we travelled up towards the border of New South Wales, letting the warm wind rush across my face and over my hot skin.

Receding into the distance I could see the electricity pylons slowly diminishing in size, their outstretched limbs holding the power lines aloft in sagging continuity. The exactness of their spacing and the repetition of their outline across the horizon was somehow reassuring. They were a familiar sight and part of the view whenever we travelled around Victoria, but I'd never given them more than a fleeting glance. I let my eyes linger on them, studying their metal outline and looking at them with renewed interest as I absorbed their unusual shape.

"Check out the pylons," I mouthed, pointing out of the window to the right.

Mark followed the direction indicated by my finger, but waited for me to continue, his face attentive.

"What d'you think they look like?" I continued.

He scanned them briefly and shrugged as he flicked his eyes back to the road.

"They look Mexican," I called back, leaning in to him so I could be heard.

He shook his head and frowned at me slightly to indicate he didn't understand.

"Look at the shape they make," I replied loudly, intrigued that I'd never noticed it before.

Mark let his eyes sweep across them a couple of times.

"They look like two Mexicans dancing, don't you think?" I asked, straining to be heard.

The shape of each pylon comprised an elongated hat shared by two bodies, their hips bumped together as if frozen in some dance, an arm thrown up on either side in a carefree salute. Mark was scrutinising them more carefully now.

"Can you see it? That bit's the hat, like a sombrero, and then the two bodies are joined at the hip?"

"Oh yeah. They do…." he said from under his wind jostled hair.

"I wonder why they're like that?" I shouted. "It can't be a random shape."

"Who knows?" He shrugged and let a smile creep across his face.

I watched them prancing across the horizon, getting gradually smaller on the unravelling terrain. It was like a winding conga line of dancers, a stolen moment from a fiesta. It made such a joyful image. The thick wires looping them together looked like veins, carrying power and light, keeping us all alive and connected. They'd always been there, dancing across the fields as we travelled the highways, threaded through the background, amongst the abundance of detail that we regularly failed to see.

Now that I'd noticed their distinctive features it had brought them to life. I turned my head as they began to fall behind us at last, a symbol of the things we took for granted even when they were right in front of us. I glanced at Mark, reaching across and letting my hand linger on his leg as he drove.

We'd navigated our way through to the end of another year, even if some things remained unresolved. For the next couple of weeks there would just be the two of us on the road, a chance to remember those early days in Tasmania and all the reasons we'd fallen in love.

"What's up ma'friend?" he asked, his words scattering across the air.

"I just can't believe I've never noticed them before."

"The Mexicans?" he teased. "I bet no-one has."

Leaning across, I brushed my lips against Mark's cheek. My hand was still on his thigh and I left it there, holding on, despite my fingers becoming clammy against his skin. After a moment I felt him place his left palm over my hand, letting it sit with mine as he drove.

Like the songs and the photographs, and like Orion, the Mexicans too would become part of our story. Even as the dancing pairs disappeared into the distance, their silent exhilaration stayed with me, opening my eyes to the life I had chosen. They were a symbol of the hidden joys everywhere, the opportunities we can so easily miss, and the privileges within our grasp that we often take for granted. I was glad of their presence on the landscape, as a warning against complacency.

I looked down at Mark's hand on mine, feeling the heat between us, remembering the moment we'd driven away from the orchard in Dilston on that dark evening. With my hand in his that first time, neither of us had wanted to let go. I was glad that it still felt the same.

*

The Newell Highway was taking us up through New South Wales where we planned to stay the night in Dubbo. The asphalt surface of the road was broken centrally by an intermittent white line and bordered by a solid stripe that indicated the edge of the highway. To the outside of that was the ragged edge of the bitumen where it met the dry earth, our tyres forming clouds of dust and grit if we strayed too far over the line. With only one lane in either direction it didn't fit my image of a major road across the state, and its untidy edges made it look like it had been constructed in a hurry.

But as we travelled over miles of flat, parched land I began to realise that in such desolation and unrelenting heat the construction of any road was an achievement, particularly with the scarcity of towns, or even service stations. We frequently drove more than a hundred kilometres between isolated townships, the road stretching into the distance in an uninterrupted straight line, across nothing but open space.

For a while there was just native grass forming a golden swell in the breeze, the road edged with wire fencing that had been stretched between rough wooden posts; but as we headed north east to Narrandera, groups of scattered gum trees broke the flat line between land and sky, and there were spindly bushes that were hardened to the arid climate. Power lines sagged loosely from post to post, their wires drooping lazily between T-shaped wooden poles rising askew from the ground, each one leaning precariously into the level distance.

At times we saw huge grass seeds like giant dandelion clocks rolling across the road; tumbleweeds that made the isolated landscape look like a deserted film set for a western, the scene overhung by a rich blue sky that held staggered layers of cloud formations.

By early evening we'd reached the old gold town of Forbes where Ned Kelly's sister was buried, stopping at the RSL Club for Sunday dinner with the locals, and sitting amongst the rows of white tables and plastic chairs with all the other weary travellers.

Eventually, having followed our progress across several maps as Mark drove, I could see we were nearing Dubbo in the darkness of the late evening. We cruised the streets looking for our motel, feeling the heat still floating up from the warm pavements and hot concrete. Although we unloaded our bags wearily at the reception of the Dubbo Palms Motor Inn, we couldn't resist sliding into the swimming pool outside, gliding quietly across the calm water and letting it cool our hot skin. Our limbs were cramped from hours of driving, and we could think of no better way to end the day, drifting on the surface of the chilled pool, and listening to the rub of insects humming under a huge canopy of stars.

The next day it was predictably warm again and it was difficult to leave the air conditioned room for the relative discomfort of a hot car. We would soon be heading up to the mountains where the air was cool, but first we were staying with Mark's grandparents for a couple of days, and that meant travelling on towards the Gold Coast with a few detours en route. Taking the Oxley Highway and then the unsealed roads to Warrumbungle National Park we drove the winding lanes, kicking up grit and dirt as we passed tree covered rock formations whose rippled shapes hinted of their volcanic past.

Stark against the blue sky we finally sighted the white dome of the observatory, taking in the panoramic view from the rocky landscape of Siding Springs, visiting its massive telescope and filling our heads with stories of quasars and distant galaxies.

Mark's European grandparents had refused to ever acclimatise to the heat and humidity of Queensland, living in a fully air conditioned unit which they rarely left, complete with enormous ceiling fans like huge plane propellers. They also had a small swimming pool in the back garden, and when we arrived in the evening, we tipped ourselves into the plunge pool despite the late hour, revelling in the gentle buoyancy after the confinement of the car. Even in the humid darkness I was planning my next dip.

In the morning I joined Mark's Grandmother for a swim in the brash sunlight, slopping my wet arms out of the water and over the rim of the pool as we wallowed and chatted. She got out when Mark appeared, stepping from the hot concrete into her plastic sandals before heading in for her morning coffee. Glancing back at us, I saw her frown at the spot where I was gripping the poolside, the water from my hands spreading and blurring on the ground. In an instant she'd bolted, and within three strides she was over me, with a leg poised, ready to strike.

"Hah!" she said, narrowly missing my fingers and slapping her shoe down.

I jumped back as she turned on her heel and retreated inside, leaving me squinting in the reflected light. Mark was backstroking in dizzying circles around the perimeter of the tiny pool as I turned to look at him. It made me think of a fly caught in a glass of water.

"What did I do?"

I heaved myself up so I could peer at the ground next to the pool. Within an inch of where my hands had gripped the side lay the remains of a squashed spider. I sized up the scrambled pieces, trying to work out its other two dimensions.

"I think that might've been a Redback," I said, sliding back into the water.

"I'd say so," he replied.

With its red striped abdomen tucked menacingly out of sight, the coin sized black spider would have been completely hidden to anyone in the pool.

Mark was diving and surfacing, puffing wide sprays of water from his mouth as he released each breath.

"Aren't they the small, venomous ones?" I asked.

"They're deadly," he said earnestly, buzzing across the pool.

I shuddered at the thought. The Redback was a relative of the American Black Widow spider.

"Well look how close it was to my hand," I fussed, indicating the drying handprints, "it could have bitten me."

"Nanna's fearless isn't she?"

He released a big breath with a loud gasp as he surfaced again somewhere near my feet, but it sounded more like laughter to me. He wrapped his arms around my waist as we floated together.

"Let's go and explore," he said, kissing my neck gently and sweeping me round in circles.

"As long as there's somewhere to swim so we can keep cool."

"We are cool...we're groovy...we're..."

But I'd pushed him under the water and he was pretending to drown, blowing bubbles to the surface.

A morning on Main beach proved too hot for our pale skins and we soon headed back to his grandparent's unit so we could visit the nearby Sanctuary Cove for lunch, a new complex that we'd discovered at the waterside. It was a modern development comprising shops and a golf course, and it had various restaurants and hotels. There were plenty of clean swept paths to stroll, but it required a certain vigilance due to the continuous traffic of motorised buggies. We were able to dodge them as they passed, but we were at constant risk of being run over in slow motion.

After a while we realised they weren't just golf buggies. Almost everyone in the Cove seemed to be trundling around in one. At the marina and the food market it became more obvious. Most of the shoppers were elderly patrons. The Cove and its manicured pathways was teeming with corpulent, well-heeled retirees.

"Why don't they just walk?" I asked Mark, in exasperation, sidestepping a perspex-covered cart that glinted in the sunshine as it rolled along.

"Probably because they're too old," he commented, following one of the doddery drivers with his eyes.

"Or because their jewellery is too heavy," I added, scanning some of the more affluent looking patrons.

"Oh, you're just jealous," he teased.

"What? Of being old and rich? Or being fat and lazy?"

"Both," he replied, watching me scrutinise the sedate migration of buggies as they swarmed around the grounds.

"I'd be fat and lazy if I had the money. Come on, let's find a restaurant and we can lick their plates."

By chance we had also passed a sign for a place called Cableski World so we decided to take a trip there the next morning. The vast car park was almost empty, but there were spaces mapped out for hundreds of cars.

"This place must get pretty busy," I said to Mark, thinking of the peak tourist season. "Imagine the money they can make when the car park's full."

A cable network had been constructed over a group of lakes, and as we walked closer to the toll booth we could see tow ropes connected to the overhead system at regular intervals.

Near the booth the ropes travelled over a pulley which seemed to briefly stall their movement on the cable above. There was a queue of skiers waiting on a ramp which tilted into the water, and as a rope reached the junction overhead the attendant snagged it. He handed it to the man at the front of the queue. It grew taut as we watched, latching onto the moving cable above and launching him into the lake. He skimmed away, followed by another skier on the next tow rope.

It was a huge stretch of water, and we could see the skiers growing smaller in the distance as they were towed around the perimeter of the lake. Any unused ropes just trailed the surface as the cable raced overhead in measured circuits. Since it was the beginning of the tourist season there was only one lake open, and they were running slow laps at 30kph that afternoon. I wondered what they considered a fast lap.

The challenge was to complete a circuit without falling over, but there was a two lap limit for continuous skiing, so you were supposed to take a break if you made it round twice. We tentatively paid the man at the booth with the assurance that we'd receive tuition at the ramp. Rather than skiing I chose a small board on which to kneel and waited in line for the attendant to hand me the next tow rope.

I was checking the rubber loops securing my knees to the board when I felt a rope being jabbed into my hand. What had happened to my tuition? My seconds had ticked, and there was no time to worry about technique.

"You've done this before?" he asked me, too late.

The loading force had reached its limit on the taut line, gaining enough recoil to make me airborne, hurling me in a flurry of limbs like something from a slingshot. I landed about three metres from the ramp. For a moment I lay face down on the surface, startled by the bracing slap of the water.

"Sorry," he yelled to the underside of my board, "I thought you'd done it before."

Winded and panting and still attached to the board at the knees, I rose to the surface in the shallows, bobbing like a piece of flotsam.

On the muddy bank I tucked the board under one arm and stalked back to the jetty, glaring at the man in the booth and ignoring his thumbs-up at my dishevelled figure.

I waited in line again on the ramp until I was at the front of the queue. I was seconds away from being jettisoned. The spring loading had reached capacity and I needed my instructions.

"Here... Hold this and lean forward...FORWARD...!"

Really? That was all he had? I was wrenched from the ramp, my shoulders absorbing the full disarticulating traction of the acceleration, and sent bouncing and slicing over the surface in my kneeling position. Somehow I was upright. I blinked away the spray produced by my board as it slapped against the water. The 30kph lap speed didn't feel very slow now.

Through narrowed eyes I could see red and white buoys scattered about the lake. So far I'd been able to avoid them but they seemed to be everywhere. Calculating the seconds I'd have to react to anything I wondered how much they'd hurt if I hit them.

There was a slight drop in tension sometimes when the rope passed over intersections in the cable network, but this seemed to be self-correcting. I'd almost reached the farthest end of the lake where the cable veered around for the turn, and I was steering into the curve determinedly. Blinking away the splashes as I skimmed the surface I felt the line go suddenly limp. I looked up as my speed slowed, shaking the flaccid rope suspiciously and wondering what had caused this interruption. For a few moments I bobbled around on my board in a position of prayer, wondering what to do. I looked around me, swivelling my head towards the distant ramp.

When the line jerked into action again I executed a perfect nose dive into the water with a graceless inevitability, still connected to my board by the straps.

It took more than ten minutes to hobble back around the shore, my wet footprints leaving a muddy trail on the dry, cracked earth. With every scorching step I cursed the attendant, feeling the hot ground burning into the soles of my bare feet. I'd just about run out of expletives when I got back to the ramp, where he was grinning at me rather ill-advisedly I thought.

"It's not a good idea to fall off at that end," he snorted, having tracked my progress as I tramped around the lake with the board under my arm.

"I didn't fall off," I said, boring my eyes into his head, "the rope went slack."

"Because you didn't go through the buoys."

"What?"

"You didn't go through the red ones."

"You didn't tell me to go through the red ones."

"If you don't go through the red buoys it stops. It thinks you've fallen off…" he recited, as if he said it quite often.

"…How am I supposed to know that?" I interrupted.

"…and it goes slack so you don't get dragged. You know. After you've fallen off."

"I fell off because it went slack, not because…" There was really no point pursuing it. I imagined how it would feel to shove him in the water.

"Oh never mind," I sighed, "I'll have another go, and I'll try to go *through the buoys* this time." Then I had another thought. "What about the white ones?"

"Oh, don't worry about the white ones," he said mysteriously.

"But what are they for?"

"You don't have to worry about the white ones. Trust me."

Mark was doing better than me. He hooted at me as he passed on his skis, ignoring the two lap limit and completing another circuit in an ungainly semi-squat. Perhaps it lacked the usual grace but he was still standing.

After I had managed a full circuit I handed-in my board, thankful to have emerged without any major injuries. I settled down to watch Mark's antics from the bank, laughing at his extensive vocabulary of whoops and shrieks as he continued to embrace the relative dangers. I raised my arm in salute when he passed again, already feeling the hurt in my arms, chest and shoulders as my overstretched muscles grumbled from the workout. Perhaps Queensland wasn't the harmless, languorous tourist destination that I'd been led to believe. Deadly spiders, heatstroke, near drownings. It was going to be an interesting fortnight.

*

The tropical Queensland scenery was lush and exotic to someone seeing it for the first time. We passed fields of tall sugar cane standing three metres high, their verdant jointed stems rippling in the wind; and we stared longingly at the green pods in the banana plantations, their leafy trees yielding crops in abundant clumps. Whole boxes of tropical fruits - mangoes and cantaloupes - were sold at the roadside for a few dollars, and as we travelled on lanes that twisted and turned through the rolling scenery we laughed at the flagrant advertising of local produce.

At any moment a ten metre pineapple or avocado could suddenly loom around a bend in the highway. The giant effigies were fibreglass models, some of them large enough for tourists to walk around inside them. It was a great way to boost sales.

When we reached Byron Bay there was an off sea breeze charging across the water, reinforcing its image as one of the greatest surfing towns. It was the most easterly point in Australia, and on the beach the wind was whipping the fine sand into dust clouds that chased along the shore and flicked into our eyes. It was a challenge to stay above the powerful, sucking waves when we went swimming, or to observe any other hazards in the depths.

There were plenty of stinging jelly fish to be dodged in the churning waters. The ever present Bluebottles were known by other names like, Portuguese Man-of-War, but my favourite of all of them was, The Floating Terror. At the mercy of the wind they would drift inland towards the shoreline, some of them already dead, lying motionless in transparent mounds. Beached and helpless on the sand they traced a scattered outline of the tide, looking like piles of jelly that had been tipped out of bowls, washing to and fro in the waves. Up close we could poke at their firm gel bodies and clusters of ropey gelatinous tentacles; but the separate filament of their sting was so long and fine that it was more often felt than seen. A sting was painful, but mostly harmless.

Most of the beaches were clearly for surfers or for capable and strenuous swimmers rather than for leisurely bathers. Waves loomed and crashed down relentlessly on our heads like walls of water. Faced with the continuous barrage we could see why it was such a hazard to venture into the sea without the extra buoyancy of a surfboard.

When I exited breathlessly from the water, the waves were still clamouring around my legs trying to draw me back. In the knee deep water I felt something brush my skin like a line of fishing twine. There was a smarting sensation and a thin red welt began to form across my calf. Although I couldn't see it in the roiling water, the slender stinging thread of a Bluebottle must have entwined my wading feet. Waving at Mark still bobbing in the water behind me, I indicated that I was heading over to the Surf Lifesavers station where I could get doused with vinegar to ease the pain. From the queue of people ahead of me I could see I wasn't the only one to have had an encounter in the waves.

\*

It was an overcast day when we said goodbye to Mark's Grandparents and began the ascent on the winding road up to the Tamborine Mountains. As we left the coastline there was a haze hanging over the high-rise buildings and the air felt thick and muggy as it flowed through the open windows, but as we climbed steadily upwards it became cooler. For most of the afternoon we dodged in and out of craft and antique stores on the mountain road, admiring the walnut furniture and beautiful china tea sets, but it was getting late and the shadows were becoming darker underneath the trees. We parked in the dwindling light, walking the earthy track that led to the tumbling Curtis Falls, the mosquitoes hungrily circling our bare legs when we reached the water. Despite their persistence we dawdled there for a while, welcoming the cool damp air in the half light, redolent with the smell of wet earth and clean mountain breezes.

We'd been invited to have dinner with Mark's uncle and his family, and after the meal they offered us some delicious homemade orange cake made by one of the boys, Mark's young cousin.

"It would have been iced and decorated, but we had a bit of a problem with the sugar," his Uncle said. "Show Mark," he instructed the boys.

They ran to the cupboard for the bag of icing sugar. It was littered with dark specks.

"Weevils," his Uncle said.

They had bored into the bag to gorge themselves, and remained in the white powder like small black apostrophes.

Sitting at the kitchen table we could already hear the soft scratchings of unseen insects rustling around the floor, setting out on their nocturnal errands now the house had cooled. The metallic clatter of spoons on plates joined the night sounds as the house relaxed on its foundations. The joists had begun to settle in the chill of the evening and we could hear the wooden beams creaking around us like old bones.

We descended the mountains in the cool of the morning, taking the meandering road down to the beach with the boys piled into the backseat. Mark had promised to deliver them to The Spit for a swim. After creeping down the steep, forested slopes with scorching brake pads I looked longingly at the waves rolling into Surfers Paradise.

"Shall we have a final dip?" I asked, watching the breakers dumping onshore. The pull of the ocean was irresistible.

"Come on! Come and bodysurf with us!" the boys shrilled eagerly.

Mark looked out at the wave crests peaking across the water and checked his watch.

"Have you boys got any sunscreen or anything?"

They were travelling light, without towels or even spare clothing.

"We've got drinks," they said, holding up two-litre plastic bottles of cordial. The contents had been frozen solid overnight and were slowly melting, the bottles sweating and beading in the heat.

"Come on then. You can have some of my BullFrog," Mark said, passing a tube of sunscreen to them in the backseat.

The decision was met with great enthusiasm, everyone disgorging from the car, keen to throw ourselves into the churning white waters and cool off even before the heat of the day had crested.

As I applied sunscreen on shore I watched the waves clattering across the jumble of heads, Mark taking the lead as they bobbed and dived. Raising an arm, he waved at me to beckon me in, and I could see his smile across the distance. He looked so tanned and relaxed, just another swimmer riding the waves. It was good to see him enjoying the sunshine with his cousins, blending into the crowd unrecognised.

I waved back as I began to walk towards the water, wading in and feeling the push and pull of its power around my legs. Our next stop was going to be the state capital with all its big city noise and humidity. I was in no hurry to get there.

## Like Two Mexicans Dancing

THERE WAS a huge and ornately decorated Christmas tree in the square in Brisbane next to the City Hall. It stood several metres high, glistening with tinsel and almost reaching the clock face on the building. In the lunchtime sunshine, with a hot breeze blowing lazily, it seemed peculiar to have a fully decorated tree. I had to remind myself that it was December and it would soon be Christmas, a month that I still associated with snow and frost.

At the Art Gallery we browsed the photographs by Bill Hensen, the paintings by Renoir and Pissarro, and admired Rodin's small bronze sculpture. It was the figure of a crouching woman, perhaps of his lover, Camille Claudel. I eyed the museum's collection of photographic artefacts including a folding Brownie Six-20 from the fifties, and a selection of swimwear from the turn of the century.

The costume sizes diminished as the years passed, each outfit having less fabric and revealing more skin. I eyed the modesty of the neck-to-knee styles from the 1920's, knitted woollen outfits that would be slow drying and heavy and highly unsuitable for bathing, and quietly thanked Paula Stafford, the pioneer of the bikini.

We stayed with Mark's friends in the city, listening to tales of clothes turning mouldy in the constant humidity and of wet shoes that never seemed to dry. Their cat, Alice, delighted in stalking the crickets which flitted into the house, depositing their dead bodies on our pillows or suitcases in a feline gesture of welcome. Their stiff papery bodies were the gifts we found when we turned down our beds for the evening.

The days were filled with the sights of the city or the briny air of the beaches, and in the warm evenings on the deck overlooking their pool our hosts barbecued fresh bream, bought in the west end. Ever resourceful, Alice watched opportunistically for a chance to seize a morsel but was usually satisfied with a crispy prawn cracker instead.

After watching music videos of Joy Division and Aztec Camera we walked in the darkness down by the river, and then doubled back through the graveyard. We saw the shadows of cane toads there, plopping in gelatinous silence between headstones, and bats as big as crows swooping animatedly

## King George Square, Brisbane

overhead, the slow flap of their wings sounding like a blanket being shaken out.

On our last evening we sat in a bar above the street talking about Christmas and what may lie ahead in the new year. Below us there were dozens of Santa impersonators perspiring in the heat, cloaked in festive red and white suits and roaming the humid, neon lit pavements.

We watched them as we sipped cold beers from glasses that beaded with moisture in the warm air, reflecting on our trip and the return journey. Mark had been gradually unwinding from the pressures of the band but within two days we'd be back to the reality of Melbourne. The album was currently in the hands of the producers for the final mixing. That meant a launch would be imminent, then more marketing, and no doubt some more touring. I hoped he felt ready for the onslaught.

*

Leaving the Gold Coast and Surfers Paradise on the thirteen hour drive to Dubbo I could see the highway unravelling into the distance in a shimmer of heat haze. Bright yellow sunflowers were growing at the roadside, their faces tipped demurely on long stalks as we passed through the Great Dividing Range. Workmen were digging the roads on stretches of the highway, giving us a leisurely salute as they waved-on the passing traffic, their skin tanned and leathery from years of outdoor work.

Mark pursued his own private war with the oversized trucks and road-trains that thundered past us. With two or three trailers and up to 40m in length, they roared along the one lane highways, sometimes hauling a cache of sheep or cows crammed into the fenced sides of livestock carriers, throwing back the ripe reek of dung as they sped by. If we were forced to overtake them Mark would hang onto the wheel grimly, his foot to the floor on the accelerator, willing the red Gemini to clear the length of the freight containers on the rig. A full minute could pass until we drew level, flanking the highly polished chrome of the prime mover at the fore, looking up at the high doors of its cabin, dwarfed by its massive bull bars.

"I hate trucks," Mark would repeat, gritting his teeth at the roar of the diesel and the swishing hydraulics. With each white knuckled manoeuvre he'd be driving in a cloud of gravel and dust, eyes half-closed, the car as far across the other side of the highway as possible without actually driving on the blanched scrub grass.

Even with all the windows down the unremitting heat pulsed through the car, forcing us to stop regularly, eager to splash our faces at rest stops or to seek out ice creams and cold drinks. There seemed to be an all pervasive smell of scorching rubber on the road and it hung in the air when we pulled over to stretch our legs, resting our hot tyres, waiting for the engine to cool slightly, and wondering when the daily temperature might begin to drop below forty degrees.

By the loose edges of the roadside we noticed the remnants of shredded tyres littering the verges like pieces of torn clothing; and we fantasized about our own sticky tyres slowly melting onto the road and leaving long black streaks, like treacle. At one point we even passed a small bushfire that had begun to blaze in the dry tinder, the smoke lingering like a beacon long after we'd passed it.

At Moree I felt Mark slowing down and then braking so he could pull over. I looked at the flat landscape all around me, and then back at Mark.

"Are you having a toilet stop here?"

He'd started to take off his clothes in the car. By the time he'd stripped to his yellow underpants I wondered if he'd decided to drive naked.

"What are you doing?" I stared at him. "Mark?"

The temptation had proved too great. He shot out of the car with a grin and onto the adjacent grass.

Swinging open my car door I laughed as he ran bare foot, heading towards a sprinkler that was watering the grass on the fringes of the park. I grabbed my camera to record the drenching just as he dived into the curtain of fine mist fanning the air.

"Come on, Ange, the water's perfect!"

"No chance. I'll stick with the spray bottle."

I gave myself a dowsing to make my point and stepped out of the car, feeling the water swiftly evaporating. But Mark had his eyes closed, turning his head from side to side, enjoying the spray and getting some relief from the heat even if it was just for a few minutes.

This was all too much for the local boys playing in the park who were obviously unaccustomed to such flagrant behaviour in the country. Mark was evidently the first person to cavort in his underwear in daylight hours in a public park, so they settled down on the other side of the road for a better view of the spectacle as it unfolded.

I knew what would follow.

"Come over here," he urged, trying to entice me into the water jets.

"No!"

"Go on, it'll cool you down," he entreated, walking towards me.

I yelped as I dodged his grasp, squirming out of the way.

"With all my clothes on?"

"Take them off." He flicked his eyebrows upwards suggestively.

I shook my head as I backed away.

"Come over and give me a hug then," he said, grabbing me in a sodden embrace.

My protests were hardly credible in the heat, especially when I felt the cool expanse of his naked skin pressed to mine, and the soft kisses that followed.

In the fading light, on the far left of the highway, we saw a storm racing with us towards Dubbo, sheet lightning in a quick succession of flashes, freeze-framing the horizon and leaving a hint of distant rain as the damp, earthy smell was carried in the air. For a while we stopped the car and stared open mouthed at the storm's light show under a vast expanse of black sky and its multitude of stars.

When we finally reached our motel in Dubbo there were swarms of desperate flies and other night insects gyroscoping around the glow of the tungsten lights, drawing invisible coils in the air, keeping a frantic orbit within the stillness of the night. It was so late that we had to wake the receptionist when we checked-in, and then evict the resident cockroach family from our room before we could shower and sleep.

"This is exactly the same room we had on the way over," I murmured to Mark.

"I thought I recognised that cockroach," he said drowsily. "They must've been waiting up for us."

Stretching out our cramped limbs on the soft cotton sheets, there was nothing better than lying under the cool burr of the air conditioning as it blasted overhead and sent us off to sleep.

We couldn't leave town in the morning without visiting the Old Dubbo Gaol with its delightfully old fashioned animatronics; mannequins replete with swivelling heads and rolling eyes, jaws champing in time with the soundtrack as each life sized model told its tale of incarceration. One tale was of a country criminal from the Back of Bourke, *where the crows fly backwards to keep the dust out of their eyes.* He received a 4 day sentence for brawling in the city. Hardened criminals were left in solitary confinement, just a pit covered by a trap door, and others were condemned to die for committing murder. I urged Mark into the wooden stocks outside, taking photographs when he pushed his head and hands through the holes and scowled convincingly for the camera.

Melbourne had been far from my thoughts but I could feel us being slowly reeled in as we headed southwards. We'd reached a latitude almost level with Sydney, about 5 hours due west of it, passing through the town of Parkes where we stopped just out of town to see the huge radio telescope and satellite dish.

The intricate mesh of its outer frame made it look like a giant shuttlecock balanced on a barrel shaped tower. At more than sixty metres in diameter, the satellite dish looked stark and out of place against the unbroken backdrop of rough vegetation, and from a distance it seemed to gape like a vast open mouth, in thrall to the sky. It had relayed the live, televised pictures of the Apollo 11 moon landing in 1969, and then Neil Armstrong's historic first steps on the moon. The thought of history being made and recorded here made us linger for a while, spellbound that it could happen in such an isolated place with all the world watching.

Our four thousand kilometre trip was almost over. Shadows lengthened as the sun fell steadily. Pieces of daylight flashed at us in a hypnotic strobe, interrupted by the tree branches at the roadside. They cast a flickering light onto the car as we drove past them. Settling back, I watched the darkness slowly claiming the finer details of the vegetation at the verges, eventually only being able to see the black shapes of cast off shredded tyres as our lights caught their outline.

Nodding with the comforting motion of the car and losing myself in recollections of our trip I wasn't sure how much time had slipped away, but after a while I started to recognise subtle changes occurring in the terrain. I could see that we had finally crossed the state line and had returned to the familiar landscape of Victoria.

In the dark I looked across at Mark's profile, his eyes staring intently at the tongue of the road poking from the cast of the headlights.

"We're nearly home," I said, although I felt my thoughts drifting to Tasmania, and then to the distant shores of England.

Mark was fumbling for my hand in the gloom, reviving all my senses with his touch. It felt like deliverance. I could feel his skin on mine in the shadowy car, the hand of rescue in the darkness, tipping the balance, pulling me gently back towards our Melbourne home.

As I contemplated the huge expanses separating all the continents, I remembered a similar moment on the Gordon River cruise, looking out through Hell's Gate. I'd glimpsed something about the water that day, as the river clashed and merged with the Southern Ocean, picturing all the seas intersecting, each with the next across the globe. With Mark's hand in mine, I thought of the oceans again, imagining them blurring together, folding over every distant shoreline so it didn't feel as if I had to make a choice. My homes weren't disconnected; they were all joined together by sea.

"It's good to be back," I said, thinking of Melbourne and the bay, where our current life was waiting for us.

"We're almost in the northern suburbs now," he said.

"Yes, almost."

I turned my attention to the horizon as we continued to rumble along the highway, focussing on the approaching city and its winking lights.

"Our home from home," he said, giving my fingers a gentle squeeze.

"It kind of makes you appreciate it more, when you've been away for a while," I murmured, thinking of the crashing seas just beyond the bay, but in the darkness it felt like I was holding fast to his hand, like an anchor.

## TISM, Stanley and Fin

OUTSIDE THE PALACE THEATRE in St Kilda the smell of the ocean lingered in the air. A few metres away, the neon-lit historic Luna Park was carved in relief against a dark sky. Within its foreshore location high rollercoaster tracks swept around its fenced perimeters, and the circular Ferris wheel was framed in silhouette. From where we were standing we could see the water glimmering in the darkness, the sea only just beyond the road and adjacent shoreline; but the busy hum of crowds pushing into the venue obscured any sound of waves that might have carried in the air.

Steps led up into the foyer under The Palace's gaudy neon lit sign, its spacious interior offering plenty of open floor space to dance, and room for the audience to clump together in front of the stage. The gig was evidently going to be well attended that night looking at the number of people pouring in.

Darren was there, going through a phase of wanting to be a professional roadie. It'd been so long since I'd seen him that in the interim his hair had grown to shoulder length. His ideas of becoming a ski instructor seemed to have come and gone. I suspected he'd be changing his mind again soon anyway. He was always living his dream, but never the same one for very long.

That evening after The Fish had played their set, we'd all decided to stay for the headliner. That didn't happen very often, but it was probably also because all their equipment was still at the rear of the stage, and they wouldn't be able to collect it until the gig was over.

It was one of Darren's favourite bands, TISM, and with such a massive audience it was difficult to find a place to stand and to have an unobstructed view of the stage. We'd squeezed onto the metal steps that led up to the balcony area on the far side of the huge room, and we were guarding our elevated position tenaciously as we balanced on the crowded stairway.

Darren's eyes were shining with excitement as he scanned the room.

"It's perfect for stage diving," he said.

He was eying the throng at the front of the stage, dancing en-masse like one body with a multitude of arms. I could just hear his voice above the deafening noise that was coming from the towering speakers.

"I'm gonna do it!" he yelled across to us.

"Go on then," I urged him, unconvinced.

"I am. This time, I'm really gonna do it."

He stood for a few more minutes, sizing up the risks and working out his point of entry into the crowd, and then he disappeared. He'd said it before. I don't think any of us believed he would do it this time either, particularly with the difficulty of getting up on the stage before the bouncers or security staff noticed. They'd haul him off to the outer limits of the crowd if they caught him, or even eject him outside the venue.

An enigma even to their fans, TISM filled the stage with almost a dozen musicians, each dancing furiously or moving with jerky, exaggerated movements to the music. They were all wearing elaborate costumes, cloaks and masks that obscured their faces. Allegedly, no-one knew their identities behind the masks, and it was argued that it was often a succession of different musicians playing the instruments.

As we watched the band, we suddenly saw a figure run diagonally across from the right side to centre stage, flashing past the vocalist at speed, before he launched himself off into the dense crowd. It was a perfect dive, like someone entering water, the figure disappearing with hair flowing and arms outstretched into the throng of heads and arms below.

"That was Darren!" I shouted to anyone who could hear me, "I'd recognise that hair anywhere."

The crowd continued to wash about, reeling and swaying with the forces generated from within, occasionally disengaging an individual from the masses and levitating it on a swell of hands. Thrust aloft, the body would ride the crest, rolled like a log above the heads of the people below until the current pulled them under again.

A few minutes later Darren reappeared, pushing his way through the crowd. I could barely hear my own voice as I tipped my head towards him.

"Well? How was it?" I pressed, eager for the lowdown.

The shuddering spasms of his cough looked like a mime, lost in the obliterating noise, but I waited as he pushed his hair back with both hands then leaned closer to my ear to reply.

"No one caught me!" he yelled against the thundering music, giving me a stunned look. "They all just moved out of the way. Bastards!"

"Not even…"

"…No! The crowd just parted, and I landed on the floor. It was awful."

His pain was genuine, but it was difficult not to laugh. I waited until he limped off to the bar with Graham, still rubbing his leg, and then I nudged Mark.

"That crowd looks pretty solid. How could everyone have had enough room to move out of the way when Darren jumped?"

Mark squinted at the compressed bodies and shrugged back.

"Just unlucky I suppose."

"Maybe he'll do better next time."

I never did see a next time, even at other gigs. The rest of us kept our distance from the crush that night, standing on the stairs, and taking turns to get beers at the bar so that we didn't lose our coveted position. Even after the encores we lingered at the back until the venue emptied, waiting to retrieve the band's amps and drums from the stage.

That was probably one of the last occasions I remember Graham being with the band. After the major changes that had occurred over the past few months, it wasn't such a shock to hear that he was leaving the Fish. He'd accepted an offer to drum for Barb Waters & The Rough Diamonds, meaning the boys could choose a new drummer and complete the full transformation of the band.

Within the network of musical connections and local relationships it was relatively simple to choose someone already known to the band; and so that was how Stanley joined the Fish, temporarily suspending activities with his own three piece band, Man in The Wood, in which he was the drummer and the vocalist.

Stanley Paulzen had a small goatee beard and a blonde, Tintin haircut. He wore cardigans with big leather buttons and holes in the elbows too large to ever try and sew up, and he had the sort of wry, dangerous wit that had assured he was also given a microphone when he performed with The Fish. Even though the drum kit is usually at the rear of the stage, often obscuring all but the head of the drummer, Stanley usually had more to say than all the boys collectively, and being at the back didn't deter him.

With the expectation that the album, Fin would soon be ready for marketing, the boys had organised a professional photographer to take individual portraits that could be included on the inner sleeve, but in addition to these Mark asked me to take some informal pictures which could be used later for press releases, as well as supplementing the album shots.

We decided to use the overgrown backyard at Stanley's house for the backdrop, depicting the boys smelling the roses that were in full bloom, and engineering a picture of Martin that gives the impression he has three hands. There was a sagging wire clothes line across the yard and as soon as I saw the pegs I handed them to Michael.

"Pretend to peg the boys onto the line," I suggested, climbing up onto the wall for some overhead shots.

The washing line picture was my favourite from the whole shoot, but it would be July, six months later, that I would receive my first and only copy of it, when it eventually appeared in one of the free music newspapers in Perth, The Drum Media (16 July 1991).

I was excited to see that I was credited as the Photographer and that the picture was attached to an interview by John Tingwell. Mark gave me a copy of the newspaper when he returned from touring Perth with the band, and he also handed me a sheet of A4 paper on which he'd photocopied a phrase from another interview. He'd magnified the text until the letters were an inch tall and they filled the paper entirely. It referred to his song, Poetry, and was filled with heartache and yearning:

> "...Another one is called Poetry, which is a love song, a ballad that I wrote because I'm in love terribly with a beautiful woman from Manchester... that's a sad song..."

In Stanley's backyard that afternoon, as we were completing the photographs for the album, we had high expectations of where we would all be in six months' time.

But the elation gradually gave way to a collective longing and despondency, and within a few months Mark's comments during the interview in Perth would capture the changed mood. By the middle of the year our outlook would be entirely different, and it wouldn't be for the reasons that any of us would have expected.

*Angela J. Dawson*

# Gigs, media and recording, 1991

AT THE START of the year war was finally declared in the Persian Gulf after the mid-January deadline, and the failure of negotiations; and so began Desert Storm and the long chase for Saddam Hussein. It was a gloomy beginning, and a far cry from the auspicious news about Mandela the year before.

Sometime before February the news on our side of the map was that The Punters Club had finally been renovated. It had been upgraded from the days of the torn, sagging couch, and instead of looking like a dank cellar as it had done previously, it now looked like a dank cellar with air conditioning and a few pinball machines.

Fortunately the Fish held the official launch of their second album, Fin, after the renovation, appearing in February in the freshly overhauled Punters Club, with Mark Adams' new band playing the support. I was pleased to see some of my photographs on the inside sleeve of the album, using the roses in Stanley's backyard, but I wasn't too happy with the layout, and how they'd been cut together. Mark was apologetic, but it was too late to make reparation. In those days of film I often handed over the roll after shooting, and therefore had no recourse in terms of copyright or ownership. It was something that I learned to regret.

For the gig, Warky had put together a band called The Plastic Tornadoes, with Eva on bass, and they played a short set to the largest crowd I could ever remember seeing at a Fish gig at The Punters Club. There was the welcome sight of previous band members in the audience, and it was a relief for everyone that former differences had been put aside so that Warky too could be included in the album launch.

The Fish had undergone a complete transformation. It was a totally different band receiving the accolades that night to the one that had recorded the first album, Swim, at Sing Sing Studios in November 1988. It was encouraging to see a capacity crowd, particularly after all the recent changes, and as I looked at the crush of people wedged around the small stage it was evident that they were still popular enough to fill a venue.

Warky's band continued to tour the local pub circuit, changing their name eventually to Hurdy Gurdy, while the Fish expected some interest in the wake of this second album, released locally as planned, on Shock Records. The new line-up and musical influences had given them fresh hope, but offers continued to fall into the hands of others more readily.

Close to home, the Helvelln boys were getting themselves noticed. One evening Jeremy invited us to the studios of Whirled Records to participate in a live film shoot. The band was recording a few songs for distribution to selected record companies, and had invited some friends to feature in the video as the audience. It was a gamble that paid off. Shortly afterwards, Mushroom Records made a move, and finally offered the band a contract.

It was cause for celebration, seeing friends being recognised, but for The Fish it was also a test of their resolve. There was little else for them to do except dig-in, keep performing, and wait for an opportunity to present itself.

IT WAS a cool evening in April, and Mark and I were walking in the Carlton Gardens adjacent to the silvery windows of the Exhibition Buildings. Like huge mirrors their glass reflected the lights and shapes of the surrounding streets. It was in these gardens that Mark had proposed to me just over a year ago. Although we were talking about the future again that night, we were also trying to navigate our way through familiar obstacles.

Engulfed by the ongoing disappointments and delays faced by the band, we'd lost sight of the joy we'd felt during those idyllic Tasmanian days. The boys were all disheartened, life was on hold, and the band was in stasis. Mark had very little income, and with only my salary it was hard to think of his proposal as anything more than a romantic notion.

I was entering my fourth year in Australia. With the passing of another year and still no change to Mark's prospects, I felt unsettled and racked with indecision about a return to England. There were times when I wished I had never left and split my life in two. I'd heard a song by They Might Be Giants called *Ana Ng* whose lyrics conveyed my sense of frustration, and illustrated my polarised thoughts – you might not want the whole world, but you always look longingly at someone else's half.

We didn't know how to reconcile our differences and the additional stress of the band was taking its toll, creating further tension between us. Nothing had been resolved when we parted that evening, and I was aware of my own reluctance to impose any sort of ultimatum. The band was due to tour Sydney and Tasmania with The Church, which meant another protracted absence, and after Mark had dropped me off outside my house and driven away, I was conscious that neither of us had set a date to meet on his return.

The omission worried me and gnawed at my thoughts. I bought a bike. I didn't want to consider the tacit agreement that seemed to have occurred that evening. Days passed without even a phone call between us, and I rode my bike around the streets and suburbs of Melbourne, spending hours cycling in the dark evenings, and travelling miles around the Peninsula at the weekends.

I rode until I was exhausted. I rode until I couldn't think; and I wrote.

## Lament

Heartsick
In the vain glory
Of the winning dark,
I remember the days
We made;
When summer
Was the only season
And colours rich
In every hue;
Where sometime
In between
The pictures
And the songs
We loved more
Than the pain
We leave behind.
Even now I hold a memory,
A piece of the past,
A hope, a dream
That love would never lose,
That my loss would never be you.
This much we know:
How to hurt each other
A wound on me
From you, forever.
Like a scar that fades
It is sometimes seen
As a silvery streak on skin.

*Angela J. Dawson*

Flyer, for Mark Adams' band, The Plastic Tornadoes

## Fin album

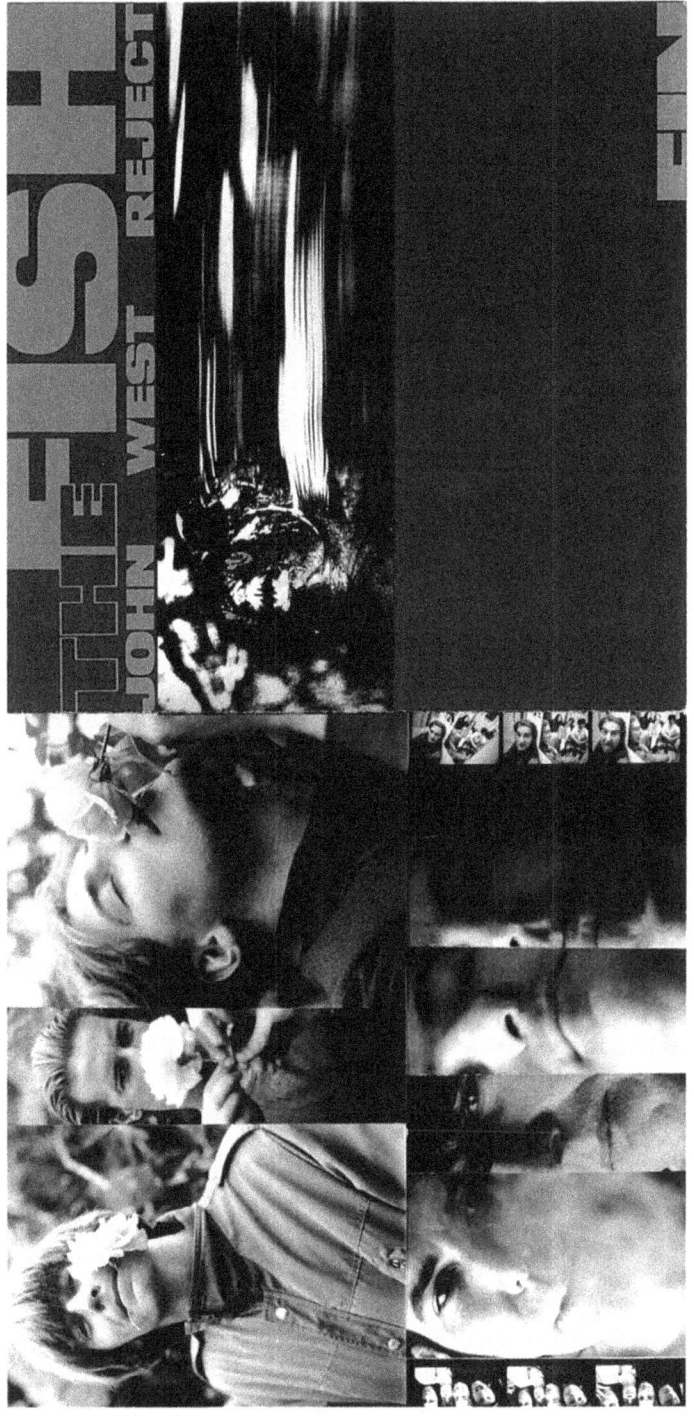

*Angela J. Dawson*

# Fin - credits for John (FOM) & Jeremy (Helvelln)

*Like Two Mexicans Dancing*

*Angela J. Dawson*

Drum Media article – with photo credit

42  16 July 1991  THE DRUM MEDIA

# THE DRUM MEDIA LOCAL

FISH JOHN WEST REJECT/MARK NARKOWICZ by JOHN TINGWELL

# REVENGE OF THE LOVE-SICK FISH

OK, what do Errol Flynn, damning environmental battles, very short cricketers with hairy top lips, Cox's Orange Pippins and The Fish John West Reject have in common? No marks, I'm afraid, if you said, 'very silly names' — the correct answer is of course, Tasmania; that island state of Australia which seems always to be shrouded in mystery, orchards and green, undulating hills.

"WE left Tasmania at the beginning of 1988", says The Fish's lead vocalist and guitarist, Mark Narkowicz on the line from Perth. "We've been based in Melbourne since then, so we don't see ourselves as a Tasmanian band anymore. We see ourselves personally as Tasmanians, but we're definitely a Melbourne band made up of Tasmanian people. My roots are important to me and I'd like people to acknowledge the fact that we come from an isolated area and made a bit of a name for ourselves. We're just an Australian independent band."

THE Fish, (as their many ardent followers refer to them nowadays), were hatched in 1985 in the form of an extravert busking duo. Narkowicz and ex-member, Mark Adams were apparently responsible for creating wild scenes of mayhem at The Mall in Launceston and in due course their popularity increased to such a level that more members and more established venues were the only answer.

"MARK Adams and I started off by playing all these whacky gospel standards and country songs while we were busking, but I've always been a fan of power pop. From there, The Fish became a bit of a monster, playing all this pop thrashabilly and people got right into it because of its aggressiveness and charm.

BY the time the band were in full flight, there were some very obvious folk influences evident in their music. With inevitable line-up changes and the subsequent inclusion of Michael and Martin Witheford in the ranks, their music took another turn back to Narkowicz's original inspiration — power pop. Their second album, *Fin*, released earlier this year is testimony of this fact. *Fin* is the sort of album which could've been released in any decade, but its roots seem to be firmly planted in the '60s, courtesy of The Fish's trademark vocal harmonies and power guitar chords. I liken it to something The Beatles would've hatched in 1965, had they been influenced by The Wondersuff.

"SOMEBODY here in Perth said today that *Fin* sounded like The Kinks and somebody else described it as mid-'60s power pop. It's very interesting that people are placing it in a decade rather than a specific genre. I can't see the '60s connection myself.

IT surely has something to do with their superb vocal harmonies. They seem to be one of the very few Australian independent bands who are making a point of using three and four part harmonies in pop tunes. The Fish use their voices as an integral instrument rather than something they have to do in order to sell records. "Vocals have always been a big love of ours. We love singing together", says Narkowicz. "But now we're also into sampling, big power chords, real melodies and real harmonies. That about sums us up."

ON stage, The Fish John West Reject are synonymous with real energy, real passion and real vitality. Most of that is personified by Mark Narkowicz. A direct result of his days as a busker in Launceston, perhaps?

"FOR sure, but it also comes from my own performer's ego, I think. When I'm on stage, I really have to satisfy that ego, but that's not to say it's a contrived thing, it comes very naturally. I love performing, I think it's a lot of fun."

THERE seems to be a common lyrical thread running through *Fin*. It's not a particularly original concept, but The Fish's concerns definitely lie in the girls, love and crumbling relationships arena. Mark Narkowicz says they should have named the album, "More Songs About Lost Love And Girls".

"BASICALLY, never go out with a member of The Fish and leave them, 'or we'll write a song about you. Our secret weapon is the revenge of the pen and paper."

SOUNDS rather frightening — the revenge of the love-sick Fish. Considering the band's original folk influences, (hardly noticeable today), and their Tasmanian heritage, it's surprising their lyrical concerns don't lean towards environmental and/or political subjects. Narkowicz, however, is quite adamant about politics in music, or rather the fact that the two don't mix.

Pop music is all about having a good time — how can you have a good time with some person shoving their political grievances down your throat while they're on stage?"

BUT as George Orwell once said, to say that politics and art don't mix, is in itself a political statement.

**THE Fish John Reject are performing at The Sandringham on July 19, The Phoenician Club on July 20 where they'll be giving away copies of their new EP, *Sick Inside* and sharing the bill with Swordfish and Splash, which should prove to be a very aquatic night of entertainment. Their last Sydney show will be at The Hopetoun on July 21. Their album, *Fin* is superb and available on Shock Records.**

photo Angela J. Dawson

# Bagging The Unknown Band

SOME days in this game just trundle by like they do for most people, other days are just extraordinarily exhilarating. The day I interviewed the Unknown Band was just plain bizarre. Let me set the scene for you. A musician stumbles up to the doors of *The Drum Media*. He's a little disoriented and ahead of the rest of the band by a good ten minutes. His disorientation is not, however, due to the usual pitfalls of living a rock'n'roll lifestyle. This man is here to be interviewed with a paper bag on his head! Moments later, led by a paper bagless manager, the rest of the troupe arrive, all 'bagged' up, barely missing bumping into walls, doors and each other as they enter our office lobby to take over the 'comfy chairs' for our interrogation. This is weird indeed.

SO, you're thinking, 'Okay, are they doing a TISM? Are they here to turn those Melbourne anarchists on their collective heads with a good dose of Sydney-based rock?' No sirree. The Unknown Band are a completely different field. Let me hand you over to the principal spokes-bag, John Bull no-Hypershit, to 'explain'. Interjections throughout come courtesy any or all of the following: — Mr X, Jimmy Wheezmuller, Murralyn Manitoe, Billy Joe Bob Whats His Name and Englebert Dinkleberry 3rd — 'cos behind the paper bags, I couldn't figure which matched which psuedonym!

"IT'S amazing you know. The only time in the whole show when the entire band get completely out of time is when I come out to dance! I'm dancing in time and these guys are all over the place. It's extraordinary. But that's the by the by. With regard to TISM, we've set our sights a little bit lower than TISM actually. We want to work! We base our concept around music the people, er, know . . . only because it's sort of easier that way. Without putting too fine a point on it, we've seen TISM and TISM are a m-i-g-h-t-y fine band, but they're aiming at a different side of the market. We're writing original stuff but we're writing stuff that's geared towards the show as opposed to throwing original songs out willy nilly.

"OUR concept is that, instead of spending 70% of a night performing stuff the audience don't know, we play stuff they know so they feel safe and secure, and then surprise them!" You're getting the picture, right? What you get over two hours of non-stop rock cabaret party is six guys playing a lot of the songs you already know with paper bags on their heads, but with a bit of a twist here and there, such as Toast Is Burning instead of Beds Are Burning, Bound For Dapto instead of Glory, The Bags Are Back In Town, You Can Leave Your Bag On and our own Bag Rap.

"WE also have this section taking all the original cuts of songs before they were released, the bits that were left on the studio floor before they were organised, so there's our Cutting Room Floor Song. All part of our very Green approach, recycling everything. The bags are, of course, biodegradable. We use unbleached paper bags which break down very easily under sweat on Murralyn over here can testify to. He is our greatest bag user. Murralyn the walking armpit. Sweats in all he does."

NOW, if bags were all the Unknown Band had to offer, they'd be pretty ho-hum, but the idea seems to be to create a 'show' that truly involves the audience. So, as the audience enters, they get a paper bag, naturally, but with the words to the songs in it.

"THERE's a sumo wrestler — The Unknown Wrestler — who also wears a mask. And there are two short people who wrestle with him. He greets people as they come in and gives them their bags with the songwords and bingo tickets, because we also have rock'n'roll bingo with Keno Ken and Book Yard Barbie. It's funny but when you've got an 18 stone sumo wrestler on the door, nobody questions the entry price!"

THEN there's the World's Worst Dancing competition, door prizes and giveaways and even some hot gospelling from the Rev Head Piles. Proudly sponsored by, who else, the Australian Paper Bag Company, you can discover the dubious joys of paper baggism and The Unknown Band next Tuesday 16 at the Great Northern in Chatswood, Thursday 18 at the Smithfield Tavern, Friday 19 at Selina's, Saturday 20 at CT's in Camden, Friday 26 at the Collector Tavern in Parramatta and Saturday 27 at Didi's before they trundle off to Adelaide, Albury, Wagga and Queensland to foist this silliness on the rest of the nation!

THE UNKNOWN BAND — PHOTO COURTESY OF THE LEADER

Inside Drum Media – gig advert, showing Ol' Shep the fish

## Inside Drum Media – Sunday gig advert

Music review for EP, Sick Inside

### THE FISH JOHN WEST REJECT
**Sick Inside**
*Shock*

WET Blanket Pop, for the benefit of the ignorant few, is a school founded in the mid 80s by a bunch of anorak clad dips from Britain who were into calm, melodic pop songs with sensitive, self deprecating lyrics, an emphasis on the ironic, and the occasional foray into the daisy-fopped 60s, or their impression of it.

The Fish John West Reject are card carrying members, producing on Sick Inside an EP the title track reminds me of a neat and tidy Jesus and Mary Chain. Same deep dead vocals, same slow careful drumbeat, same poignant strum. The B-side is more upbeat, on a wiggler in the politest possible way. With the pathos-ridden It's My Birthday, check out the deadpan "flip flop, tick tock" and the chorus Mother Hold My Coat, this one is strictly for lovers of the lonesome, for those who believe in the inherent beauty of sadness, and the swoon of lost love's song. Wrap yourself up in something warm and mushy, and hibernate till summer. The awesome, the majestic have been replaced by the kitchen sink. Pedestrianism rules, ok.

— SIMON KILLALEA

From a card made by Mark, B&W photo - unknown source

*Like Two Mexicans Dancing*

# Royal Derby Hotel

MAY THE FIFTH was Mark's birthday, a Monday, and I had decided I couldn't let it pass without some acknowledgement. I planned to leave a gift, riding my bike through Carlton on a beautiful sunny Sunday morning and picking up some flowers from one of the many florists in the area. Knowing that the security door to the apartment block was rarely closed, I planned to leave them outside his door so that he'd have them for his birthday the following morning.

When I arrived, the building was quiet and I was able to stride the stairs to the second floor unseen, pausing outside the familiar door before laying the flowers down next to it. I left a card with them so that he would know I'd remembered the exact day, then returned to the empty streets and my cycling. April and May felt like the longest months.

In the gig guide at the end of May I noticed that the Fish were playing at the Royal Derby Hotel, supported by a new band, The Somerfields. The lanky guitarist, Gary Aspinall, from The Killjoys had formed this new band, and I'd met him on the occasions he'd operated the stage lighting or the mixing desk during Fish gigs. I was curious to see the Fish play again, and after six weeks apart I felt ready to see Mark, ready to test the parameters of this separation and decide if the break had helped us reach any decisions. Neither of us had made any declarations about our future.

I wasn't surprised that I felt nervous standing at the door of the pub. It was odd having to pay at the front door when I would have normally been backstage with Mark, hanging around for the sound check. Once inside I studied the crowd for familiar faces, feeling conspicuous in the clothes that I'd chosen to wear, the bold black and white striped jeans that would look obvious even in the darkened room. I hovered at the back near the bar, watching The Somerfields complete their set and sipping a drink absently.

Before the Fish played there was the usual break for equipment to be rearranged and sound levels checked. I could see various band members mingling with the crowd, and in the dim lighting I could pick out Gary's profile and his swept back hair. I smiled as he approached me but he walked past without a glance. I convinced myself that in the noise and general din of music and conversation he would have been too distracted to notice me. No one had been expecting me to turn up that evening and he probably hadn't recognised me anyway after my long absence. But then Stanley surfaced from out of the gloom and did the same thing.

Perhaps I wasn't ready for all this after all. I could feel my heart starting to beat faster with humiliation, but I couldn't believe that everyone would ignore me. Feeling crushed I slipped through the crowd to look for the bathroom so that I could have some time to organise my thoughts and compose myself. I stood leaning against the wall and staring at the grimy wash basins, running the scene over in my mind until I realised some of the girls entering the bathroom were coming back for a second, and then a third visit. To avoid any questions about me lingering there for so long I slid out into the crowd again, realising that the band was getting ready to play. I was eager for them to begin their set so that that people would swarm to the front, making it easier for me to blend in amongst the press of bodies. I hovered uncertainly, waiting for the room to be dimmed for the stage lights.

Under the spotlights I saw Mark stride across the stage and then disappear into the audience momentarily before reappearing within touching distance of where I was standing. He didn't acknowledge me, speaking briefly across the bar to one of the staff and then returning to the stage where he picked up a guitar and swung the strap over his shoulder.

It was like a slow death. I was looking into a future in which I no longer belonged. I felt out of place. My heart was still beating wildly as I watched Mark play, taking in his movements on stage and the familiarity of his voice, listening entranced as they moved from song to song, looking for any small clue that he may be aware of my presence.

They played Michael's song, *Isobel* and another that was called *One Of Your Bets*. Listening to the lyrics as they played I thought of all the gigs I'd attended, and I could feel my eyes beginning to blur with tears.

After all this time I'd been certain I would enjoy seeing the band, but now I was just heartbroken and wretched. All the strength and resolve I imagined I'd been gaining during the weeks of self-imposed isolation was a fragile deception when put to the test. I couldn't bear to wait for the last song, and so with a final glance from the doorway, I left.

Walking in the cool, shadowy streets was a relief as I tried to untangle my confused thoughts, but although I arrived home tired and scattered my clothes across the floor, I lay in bed staring at the darkness until my eyes burned; and even then I couldn't sleep.

The next morning I paced and I replayed all the details of the previous evening. I had to know the truth; whether he'd seen me there, whether he'd decided to never speak to me again. Even if I was correct, anything would be better than this uncertainty. I had to talk to him.

"Hello?" The voice sounded sleepy when he eventually answered the phone, following several rings. My heart was skipping erratically.

"Hi, did I wake you?" I tried to keep my voice steady.

"Hey, hi…"

His voice was soft and full of recognition. It was warm and welcoming.

"No, that's okay," he murmured, "it's great to hear from you."

"I just wanted you to know that I liked the new songs you played last night."

"Thanks," he started, before checking himself. He sounded genuinely surprised. "Hang on….You were *there*?"

I released my held breath with a grateful sigh.

"Yes, I was there. Didn't you see me?"

"No, I…had…no idea…"

I was half laughing as I interrupted again.

"…But how could you miss me in those black and white pants?"

"I didn't see you," he continued. "You came to the gig? Why didn't you say hello?"

A surge of relief washed over me.

"I really wanted to come…I know it's been ages…" I said, feeling my heartbeat slowing down. "I still can't believe you didn't see me. Stan *and* Gary walked past me as if I was invisible. I thought maybe you were all ignoring me?"

"No! Why would I do that?"

I loved hearing his voice and being able to talk to him again. There seemed to be so much to say. With all the things that had happened over the past few weeks we decided to catch-up, cruising through Abbotsford together on our bikes and then dropping in to The Retreat Hotel to have an afternoon beer in the dim interior.

Known as the hotel in which *The Sullivans* television series had been filmed it was one of my favourite pubs, small and cosy, filled with cushioned nooks, and popular for its English beer on tap. We found a corner and chatted for hours, watching the locals at their stools by the bar, and eyeing the steaming plates of food arriving from the kitchen. Mellowed by the beer, neither of us were in a hurry to leave, but we decided to take the bikes home and then go to a gig later that night.

I wasn't sure what was happening, and couldn't seem to find the right words to ask Mark directly. It felt like reconciliation, as if the last few weeks had been an aberration, but when I rode away in the scant warmth of the autumn sunshine I hardly dared to have any expectations. I was just focussed on getting back to him, and spending the evening together.

It held all the suspense and delight of a new romance. Although we watched The Underground Lovers and then The Somerfields play, for most of the time we ignored the bands as we continued to talk, intoxicated by the pleasure of being together again, finally returning to Mark's flat to share a late dinner.

There was hardly a sound in the air outside. Having steadily closed the gap between us, we were curled up together on the swivel chair in the lounge room in the early hours of the morning. We had talked enough, and I was sitting on his lap with my back to his chest, watching the candles flicker their light against the far wall. The familiarity of this room and his embrace had lulled me to a sense of calm. I'd expected to go home after the gig, but I hadn't been able to bring myself to leave. It was comforting to be so close, and I could feel the warmth of his touch as he stroked my arm tenderly, welcoming the proximity of his body where I could feel his chest rising and falling against my back.

My face was beginning to flush, and I was aware of my breath quickening as all my senses began to focus on his hand trailing across the inside of my elbow. It was irresistible, that place where his skin met mine. Leaning against him with eyes closed, my emotions were running out of control as his hands began to wander over my body. I could feel the questions on his fingers with each caress, unsure of the boundaries now, advancing cautiously. Time seemed to have a strange momentum, slowing as I traced his contours, quickening as I felt him reach beneath my layers of clothing. The heat of my desire and longing took my breath away, rendering me speechless as it flared through every nerve ending. It was unbearable and exhilarating, wordlessly letting him go further, willing him to continue, as if speaking would break the spell.

We teetered on the cusp of the suspense, holding back and then rushing forward, eager but afraid. It was like freefalling to an unknown place, feeling my heart speeding through the minutes, feeling the lightness in my stomach and the butterflies thrumming above my navel.

The compulsion became an urgency then, and we fell into it, letting it consume us as we started to make love raggedly, unselfconsciously, generating a passion that I'd never known. I could feel myself being transported by exquisite sensations; alternating between sadness and bliss, euphoria and loss, feeling a sob building within my chest and overwhelming me. As I moved on his lap listening to a sound in the darkness, I realised it was my own voice laughing uninhibitedly, crying uncontrollably. The intensity of my emotions was terrifying and unstoppable. I was so afraid of how my desire had made me lose control, afraid of how deep it was taking me, to this new and uncharted place. But it had come too far now, there was no way back; I was losing myself entirely to the rapture of it all, and I could finally do nothing but admit defeat.

It was such a sweet surrender. I was still trembling as we clung together, our shadows flickering in the candlelight on the wall opposite, rocking gently and merging together like one body. I could feel tears rolling down my face and I could hear Mark's voice imploring softly, asking over and over if he'd hurt me; but I couldn't speak after what had just happened. It felt as if he'd wrested something from me that I'd been trying to keep in check for the last few weeks because I was so afraid of the power it had over me. It coursed through me now. There was a stark honesty to it, an inescapable certainty. Every part of me felt bound to him; I belonged to him.

He held my naked body against his until I stopped crying, cradling me in the darkness and waiting for me to say something.

"Are you alright Ange?"

There was such a tenderness to the way he was holding me that I thought my heart might break. In my chest I could feel its erratic rhythm, driving the tempo of my blood. As my breathing slowed I whispered to him softly.

"Yes, I'm alright…"

But how could I begin to tell him?

"It's just…that I love you, so much… more than I ever knew. I don't even know how to tell you. There are no words for it."

*Like Two Mexicans Dancing*

# Winter and Jesus Jones

JUNE WAS FILLED with the glory of love and desire, raw passion and tenderness. Although it was a winter month I was flooded with such intoxicating emotions that I barely registered the cold weather. In the evenings we continued the rounds of live music, bumping into Martin or Andrew who were often out gigging at the same venues, ignoring their raised eyebrows and their queries about the resurrection of our relationship.

At the beginning of the month we went to Melbourne University to see Jesus Jones. Whenever we turned on the radio the local stations were playing tracks from the current album, Doubt, and for days we'd been hearing Mike Edwards' familiar voice coming through the speakers with *International Bright Young Thing*, and *Right Here, Right Now*.

Having arrived too early at the huge, empty hall we'd retreated to the student coffee shop downstairs to buy drinks. At one of the tables there was an unkempt man tearing into a meat pie with his hands, having a very loud and animated conversation, and chatting gregariously in between bites. There was a strong, familiar burr to his voice that confirmed he was from the North of England, and as we joined the discussion we discovered he was the Sound Technician for the band.

Chronic deafness was an occupational hazard for most Technicians; a less attractive side of live performance, and probably the reason for his noisy banter and raucous anecdotes. I could see it was going to be an ear splitting gig if he was going to be setting the levels that night.

The support was by the Sydney band, Clouds, and locals, The Underground Lovers, who were first on stage that night. By the time they'd finished playing, the hall had transformed from echoing emptiness into shoulder-to-shoulder students, and the floor was wet and slippery with spilled drinks.

Jesus Jones began their set with a light-show of lasers and strobe lights, Al Doughty wielding his bass with a blur of blonde dreadlocks. Bare-chested, we watched him gyrate and whirl his heavy mop of hair to the throb of the music. For more than an hour he twirled his head, tossing and rotating it to the songs as he balanced in a wide stance, stabbing at the bass strings. With the uninterrupted velocity of his head banging I didn't know how he managed to play with such accuracy. The spectacle made my neck ache, but it was clear that the show and his pounding bass enthused the already passionate fans.

In the crowd at the front a tightly packed throng of people were dancing frenetically, all elbows and tearing fists, bagatelle body slamming and thrusting chests. Boys occasionally emerged from the pack with just the collar of their T-shirt remaining, like a necklace above their bare chests, ravaged by the push and shove from the mass within.

We watched as a body was occasionally birthed upwards from out of the horde, surfing the crowd on the waiting arms overhead, or oozing out at the front of the stage. From there they'd dive back onto a sea of upraised hands that log rolled and washed them to-and-fro until they were finally absorbed again into the thrashing crowd. It made me think of the TISM gig and all of Darren's aspirations.

The gig was finally brought to a close with the song, *Blissed*, the sound by then having reached an uncomfortable intensity that could only be endured with earplugs, the room rank with perspiration and intolerably hot despite the cool weather outside. As soon as the main lights came on and cast their harsh stare on the carnage and detritus in the hall, we swarmed gratefully out on to the campus, our damp shirts quickly growing cold against our skin, our ears glad of the quiet but shocked by the hushed night air.

Walking back to the car arm in arm, it was one of those few nights when we could leave together after the final song, chatting about the highlights and comparing favourite moments. There was no equipment to pack away, no lingering until the early hours of the morning. Both of us were content to be punters for the night, blending seamlessly with the crowd, happy to be caught in the lull until Mark's schedule would take him away again.

\*

A week later The Fish were at The Club, continuing their album launch, this time offering their handmade *Finzine* magazine to everyone that attended. It included '50 crap things you don't really need to know about The Fish', as well as a complete recording history. It incorporated a page written by each of the band members, allowing them to provide some personalised facts and comments.

Mark's page was filled with credits and acknowledgments, as well as his musical influences. When I saw references to The Violent Femmes, Jonathan Richman, and T-Bone Burnett, I slid effortlessly into memories of his gentle serenades. Scanning the list of bands with whom they'd played provoked other memories - the acrimonious start to the UB40 tour; the night when Martin had his white Rickenbacker autographed by Harry Dean Stanton; the Violent Femmes gig.

They'd played with the Femmes at The Palace in November 1990. Mark had been so excited about the gig, and everyone had been in such high spirits afterwards. From the wings in the backstage area, I'd been able to stand away from the crush pressed to the front of the stage and take photographs. It had been a highlight for the band, and had preceded our trip to Queensland by only a couple of weeks.

To be promoting a second album with such a catalogue of past achievements seemed to augur well for the future. I knew the band would be hoping for increased sales on the back of all the recent launches, even if their resolve had been continually tested since the first album.

With a thrill I saw that I was included in the list of tributes on Mark's page, smiling when I noticed he'd added another tiny comment in the top left corner, a cryptic reference to our incredible and passionate reunion. It said simply, 'Try it in a swivel chair'.

There was also a bible reference, Ecclesiastes 11:9

I looked it up later, and was surprised by what it said:

*'Be happy, young man, while you are young, and let your heart give you joy in the days of your youth. Follow the ways of your heart and whatever your eyes see, but know that for all these things God will bring you to judgement.'*

Supporting Violent Femmes – The Palace, Nov 1990

(From L: Michael, Martin, Mark)

## Violent Femmes: The Palace, Nov 1990

*Angela J. Dawson*

From *Finzine* magazine

T-Shirt logo, with Ol' Shep the fish

*Angela J. Dawson*

# Ride

ON A SUNDAY evening at the end of June we were back at the beach, on the familiar streets of St Kilda, awaiting the only gig in Melbourne by English shoegazing band, Ride.  Originally the gig had been booked at The Old Greek Theatre on Bridge Road, but it had been cancelled after the theatre's sudden and mysterious demise that same month.  The official line was that it had burned down, but there were rumours of arson.  All the same, a *To Let* sign had been placed outside what was left of it, and all the bands that had been listed to play there had been rescheduled to other venues.

The Old Greek in Richmond held many memories as a quirky Art Deco venue, and was a regular on the gig circuit.  We'd seen countless bands there and shared our evenings with other local musicians, including fellow Tasmanians, the Wild Pumpkins At Midnight.  Inside the congested hall its wooden floors were set at an angle sloping progressively downwards towards the stage, and this always ensured a good view of the stage even from the back.  But if you dropped something in the crowd - a pen, some coins, your keys - the gentle gradient of the floor ensured its permanent disappearance.  Your possessions would be propelled down the incline between the dense mass of legs and feet and be lost forever.  For the same reason it was never a good idea to sit on the floor, however much your legs ached from standing.  Spilled drinks behind you travelled quickly.

Confusingly supported by the local band, Ripe, the Oxford boys of Ride had been slotted into The Palace schedule at short notice and had a playlist of new songs that would ultimately be on their second album, Going Blank Again, planned for release in March 1992 on Creation Records.

After the support set, Ride appeared with a backdrop of rainbow colours at the rear of the stage, the stripes shifting like light coming through venetian blinds, the customary dry ice fog seeping stealthily over the edges of the stage and fingering the floor below.  In front of it all Mark Gardener stood calmly in the strobe lights, jump-starting his guitar, raking and swiping at the strings, the ultraviolet lights whitening our teeth and picking out tiny flecks on our black clothes.

### Like Two Mexicans Dancing

A single keyboard note echoed in tremulous reverb, joined by the pulse of the bass, its narrative pounding in our chest cavities as we crashed into a powerful eight minute *Leave Them All Behind*. Stacked vocal harmonies looped through layered guitars, the patterns building and repeating to a dissonant crashing end. As they segued into *Going Blank Again* we didn't have any sense of the night being so precious, oblivious to the conflict within the band that would soon pull them apart. No-one could have known, as we watched them perform with cool detachment, that the demands of such extensive touring would be the catalyst for their demise.

When their debut album, Nowhere had been released in 1990 at the height of the heavy-fringed, anorak wearing era, a little piece of history had been burned into one of the tracks. The British Poll Tax Riots were raging outside the studios at the time, and during the recording of the song, *Paralysed* the crowd-noise had been captured in the background.

This pending second album would be where the cracks started to show, and these remaining gigs would become part of their own history. Beyond the third album, Carnival of Light, the band would dissolve. In 1995, Andy Bell would relinquish his guitar, and he would go on to play bass for Oasis. It wasn't a prospect that we could have imagined for them that night.

As the jagged edges of the feedback soared and the sound reached a painful level of noise, I worked-in my foam earplugs, speculating on the 10,000 miles the band would soon be travelling to return to their home town. Seeing an English band was an acute reminder of my distant origins and I keenly felt the pull of my homeland at times like this, beset with questions about where my long term future lay. It was impossible to resolve. The way forward was indefinable and filled with challenges. There were no time frames for Mark's success. I didn't know what would happen next, or how long we would need to wait.

*

In the weeks that followed our reconciliation, we continued to chase the dream of commercial success with every band we saw, taking in the vibe, feeling a displaced, vicarious sort of pleasure as we watched them play. We were transported by our rekindled relationship, savouring our renewed romance as we indulged our musical passions, clinging to a concept of the life we wanted, and imagining all the possibilities.

It was a Utopia in which we were left to linger, where everything was enmeshed; but we really didn't have anywhere else to go. We were caught up in all the indecision, and trapped by the threads of our past.

# Helvelln

IN AUGUST, Jeremy, Nick and Andrew released their self-titled album, Helvelln on Mushroom Records. Mark was credited for his backing-vocals on three of the tracks, and Chris Wilson featured on harmonica. From the beginning, the label wanted Jeremy to add new members, keen to expand the band beyond the founding trio. There was even pressure to replace one of the original three, dividing their loyalties and testing their friendships. The coveted record deal could come at a high price sometimes.

Grappling with the opportunities occurring in front of us and the contrasting apathy towards The Fish, Mark and I continued our mutual addiction. We were energised by charged encounters that kept our lives entangled, but it was just a distraction that enabled us to overlook the slow unravelling of everything else. Friends were making progress while they were still standing on the side lines. The band continued to be ignored, to Mark's perpetual frustration, and yet we all felt they were stronger than ever with Michael's influence and his song writing. Their current line-up should have been cause for celebration, a chance to explore new directions, but I had never seen them so defeated. We were all wondering how much longer they would need to hold out when things suddenly moved even closer to home; closer to Mark's home anyway.

We'd grown accustomed to hearing John play his keyboard in the flat above Mark's apartment. On lazy afternoons, when we'd still be in bed after a gig the night before, his melodies would float down to where we lay, filtered sunshine slicing through the louvred screens in the bedroom, the blinds blowing outwards in the light breeze. John shared his news about FOM when he crossed paths with Mark on the stairs one day, confirming they were being pursued by a record company.

In the end, FOM would be the first band to sign to the short lived Raw label, an affiliate of Sony Music Australia, releasing their four track EP, Hog Heaven in 1992.

That was as close as it got. Shortly afterwards, Mark told me he'd decided to break up the band. After a final gig in October at The Club on Smith Street, he planned to return to Tasmania and complete the Teaching Diploma that he'd deferred for so long. Knowing the importance of the band to Mark, I realised he would have considered every option first before deciding to leave Melbourne. His imminent departure for Tasmania demonstrated his resolve to move on, and it finally offered a way out of our dilemma.

Despite the finality of the decision, I felt myself resisting the consequences. There had been a few difficult conversations, and they'd revealed some interesting truths.

"Teaching?" I asked, with dismay.

"I need to finish my Diploma. The band has never had enough…"

He blew out a heavy breath, before he continued.

"There's just no point anymore…when we're being continually overlooked."

"But you'll be…living in Tassie? For months; maybe for a whole year?"

"I have to go back to the same college in Launceston where I deferred. If I'm going to teach, I need to get my qualifications."

I couldn't imagine it. The end of the band. My own sadness and disappointment was suffocating; Mark must have felt broken. I wasn't sure what it meant for us now.

"I'll be the same person. Just not a musician." He looked at me pointedly. "I hope that's not the only reason you'd want to be with me, Ange."

I felt cornered.

"I don't know you as anything else. That's who you were when we met. It's who you are to me, who you've always been."

I looked at him sadly, both of us at a loss, wondering what to say.

"I had dreams about it too you know, about the life we'd have," I said.

"We can still be together. It'll be a different life, that's all."

I could feel his eyes on me as I dropped my gaze to the ground.

"It's not just that," I declared, "there are so many other things to consider."

"What d'you mean?" He tipped his head slightly as he looked at me.

"Will you come back?"

He raised an arm towards me as he replied, "Ange….I'm not saying…"

"Don't." I moved a step back. "I live here now, Mark. My job's here. So…what? We'll visit? We'll write? Or is this it?"

I realised he hadn't actually asked me to go with him. He ran his hand through his hair and tried to take my hand as I continued.

"I'm just so shocked that you're giving up. I've invested so much in this as well. I moved here to be with you, to pursue all this. Are you really sure this is what you want?"

"It's not what I want." He paused, and sighed despondently. "But it's how it is."

If he went back to Tasmania I wasn't confident we could survive the separation of living so far apart again. It felt like he was giving up on us, as well as the band.

"You won't change your mind then?"

"No."

It was heart breaking, everything being pulled apart after such a long struggle to hold on to it.

"But you could come back here, after you've graduated?" I asked.

"I have to study first." He paused, and I waited. "If I can get a job, yes."

I searched his face, as if it might somehow contain the answers to all my questions.

"So it could be more than a year?"

When I was living in Tasmania, the long wait for my visa had seemed interminable, but that had only been for six months. Now I didn't know how long he'd be gone, or if he'd even come back. Throughout all of this, we'd always waited for each other, whatever had happened, however long it had taken. I had to choose now. I either stayed or followed, I either waited or I moved on.

"It's a long time," I said.

"It's only an hour away."

Helvelln, self-titled album (cassette) - 1991 Mushroom Records Pty Ltd

*Like Two Mexicans Dancing*

This page, & previous:- cassette inlay
(with incorrect spelling of Mark's surname)

*Like Two Mexicans Dancing*

## LAUNCESTON WEEK
### ENTERTAINMENT AND VISITOR GUIDE

# Fish to farewell Tasmanian fans

**By CHRIS COPAS**

ONE of Australia's most innovative and refreshing bands, the Melbourne-based FISH JOHN WEST REJECT, have decided to call it quits.

The band, which formed in Tasmania in the mid-'80s, says that the decision was catalysed by a long-running personal disagreement between a record company executive and its former Sydney manager.

Guitarist Martin Witheford said last week that the band's album Fin, released on Melbourne's independent Shock label in June, 1990, "really came out eight months late, by which time the impetus had gone."

The band, despondent over treatment from major companies and frustrated by its lack of commercial success despite critical acclaim, will disband about the middle of October.

However, before then, they'll play one final Tasmanian tour, kicking off tonight (Wednesday) at the Uni campus in Launceston.

The band will then line up at Lugoni's, the new alternative venue on the first floor of Lloyd's Hotel, in lower George St, this Thursday night.

Venue organiser David O'Byrne said that the gig would be a special one for Fish fans, with special giveaways of collections of the recordings of the band, on album and single.

The Fish will also play at the Uni campus in Hobart on Friday night, and at the Wheatsheaf Hotel, Hobart, on Saturday night.

"We are sick of touring and playing constantly, but seemingly banging our heads against a brick wall," Witheford said.

"All our recorded material has met with heaps of critical acclaim from all over the country, yet we are constantly ignored by major record companies.

"We are by no means the only band in this situation, but we work harder than a lot of independent bands."

Witheford said that the Fish John West Reject had been offered a contract with a major concern in April, 1990, but it had been withdrawn because the company's boss had been feuding with the band's then-Sydney manager for more than 15 years.

"It set us back on our heels by almost a year," he said.

Witheford and singer and guitarist Mark Narcowicz will continue together as a duo, but mostly in the studio.

Drummer Graham Rankin and bass player Michael Witheford will also work separately as a duo.

The Fish started as a busking duo of Narcowicz and Mark Adams in Launceston in 1985, and by 1987 had grown into a four-piece outfit including bass player Andrew Viney and drummer Rankin.

They moved to Melbourne in 1988, and have since issued two cassette albums, three singles, a four-track extended play and two fully-fledged albums, also on Compact Disc.

Their recorded work has also appeared on numerous compilations, including the RRR FM collection of rising Melbourne bands Used And Recovered By in 1989.

Adams left the band early in 1990, and Viney followed soon after.

Michael Witheford, then resident in Melbourne, was recruited first, followed by brother Martin, then working in a Launceston band.

He would make his debut with the band in Perth, while they were supporting UB40 on a national tour.

The band's last album Fin, seemingly destined to become a collector's piece, is available in all formats through Shock Records.

• Melbourne-based band, the Fish John West Reject, will play at the University's Launceston campus tonight.

*Angela J. Dawson*

# 18 October 1991

I'D NOTED the date for the final gig in my diary - it was a Friday. The Club on Smith St, Collingwood held many memories of past shows. Before he joined the Fish, I'd even seen Stanley play there with his band, Man In The Wood, so I looked forward to returning to its familiar surroundings.

I arrived early, glancing up from the entrance to the stairs that sagged a worn path to the upstairs bar, the torn carpet and faded paintwork broken only by the coloured posters advertising past and future bands. From street level I tramped up the steep staircase, wondering why a relatively large venue would have such a plain and unobtrusive doorway.

The staircase opened out to a large room with a bar and pool tables and a small space for musicians to play. Whenever the main gig finished downstairs there'd usually be someone strumming a guitar here into the late hours. In fact, a long time ago I'd watched a trio of musicians playing enthusiastically, crammed into a corner of this room. Their drummer had spent the night chasing his kick-drum across the floor because they'd forgotten to bring enough sand bags to weigh it down. That had been Helvelln in their hey-day.

I smiled at the thought, crossing the length of the room to the far corner where another door led to a metal staircase. These steps veered back down into the depths of The Club where there was a second bar and a stage at the far end of a cavernous room. The shabbiness of the venue was more evident when it was empty. The soul of the place returned when the crowds filled its echoing spaces, but it leaked out onto the dark street whenever they dispersed.

In the daylight the huge rooms stared lethargically with an empty patience, waiting for their nocturnal rousing, for the songs that would bring them to life each night. The sound of so many bands had been leeched into the brickwork; hours of musical history had been infused into the substance of the walls. Memories materialised with a strength that made them feel palpable. I could almost touch the past here.

Everyone who had ever been involved with the band was in the audience. From the cameo roles, to those who had launched this great production in the beginning, they were all returning for the credits. I could see Graham in the crowd, his long black hair shaved off completely, wearing his characteristic black leather jacket with a black T-shirt. He was still drumming for The Rough Diamonds and I hadn't seen him since the day he'd handed over to Stanley. Even Graham's previous girlfriend, Cathy had appeared like a distant memory from that warm summer evening, when she had invited me to join the band in Princes Park in Launceston. Her boy was probably about two years old now; Graham's son born into those early days of hopefulness and expectation.

I listened as Warky's band, Hurdy Gurdy played a brief support, excusing my way through the crowd towards the back of the room where I found Harve and Di, grateful for familiar faces after arriving on my own. There would be a long wait until the Fish appeared; too much time for doubts to arise. Over the last few weeks Mark and I had tried to disconnect, but I didn't feel confident about my resolve. I knew I would yearn to be with Mark when I heard all the familiar songs again. Having been propelled into a passionate reunion after our last separation, I wasn't sure that it would be any different this time. Even with the reality of his departure we hadn't completely discounted all notions of being together. We couldn't seem to let go of that glimmer of hope that lay somewhere in the future.

He looked relaxed when he emerged, wearing a suit and tie, his hair slicked back into a pony tail, smiling generously as the band launched into an acoustic version of *Invitations* on behalf of Andrew, who was strangely absent.

There was a transition as they moved into a couple of Michael's songs, beginning with a new one called *Flames*, and then changing pace again for some of the familiar cover versions, like Jonathan Richman's *Roadrunner*. I listened to lyrics that I knew so well I could sing them myself, feeling a combination of nostalgia and regret. But when I heard the opening lines of *Caution Rings* my heart began to race. Weaving my way forward through the crowd, I wanted to get up close and see Mark singing, as I always did.

In the centre of the room where the press of people was surprisingly less, I'd been watching Mark's lips and grappling with my shifting emotions when I caught sight of Darren grinning at me, his head nodding to the music. I smiled back, unable to talk in the sheer volume surrounding us, but glad of the noise as I felt my eyes begin to blur and the room start to shimmer. This would be the last time I'd hear *Caution Rings* played live.

I never tired of hearing the chorus, taking me back to that bright summer day when Mark had been busking. But as I followed the lyrics, I realised they were singing Michael's revised version, the one they'd recorded for the album. I felt profoundly sad. It cut me from the story as if I'd never been there. Mark's chorus only existed on the limited edition of The Orchard they'd released as a cassette in 1989. It was all I had. I listened with a sense of mourning for all the disappointments, for the losses and the sacrifices that had brought us to this point.

The final few songs in the set were like an exposition of their musical history. First Warky joined Mark and the Witheford brothers on guitars, and then Graham and Tim joined Stan on drums, the three of them crowding the drum kit to chase a frantic pace through the music. Andrew's absence was the only piece missing from their story. I gazed at them all on stage, seeing glimpses of the early days and remembering the occasions I'd seen them at their best. After this gig, it was all over.

Darren was leaving the venue early, his long hair swinging as he moved through the crowd, striding towards the rear steps as the music rose to fill the room and wake the ghosts of the past. I looked again at the stage and scanned the crowded room, dwelling on my misgivings, floundering at the prospect of letting it all go. Darren had managed it. He no longer had any responsibility for the band and was just a member of the audience like everyone else. He'd already deleted himself from their future. Even though I wavered indecisively, I already knew what I'd need to do. I'd have to go back to the beginning. It was only from there that I'd be able to see the way forward.

# How The Fish John West Reject went off

### The lost innocence of a Tasmanian success story

The Fish John West Reject, arguably Launceston's most successful musical export, played its farewell show in Melbourne on October 18. It was an untimely end for a band which survived internal problems and fickle reactions at home to be on the brink of a major recording contract... RICKY EAVES spoke to founding member Mark Narkowicz about a band's loss of innocence... Ricky Eaves

• The Fish as they were, pictured above, from left, Narkowicz, Viney, Adams and Rankin (front); and as they were at the finish, from left: Michael Witheford, Narkowicz, Martin Witheford.

THE contract was on the table... a three-album deal with major record label Mushroom needed only a signature.

For Mark Narkowicz, singer, guitarist and last remaining founding-member of The Fish John West Reject, it should have been a culmination to years of writing, touring and learning.

Instead, the contract would remain unsigned; the spirit of the band was hence cast into the limbo of an industry where momentum and the 'current vibes' are everything.

"It fell through because of personal differences between certain people at the record company and a person associated with the band. We had pushed for a major label contract and we toured to Sydney constantly, but it was for nothing."

Ragged from endless touring and devoid of faith in the industry, they recorded their second album, Fin, regardless; it was self-funded like the first album, Swim, which sold more than 5000 copies.

The Fish then wound down to an agreed, though sadly premature, end last month.

□ □ □

The decision and money-making offices of Mushroom records were a far-cry from the enigmatic "Muse" in Launceston, an underground basement venue that first gained The Fish a following in 1986. That venue, in Charles St, was reduced to folklore when it was condemned as a fire-hazard in 1987.

The band which recorded Fin was also very different to the Christian busking act in the Brisbane St Mall in 1985. The original nucleus was Narkowicz, then a TSIT student and now a teacher, and social worker Mark Adams, whom he met at a church meeting.

Their first-ever show was as a folk duo performing at what was then Lloyds Hotel's Warm Sporran Folk Club.

Andrew Viney, formerly of Burnie band Noddy's Revenge, joined on bass in 1986. He left only last year to dedicate his time to his sons Matthew and Tim, for whom he is a single parent.

"The original Fish were all good Christian boys. We played gospel and folk music — Leadbelly, Woody Guthrie, that sort of thing — we had a real essence and a sense of what we were about," said Narkowicz.

First drummer Tim Gleeson was replaced by Graham Rankin shortly before the band left Launceston in '88.

The Fish had provided the freshest burst of original pop music and performance that Launceston had seen before relocating to Melbourne.

They immediately found a following. They appeared on ABC music programs Rage and Countdown Revolution; they played before 10,000 people supporting English band UB40 in Melbourne last year.

□ □ □

Coming home to Launceston created dilemmas for the band, caused partly by tall-poppy syndrome and local indifference to original music.

Some Fish faithful though were disappointed that the band had evolved from its original "hackabilly" style of folk-pop to a more conventional format.

The change happened when Mark Adams left the band in March last year, due to personal and musical differences with Narkowicz.

Narkowicz admits the break-up had been nasty, but would say no more. Adams now leads Melbourne band Hurdy Gurdy, which is touring Tasmania.

When Viney left, Narkowicz' old Launceston friends Martin and Michael Witheford took over on guitar and bass respectively and penned much of the Fin album.

Narkowicz maintains the Fish had a raw deal locally. "I'd heap shame on promoters and venue owners here. At times, we could only play Nick's Bar (Hotel Tasmania) on a Sunday. Radio too — we were the most successful Launceston band ever, but were rarely played."

Narkowicz intends teaching in Melbourne. He and Martin Witheford will continue recording together, while Michael Witheford freelances for the music press.

"If the Fish are to be remembered for anything, then I would prefer it was for one good song than for 100 live shows. The songs were what we were about," Narkowicz said.

## 'The contract was sitting on the table ready to be signed

Angela J. Dawson

# Rood and Roods

JAMES WAS drawing deeply on one of the Indonesian cigarettes to which he was so partial.

"It's really good to be here, Roody."

"Well, you could come back and live here you know."

We were sitting in his living room in Launceston, surrounded by cardboard boxes. They formed half built walls, stacked across the floor, distended and bulging with years of accumulated possessions and gadgets.

"D'you still have that pickled onion grabber thingy?" I asked.

"Oh, somewhere, in one of those," James said, waving at the collection of boxes teetering in front of us.

We were in imminent danger of being engulfed by a tsunami of utensils, appliances, soft furnishings and other mysterious contraptions.

"Do you really need all this stuff?"

He made a controlled noise in the back of his throat, like a worried chicken.

"You should see the bedroom."

The tip of his cigarette glowed orange as he inhaled.

"I thought you'd given up?" I challenged, watching him release a cloud of smoke.

"Yes well, it's the first drag that's hard to give up."

"HE loves it?" I queried, knowing his proclivity for anything hedonistic.

He quickly rose to the challenge.

"SHE loves it…!" he threw back, no doubt thinking of something lewd.

"…WE ALL *love it*!" we shrieked in unison.

James leaned forward as he gave the last consonant extra emphasis, before sinking deeper into his armchair with a satisfied grin.

"Actually she doesn't love it - Carolyn. I'll have to stop when we get married."

His initial concession had been to exchange normal cigarettes for the allegedly milder Indonesian ones as an interim measure, but Carolyn had never liked James smoking. The next stage was to cut down, but I knew he was finding it hard to cease altogether.

"So, when are you coming back here?" James asked, eyeing me provocatively.

"To Launceston? Oh, you know I'd love to Roody." I paused. "I'm very fond of the old place, and Melbourne's been such a headache lately."

"You could buy a house here around the corner from ours, and grow lots of bowel fodder in the garden, and walk over whenever you liked, and Callie would make scones, and you'd be able to drop around for afternoon tea with us on a Sunday. We might even get a dog."

He took a breath and smiled, watching my reaction. I could hear Carolyn whistling loudly in the kitchen, hitting each note perfectly.

"I could," I sighed. "It'd be brilliant. But it'd have to be different because a lot of the memories here would make me feel sad. It'd be like digging up all of the past, and that is, after all, what I'm trying to avoid at the moment."

A week had passed since that last gig at The Club, and I'd flown over to Tasmania to spend the weekend with James and Carolyn, timing my visit coincidentally with their house moving. They would be leaving the steep incline of Elizabeth Street for their new home on the equally vertigo inspiring gradient of Howick Street, adjacent to the hospital. With all the scaling of hills between houses, Cecil the silver Suzuki was almost down to the blocks on the brake pads. From the rear seat I'd been watching as James pummelled the pedals, counting on the gears to control our deceleration as we pelted down the dizzying slopes. It left our stomachs lurching as we scooped down sheer roads, freefalling towards the dip and then looping into the upswing. Lemmings, I thought. This is what it would feel like as they plummeted, even if they wouldn't be doing it in a Suzuki.

We'd been packing boxes and cleaning all day, deciding at this point to sit down amidst the clutter and estimate the amount of tidying yet to follow. Carolyn, ever conscious of our needs, appeared with a plate of assorted homemade biscuits. She had a lurid green fluid in a glass tumbler that I stared at suspiciously, narrowing my eyes as I sized it up. It was the colour of dishwashing liquid, an otherworldly luminescent colour, like something out of the movie, Alien.

"Is that…?" I began, fumbling for an appropriate noun before I could continue. "What. Exactly. Is. That?"

"Cordial."

"It's not for me is it?" I was trying to imagine the sort of flavour you could expect from such an odious hue.

She sipped it, to my relief, and handed me the plate. Her aversion to tea and coffee was a long standing affront to my caffeine dependence and seemed incongruous to any English tea drinker. James's mind had obviously made the transition to food at the appearance of the plate.

"Melbourne doesn't have a German Patisserie," he said tangentially.

"Well that's hardly a good reason for me to leave."

"But you know the Patisserie does make the best sausage rolls," he taunted, in reference to the Launceston shop, licking his lips salaciously. It was one of his favourite places.

"You could say the same about the vindaloo pies they sell at that grocery store in town. You can't get one of those outside of Launceston but it's not enough to make me move interstate," I challenged, smiling at him.

"Well," he bit into a biscuit, and mumbled through the crumbs, "don't say we didn't ask."

The three of us were resting casually in the back room now, overlooking the garden, sitting on the remnants of things yet to be packed and feeding our collective cravings for drinks, sugar and cigarettes. Without warning, James launched himself out of the chair in which until then he'd been reclining serenely. The sudden show of energy was quite out of character. Experience told me it was the sort of aberrant behaviour that warranted some scrutiny. With a mutual glance, Carolyn and I shifted ourselves in the clutter, settling back for a better view.

James had bolted out of the room but returned swiftly with an aerosol from the kitchen. At arm's length, he pointed the can at a chosen target and began spraying the floor in a series of staccato bursts, his arm pulling back every time like the recoil from a gun, his shrieks perfectly choreographed with each burst of spray.

"Aaah... Aaah... Aaah...!" he bellowed, his voice becoming more and more strident.

A type of Irish step dancing accompanied all this, a complex sequence of rapid leg movements that involved pogoing around a central spot on the floor. There was some sort of invader in the midst of the drama, and as James hopped around like someone on molten sand at the beach he was ensuring his assailant couldn't vault the gap and latch onto his unprotected hands or feet.

By then my interest had been sufficiently piqued to make me get up and move towards this dangerous creature, now almost completely buried under an avalanche of white aerosol powder. James was shaking the can vigorously for a final onslaught, but he appeared to have drained the contents to the last ozone depleting molecule.

"James," I put a restraining hand on his arm. "I think it's dead."

Ignoring me, he managed a last flourish with the aerosol, leaning at an oblique angle and pumping a few doses of spray as he uttered each word.

"Dirty. Filthy. Thing."

Carolyn seemed unconcerned, continuing to nibble her biscuit calmly and watching the drama as if she already knew the script.

"What is... erm..." I peered at the ground. "What was it?"

"A spider!" he roared, with undisguised revulsion. "A dirty, big, mother of a thing. Look at it!"

His aversion to spiders was unsurpassed. It could result in a call to action and an onslaught that would make the massacres of Genghis Khan pale, until the thing was finally annihilated. Carolyn had also decided to move and we both tried to identify the corpse, squinting at the white mound, while James went outside to the garden muttering something about retrieving a stick.

He re-appeared around the door jamb with an excessively long stick that was the best part of an entire tree limb, and which I would have called a branch. A few more minutes of skipping around followed as he tried to spear the spider remains onto the end of the branch from a distance of about six feet away. It had been a good show so far.

"You won't be able to even see it from back there."

It was like watching one sided jousting.

"You'll be sorry when it bites you."

"It can hardly bite me when it's just been smothered. It would have been asphyxiated after the first ten sprays."

"Well, you can never be too sure."

He was manoeuvring the limp spider outside onto the patio, having impaled it on the tip of the tree bough, where he then smeared it onto the warm concrete and finally stepped on it to reduce it to the basic atoms of its previous existence.

"There," he said, evidently proud of taking command of the situation, and peering at the damp smudge under his toe. "I've probably just saved your lives."

AS WE MOVED boxes into the new house, James gave me a vague insight into the world of mortgages, recounting the tale of how he'd approached the bank for a loan in order to buy the house on Howick Street. Although real estate was more affordable in Launceston he'd still needed to convince the bank manager he could afford the sixty thousand dollar mortgage.

"So I asked him how much I'd need for a deposit, and he asked me how much I'd got…"

I raised my eyebrows, waiting for the story to unfold.

"…and I said, not much…and he said, yes but how much exactly?"

"And?"

"And I said I only had a few hundred dollars, and then he wanted to know how many hundred."

"So how many did you have?" I asked, heaving a box down onto the floor.

"Three."

"You got a loan for a house for a three hundred dollar deposit?"

He nodded, with a smirk.

"Plus membership to the Secret Sect, highly coveted in this region I'll have you know."

I shook my head in disbelief.

"You must have an honest face, James."

"Well, mum gave me a bit more towards it," he admitted. "Pre-wedding gift."

"Ah… so you'd better not default on those payments. How does Callie feel about living with your Mum?"

I put down another box and looked around at the interior of the new house. It would need extensive work to decorate and repaint the garishly coloured bedrooms. Both James and Carolyn were keen homemakers, and as well as Callie's talent for baking and condiments they were skilled in the art of stencilling and sewing, tapestry and picture framing, upholstery and curtain making. James was eager to tackle any household task with his vast array of gadgets and labour saving devices, and Callie had already started new projects, making raffia hats and soft toys. It explained the glass eyes I'd found on the kitchen bench.

When Carolyn and I returned with the last of the boxes, James had already moved the fridge and was using his cordless drill to tackle the rusted screws in a wooden alcove, trying to widen an area to accommodate it. We left him pulling things apart in the kitchen, but when I checked on his progress a few minutes later he was grinning about something.

"Have a look behind the microwave."

I looked at him suspiciously and then at the microwave that he'd put onto the bench.

"Go on, have a look," he urged.

"Why? Is there going to be another pest control moment?"

"The man that lived here had a microwave there too, in exactly the same place on the bench."

"It's alright," Carolyn added, from across the room, "you're safe to have a look. He's a Painter, but I don't think he practised his trade much at home."

I peered behind it and could see a white square of unpainted wall that perfectly matched the size and shape of the microwave.

"He didn't paint behind it?"

"He painted around it. Obviously couldn't be bothered moving it. Doesn't it look weird?" Carolyn said.

"Good job we've got a microwave the same size as the gap," James said through clenched teeth, breaking into a sweat as he tried to wrench off a piece of the alcove that he'd managed to loosen.

"Come and look at the bathroom." Carolyn was beckoning for me to follow her.

From the doorway I could see one of the walls had a large rectangle of paint in a different colour to the rest of the room.

"He had a cupboard in here against the wall when we looked at the place. He must have done the same thing. Maybe to save a bit of paint!"

When we returned to the kitchen James had finished his first small project. The alcove had been widened, the wood splintered crudely along one side where he'd finally pulled it free, he had a large dusty smudge on his face, but the fridge was in place now and plugged in. He'd retrieved a bottle of red wine and some glasses from a box in the lounge, and he passed them around to us as he rummaged for a corkscrew.

"Let's drink to a new paint job; and to the official Sect Marital Abode."

"I'm so glad I could be here for this. I've really enjoyed helping you move in," I said, taking my glass. "It's been great - packing boxes, scrubbing my fingers to the bone, watching James execute spiders…"

"Thanks for helping," Carolyn sighed, surveying the mess. "I'm back to work tomorrow - on an early - so you'll have to carry on without me."

"What about you, James?" I asked.

"I was thinking of going to visit The Fruit Bat; if you fancy a drive to Ulverstone?"

IT WAS ONE of those bleak days, when the sun never breaks through the white sky, the diffuse light flattening the colours of the landscape and leaving just a few shades of green. We were heading towards the north coast to see James' parents. The Fruit Bat was his mother, and she'd been storing a few things that James wanted to retrieve and use at their new house.

The overcast sky and colourless landscape made me feel tired, but I was content to be jostled along the quiet road to Ulverstone as James drove.

"Sometimes I wish I'd never left here."

James glanced at me as he kept a steady speed.

"I suppose I always knew I'd leave eventually, but I couldn't imagine what would take me away; until I met Mark."

"Who's stopping you from coming back?"

My breath came out in a long sigh.

"I don't know. It would never be the same."

I stared listlessly through the window.

"It'd be too hard to recapture what I had; but when I'm here…it's so peaceful. Nothing like Melbourne," I admitted wistfully.

James cleared his throat, but said nothing.

"Of course Mark will be coming back here, to live for who knows how long."

I'd already told James about the band breaking up.

"Isn't that a good reason to come back?" he asked.

I watched the scenery pass for several minutes.

"I think Mark and I have finally split up."

He waited for a moment.

"You…think?" James repeated carefully.

"Well, neither of us have said anything, just like last time, but the way things have been going…" My voice trailed away.

"So you don't want to try, to come back here and be with him and see what happens?"

"I don't know. I love him, Roody. And I know he loves me."

I stared at the road sadly.

"But we can't seem to figure out our future. Everything's been so up in the air. I don't know what to do. I haven't known what to do for a while. It's like I've been waiting for something to happen to help me decide," I said miserably.

"Has he asked you to come?"

"Not really. Not in so many words. I mean we haven't had that talk."

"You haven't left him… and he hasn't left you… but it's all over?"

"It's sort of assumed."

"Look, we don't really know Mark very well. He didn't socialise with us much."

James flicked a glance at me, and I could tell he was trying to be tactful.

"I mean, we never spent a lot of time with both of you…together," he elaborated.

I considered what he'd just said for a moment.

"Do you think Mark doesn't like you?"

"Erm," he was trying to light a cigarette so he didn't have to look at me.

"Roody?"

He inhaled deeply and rolled the window down further as he released the smoke.

"I didn't know you felt like that," I said unhappily.

"Well, I'd hardly tell you, would I?"

"It's all over now anyway, so it won't matter."

"I've heard that before," he said softly, tipping his head slightly towards me.

"But it's different this time. Everything's come to an end; the band splitting up, Mark leaving Melbourne and returning to college. It's just the way everything seems to be going. It's like he's given up on everything. And I'm so tired of it all sometimes, trying to prove I love him enough."

James glanced at me. "So what will you do?"

"Nothing. Probably. I don't think I need to do anything. He'll just go, and that'll be it. I'll be in Melbourne."

As soon as I'd said it, I was struck by the harsh reality of the words, and I could feel my eyes stinging. A few moments passed before James spoke again.

"I suppose I was a bit jealous of Mark in a way."

"Why?"

"Because he took you away from us."

I thought of James' tearful drive to the ferry when I left Launceston.

"But it didn't stop us from being friends," I contested.

"No, I know. We'll always be friends."

He drew on the cigarette so that the tip glowed orange against the white backdrop of sky, and tapped the ash lightly into the buffeting winds of the open window.

"To be honest, Roody, I think Mark was a bit jealous of you too, you know, of our friendship. He never really understood all the Sect stuff, or what we were laughing about half the time. I think he found it all rather stupid."

"It'll all work out in the end. And as long as you're okay with whatever happens, you'll be alright. Perhaps we'll get to see you more often now?"

"Yeah, well, if he did take me away from you, I'm giving myself back. You'll be sorry."

At Overton, the house where his parents lived, James's elderly father was taking a batch of scones out of the oven for afternoon tea, and as we rummaged in the shed for dusty possessions, retrieving furniture from under the house, the rich smell of baking wafted out across the garden from the open windows. We quickly piled the assortment of items into the car and returned to the kitchen where we were faced with a plate of scones, still hot from the oven, and a pot of tea. Clearly James had acquired his domesticity genes from his Yorkshire father. Drawing wooden stools up to the kitchen table, we sat in the oven warmed room and looked out at the steep garden landscape, sloping down to the stream below. James was talking about how he used to play in the stream as a young boy, but I was looking at the rolling Tasmanian landscape, and thinking of the past.

For the last few days I'd been reliving so many memories. I'd walked through the Gorge at night, lit by the dull glow of lamps that cast their yellow light on the dusty pathways. I'd listened to the piercing shrill of the peacocks, echoing with mournful clarity from The Basin just as they had done nearly three years ago when Mark and I had walked together nervously for the first time. I'd hoped to find answers here, thinking that by retracing my footsteps, I might find my way again, or I might find something I'd missed.

Around town I'd looked for the tatty remnants of old posters advertising Fish gigs, and found they'd finally succumbed to the depredations of time and weather. Any faded pieces I'd seen on previous visits had been torn from the walls or pasted over, their historic purpose lost on the new bands advertised there now.

Launceston would always fill me with a deep sense of longing. I'd made my first home here on these shores, and I knew I'd feel forever grateful for that foundation, for its days of innocence and yearning. But like the posters around town, the fragments of my life and the home I'd made here had also gone, long ago.

All too easily I'd become snagged in those memories again as I'd been trying to work loose the ties that bound me. I didn't want to forget where I'd come from, but neither did I want to be held captive by my past.

Even as I circled the range of possibilities, wondering what to do, I could see that everything was more complicated than it seemed, it was wheels within wheels, interconnected and inseparable, making it impossible to unravel all the emotions and motivations. The sharp edges of my resolve blurred whenever I tried to make a choice.

I hadn't been seeking restitution. I knew I couldn't go back, but I could make repairs to the original, recreate a better model. The alternative was to forge a new path. The doors to the past and the future were both here, but first I needed to decide which one I'd step through.

Ticket for gig at The Palace, St Kilda

```
WONDER    | Triple J, Lees & West         | WONDER
STUFF     | present THE WONDER STUFF      | STUFF
$20+b/f   | +The Hummingbirds & Crystal Set

PALACE    | THE PALACE                    | PALACE

NOV 22    | FRIDAY 22 NOVEMBER 1991       | NOV 22
8 PM      |         8.00 PM               | 8 PM
          | UNDER 18'S NOT ADMITTED       | $20+b/f
NO.  367  | GENERAL ADMISSION      367    | NO.  367
```

# Always

A MONTH AFTER my visit to Tasmania I was waiting for Mark to collect me in the red Gemini. Tempted by the listings in the international music gig guide, we'd secured tickets to see English band, The Wonderstuff playing at The Palace in St Kilda.

Since my trip to Launceston we'd been counting down the days until Mark's departure and his return to full time study in Dilston. My second Christmas in Melbourne was approaching, and we'd already had the sort of hot gusting winds that often culminated in thunderstorms, bringing some relief to us on those humid afternoons. I'd seen less of Mark as he'd been packing his possessions and preparing to transfer his life across The Strait, but we were excited to be seeing the band together that night. As soon as he arrived, I could feel the anticipation that always preceded a gig, but also the gentle affection between us as we shared stories about the last couple of weeks.

The two lanes of Queens Road swept alongside Albert Park Lake on the right, and on towards St Kilda. In the twilight I could see cars nosing around Lakeside Drive as it wound around the water, their headlights highlighting the curves as they scooped through the park. My eyes had been taking in the view but they dropped to Mark in the foreground, sitting behind the wheel. I could feel the powerful tug of familiarity, and the urge to reach across, to rest a hand on his leg as he drove. As we circled around looking for somewhere to park we were already high on emotions that we'd been trying to keep in check, sensing the gravitational pull of attraction and the path we seemed compelled to follow, constraining us to remain bound together.

At The Palace, we were faced with all the usual faces in the crowd. Harve and Di smiled questioningly at us when we appeared together. Mark's previous girlfriend was there, emerging from a past they'd shared before my arrival on the island. She'd taken the trip over from Launceston to come to the gig.

We listened to the set of familiar songs, *Size of a cow*, and *Don't let me down*, and the lilting refrain of *Caught in your shadow*, but I was lost in my thoughts all night, flicking through countless images and trying to reach some sort of decision.

On the way home it felt so easy to be with Mark again, sitting close to him in the confines of the car, taking in the mannerisms of his driving and the intimacy of our situation.

"Ange...?"

"Hmmm."

"Will I see you in Launceston? When you come over for the wedding?"

James and Carolyn had set the date for a January wedding, and I was one of the bridesmaids.

The next few weeks would be testing. There was still so much about our future that was uncertain, but he was lighting a beacon, keeping us connected. It felt like a glimmer of hope.

"I don't know. It'd be nice, but perhaps we should wait and see, don't you think?"

I wasn't sure if he'd decided where he'd be living after his studies, whether he'd stay in Tasmania. I didn't want to contemplate all the months ahead, and how I would fill my days.

"Do you think...when we meet up again in the future, we'll make love for old times' sake?"

The question sat there for a moment, posed for a time when we might no longer be together. I didn't know. Would we?

"I don't think so," I replied gently, mistrusting my own uncertainty. "I don't think it would be a good idea. Why do you ask?"

"Oh, I was just wondering."

He pulled over at the side of the road by my Parkville house, with the engine idling. He was looking at me with the usual expression, the same one his face had always held whenever he had stared up to my window in Launceston. Even in the shadows I could see the tenderness in his face. I knew that I could kiss him, that it would be so easy, that he would let me. He was waiting to see what I would do.

The engine hummed in the quiet street. My arm was resting lightly on the door as I paused, wondering what would happen next.

"Thanks, for driving me. For the lift."

I stepped lightly out of the car and closed the door. I took a breath, and let it out. The first one I would take as I watched him go, driving away from me for the last time. The taillights gleamed in the darkness as he paused at the end of the street, the indicator blinking left. Across the road the old terrace shrugged between its neighbours in the darkness, waiting for me to step inside. The Gemini was turning into the traffic on Royal Parade, pulling away from the junction and I knew Mark would be able to see me in the rear vision mirror, still standing on the street. I waited until he'd turned the corner, and then crossed the road, inhaling the cool air and listening to the hum of the hospital behind me.

High above me, scattered stars reflected the light of a distant sun. I turned on the spot, my eyes scanning the patterns in the blackness, thinking of promises made, of the feelings we had tried for so long to relinquish but they had endured.

I had somehow found true love and it had brought me such happiness and sorrow. Perhaps I was fortunate to discover what many others seek, yet may not always find. Love is the one truth that completes us, yet leaves us entirely naked, with the strength to break and expose us. It is the most illuminating of all our human characteristics, the one for which songs are played and poetry written. Despite the primal fears that it aroused, and its brutal wounds, it contained the blissful heights of enchantment to which I would always want to return.

Since I began writing at my desk in the summer of 1993 I have travelled and I have loved, passionately but evanescently, never falling as deeply as I did when my young heart skipped through that first summer. Love can only be felt for the first time once. Perhaps it is that first experience that is so hard to forget, when life is unutterably joyful, when the highs and lows are so extreme and visceral.

I think often of the raw wilderness and simplicity of my life in Tasmania. I remember how love manifested, and how it unfolded me for the first time. It continues to exist within me like an eternal flame, sometimes flickering, sometimes substantial. Sustained by memories or dimmed by time, its flare is bearable for the most part, until an unsolicited ache is stirred by a fleeting thought, a familiar phrase, or a certain song. It is only now, when I reflect on everything, that I can truly understand the everlasting characteristics of real love, the silent way it waits within me, and its eternal nature.

So it follows that I will always find my heart returning to that rapturous moment of youth and all of its discovery; those transcendent days of first love, never forgotten, and somehow never eclipsed by any other light, however brightly it may seem to burn.

Music is an open portal to the past. It's usually the songs that evoke those passions and stir that wistful longing for the past. Sometimes it can be just from the smallest detail, like a shell on my windowsill, or a busker on the street.

The stars are my greatest weakness, and there are so many clear nights here when I can see Orion. But it's when I see the pylons in the fields, retreating off into the distance, that I am transported. It reminds me of our laughter all those years ago when I told you they were like two Mexicans dancing. It reminds me of what I once had, and what I will always have, deep within my heart.

*Angela J. Dawson*

# Addendum

ABOUT SIX MONTHS later, in May 1992 I met Mark again in Launceston at the Hard Times Café, across the road from Rosie's Bar where we had met for a first date more than three years ago. Afterwards, we drove across the city and then walked in the dark Gorge under a half moon, watching the waters racing in torrents under the bridge just as we'd done on that first night. For more than five hours we stirred the deep waters of our past again, talking about the time we'd shared during that unforgettable summer.

I wanted to be certain that we had meant as much to each other as I thought. But I also wanted to reassure myself I had made the right decision. As we relived all the memories that had begun in Launceston, he assured me that he had loved me. Loved. He had finally released me.

My tears began in the moonlight that night, knowing beyond a doubt he was no longer mine. The certainty of it broke my heart. It was only then that I really saw the magnificent, saturated Technicolor of the love I had forsaken.

# So the story goes

By May 1993, a year later, I'd already started writing about everything that had happened, thinking it would bring some sort of resolution and closure to that chapter of my life. After all, the past was really a prologue, a starting point for all that would follow.

I had a brief meeting with Mark around that time, to give him a collage I'd made for his birthday, when I heard he was visiting Martin in Melbourne. Although I realised it was the end of our story, I knew I would always grapple with the outcome, and that my thoughts would often stray to those bright, idealistic days.

I didn't expect to ever see him again.

Introducing *the* **alternative.**

birthday experience ... QUALITY SO GOOD YOU CAN WIPE IT OFF ON THE KERB ... No...!

It's NOT **$150,000** ... it's NOT a  ... it's not even a (SAVAGE)

but it's Cholesterol Free ... it's full of Dietary Fibre and it's LIKE A BREATH OF FRESH AIR IN A ROOM FULL OF FARTS

Hope you had a fun day **OF GUN SLINGIN' COW POKIN' ROOTIN' TOOTIN' & PARTYIN'** in the **great outdoors** with people who know how to PLUMP YOUR LASHES ... & have <u>APPROVED</u> your **PARTS**.

Life ... it has AN EXCEPTIONAL EFFECT ON WRINKLES ... but then... **All too often,** so do **politicians or bankers.**

Here's to the **happy endings...**

from a **WILD** & **ECCENTRIC** tart. xxx

This entitles the bearer to two cups of coffee and/or several large slices of cake, a couple of bagels & a banana smoothie ... depending on who's paying the bill.
( VALID UNTIL 1995 )

PaGE FouR

## The Fish John West Reject were:

Mark Narkowicz
Mark Adams
Tim Gleeson
Andrew Viney
Graham Rankin
Martin Witheford
Stanley Paulzen
Michael Witheford

(Manager, Gary Minato;  Roadie, Darren Christensen)

## By 1993:

Tim was living in Tasmania
Michael was in his own band, Lust in Space
Martin returned to his career in pathology, at a Melbourne hospital
Graham was probably drumming for one band or another
Andrew was playing gigs with Harve's band, Tender Engines
Mark Adams had his own band, Hurdy Gurdy
Stan was living in The Punters Club, when last seen
Mark had married, and was working as a Music Teacher

# Lust In Space are rocking back in town

● Lust In Space is Lynch, Witheford and Lally.

WHAT more can I say about Lust In Space, the Launceston-birthed power trio whose brilliant debut album Glamnesia is nothing less than a piece of melodic punk-pop art?

Nothing much more than tell you that LIS — Michael Witheford, Alex Lynch and Phil Lally — are back in town for a gig at the Trades Hotel on Friday (for Burnie fans it's Saturday at The Club).

So for the rest of this story I have turned to the pages of the October issue of Rolling Stone, where a delirious Mark Demetrius describes Glamnesia in the following understated manner —

The debut album Glamnesia kicks like a mule and has the exquisite balance of historical perspective and sparkling freshness which characterises the purest rock and roll. It's rare to hear glam/hard-rock played without cliche these days, and even rarer to find it imbued with intelligence and wit.

Lust In Space are simultaneously elemental and plush. They sound like everyone and no-one. They recall Mott The Hoople, the Sex Pistols and The Beatles, among others, but their overall sound is distinctive.

If that's not enough to intrigue you, they've got rollicking drums and dirty guitars.

Some of the lyrics are a bit suggestive too: "You make me swell to twice my size." "I'd better shut up and move on to another CD, but my heart's not in it.

If you think such a rave review is rare, then realise that the chance to see LIS live in Launceston is has a similar Tasmanian Tiger quality.

*Angela J. Dawson*

# Author's note

This is a work of non-fiction, based on real events, but it is by no means a comprehensive account. It is based on my own experiences and memories of the time I spent with the people that feature in the story. It was compiled from diaries, personal photographs and correspondence, and has had many incarnations since its inception. I wrote the original transcript using a portable typewriter, and over the next 5 years the manuscript was edited and retyped twice, entirely on paper.

Over the years the manuscript remained in a box, transported with me wherever I travelled - to the UK, to the Northern Territory, and to America. It is a story that I have carried with me in every sense.

In the mid 1990's, with the proliferation of computers, it was re-typed and transferred to floppy disc. Ultimately it was moved to a hard drive and then expanded to include scanned images. In a digital era it has been much easier to add relevant graphics, allowing me to restore and upgrade the original format and present it in a way that I could not have done in the past.

Many years have passed and the story of that brief and glorious time has remained untold. However, in 2015 when I had decided it was time to publish the story and I had begun revisions on the manuscript, Mark unexpectedly made contact for the first time in many years. It provided the incentive to finally release my memories of that time, while there are still people who would remember TFJWR in their heyday.

Although the story has been edited, extended and upgraded, I have been reluctant to make significant changes to the tone and character of the narrative. Having captured the sense of wonder and excitement with which the world is experienced at the age of 23, it would not be possible to re-frame or reconstruct it so many years later without altering it entirely.

# Acknowledgements

Thanks to all band members and friends of The Fish John West Reject, including Darren Christensen, for all the driving and late nights. I hope you found that dream girl in the end.

To my friend and fellow Writer, Christine, *Ms M*, thank you for all the encouragement and pots of tea. It's a long journey that we are compelled to make, but one that's filled with countless joys.

I would like to express my appreciation to Derek Murphy at creativindie.com, who generously and selflessly shares his knowledge with other aspiring writers. His tips and tutorials have been invaluable for the long and daunting task of preparing and formatting material. On those difficult days it has helped me to keep going.

Some time ago, during this long process, a couple of friends assisted with the typing of the manuscript when I was too daunted to do it for the fourth time. Thanks to Helen *(Thing)* and Kylie, for moving me from paper to computer a couple of decades ago.

When I first made the trip over here to the other side of the world, I used to write long letters and mail them to my grandfather, Eric Thomas. As he read all my stories he was the first one to suggest that I write a book. So here it is Grandad, at last. I just wish you could be here to see it.

Thank you to my sister, Julie for indulging me by reading all this a long time ago, and to my parents, Andrea (1937-2014) and Keith Thomas, who gave me wings, knowing I might fly away. Even the other side of the globe isn't that far anymore.

For love and friendship I am so grateful to Rood and Roods, my Tasmanian family. Every time I return to Launceston it feels like coming home.

Thanks to Mark, well, for everything. I wish you every happiness. Everyone should hope for a love like that just once in a lifetime.

*Angela J. Dawson*

# List of inserts

**Photographs** by Angela J Dawson, (private collection) except publicity shot

**Publicity shot**, B & W, copyright © Mercury Hobart Tasmania (Newspaper), reproduced with permission

**Collages, cards and sketches** by Angela J Dawson

**Poems** copyright © Angela J Dawson 2016: *Orion's Belt, Tin Roof Rain, Softly, Lament*

**Scanned musical memorabilia** copyright © TFJWR, reproduced with grateful thanks to Mark Narkowicz and TFJWR (vinyl/cassette covers, lyric excerpts)

**Nan Witcomb** excerpt – thank you, Nan, for your permission to use your words from ***The Thoughts of Nanushka Vol VIII, Rainbows are for Everyone*** copyright © Nan Witcomb 1980

**Lyric** excerpt from *Lovesong* **by The Cure**, reproduced with permission from Universal Music

**Lyric** excerpt from *Poetry*, **T-Bone Burnett** - before going to print, all reasonable effort has been made to contact the copyright holders. Please contact the Author for any copyright claim in relation to the excerpt used.

Cassette cover of **Helvelln** album reproduced with permission from Pierre Baroni, Jeremy Gronow, and Polly Borland (courtesy Murray White Room, Melbourne)

**Newspaper articles reproduced, with permission from the Writers:**
* (indicates the paper/journal is no longer in print):
* *A Fishy Tale* Byron Smith, Juke Magazine, 6 May 1989
* *Fish Molly Meldrum Accepted* Michael Dwyer, X-Press Magazine, Perth, 1991
* *Revenge of the Love-Sick Fish* John Tingwell, The Drum Media, 16 Jul 1991
*How the Fish John West Reject went off* © Ricky Eaves, undated
*Lust in Space are rocking back into town* Author unknown, undated
**except (unable to contact/unreachable):**
*Fish to Farewell Tasmanian Fans* Chris Copas, Launceston Week, 2 Oct 1991
*The Fish Devonport crowds didn't reject* Russell Jarvis (dec), The Weekender, 21 Jan 1989

# Music

As Molly would say, do yourself a favour - make yourself a mix tape of that era. Songs mentioned in the story, and others on our playlist:

The Cure *Lovesong / Pictures of You*
The Go-Betweens *Cattle and Cane*
The Beat Farmers *Happy Boy*
Jonathan Richman *My Jeans / Chewing Gum Wrapper*
The Proclaimers *500 Miles*
The Jesus & Mary Chain *Sidewalking*
T-Bone Burnett *River of Love / Shake yourself Loose*
Frank & Nancy Sinatra *Somethin' Stupid*
Nick Cave *Something's Gotten Hold of my Heart*
Violent Femmes *Two People / Good Feeling / Gone Daddy Gone*
The Communards *You Are My World*
Inspiral Carpets *This is How it Feels*
Billy Bragg *Levi Stubbs Tears / Love Gets Dangerous*
Ride *Twisterella / Leave Them All Behind*
Hoodoo Gurus *Come Anytime / Bittersweet*
Hunters & Collectors *When the Rivers Run Dry / Throw Your Arms Around Me*
The Pixies *Debaser / Monkey Gone to Heaven / Hey*
Helvelln *Elvis / Subway Girl / Cruelest Plague*
Aztec Camera *Oblivious*
The Railway Children *A Gentle Sound / Brighter*
The Lilac Time *Black Velvet*
Hurrah! *The Sun Shines here / Celtic / I'll be Your Surprise*
Jesus Jones *Right here, Right now*
The Wonderstuff *Caught in My Shadow / Don't Let Me Down, Gently*
The Rainyard *So Happy Now / Another Yesterday*
The House of Love *Shine on / Christine / I don't know Why I Love You*
Primal Scream *Velocity Girl / Damaged*
The Chills *Pink Frost*

And of course, the full back catalogue of The Fish John West Reject.

## About the Author

Growing up in Manchester, England, Angela pursued her passion for indie and local music, radio production and creative writing. In Melbourne, she went on to study Copywriting and Scriptwriting, attended workshops with Jimmy McGovern, and completed Melbourne University Filmmaking Summer School.

In 2012 she won the national WB Yeats Poetry Prize for Australia with the poem, *Restitution*. Her poem, *Apart: Nov 1915* was included in the '100 Years from Gallipoli Poetry Project' (Graeme Lindsay) that toured New Zealand, Sydney and Tasmania in 2013/2014. Her poem, *Skating by Moonlight* was shortlisted for the NSW Lane Cove Literary Award 2014 (Waterbrook Poetry Prize)

She has appeared regularly at numerous venues in Melbourne since 2000, and in 2012 her poetry was featured on the 3CR community radio programme, *Spoken Word* (with Santo Cazzati).

She still lives in Melbourne, close to the water, where the oceans mingle and connect her three homes, living the life that Tinka had predicted. This is her first book.

*Like Two Mexicans Dancing*

Angela J. Dawson

*Like Two Mexicans Dancing*

www.ingramcontent.com/pod-product-compliance
Lightning Source LLC
Chambersburg PA
CBHW062108290426
44110CB00023B/2745